THE BLACK IMAGE
IN THE WHITE MIND

Also by
George M. Fredrickson

THE INNER CIVIL WAR
Northern Intellectuals
and the Crisis of the Union

WHITE SUPREMACY
A Comparative Study of American
and South African History

George M. Fredrickson

THE BLACK
IMAGE IN THE
WHITE MIND

*The Debate on Afro-American
Character and Destiny,
1817-1914*

WESLEYAN UNIVERSITY PRESS

Copyright © 1971 by George M. Fredrickson
Introduction to the Wesleyan Edition copyright © 1987
by George M. Fredrickson

This book was first published by Harper Row, Publishers

LIBRARY OF CONGRESS CATALOGING-IN-PUBLICATION DATA
Fredrickson, George M., 1934–
  The Black image in the white mind.
  (Wesleyan paperback)
  Includes bibliographical references and index.
  1. Afro-Americans—History.   2. Prejudices—United
States.   3. United States—Race relations.   I. Title.
[E185.F836 1987]   305.8′96073′073   86–19022
ISBN 0-8195-6188-6 (pbk.)

WESLEYAN UNIVERSITY PRESS
Published by University Press of New England,
Hanover, NH 03755

Manufactured in the United States of America

Wesleyan Paperback, 1987

5   4

FOR HÉLÈNE

Contents

Introduction to the Wesleyan Edition
of *The Black Image in the White Mind*

The publication of a new edition of *The Black Image in the White Mind* provides me with the occasion for some general reflections on what I thought I was doing when I wrote the book and how I view it in retrospect.

When I began work on the project in the mid–1960s, I conceived of it primarily as the exploration of a neglected aspect of American intellectual history, rather than as a contribution to Afro-American and Southern history. My first book, *The Inner Civil War: Northern Intellectuals and the Crisis of the Union*, published in 1965, had proved of some use to Civil War historians but had had a greater impact on those concerned with general trends in American intellectual and cultural development during the nineteenth century. *The Black Image*, however, turned out to be a work much more meaningful and influential among scholars and students of the history of the South, the sectional conflict, and race relations than among mainstream intellectual and cultural historians. To some extent this result may raise questions about the usual boundaries of intellectual history. Yet it was due in part to a shift of my interest from "the life of the mind" per se to the problem of how ideas become instruments of group advantage or domination. In short, I moved beyond the history of ideas and toward the history of ideologies and their role in the historical process. This change in direction was a response to concerns and pressures of the 1960s, a decade that aroused much scholarly concern with the ideological origins of contemporary injustices.

This book was one of a number of studies of the sixties and early seventies that reflected an intense historical and social-scientific preoccupation with the devastating effects of racism on American society, past and present. When it came out in 1971, the civil-rights movement of the 1960s had run its course, with results that were disappointing to those who had anticipated the full triumph of racial egalitarianism; the urban riots of the last half of the decade strongly implied that many blacks were disillusioned with the integrationist reformism of the early to middle sixties, an implication that was made explicit by the rise of black power and black nationalist ideologies. Among liberal whites there was either a sense of despair about race relations or a decisive shift of attention to other issues, especially to the war in Vietnam. *The Black Image in the White Mind* reflected the mood of frustration and pessimism about black-white relations that was particularly strong among those who had identified fervently with the civil-rights movement. One reviewer described the book as "somber," and others noted its compatibility with black nationalist views on the enduring power of racism in American life. The undeniably somber concluding paragraphs and the tendency throughout to find white-supremacist warts on white racial "liberals" of the past were obviously influenced by a sense of the failure of American liberalism that had been exacerbated by the Vietnam war. I would be the last to deny, therefore, that the work was to some extent a product of its time, influenced by the concerns of that era. Indeed, throughout the book the method used of relating ideas to their social and political context would prevent me from claiming personal immunity from a degree of "presentism."

I would, however, be unwilling to concede that the study is outdated in more than a superficial way, or to a greater degree than historical works dealing with apparently safer or cooler subjects. I consciously tried—for the most part successfully, I think—to avoid being polemical or preachy, adopting as a model for how to study the history of racism my notion of how a medical scientist might undertake the study of some hideous disease. Whatever the fate of some of its interpretations, the book remains, at the very least, a useful and balanced description of white thinking about blacks in the nineteenth and early-twentieth centuries. As the fruit of broad research into the annals of racialist discourse, it will retain the ability to inform students of the subject even if they approach it from very different vantage points.

A perspective influenced by the concerns of a particular moment need not be misleading. Indeed, the conditions of the late 1960s probably permitted a more candid and realistic view of the history of American race relations than is likely in other eras, in which the dominant impulse may be evasion or complacent celebration of progress. It might even be argued that the more recent tendency of historians to make cultural racism a secondary or epiphenomenal aspect of "class" relations is the latest device for avoiding the full dimensions of the problem. Recent efforts to dismantle affirmative action and other programs aimed at making racial equality a substantive reality rather than a mere legal norm could be interpreted as resulting partially from the persistent vitality of racist myths and stereotypes.

I prefer to rely on another line of defense—the view that all historical interpretations are necessarily partial in the sense that they address only part of a complex reality. This book is no exception; it focuses on the limitations and shortcomings of white racial thought when viewed from a modern egalitarian perspective. Such an enterprise was, and remains, useful because it helps to undermine the debilitating myth that our ancestors had the answer to our problems and that we therefore do not have to think about them in fresh and creative ways. But if I were to rewrite the book today, I would shift the emphasis somewhat in the direction of a greater tolerance for past white efforts to better the situation of blacks. These efforts were obviously flawed or inadequate when judged by modern ideas about race and reform, but our own failures to achieve racial equality or even to think clearly and incisively about how to achieve it should make us more understanding of the inability of past reformers to break out of the bounds set by the culture and ideology of their time. Although my descriptions and interpretations of the racial thought of abolitionists, Radical Republicans, and interracial liberals of later periods still strike me as persuasive in the main, I would now soften the tone somewhat and avoid a touch of cynicism I can no longer justify. My later work, comparing white supremacy in the United States and South Africa, has given me a stronger sense that something of enduring value was achieved by abolitionists, Radicals, and liberals; had they not struggled for some ideal of racial justice, conditions today would clearly be a lot worse than they are.

This newer sense of what was accomplished *despite* the limitations of vision and commitment that I documented might make a thoroughly revised version somewhat less somber and pessimistic than the original, although it would hardly turn it into a celebration of American progress and virtue. I am not sure that such a newer perspective would be better or more illuminating than the original, but it would bring out some trends of thought on the role of blacks in American life that are perhaps underemphasized. More particularly, it might show more clearly than it does that ideologies of a more general character than those concerned explicitly with race were often of greater consequence for the circumstances or prospects of Afro-Americans than the speculations about the intrinsic character or ultimate destiny of blacks that I made it my special responsibility to uncover. For example, more general attitudes, toward labor, labor systems, and working classes should probably have received more attention than they got.

I would not want this admission to be interpreted as a surrender to critics who would substitute a "materialist class analysis" for what they at times have taken to be my "idealist race analysis." In the first place, a close reading of the book will reveal that considerations of social class do enter the argument decisively at several points. What I called "herrenvolk democracy," for example, is not treated as an idea that comes out of the air to determine social and political reality; rather, it is shown to be shaped and empowered by social reality, including class relationships. Where I part company with my (mostly) Marxian critics is in my conviction that the most useful approach for the historian of racism is to study the interaction between culture—preexisting beliefs, values, and attitudes—and social structure, defined as the stratification of classes based on relationship to the market or the means of production. Race awareness and racism, in my view, are the products of a complex interplay between culture and society that defies monocausal—strictly "idealist" or strictly "materialist"—explanations. This theoretical orientation was what I was implying or groping for in *The Black Image*, and I regret that I was not able to make it more explicit.

Another limitation of the book, which has troubled me more than it has my critics, is unfortunately inherent in the way the subject was defined. By focusing almost exclusively on what whites thought about blacks, I may have conveyed the impression that black thinkers and writers in that period made little or no contribution to American racial discourse and imagery. To a great extent, of course, black efforts to define America's racial reality were ignored by whites as special pleading or as the product of limited or clouded intellects. But historians of black thought have revealed a rich vein of theory and speculation about racial character and destiny that was not hermetically sealed from what white publicists, ideologues, and social thinkers were saying at the same time. Nor was it merely reactive. The tendency, which I have shared with historians of Afro-American thought, to accept the color line as the division of discourse has had the unfortunate result of segregating an aspect of our cultural history that was, in fact, biracial. Some black thinkers—most notably Frederick Douglass, Booker T. Washington, and W. E. B. Du Bois—had a major impact on some segments of white opinion, and such white radicals as William Lloyd Garrison, Wendell Phillips, Thaddeus Stevens, and Albion W. Tourgée defined racial issues in ways that many blacks found compelling. No one would think of writing about racial thought in more recent times without giving central attention to the ideas and images of Martin Luther King, Jr., Malcolm X, A. Philip Randolph, James Baldwin, and Ralph

Ellison. What is needed in future scholarship on the intellectual history of race relations is greater effort to chart the flow of dialogue and debate across racial lines in an effort to capture the full range of the discourse and also to determine where its boundaries were, what it was that was salient only for an ingroup audience and what could be appreciated and even appropriated by the "other."

Perhaps closer attention to language, as recommended by currently fashionable schools of literary theory, will prove helpful in understanding how Americans, both white and black, established modes of discourse based on racial assumptions that then had an enduring effect on the world because of the extent to which they predetermined the very categories or forms that we use to think about the world. Whatever new methods and perspectives emerge in the study of "race" as a mental and cultural phenomenon, there can be little doubt that the subject will retain its importance and fascination. If this book continues to be a source of information, ideas, and hypotheses for those who are interested in racial thinking and imagery, past or present, the author will be satisfied.

Acknowledgments

I thank the staffs of the following libraries for assisting me in the research for this volume: Harvard University, the Library of Congress, the New York Public Library, Oberlin College, Emory University, Atlanta University, and Northwestern University. I have a special debt of gratitude to Miss Marjorie L. Carpenter of the Northwestern University Library, who demonstrated extraordinary efficiency and ingenuity by tracking down innumerable rare books and pamphlets and making them available to me through interlibrary loan. I would also like to express my thanks to Mrs. Richard Potter for typing the manuscript. Christopher Lasch and C. Vann Woodward put me heavily in their debt by reading the completed manuscript and making many valuable suggestions for improvement. I also benefited greatly from Christopher Lasch's encouragement from the very beginning of the project and from his willingness to act as a sounding board for my ideas while the work was in progress. As always, Jeannette Hopkins of Harper & Row was an exacting and very helpful editor. Finally, I wish to thank the John Simon Guggenheim Foundation and the Northwestern University Research Committee for the financial support that made the writing of this book possible.

Preface

During the nineteenth century, race-thinking emerged for the first time as a central current in Western thought. Previously whites had encountered other races in the course of "the expansion of Europe" and had characteristically subjugated, enslaved, or exterminated them. Out of these brutal and crassly exploitative contacts developed a set of attitudes about dark-skinned peoples which were "racist," if racism is regarded as synonymous with race prejudice and discrimination, but which might be considered preracist or protoracist, if one defines racism in a more restricted way—as a rationalized pseudoscientific theory positing the innate and permanent inferiority of nonwhites. Racism in this second sense had some roots in the biological thinking of the eighteenth century but did not come to fruition or exert great influence until well along in the nineteenth. In large part this book is a study of the development of intellectualized racist theory and ideology as it was applied directly and programmatically to the "problem" posed in the white mind by the presence of millions of blacks in the United States. It is also, however, a study of countertendencies, an examination of racial concepts, images, and proposals that deviated in some way from those associated with the "hard" racism of the inherent-inferiority school. In attempting to describe and interpret the debate that developed between spokesmen for differing conceptions of Afro-

American character and destiny, I have found that disagreement occurred within a narrowing consensus; for pseudoscientific racism or its equivalent tended during the period of this study to increase its hold on the American mind and to infect even those whites who resisted its full implications.

Although I have tried to describe the essential content of the various racial theories that were advanced, I have not gone deeply into details of interest mainly to the historian of science or anthropology. My principal concern has been with the relationship of racial doctrines and images to general social and intellectual developments and especially to the great historical conflicts involving the status of the black man in the United States. This is not, then, a pure "history of ideas" but rather a study of ideas in action, as they were espoused and applied by race-conscious intellectuals, pseudointellectuals, publicists, and politicians—men who spoke, to some extent at least, for particular groups and interests. Hence my emphasis has been on aspects of race-thinking that were most readily communicated to a fairly large public and on the broad policy implications of what were regarded at a given time as authoritative white opinions on black character and potentialities.

Central to the whole undertaking has been an effort to describe the interplay of basic racial conceptions with social or political ideologies as they manifested themselves in an era which saw the conflict over slavery and the Union, the tragic failure of Reconstruction, and finally the achievement of sectional reunion, largely at the expense of the Negro. The controversy surrounding the American Civil War led to a complex interaction between racial doctrines and broader ideological currents. As I studied this interaction it quickly became apparent that differences in larger social aims sometimes resulted in divergent applications of what were basically similar conceptions of the black man's essential nature.

Attention has also been devoted to one aspect of American race-thinking that previous scholars have largely ignored—racial prognostication. I have found that differing predictions made about the ultimate destiny of American blacks reveal much about essential white attitudes; often they reveal biases that may be obscured by positions taken on immediate issues. Taken together, they suggest the tragic limitation of the white racial imagination of the nineteenth century, namely its characteristic inability to visualize an egalitarian biracial society.

The book has been organized around a sequence of interrelated but distinguishable conceptions of black character and destiny—associated in most cases with a particular section, group, or movement. I have tried to arrange them chronologically, so far as possible, in the order of their emergence into the arena of public controversy. Studied in this fashion, the debate can often be seen as proceeding dialectically, with one conception provoking another which may then force some modification of the first. But the dialectic, if it can be called that, was not inherent in the ideas themselves but resulted from the interaction of prior conceptions with historical developments and changing circumstances. In part this was a dialogue which resulted from differing views of Northern and Southern spokesmen on the Negro's place in American life, but there were also important intersectional alliances, not to mention disagreements *within* each section on the nature and significance of racial distinctions. It should be reemphasized, however, that underlying most of these differences of opinion were certain common assumptions which established the boundaries of the debate and laid bare the limitations of almost all white perspectives of black America.

Perhaps something needs to be said about the chronological limits of this study. It covers the period from the earliest beginnings of the nineteenth-century controversy over slavery to the era of the First World War. I therefore begin at a point when formalized racism was still in an embryonic stage and end when it had reached a peak of power and influence—just before it began to be seriously challenged by the new liberal environmentalism of the twentieth century. Although I touch on more recent developments in the final chapter, this work is basically an account of the rise of racism but not of its subsequent fall from intellectual respectability. It would take another book as long as this one to do justice to the gradual decline of openly espoused ideological racism, the triumph, in some circles at least, of an environmentalist conception of human differences, and the appearance, despite these intellectual developments, of ominous new patterns of racial discrimination and antagonism.

THE BLACK IMAGE
IN THE WHITE MIND

Chapter One

•

Prejudice and Reformism: The Colonization Idea and the Abolitionist Response, 1817–1840

IN THE YEARS immediately before and after 1800, white Americans often revealed by their words and actions that they viewed Negroes as a permanently alien and unassimilable element of the population.[1] Yet articulate whites of that period were characteristically unable, and perhaps even unwilling, to defend their anti-Negro predispositions by presenting anything that resembled a "scientific" or philosophical case for the innate moral and intellectual inferiority of the black race. In the 1780s, Thomas Jefferson, alone among the spokesmen for the American Enlightenment, had moved in this direction by arguing that blacks were probably inferior to whites in certain basic qualities, but he conceded that all the facts were not available and that final judgment on the question ought to be suspended.

"The opinion that they [the blacks] are inferior in the faculties of reason and imagination, must be hazarded with great diffidence," he wrote. No hypothesis could be verified until more scientific investigation of racial differences had been carried out: "I advance it therefore as a suspicion only, that the blacks, whether originally a distinct race, or made distinct by time and circumstances, are inferior to whites both in body and mind." In

1. See Winthrop D. Jordan, *White Over Black: American Attitudes Toward the Negro, 1550–1812* (Chapel Hill, 1968), Parts Four and Five, especially Chapters XI and XV.

the words of Winthrop Jordan: "Until well into the nineteenth century Jefferson's judgment on that matter, with all its confused tentativeness, stood as the strongest suggestion of inferiority expressed by any native American."[2]

American *racial prejudice* had of course manifested itself in various forms as a concomitant of slavery since the seventeenth century, but *racism*—defined here as a rationalized ideology grounded in what were thought to be the facts of nature—would remain in an embryonic stage until almost the middle of the nineteenth century; for the environmentalism that was characteristic of Enlightenment thinking about human differences persisted even after the campaign against slavery it had helped create during the Revolutionary era had lost most of its momentum. In one sense, it can be said, the environmentalist philosophy was beginning to erode by 1810; by then, increasing doubts were being expressed about the naïve eighteenth-century theory that differences in pigmentation were a comparatively short-range result of climate and other environmental factors. What Winthrop Jordan sees as "an end to environmentalism" in the period 1800–1812 was actually a gradual undermining of what he elsewhere more accurately describes as "an extremely environmentalist posture," one which ascribed differences in *skin color* to the immediate effects of "climate, state of society, and manner of living." The belief that black mental, moral, and psychological characteristics were the result of environment was not effectively challenged in this period and persisted as a respectable ethnological doctrine until the 1830s and 1840s.[3]

For its full growth intellectual and ideological racism required a body of "scientific" and cultural thought which would give credence to the notion that the blacks were, for unalterable reasons of race, morally and intellectually inferior to whites, and, more importantly, it required a historical context which would make such an ideology seem necessary for the effective defense of Negro slavery or other forms of white supremacy.

Although gradual emancipation had been instituted in the

2. Thomas Jefferson, "Notes on Virginia" (1784), in *The Life and Selected Writings of Thomas Jefferson*, ed. Adrienne Koch and William Peden (New York, 1944), pp. 256–262; Jordan, *White Over Black*, p. 455.
3. Jordan, *White Over Black*, pp. 533–538.

North, slavery in the South had survived the Revolutionary era and the rise of the natural-rights philosophy without an elaborated racial defense—without, indeed, much of an intellectual defense of any kind; for the institution had never actually been seriously threatened. Antislavery forces had been so weak and hesitant in the post-Revolutionary South that emancipation proposals had not even come up for full public consideration, even though there was little difficulty at the time in gaining theoretical assent from many slaveholders to the abstract proposition that slavery was an undesirable institution which posed a threat to republican government, national unity, and economic progress.[4] The difficulty of turning such beliefs into action came not only from the obvious reluctance of slaveholders to give up the immediate economic and social rewards of bondage but also from the growing awareness, even among those most strongly opposed to slavery as an institution, of the power of white "prejudices" and the likelihood that freed blacks would run up against barriers to equality which would inevitably make them a dangerous and degraded pariah class.

A recognition that most whites had an emotional antipathy to the idea of black and white equality, as well as forebodings that blacks would emerge from slavery with moral faculties benumbed and with vengeful attitudes toward whites that would be exacerbated by the new and more competitive situation, had led Jefferson and many others to deny the feasibility and safety of emancipating large numbers of blacks on the soil, although they speculated on the possibility of avoiding race war by eventually combining emancipation with the colonization of blacks outside the United States. As Jefferson put it in *Notes on Virginia,* it was impossible to "encorporate the blacks into the

4. Robert McColley's *Slavery and Jeffersonian Virginia* (Urbana, Ill., 1964) documents the limitations of the antislavery impulse in post-Revolutionary Virginia. But his conclusion that proslavery Virginians relied significantly on a racial argument and handed down "the model theory of American racism" to subsequent generations (p. 188) is misleading because it is based almost entirely on Jefferson's exceptional and tentative statements about black inferiority. Taken as a whole, McColley's book actually supports the view that antislavery forces were weak and hesitant in the face of the powerful social and economic interest represented by slavery—so weak that there was no need to develop and promulgate an articulated racism in order to sustain the institution.

state," because "deep-rooted prejudices entertained by the whites; ten thousand recollections by the blacks of the injuries they have sustained; the real distinctions nature has made; and many other circumstances, will divide us into parties, and produce convulsions, which will probably never end but in the extermination of one or the other race."[5]

The belief that the Negro, if freed, would remain an alien and troublesome presence seemed confirmed in the early nineteenth century by the situation of those blacks who, after the Revolution, had been emancipated in the North or manumitted privately in the South. It was the son of one of the leaders of the successful emancipation movement in Connecticut who suggested in 1834 that the manumissions of the late eighteenth century may have set back the cause of emancipation nationally. The bad "practical effects" of these actions were a consequence of "the corrupted characters of the manumitted slaves"; their change in condition "was fruitful in crime, but rarely productive of happiness."[6]

Indeed, from the very beginning of the gradual emancipation process in the North, the conduct of newly freed Negroes was an embarrassment to some of those who hoped most fervently for the rapid demise of slavery. In 1798 a group of New Jersey abolitionists reported that many free blacks were "given to Idleness, Frolicking, Drunkeness, and in some few cases to Dishonesty." In 1806 a leading Pennsylvania abolitionist described most Philadelphia Negroes as "degraded and vicious," and two years later the New York Manumission Society announced that it viewed "with regret the looseness of manners & depravity of conduct in many of the Persons of Colour in this city."[7] Of course these humanitarians generally attributed black depravity to environ-

5. *Life and Selected Writings of Thomas Jefferson,* ed. Koch and Peden, p. 256. Jordan discusses the origins of the colonization idea and the thinking behind it in *White Over Black,* Chapter XV.

6. Ebenezer Baldwin, *Observations on the Physical, Intellectual, and Moral Character of Our Colored Population* (New Haven, 1834), p. 41. Baldwin was the son of the Reverend Ebenezer Baldwin who was an antislavery spokesman in Connecticut as early as 1773. The elder Baldwin is mentioned in Arthur Zilversmit, *The First Emancipation: The Abolition of Slavery in the North* (Chicago, 1967), p. 107.

7. Quoted in Zilversmit, *The First Emancipation,* pp. 223–224.

mental factors—the heritage of slavery and the conditions under which free Negroes were forced to live. But they nevertheless unwittingly provided an argument against further acts of liberation: if it was true that American society turned free Negroes into a "depraved population" by refusing them decent treatment and adequate opportunities, then "practical" men might be led to conclude, on the basis of this consequence alone, that emancipation was undesirable.

The Northern image of the free Negro as a social danger came into sharper focus as time went on. In Massachusetts, a state with a very small black population that had abolished slavery almost without controversy, a serious concern with free-Negro "depravity" developed in the 1820s. In 1821 the legislature appointed a committee to look into the possibility of restricting Negro immigration, on the grounds that blacks constituted "a species of population" that could "become both injurious and burdensome."[8] In 1826 the Board of Managers of the Boston Prison Discipline Society, an organization for penal reform, pointed out in their first annual report that Negroes constituted a disproportionately large percentage of the prison population of the Northeastern states and concluded that "the first cause existing in society of the frequency and increase of crime, is the degraded character of the colored population." The use here of the adjective "degraded," which was constantly applied to free Negroes during this period, suggested that there was some ideal of manhood from which the Negro had fallen or to which he might be raised, and the Prison Discipline Society readily conceded that an appropriation for black education equal to the cost of maintaining black convicts "would very soon raise their character to a level of whites, and diminish the number of convicts from among them, about ten fold." But the Boston prison reformers had no real expectation that such an ambitious program of Negro uplift would be adopted, and they moved quickly to endorse an alternative solution—the removal of the free blacks by colonizing them abroad. In advocating this approach to the problem, they were falling in line with the "enlightened" philanthropy of the day which had settled on African colonization as the panacea

8. *Ibid.*, p. 225.

that would not only solve the free-Negro crisis but also open the way to the gradual extinction of slavery.[9]

The new colonization movement, which began with the founding of the American Colonization Society in 1817, was in many respects typical of the benevolent movements which burgeoned between the War of 1812 and the late 1820s. Like the American Education Society, the Home Missionary Society, the American Bible Society, and the American Temperance Society, it developed as part of a conservative response to a changing social situation, drawing most of its initial inspiration and support from two interrelated groups—the Protestant clergy of the major "evangelical" denominations and the adherents of the declining Federalist Party. The clergy, adjusting to the separation of church and state resulting from the Revolution, was turning to voluntaristic methods, such as controlled revivals and organized benevolence, in order to maintain the authority of religion and curb the tendency to "anarchy" and moral laxity supposedly fostered by westward expansion and the growth of democratic ideas and practices. Federalists, still attempting to rebound in some way from their defeat in the election in 1800, were eager to support movements to restrain the "dangerous" propensities of the common people. If clergymen supported the new benevolence as a substitute for the old church-state relationship, Federalists were seeking in it a way of regaining some of the social control that had been lost with the decline of the hierarchical society and deferential politics of the colonial period.[10]

9. *First Annual Report of the Board of Managers of the Boston Prison Discipline Society* (Boston, 1826) , pp. 35–38.

10. The essentially conservative character of the original benevolent impulse has been demonstrated by a number of recent books. Among them are John R. Bodo, *The Protestant Clergy and Public Issues, 1812–1848* (Princeton, 1954) ; Clifford Griffin, *Their Brothers' Keepers: Moral Stewardship in the United States, 1800–1865* (New Brunswick, N. J., 1960) ; Charles I. Foster, *An Errand of Mercy: The Evangelical United Front, 1790–1837* (Chapel Hill, 1960) ; and Charles C. Cole, *The Social Ideas of the Northern Evangelists, 1826–1860* (New York, 1954) . On the new responsiveness of Federalists to evangelical religion at the beginning of the age of organized benevolence, see David Hackett Fischer, *The Revolution of American Conservatism: The Federalist Party in the Era of Jeffersonian Democracy* (New York, 1965) , pp. 48–49.

The Colonization Society, like the other benevolent organizations, originated through the initiative of a clergyman—the principal instigator was the Reverend Robert Finley, a Presbyterian of Baskingridge, New Jersey—and once established it received the overwhelming support of the evangelical establishment and the Calvinist clergy. It became customary by the 1820s for many Northern ministers, especially Congregationalists and Presbyterians, to give special Independence Day sermons endorsing the cause of African colonization and seeking support for the society's Liberian colony, which received its first settlers in 1822. The specifically religious appeal of the movement came from its claim to be a missionary enterprise. A colony of converted ex-slaves would, it was argued, contribute to the conversion and "redemption" of Africa. The idea also won the immediate support of Federalists, especially those from the upper South and the border states. Among the prominent Federalist leaders who took an active role in the movement were Robert Goodloe Harper of Maryland, a politician and general, who suggested the names Liberia and Monrovia; Charles Fenton Mercer, a leading Virginia Federalist of the younger generation; and Elias Caldwell of New Jersey, clerk of the Supreme Court, who served both as editor of a Federalist party paper and as first secretary of the Colonization Society. Typical of the early leadership was Francis Scott Key of Maryland, who, after giving up the idea of a political career as a Federalist because of his revulsion against the new democratic tone in politics, sought a corrective to what he considered the "vicious" state of contemporary society through his work in the American Bible Society, the American Sunday School Union, and the American Colonization Society.[11]

For men of this background and mentality, the free Negroes were bound to present a problem, in that they constituted an-

11. P. J. Staudenraus, *The African Colonization Movement, 1816–1865* (New York, 1961), Chapters II and III, *passim,* and pp. 119–120. Staudenraus's thorough and judicious volume is the necessary starting point for any re-evaluation of the colonizationists. A general account of the colonization movement which has been completely superseded by Staudenraus is Early Lee Fox, *The American Colonization Society, 1817–1840* (Baltimore, 1919). For further information on Harper, Mercer, and Caldwell—prominent colonizationists who were also leading Federalists—see Fischer, *Revolution of American Conservatism,* 36–38, 364–365, 385.

other inadequately controlled and unpredictable element in a social situation that seemed to offer many threats to order, stability, and hierarchy. General emancipation in the North and the manumission of many slaves in the upper South had been aspects of a general loosening of traditional social controls which had begun in the Revolutionary era, and here as elsewhere conservative men had to face the consequences of a new order in society and politics. On the surface at least, the colonizationist attitude toward the free Negro often resembled the attitude of contemporary philanthropists toward drunkards, infidels, and people moving west too fast for the churches to keep up with them. Like other newly and perhaps too hastily liberated elements, they constituted a threat to the order and decorum of society. "There is a point," wrote one colonizationist, "beyond which the peace of society cannot permit the increase of the elements of commotion." With the growth of the free black population, that point seemed about to be reached.[12] In the North the problem was the one pointed out by the Boston Prison Discipline Society in 1826, namely that blacks allegedly contributed to the idleness, disorderliness, and criminality of the urban poor; in the South there was an even more pressing danger. As Robert Goodloe Harper pointed out in 1817, "the free people of color" were "a nuisance and burden," not only because their poverty brought the social costs of pauperism, vice, and crime but also because they "contribute greatly to the corruption of the slaves, and to aggravate the evils of their condition, by rendering them idle, discontented, and disobedient." The dissatisfaction they inspired could eventuate in "direct resistance" to the master's authority.[13]

The danger of slave unrest and rebellion in the South was a recurring theme of colonizationist literature. But it would be wrong to conclude from this that all, or even most, of the leading exponents of colonization wanted to remove the free Negro

12. *African Repository,* IX (January, 1834) , 322. For my analysis of colonizationist thought, I have made considerable use of the *Repository,* which was the official organ of the American Colonization Society.

13. Robert Goodloe Harper, *A Letter from General Harper of Maryland, to Elias Caldwell, Secretary of the American Society for Colonizing Free People of Colour, in the United States, with their own consent* (Baltimore, 1818) , pp. 9–11.

merely to provide for the safety and security of the institution of slavery—as the abolitionists charged in the 1830s. On the contrary, many of them saw the danger of bloody rebellion and a repetition of the "scenes of San Domingo" (Haiti) as inherent in servitude itself; for this and other reasons they represented their cause as the only practical long-range solution to the menace of slavery. In 1828 a statement of the Connecticut Colonization Society pointed to the possibility that if slavery were not abolished by the gradual and voluntary means that colonizationists advocated, it would come to an end as a result of "violence and insurrection."[14] Henry Clay, the major political spokesman for colonization, also argued that the slave system contained within itself the seeds of insurrection and race war.[15]

In the same letter describing the free Negro as a threat to the peace of the plantation, Harper defended colonization precisely because "it tends, and may powerfully tend, to rid us, gradually and entirely, in the United States of slaves and slavery: a great moral and political evil, of increasing virulence and extent."[16] In 1830 the Reverend Robert J. Breckinridge, a principal advocate of the movement in Kentucky, declared that "the political moral of the Colonization Society is strikingly plain. It has taught us how we may be relieved of the curse of slavery in a manner, cheap, certain and advantageous to both parties."[17] Other leading colonizationists were equally frank about their desire for the gradual destruction of the slave system. Their oft-repeated argument was that the main obstacle to gradual emancipation came from white opposition to a free Negro population within the United States and that colonization would encourage voluntary manumission at an increasing rate by offering a way of freeing slaves without augmenting the "degraded" classes of society.

Confusion among historians about the long-range intentions of the colonizationists has arisen primarily because they sought support in the deep South by disclaiming any intention of inter-

14. *African Repository*, IV (June, 1828) , 119.
15. Staudenraus, *African Colonization*, p. 139.
16. Harper, *Letter*, p. 11.
17. Quoted in Staudenraus, *African Colonization*, p. 144.

fering directly with the institution of slavery. They meant that their own program—transporting free people of color to Africa—did not constitute a challenge to the "right" of slaveholders to control their human chattels and dispose of them as they saw fit; but they generally made it clear that their real aim was to increase voluntary manumissions as part of a movement toward the total elimination of black servitude in the United States. These aspirations were stressed in the second issue of the *African Repository*, where a general description of the purposes of the American Colonization Society was provided. The society, it was emphasized, was working *"directly"* only for the removal of free Negroes. "If, however, in its progress, it should exhibit the benefits that would accrue both to master and slaves by a voluntary dissolution of the bonds which unite them, should convince the Southern people that emancipation might be safe, practicable, replete with blessings, and full of honor, where in this great republick, is the candid and Christian man who would regret the effects of the moral influence?" The American Colonization Society, the same article continued, "interferes in no wise with the rights of property, and hopes and labors for the gradual abolition of slavery, by the voluntary and gradual manumission of slaves . . ."[18]

In 1830 the *Repository* replied to attacks on its program emanating from proslavery circles in South Carolina by emphasizing once again the narrowly focused and voluntaristic nature of the organization's immediate objectives. The *Repository* refused to deny, however, "that the society has expressed the opinion that slavery is a moral and political evil, and that it has regarded the scheme of colonization as presenting motives and exciting a moral influence at the South favorable to gradual and voluntary emancipation." It was in fact this implication of the colonization program that had "secured to it the countenance and patronage of our most profound and sagacious statesmen, and given to this scheme a peculiar attractiveness and glory in the view of the enlightened friends of their country and mankind."[19] Colonizationist spokesmen may have been deluded

18. *African Repository,* I (April, 1825) , 34, 39.
19. "South Carolina Opinions of the Colonization Society," *African Repository,* VI (September, 1830) , 205.

about the actual consequences of their program, but there is no reason, in most cases, to doubt their sincerity. Their purpose was to bring about emancipation in a way that was congenial to conservatives; "not," as a Connecticut clergyman put it, "by some sudden convulsion, demolishing the fabric of society, but by the tendencies of nature and the arrangements of Providence, slowly yet surely accomplishing the happiness of man."[20]

Slavery was considered an evil by colonizationists not because they had any empathy with the sufferings of the slaves—they were notably deficient in this regard—but because they viewed it as an economically unsound and dangerous institution, incompatible in the long run with the prosperity, peace, and security of society. In a speech before the Kentucky Colonization Society in 1830, Henry Clay, who had taken a leading role in the movement from the beginning, catalogued the economic evils of the institution as an inefficient system of labor and then went on to present his view that slavery was a potential state of war that would eventually erupt into open conflict. It was probable, he argued, that slave insurrections would increase in the future; for Negroes "are rational beings like ourselves, capable of feeling and reflection and of judging what belongs to them as a portion of the human race. By the very condition of the relation which exists between us, we are enemies of each other." The blacks, he continued, were well aware of their grievances, and only the power of the whites kept them from avenging their "wrongs."[21]

Clay's remarks suggest that at least some of the colonizationists of the 1820s and 1830s did not share the belief of later racists in the inherent slavishness and irrationality of the Negro: as "rational beings like ourselves," Negroes reacted to slavery precisely as white men would react—hence the danger of insurrection. But

20. Quoted in Staudenraus, *African Colonization*, p. 119. For a balanced assessment of the moderate and sometimes muted antislavery sentiments of the colonizationists, see Frederic Bancroft, "The Early Antislavery Movement and African Colonization," in Jacob E. Cooke, ed., *Frederic Bancroft: Historian* (Norman, Okla., 1957). "In reading countless official reports, documents, and articles of various kinds," Bancroft reported, "not one positively proslavery official word has been found. The general tenor of it all was at least mildly, often positively, antislavery. And about four-sevenths of the real colonists before 1852 had been emancipated in view of emigrating to Africa" (pp. 189–190).

21. *African Repository*, VI (March, 1830), 11.

if blacks were fully rational, it might be asked, why was it not possible to educate them up to the level of the whites, thereby opening the way to gradual emancipation without colonization? Because the colonizationists were unwilling to undertake this task or envision the possibility of its accomplishment, the analogy between their movement and other benevolent enterprises ultimately breaks down. The white drunkard, criminal, or infidel could be persuaded by missionaries and philanthropists to reform and become a respectable or harmless member of society, but not the emancipated Negro. To understand exactly why the theorists of colonization believed that the Negro alone could not be assimilated, it is necessary to look more closely at their racial ideas and assumptions.

II

One of the most surprising and unexpected features of the more sophisticated and philosophical kind of colonizationist propaganda was its respectful, even complimentary, way of describing Negroes when it was a question of their innate racial character and capacity rather than their "degraded" condition in America. The movement undoubtedly had supporters who accepted the popular notion that blacks were somehow naturally inferior, but unequivocal racists of this type did not exercise control over what might be described as the official line of the American Colonization Society. One can go through much of the literature of the movement from 1817 to the late 1830s without finding a single clear and unambiguous assertion of the Negro's inherent and unalterable inferiority to whites. When blacks were described as "degraded," it was usually made evident that the degradation resulted from circumstances and not inherent traits. Calvin Colton, a colonizationist writer who has been described by one historian as a believer in "the basic inferiority of the Negro," made it clear in his 1833 book, *The Americans,* that blacks were "degraded" and inferior for the same reasons that lower-class whites in England were "degraded" and inferior. In his pamphlet *Colonization and Abolition Contrasted* (1839), Colton raised the question of "whether the African is naturally inferior to the European," and stated that he could not "maintain it in the affirmative under all the disadvantages of his condition." "His long-depressed and inferior *condition*," he went on, "is sufficient . . . to account for his present *actual* inferiority of intellect and moral force."[22]

Along with such assertions of the Negro's *de facto* cultural inferiority, there were many statements which strongly affirmed a basic equality of human capacities. The first issue of the *African Repository,* which appeared in 1825, featured an attack on those who believe that the Negroes are "a distinct order of beings; the connecting link between men and monkees." This idea is disproved, the article went on, by the record of the great "Ethiopian" and "Cushite" civilizations of the ancient world: ". . . at a time when the rest of the world was in a state of barbarism, the Ethiopian family were exhibiting prodigies of human genius." In presenting the case for a proud Negro past, which would be used over and over again by ethnological defenders of the Negro—white and black—throughout the century, the *Repository* pointed especially to the Egyptians, whom Herodotus had described as black, and concluded that the basic arts and sciences may therefore have originated with the Negro race. Another article in the same issue indicated that contemporary Africans had exhibited similar capacities; tribes like the Soosoos had revealed to travelers a highly civilized way of life. A final section,

22. [Calvin Colton,] *The Americans* (London, 1833), p. 375; *Colonization and Abolition Contrasted* (Philadelphia, 1839), p. 5. That Colton "accepted the basic inferiority of the Negro" is maintained by Lorman Ratner in *Powder Keg: Northern Opposition to the Antislavery Movement* (New York and London, 1968), pp. 34–35. If Ratner means simply that Colton believed in the *de facto* cultural inferiority of American blacks, he is on safe ground; but if he means, as he seems to, that Colton believed that Negroes as a race were inherently and unalterably inferior, he cannot demonstrate this from Colton's own words. If "racism" is defined as a belief in *de facto* Negro inferiority and opposition to black aspirations for equality in the United States, then Colton indeed was a racist in the same sense that some present-day theorists of "cultural deprivation" can be considered "racists"; but if racism is defined as "a doctrine that inherent differences among the various human races determine cultural or individual achievement" (*The Random House Dictionary of the English Language*), then it is not at all clear that Colton was a theoretical racist.

entitled "Specimens of African Genius," reprinted an admiring description of the pomp and display found in the court of King Yaradee, a great West African monarch.[23]

Colonizationists of the 1820s and 1830s often presented such eulogies to "the African genius." Sometimes they were so eloquent that their abolitionist rivals of the 1830s could not resist quoting them. In 1833 the diplomat and reformer Alexander Hill Everett addressed the Massachusetts Colonization Society on the Negro character and was cited at length, as providing the last word on the subject, in a pamphlet by the abolitionist Samuel May. Everett rejected as "a miserable heresy" the belief that the Negro was "incapable of improvement and civilization, and condemned by the vice of his physical conformation to vegetate forever in a state of hopeless barbarism." Like the *Repository*, he invoked the black Egyptians of Herodotus as the progenitors of civilized life. "So much," he concluded, "for the supposed inferiority of the colored race, and their incapacity to make any progress in civilization and improvement."[24]

The following year a Connecticut colonizationist, Ebenezer Baldwin, published a pamphlet refuting in detail all known arguments for Negro inferiority. Attributing Negro degradation entirely to the effects of slavery, Baldwin affirmed that "Africans seem at least equal, according to their advantages, to the whites," and went on to provide examples of individual distinction among Negroes of the past, pointing to achievement in literature, law, science, mathematics, and statesmanship. In an extraordinary section he attacked the still rudimentary theories of "physiognomists and phrenologists" who deduced Negro inferiority from facial angle and cranial thickness, arguing that there was no evidence of a connection between such physical characteristics and talent or intelligence. Baldwin's colonizationist pamphlet, which explicitly attacked the abolitionists as impractical visionaries, was probably the most cogent and thorough defense of racial equality as a fact of nature that appeared in the 1830s.[25]

Another colonizationist writer who was openly and aggres-

23. *African Repository*, I (March, 1825) , 7–12, 19–21, 30–32.
24. Quoted in Samuel J. May, *The Right of the Colored People to Education Vindicated* (Brooklyn, 1833) , pp. 19–20.
25. Baldwin, *Observations*, p. 13 and *passim*.

sively egalitarian in his basic racial views was Frederick Freeman of Pennsylvania, an Episcopal rector whose book *Yaradee*—named for the impressive African monarch who was a favorite of colonizationists—went through several editions. Writing in 1836, Freeman maintained that Africans "are as capable . . . of the finest sensibilities as we are; as capable of appreciating and enjoying the endearing relations and blessings of life; as capable of self-government, and eminent attainments in knowledge, usefulness, piety, and respectability." He pointed to the great achievements of ancient "Ethiopians" and contended that the supposed indolence of contemporary inhabitants of Africa was due entirely to a natural abundance that made work unnecessary; where Negroes lived in a harsh environment, as in Senegal, they were as industrious as any people on earth.[26]

This tendency of colonizationists to celebrate the basic Negro character seemed to their critics to be hopelessly at odds with their image of the miserable, degraded state of the American free blacks and with their desire for a total separation of the races. Proponents of colonization met charges of inconsistency in their view of the black character by affirming a basically environmentalist explanation for free-Negro degradation. As Henry Clay put it: "The free people of colour are . . . the most corrupt, depraved, and abandoned element in the population"; but this "is not so much their fault as a consequence of their anomalous condition."[27] "Their degradation," Freeman wrote, "is the natural consequence of their unfortunate situation, and not the result of any inherent depravity in their natural constitution, or of deficiency of mental faculties."[28] Calvin Colton, as we have seen, contended in 1839 that the Negro's "long depressed and inferior *condition* is sufficient . . . to account for his present *actual* inferiority of intellect and moral force." Present white superiority, he continued, was "accidentally derived" from the unequal historical relationship that had developed between the races.[29]

Such explanations did not fully dispose of the problem of how

26. Frederick Freeman, *Yaradee: A Plea for Africa, in Familiar Conversations on the Subject of Slavery and Colonization* (Philadelphia, 1836), pp. 173, 16–17, 34–43, 47.
27. *African Repository*, VI (March, 1830), 12.
28. Freeman, *Yaradee*, p. 173.
29. Colton, *Colonization and Abolition Contrasted*, p. 5.

one got self-reliant Liberian colonists from such a depraved population, but all that was really needed was a further and more radical extension of the environmentalist logic. According to the Reverend Robert J. Breckinridge of Kentucky, "no friend of colonization has ever said that their vices or crimes were of such a nature as to be incapable of reform. They result, so far as they are peculiar to them, from the peculiarities of their condition; and when the condition is changed, the vices disappear."[30] When American Negroes set foot in Africa, it was argued, they would soon become new men, because they would no longer be hampered in their efforts to improve themselves by white prejudice and discrimination. In the words of Robert Goodloe Harper: "They would soon feel the noble emulation to excel, which is the fruitful source of excellence in all the various departments of life; and under the influence of this generous and powerful sentiment, united with the desire and hope of improving their condition . . . they would soon rise rapidly in the scale of existence, and soon become equal to people of Europe, or European origin, so long their masters and oppressors."[31]

Colonizationist thought illustrates the sometimes forgotten fact that social environmentalism—the belief that human character and values are shaped or predetermined by social and cultural conditions—can be put to extremely conservative uses. If the American social environment allegedly acted on free blacks in such a way as to turn them inevitably into a class of miserable paupers and criminals, it also turned whites into unalterable Negrophobes. White racial prejudice, which many colonizationists were quite willing to see as basically historical and cultural in its origins, was viewed by them as the real key to the problem, the principal factor which prevented blacks from realizing their true capacities as long as they resided in the United States. Some colonizationists stated explicitly that it was prejudice and not black inferiority which created the Negro problem.[32]

Their concept of the permanency of white American racial antipathies, however, reveals that their brand of cultural deter-

---

30. *African Repository*, IX (January, 1834) , 325.
31. Harper, *Letter*, p. 18.
32. See Staudenraus, *African Colonization*, pp. 120–121.

minism was based implicitly on the ultraconservative notion that popular attitudes that appear to be persistent and deep-seated are in fact unchangeable. It was partly because they could not visualize basic alterations in the observed values of a people that they characteristically described American racial prejudice as "invincible," "too deep to be eradicated," or removable only through divine agency. Henry Clay, for example, attributed all vices of free Negroes to the fact that the "invincible prejudices" of the whites denied them equal participation in society.[33] Perhaps the most dramatic statement of the colonizationist view of white racial bias as a permanent aspect of American culture appeared in a report of the Connecticut Colonization Society, reprinted in the *African Repository* in 1828:

> In every part of the United States, there is a broad and impassible [sic] line of demarcation between every man who has one drop of African blood in his veins, and every other class in the community. The habits, the feelings, all the prejudices of society—prejudices which neither refinement, nor argument, nor education, nor religion itself can subdue—mark the people of colour, whether bond or free, as the subjects of a degradation inevitable and incurable. The African in this country belongs by birth to the lowest station in society; and from that station he can never rise, be his talent, his enterprise, his virtues what they may.[34]

Often the analysis went no farther than this: prejudice and discrimination were fundamental facts of American life and seemingly always had been; therefore what right had anyone to expect a change? But when theorists of colonization probed more deeply, they attributed the apparently universal revulsion of whites to Negro equality to two interrelated factors, the differences in social background and pigmentation between the races. The fact that the Negro was, or had been, a slave and that the color of his skin was a permanent sign of his origin was enough to prevent for all time his acceptance as a social equal. As Harper put it, the blacks "are condemned to a hopeless state of inferior-

33. *African Repository*, VI (March, 1830), 17; see also IX (January, 1834), 334, and Freeman, *Yaradee*, pp. 171, 173.
34. *African Repository*, IV (June, 1828), 118.

ity and degradation by their color, which is an indelible mark of their origin and former condition, and establishes an impassible barrier between them and the whites."[35]

Insofar as colonizationists affirmed or implied that there was an inevitable and legitimate white prejudice against a black skin, they succumbed, in this one respect at least, to a protoracist form of biological determinism. But some of them emphatically denied that color was an important factor, in and of itself, and attributed racial antipathy entirely to the social effects of slavery.[36] The difference of opinion that existed within the movement on whether white revulsion to a black skin could be justified in principle is revealed by a sampling of comments on the question of whether racial prejudice could properly be described as wrong or immoral. Breckinridge of Kentucky, speaking probably for many Southern and border-state colonizationists, did not see anything "morally wrong" with an aversion to close contact with "persons, who from their physical organizations create disgust."[37] Calvin Colton, on the other hand, pictured racial prejudice in 1833 as simply a bias against low social status which is "doubtless as wrong, as it is natural."[38] The Reverend Lyman Beecher, representing the left wing of the Northern movement in 1834, went further and forthrightly denounced racial prejudice as "unreasonable" and "wicked." But this judgment did not prevent him from affirming the basic proposition of the colonizationists; for he went on to describe this prejudice as extremely "obstinate," and concluded by asking: ". . . is it any less obstinate because it is criminal?" Despite some recent theological deviations, Beecher remained enough of a Calvinist to believe that the eradication of sin was no easy matter, and he defended colonization and opposed "emancipation of all slaves on the soil" because whites were too full of "wicked" prejudices to allow the freed Negro to make any progress in the United States.[39]

Views like those of Beecher and Colton provide evidence that

35. Harper, *Letter,* p. 6.
36. See, for example, Baldwin, *Observations,* p. 5; and Alexander Everett in May, *Right of the Colored People,* p. 20.
37. *African Repository,* IX (January, 1834) , 323.
38. [Colton,] *The Americans,* p. 382.
39. *African Repository,* X (November, 1834) , 282.

the colonizationists' belief in the invincibility of prejudice could be more than an expression of their own antipathy to Negroes. It was also, and in some cases principally, an application to the race problem of fundamental conservative ideas emanating from the Calvinist and Federalist traditions. Thoughtful spokesmen for colonization did not believe, first of all, that all social problems could be solved in an ideal fashion. The philanthropist, wrote Ebenezer Baldwin, must recognize "the limits prescribed to the efforts of benevolence, arising from physical and moral circumstances" and "regulate his measures by prudence, and temper his ardor with discretion."[40] Since neither man nor society was perfectible, reformers had to be careful to stay within the realm of the possible; and in order to do this, they needed a realistic and unsentimental perception of the nature of their society and what might be expected from it. As conservatives, they assumed that whatever was genuinely traditional and "deeply rooted" in the life and thought of people could not—and probably should not—be changed. Since human thought and action were largely determined by an inherited fabric of well-established customs, institutions, and prejudices—which it would be foolish and dangerous to think of altering in any fundamental way—necessary reforms in the broad social interest, such as the eventual elimination of slavery, had to come about gradually and in such a way as not to fly in the face of firmly held beliefs or upset the equilibrium of society. It was possible to conceive of the ultimate elimination of slavery because for the colonizationists slavery was an anomalous institution that did not fit the basic American social pattern. The color line, on the other hand, was so deeply implanted in the national mentality that there was no reason to expect its disappearance. American society, the argument implied, was a corporate entity into which the black group had never been and never could be incorporated. This situation created the probability of conflict and chaos, unless a collective solution was found that would remove this disturbing element without upsetting the existing and legitimate interests of the various elements constituting the social fabric.

There were, of course, many who lent support to the move-

40. Baldwin, *Observations*, p. 5.

ment not because they had analyzed the problem in such a fashion but because they themselves simply manifested in acute form the anti-Negro sentiments that the theorists took for granted. On the local level, especially in the upper South and the Midwest, the movement readily degenerated into a crude deportationism aimed exclusively at the removal of free Negroes. In a sense, as Frederic Bancroft has suggested, the leaders engaged in the dangerous and, in the end, self-defeating policy of trying to use and manipulate Negrophobia to serve what they regarded as a larger humanitarian purpose.[41]

If their rhetoric was any indication of their beliefs, the principal spokesmen for the national colonization movement actually drew mainly on a kind of conservative "realism," which did not require a doctrine of innate racial differences and antipathies, when they characterized the American racial environment as intractable. And there was, it must be conceded, empirical evidence to bolster their point of view. Americans had discriminated in one way or another against Negroes since early in the colonial period. It was also true that free blacks of the early nineteenth century were almost universally denied access to public institutions and full rights of citizenship; and from the standpoint of the 1820s and 1830s, anti-Negro sentiment seemed to be on the upswing as violence against free blacks became commonplace and some Northern states acted to restrict or eliminate Negro suffrage.[42] It was not difficult for a man of benevo-

41. See Gordon E. Finnie, "The Antislavery Movement in the Upper South before 1840," *Journal of Southern History*, XXXV (August, 1969), 319–342; and Eugene H. Berwanger, *The Frontier Against Slavery: Western Anti-Negro Prejudice and the Slavery Extension Controversy* (Urbana, Ill., 1967), pp. 51–58. Finnie, however, tends to miss the statement of long-range antislavery intention that was often tacked onto the end of an apparently deportationist argument. According to Bancroft: "The actual plan was to build on the prejudices because it was feared that the prejudices could not be overcome and because it was hoped that they could be used to advantage." He notes also that the national society "was officially more humanitarian and kindly toward Negroes, free and slave, than many people who supported it." (Cooke, *Frederic Bancroft*, pp. 189–190.)

42. On the colonial origins of discrimination see Jordan, *White Over Black*. Leon F. Litwack, *North of Slavery: The Negro in the Free States, 1790–1860* (Chicago, 1961), is an excellent account of racial discrimination in the antebellum North.

lent but basically conservative inclinations to conclude that the black man had nothing to hope for as long as he remained in the United States, and that if there was any solution at all to the racial situation it had to come from separation. If one accepted certain conservative assumptions about man and society, the colonizationist image of America as a permanently prejudiced nation had great cogency.

III

Evidence that the colonizationist analysis had a logic that transcended crude Negrophobia can be found in Alexis de Tocqueville's observations on the racial situation in the United States. Arriving from France in 1831 when the movement was at the height of its popularity, Tocqueville made a point of discussing white-black relations with leading colonizationists. One of them, John Latrobe of Maryland, succinctly described the situation to him as he saw it: "The black and white population are in a state of war. Never will they mingle. One of them will have to yield place to the other."[43] Tocqueville was powerfully influenced by testimony of this kind and presented in *Democracy in America* what amounted to a full and articulate statement of the colonizationist view of American racial realities. Although he ultimately concluded that colonization itself was impractical as a solution to the problem that the colonizationists had perceived, Tocqueville paid tribute to the movement as based on "a lofty and fruitful idea."[44]

The colonizationist view of the world did not, of course, imprint itself on Tocqueville's mind as on a *tabula rasa;* for he came to America with a set of attitudes that predisposed him to sympathize with the colonizationists. Even more than the protagonists of American benevolence, he was an aristocrat trying to come to terms with a new and more democratic state of society

43. George Wilson Pierson, *Tocqueville and Beaumont in America* (New York, 1938) , p. 516.
44. Alexis de Tocqueville, *Democracy in America,* ed. Phillips Bradley (New York, 1956) , I, 392–393.

and politics. In addition, he was at one with the theorists of
colonization in regarding slavery as an evil and in holding essentially environmentalist views of racial differences—opinions
which did not prevent him from ascribing great power and
permanence to racial prejudice.[45] Furthermore, Tocqueville's
own observations seemed to confirm the notion that American
Negrophobia was widespread and "deeply rooted." In carrying
out his mission to inspect the American penal system, he found
the color line drawn even among those deprived of their freedom
because of crimes against society. It was surprising at first to
discover that prisons separated white and black convicts or that
the Philadelphia House of Refuge, a kind of reform school for
young delinquents, refused to admit Negroes on any basis (as the
director explained, "It would be degrading to the white children
to associate them with beings given up to public scorn"); but
everywhere Tocqueville went he found similar examples of racial
antipathy and discrimination in all areas of life.[46] He was forced
to conclude that racial prejudice actually increased with emancipation and was worse in the "free" North than in the slave
South. Furthermore, he could observe with his own eyes the
condition of the "freed blacks," whom he described as "condemned by the laws and public opinion to a hereditary state of
misery and degradation."[47]

It was from such observations, therefore, as well as from the
testimony of conservatives of the colonizationist type, that

45. Tocqueville's personal views on the origin and permanence of racial
differences do not come through clearly in *Democracy in America*. Some
commentators have concluded that Tocqueville was himself a believer in the
concept of inherent black inferiority. A careful reading of *Democracy in
America* suggests that he was arguing in effect that the belief in Negro
inferiority was a self-fulfilling myth that prevented blacks from improving
themselves and thereby disproving the image that whites had of them. In the
1850s Tocqueville corresponded with Count Joseph Arthur de Gobineau, the
father of European racism, and emphatically denied the latter's contention
that racial differences were innate and unchangeable. Tocqueville himself
subscribed to the eighteenth-century belief that mankind "belongs to a single
species" and that human variations are the products of "secondary and
external causes." (See Alexis de Tocqueville, *The European Revolution and
Correspondence with Gobineau*, ed. John Lukacs [New York, 1959], pp.
221–224, 227–229, 294, 305–306.)

46. Pierson, *Tocqueville and Beaumont*, pp. 512–515.

47. Tocqueville, *Democracy*, I, 299, 373.

Tocqueville derived his analysis of the American racial situation. His major point was that the progenitors of Negro slavery had entailed upon their descendants a race problem for which emancipation provided no answer. The abolition of slavery, as he saw it, was always followed by the necessity of absorbing the ex-slaves into the community, which meant in effect reconstructing society on a new basis. This had to be done because no society could maintain public peace and tranquillity with a large and permanently discontented pariah class in its midst. In the ancient world it had been possible to reconstitute the community after emancipation because there had been no visible sign of slave origin to keep alive for very long the inevitable social prejudice against freedmen and their descendants. But in the United States, as in other parts of the New World, slavery had been reserved for men of a different color, and this conjunction of servitude and color, which made the ex-slave readily and permanently identifiable, had planted the seeds of disaster by creating a problem of race more fundamental and difficult to solve than the problem of slavery. On the basis of what he had seen and heard of white American attitudes toward the free Negro, Tocqueville described what seemed likely to remain the situation so long as whites and blacks attempted to inhabit the same territory: "The two races," he wrote, "are fastened to each other without intermingling; and they are alike unable to separate entirely or combine," and he suggested that this situation constituted "the most formidable of all the ills that threaten the future of the Union."[48]

Tocqueville's vision of the future of the blacks in America was cataclysmic. Slavery would inevitably come to an end, he predicted, because it was incompatible with modern civilization and the trend of world opinion, but emancipation would be followed by a race war which would result in the extermination of the blacks except possibly "along the coast of the gulf of Mexico," where they might have the numbers to hold their own.[49] The only conceivable alternative was social acceptance accompanied

48. *Ibid.*, 370–372.
49. *Ibid.*, 390–392, 397. Tocqueville's prediction of race war derived in part from his consciousness, as a Frenchman, of the Haitian experience.

by the possibility of intermarriage; and this was ruled out by the fact that a sense of the physical differences between whites and Negroes, when combined with historically derived prejudice, made such contacts unimaginable: "His physiognomy is to our eyes hideous," Tocqueville wrote of the Negro as he was usually perceived by the white man, "his understanding weak, his tastes low; and we are almost inclined to look upon him as a being intermediate between man and the brutes." "To induce the whites to abandon the opinion they have conceived of the moral and intellectual inferiority of their former slaves," he added in a footnote, "the Negroes must change; but, as long as this opinion persists, they cannot change."[50] In presenting this early description of a "vicious circle" in black-white relations, Tocqueville, unlike later and more optimistic exponents of the idea, left no doubt that he, like the colonizationists, saw no effective way to break the circle as long as America remained a biracial society.

Although Tocqueville was convinced that the colonization movement had a correct perception of the dangers to America of an oppressed black population, he found its solution to the problem totally unrealistic. Even if colonizationists had a government subsidy, he contended, they would never even be able to send enough blacks to Liberia to drain off the natural increase of the slave population. If the Federal government undertook to purchase slaves for colonization, the cost would turn out to be enormous and unacceptable to the North, unless the price was fixed at a low level—but that in turn would lead to the South's rejection of the plan.[51]

Implicit in Tocqueville's assertion of the futility of colonization as even a partial remedy to the growth of a potentially dangerous slave population was his overriding sense of the United States as a decentralized democracy without agencies powerful enough to carry out costly new programs in the face of a public opinion which reflected only immediate interests or in opposition to localized groups which claimed a veto power over the actions of the Federal government. In considering the future of democracy in general, Tocqueville deduced from the Ameri-

50. *Ibid.*, 372, 372n.
51. *Ibid.*, 393, 393n.

can example that equality of condition and the "restless" pursuit of wealth and status to which it gave rise made liberal democracies peculiarly resistant to basic reforms; for men obsessed with their own uncertain economic and social position tend "to regard every new theory as a peril, every innovation as an irksome toil, every social improvement as a stepping-stone to revolution, and so refuse to move all together for fear of being moved too far."[52]

In a certain sense, this was a plausible description of the tendency of Jacksonian America, despite the appearance of innovation, because the democratic political and economic reforms of the age were designed to remove the last remaining barriers to a "natural" egalitarian order (for whites only, of course), which once achieved would supposedly require no further alteration. This process of democratization also involved the destruction or weakening of such centers of power and authority as might be capable of initiating and carrying out major reforms on a national scale. In attempting to resist a democratic trend that reduced the power of government and the possibility of elite direction, the colonizationists were in fact espousing aims and methods that were inappropriate to the voluntaristic society and *laissez-faire* economy that were coming into existence. The colonizationists were out of step with the political trends of the 1820s and 1830s primarily because their program required massive Federal aid and central direction. They differed in this key respect from the other benevolent movements which had been able to adjust more completely to the voluntaristic pattern of nineteenth-century America. Because the magnitude of their task forced them to look to the government for subsidization and guidance, the colonizationists ended up advocating what was basically a Federalist scheme in an era when Federalism had been discredited and when the last remnants of Hamiltonianism were being overthrown.

The first intense opposition to colonization came in the 1820s from the slaveholding states of the deep South. Seeing in colonization a long-range threat to slavery, South Carolinians in particular used the popular argument of states' rights to oppose any effort to subsidize a program of free-Negro removal that might

52. *Ibid.*, II, p. 277.

lead to gradual emancipation. Various efforts of the mid-1820s to initiate Federally supported colonization won the endorsement of several Northern state legislatures but failed to win Congressional approval because of the deep South's angry rejection of the scheme.[53]

With the triumph of Andrew Jackson in 1828, a new and less sectional basis for opposition appeared: Jackson's later destruction of the Bank of the United States and his rejection of internal improvements were part of a process of narrowing the scope of Federal action that also blocked once and for all the efforts of the Colonization Society to get substantial support from the government. The concept of positive government in what conservatives defined as the national interest did not, of course, entirely disappear in this period, but survived in modified form as "the American system" of Henry Clay and the Whigs; and it was no accident that Clay was a leading colonizationist, because the tariff, internal improvements, the Bank of the United States, and colonization were all part of the same program. Indeed, colonization became tied explicitly to the American system in 1832 when Clay, having failed to win support for Federal programs, proposed in Congress that funds derived from sales of public lands be distributed among the states "for education, internal improvements or colonization." The bill passed the House and Senate but was vetoed by Jackson, and hence subsidized colonization, like the bank, the tariff, and the internal-improvement schemes, became a casualty of Jacksonian democracy. Since the Jacksonians showed on the whole even more distaste for the black population than did the Whig colonizationists, their opposition can scarcely be attributed to a belief in the possibility of racial brotherhood in America. Given the prevailing assumption, shared by both the proponents of colonization and their political enemies, that a racially egalitarian society was inconceivable, it must be concluded that colonization was doomed as a Federally subsidized program because it constituted

53. On Southern opposition to colonizationism see Staudenraus, *African Colonization*, pp. 169–177; and William W. Freehling, *Prelude to Civil War: The Nullification Controversy in South Carolina, 1816–1836* (New York, 1966), pp. 122–126, 196–199.

an effort at positive national action under the leadership of an elite at a time when such an undertaking was rendered impossible by an increasing emphasis on *laissez faire,* decentralized democracy, and states' rights.[54]

Failing to achieve its political objectives, the movement was forced by the early 1830s to pursue its aims as a private philanthropy; and with its loss of all standing in the deep South it necessarily devoted all its attention to the border states and the North. But in the latter area a new source of opposition developed that provided the final blow that eventually reduced the movement to irrelevance even among leading proponents of philanthropy and reform. A new reform spirit was now developing in the North that found abhorrent the basic premises of colonization. The rise of the abolitionists in the 1830s was a sign that conservative, neo-Federalist philanthropy was going out of fashion and that Christian reformers were now looking beyond the corporate hierarchical society of the Federalists and Calvinists to reforms that reflected new aspirations for the liberation of the individual from the historical and institutional limitations taken for granted by conservatives.

IV

William Lloyd Garrison, who after 1830 denounced the American Colonization Society in the same harsh and uncompromising way that he castigated slaveholders, led the abolitionist assault on colonizationism. In the *Liberator,* founded in 1831, and in his book *Thoughts on African Colonization* (1832), Garrison charged that the movement was a proslavery plot, designed to rid the South of the troubling presence of free Negroes; subsequently this position was endorsed by the American Anti-Slavery Society, which was founded by Garrison and others in 1833. Perhaps Garrison's single most important contribution to the development of an antislavery movement was that he thus succeeded in discrediting colonization in the eyes of a vanguard of Northern humanitarians. If he went too far in attributing conscious pro-

54. See Staudenraus, *African Colonization,* pp. 184–187.

slavery intentions to the colonizationist leaders, there was truth in his charge that the movement actually buttressed the slave system it purported to attack. During the 1820s only 1,420 Negroes had been transported to Liberia, and many of these were not manumitted slaves. Such a trickle could have no real impact on the future of slavery; its actual function, if not its intended one, was to provide an outlet for humanitarian feelings at a time when slavery was in fact developing and flourishing in the South.[55]

The real issue, however, was not the success or failure of colonization but its basic morality. The abolitionists of the 1830s charged that the colonizationist doctrine of ineradicable prejudice was un-Christian. To rule out the possibility of a racially egalitarian society was, to their way of thinking, a willful and perverse denial of both the Gospel and the Declaration of Independence. The controversy that then erupted in Northern reform circles was not, as is sometimes supposed, a dispute over the inherent capabilities of the Negro; as we have seen, prominent advocates of colonization often shared, in theory at least, the abolitionist belief that American Negro deficiencies were the result of a repressive environment. Rather it was a debate on the separate issue of whether white Americans could be expected to overcome their antipathy to blacks and achieve interracial equality and brotherhood. As "practical" conservatives with a powerful sense of the limitations of reform, the leading colonizationists regarded prejudice as too deeply rooted to be eliminated. The abolitionists, on the other hand, were idealistic Christian reformers who believed that racial antipathy, like other "sinful" human dispositions, could be overcome.

For those who fully subscribed to Garrison's radical views, such a doctrine tended to be part of a generalized "perfectionist" or millenarian reformism. "My Bible assures me," Garrison wrote in *Thoughts on African Colonization*, "that the day is coming when even the 'wolf shall dwell with the lamb, and the leopard shall lie down with the kid, and the wolf and the young lion and the fatling together'; and, if this be possible, I see no cause why those

55. John L. Thomas, *The Liberator: William Lloyd Garrison* (Boston, 1963) , pp. 92–100, 143–154.

of the same species—God's rational creatures—fellow country-men in truth, cannot dwell in harmony together." Garrison went on to affirm that "there *is* power enough in the religion of Jesus Christ to melt down the most stubborn prejudices, to overthrow the highest walls of partition, to break the strongest caste, to improve and elevate the most degraded, to unite in fellowship the most hostile, and to equalize and bless all its recipients."

Aileen S. Kraditor has recently challenged the view that the perfectionist radicalism of the Garrisonians was shared by most abolitionists. But even the more moderate abolitionists, some of whom made tactical concessions to racial prejudice or revealed at times their own residual anti-Negro feelings, rejected the coloni-zationist concept that racial prejudice was a permanent and insuperable fact of American life.[56] All would have accepted without hesitation the formulation of William Jay, a relatively conservative abolitionist pamphleteer, who simply asked the colonizationists if it was conceivable that Christ had commanded men to love one another without giving them the power to do it.[57]

The view that Christian brotherhood was actually and im-mediately attainable was thus the key to the abolitionist view of race relations. But why, it might be asked, did the concept of an all-embracing Christian love, which had been latent in the Gospel from the beginning, suddenly become the inspiration for radical reform in the United States during the 1830s? The intel-lectual side of this development is now well understood by historians. The abolitionists' belief in interracial fraternity, like their doctrine of immediate emancipation to which it was so closely related, was part of a general radicalization of reform that took place in the 1830s, under the stimulus of religious develop-ments that suggested a higher valuation of the moral capabilities of the individual and that pointed, by implication, to the per-fectibility of society as a whole. A new evangelicalism, freed from Calvinist concepts of original sin and predestination, posited self-

56. William Lloyd Garrison, *Thoughts on African Colonization* (Boston, 1832), pp. 143–154. The best general discussion of Garrisonian perfectionism is Thomas, *The Liberator,* especially Chapter 12.

57. Aileen S. Kraditor, *Means and Ends in American Abolitionism: Garrison and His Critics on Tactics and Strategy, 1834–1850* (New York, 1969), *passim;* William Jay, *Miscellaneous Writings on Slavery* (Boston, 1853), p. 373.

regenerating individuals who were able, on their own initiative, to repent fully of their sins and experience a "second birth." According to revivalists like Charles Grandison Finney, a genuine conversion experience must be followed by a life of strenuous Christian endeavor—and to some this meant warring against the institutionalized "sins" of society. Thus slavery and racial discrimination, along with intemperance, war, and other collective evils, came to be regarded, not as social imperfections to be controlled and cautiously alleviated, but as sins which could be totally eliminated if all the individuals involved repented and immediately ceased to support institutions and practices out of harmony with the Gospel of Christ. Under the influence of this new evangelicalism, the basic character of reform changed: the gradualism and tolerance of temporary imperfection that had been characteristic of the thought of the Enlightenment was replaced by the immediatism and perfectionism of "romantic reform." As a result, movements that began under the aegis of conservative philanthropy were transformed or fragmented in the 1830s. Temperance became total abstinence; a pacifism that objected to offensive wars only was challenged by the advocates of "nonresistance"; and the colonizationalist movement was denounced by abolitionists who had formerly supported it.[58]

Reinforcing this intellectual change was a transformation of the social and economic basis of American life that had major consequences for American ideology. The colonization movement, as has been suggested, operated on the assumption that society was a corporate entity, composed of mutually dependent classes and groups living in a permanent and harmonious relationship. The blacks, it was alleged, could never be incorporated into such a society because they were—and always would be—rejected by "every other class in the community." As for slavery,

58. The pioneering study of the religious basis of abolitionism is Gilbert Hobbs Barnes, *The Antislavery Impulse, 1830–1844* (New York, 1933), Chapter I. Two brilliant recent essays which deal with the intellectual aspects of the radicalization of reform in the 1830s are John L. Thomas, "Romantic Reform in America, 1815–1865," *American Quarterly,* XVII (Winter 1965), pp. 656–681; and David Brion Davis, "The Emergence of Immediatism in British and American Antislavery Thought," *Mississippi Valley Historical Review,* XLIX (September, 1962), 209–230.

it was not considered a permanently viable social relationship, because it tended in the long run to set one group at war with the rest of the society. To some extent this concept of the social order as a closely woven but diversified fabric, with slavery as the major flaw in the pattern, was rooted in the realities of colonial and Federal America. As long as a sense of class prerogative and class deference remained, as long as churches, charter monopolies, and professional associations had an acknowledged affiliation with government and hence an official and influential place in the collective scheme of things, and as long as subordinate groups did not become too restive, the conservative corporate ideal seemed viable.

But by the 1830s such conditions no longer existed or seemed likely to be re-established. A series of interrelated developments had by then destroyed or weakened the corporate entities of colonial America and had led to a new emphasis on the individual and his potentialities which had some basis in social and economic conditions. On the fundamental level of economic ideas and practices, increasing access to the manifold sources of wealth offered by an expanding nation led to the rise of a new class of small entrepreneurs and the national triumph of *laissez faire*—a policy viewed by Jacksonians as offering greater opportunity to the individual because governmental regulation traditionally meant special privileges for established groups. In the realm of society and politics, this was the era when a sweeping egalitarianism removed the vestiges of social deference and political rule by quasi-hereditary elites. One man's birth and background were now supposedly as good as another's, and individual claims to leadership and influence had, in theory at least, to be based on an earned reputation for the right personal qualities. Evangelical religion, which now opened the possibility of conversion to any man who would attend a revival meeting, and "romantic reform," which emphasized the rehabilitation of individuals through an appeal to their consciences, were both clearly related to this larger ethos of egalitarian individualism. Thus the abolitionist belief in the moral perfectibility of man can be seen as an extreme and "spiritualized" reflection of the prevalent world view, which in essence saw the individual as the master of his own destiny.[59]

The abolitionist movement, however, was not of one mind about the full meaning of individual perfectibility. For a radical wing that looked to Garrison for leadership, it eventually came to mean nothing less than becoming like Christ himself—"perfect as your Father in Heaven is perfect"—a doctrine that led to a rejection of all earthly government and temporal allegiances.[60] If Garrison's literal Christian perfectionism and quasi anarchism represented the logical outcome of abolitionist thought, it is clear that most abolitionists never got to this point. The majority, and especially most of those who broke with Garrison when the antislavery movement divided into two organizations in 1840, adhered implicitly to a less pure ideal which reflected some confusion of Christian idealism with characteristic American middleclass values. For many antislavery spokesmen, it would seem, the model for a total realization of human potentialities was simply a middle-class New Englander, transplanted perhaps to another region, who had the proper religious commitments, "Yankee virtues," and benevolent concerns.[61]

59. A provocative exposition of the thesis that this period was characterized by a form of "institutional breakdown" appears in Stanley Elkins, *Slavery: A Problem in American Institutional and Intellectual Life* (Chicago, 1959), especially pp. 27–32. In *The Contours of American History* (Cleveland, 1961), William Appleman Williams provides a suggestive economic interpretation of the decline of "corporate" values and practices in the face of a new *"Weltanschauung of laissez-faire"* in the period after 1819 (see pp. 227–283). Although Williams and Elkins start from apparently quite different ideological positions, they actually come to comparable conclusions about the breakdown of older corporate forms and values and the pervasive influence of an individualistic, *laissez-faire* outlook in the antebellum period.

60. See Thomas, *Garrison*, especially Chapter 12.

61. Aileen Kraditor describes the non-Garrisonian abolitionists as "reformers rather than radicals," who "considered Northern society fundamentally good." The Garrisonians, on the other hand, "believed that American society, North as well as South, was fundamentally immoral, with slavery only the worst of its many sins, and . . . looked forward to a thorough-going change in its institutional structure and ideology" (Kraditor, *Means and Ends*, p. 8). The only difficulty in such a formulation is that it appears to exaggerate the radicalism of the Garrisonians by implying that they were root-and-branch opponents of the prevailing ideology. Actually even the Garrisonians did not question the capitalistic, free-labor *economic* basis of Northern life; they were, it seems obvious, bourgeois radicals and not socialists.

V

Whether their concept of individual freedom and perfectibility was a mandate for radical social change or the complacent assertion of an existing norm, it was clear that the abolitionists accepted the view of society that was triumphing in the 1830s—the notion that the basic social unit was the individual—and then attempted to prevent such a conception from becoming a license for uncontrolled selfishness by infusing it with religious and ethical aspiration. It was on the basis of such convictions and desires that they put forth their interpretation of the interrelated problems of slavery and race. Where the colonizationists saw slavery as a social and economic evil that had taken such deep root in national life that it could be eradicated only by a cautious, indirect, and gradual approach, the abolitionist vanguard regarded slaveholding as an individual sin and called upon slaveowners to repent and give immediate freedom to their bondsmen. Thus reform, which the colonizationists in their own inadequate and equivocal fashion had seen as a corporate and social undertaking, became individualized, a matter primarily of personal decision and moral example. At the same time, the very reason for objecting to slavery was altered. Where the colonizationist condemned slavery in his calculating and prudential fashion because he saw it as a threat to the prosperity and safety of society, the abolitionist acted from moral fervor and humanitarian sentiment—he sought empathy with the slave as a human being and tried to participate vicariously in his suffering.[62]

For abolitionists, the full horror of slavery came not only from

62. On the abolitionist concept of individualized reform and their emphasis on empathy with the slave, see Kraditor, *Means and Ends,* pp. 237–255. Although I agree with Miss Kraditor's formulation of abolitionist doctrines, I am not so ready to excuse the philosophical limitations and ambiguities of their approach to reform on the grounds that they were "agitators, not systematic thinkers" (p. 255). It is perfectly legitimate, in my opinion, to evaluate a radical movement, past or present, by critically analyzing its underlying philosophical rationale in terms of both the consistency of its doctrines and the efficacy of its methods.

the flagrant physical cruelty that they often documented but also from the fact that the slave, unlike other Americans, was denied a chance for moral, religious, and intellectual self-development. As the great abolitionist crusader Theodore Weld wrote to Garrison in 1833, God had given to every man the right to be *"a free moral agent,"* and "he who robs his fellow man of this tramples upon right, subverts justice, unsettles the foundation of human safety, and sacrilegiously assumes the prerogative of God."[63] In the words of Elizabeth Chandler, a Quaker writer and former associate of Garrison: ". . . it is in the very nature of slavery to cast a benumbing influence over its unhappy victims,— degrading every nobler faculty, and freezing up the well springs of intellectual excellence."[64] By thus thwarting the slave's self-development, servitude inevitably drove him to the very depths of depravity. "From the moment the slave is kidnapped," wrote the abolitionist writer Lydia Maria Child in 1833, ". . . the white man's influence directly cherishes ignorance, fraud, licentiousness, revenge, hatred and murder. It cannot be denied that human nature thus operated upon, *must* necessarily yield, more or less to all these evils."[65] The Unitarian reformer James Freeman Clarke made the same point in 1842 in a sermon on slavery:

> A worse evil to the slave than the cruelty he sometimes endures, is the moral degradation that results from his condition. Falsehood, theft, licentiousness, are the natural consequence of his situation. . . . He goes to excess in eating and drinking and animal pleasures; for he has no access to any higher pleasures, and a man cannot be an animal without sinking below an animal,—a brutal man is worse than a brute. An animal cannot be more savage or more greedy than the law of his nature allows. But there seems to be no limit to the degradation of a man. Slavery is the parent of vices. . . .

63. Theodore Weld to William Lloyd Garrison, Jan. 2, 1833, *Letters of Theodore Dwight Weld, Angelina Grimké Weld, and Sarah Weld, 1822–1844,* ed. Gilbert H. Barnes and Dwight L. Dumond (New York, 1934), I, 98.

64. Elizabeth Margaret Chandler, *Essays, Philanthropic and Moral* (Philadelphia, 1836), p. 7.

65. Lydia Maria Child, *An Appeal in Favor of that Class of Americans Called Africans* (New York, 1836), p. 16. (First published in 1833.)

Cowardice and cruelty, cunning and stupidity, abject submission or deadly vindictiveness are now as they have always been the fruits of slavery.[66]

Such statements revealed something about the abolitionist conception of the relationship between individual responsibility and social circumstances. Most obvious was what seemed to be a thoroughgoing environmentalism, reflected in the willingness to attribute Negro depravity entirely to slavery. But along with this sense of the degrading effect of the institution, there was the unmistakable note of moral disapproval in the description of the slave's "vices" and "excesses." A sin apparently remained a sin whether it was forced on the individual or not. Of course there is no real mystery about this, since the abolitionists were Christian moralists first and sociologists of slavery second. What made slavery such a detestable condition was not simply that it created a bad environment; it was such a severely limiting condition that it was incompatible with the fundamental abolitionist belief that every man was morally responsible for his actions. It was a unique case of determinism and predestination in a world allegedly composed of free men who were personally responsible for their own moral character and social situation. It is possible, therefore, that one of the reasons the abolitionists of the 1830s and early 1840s hated slavery so much was that it cast doubt on their basic view of human nature as self-regenerating.

Tension between environmental determinism and a belief in human freedom and responsibility was strikingly evident in the characteristic abolitionist view of the free Negro and his situation. Antislavery authors, by and large, admitted that the colonizationists were right in seeing the free blacks as, in some sense, a degraded population. As William Jay put it, "the free blacks have been rendered by prejudice and persecution an ignorant and degraded class."[67] Richard Hildreth, an abolitionist writer and historian, went so far as to confess that it was very difficult to answer the argument against emancipation that derived from the

66. James Freeman Clarke, *Slavery in the United States: A Sermon Delivered on Thanksgiving Day, . . . 1842* (Boston, 1843), pp. 8–9.
67. Jay, *Miscellaneous Writings*, p. 57.

present condition of the free Negro population.[68] Even Garrison, who generally defended the freed blacks against the more extreme attacks on their virtue, conceded that "it would be absurd to pretend that as a class they maintain a high character" or "to deny that intemperance, indolence, and crime prevail among them to a mournful extent."[69]

Abolitionists, of course, firmly believed that such degradation had its origin in "prejudice and persecution" and was, therefore, in no sense the result of racial attributes. But they characteristically regarded such racial injustices as hindrances rather than as insurmountable barriers to free-Negro progress in the North. Hence they felt no qualms about exhorting Northern free Negroes to self-improvement, believing apparently that a discriminatory environment did not fully excuse them from failure to elevate themselves. It was in this vein that a writer in the *Liberator* addressed the free blacks in 1832. After taking note of the colonizationist claim that Negroes constituted one-sixth of the convict population of Massachusetts, he went on as follows: "If this be so, it is time for you to awake. . . . Be industrious. Let no hour pass unemployed. . . . Be virtuous. . . . Use no bad language. Let no foolish jesting be heard from you, but be sober men who have characters to form for eternity. . . . In a word, endeavor to be good Christians, and good citizens, that all reproach may be taken from you, and that your enemies, seeing your good conduct, may be ashamed. Thus you will aid your friends in their endeavors for your good. . . ."[70] Shortly after the founding of the American Anti-Slavery Society in 1833, the executive committee of the organization instructed its agents to teach to free Negroes "the importance of domestic order and the performance of relative duties in families; of correct habits; command of temper and courteous manners." They were also to instill "industry and economy; promptness and fidelity in the fulfillment of contracts or obligations . . . and encourage them

68. Richard Hildreth, *Despotism in America; or an Inquiry into the Nature and Results of the Slaveholding System in the United States* (Boston, 1840), p. 183.
69. Garrison, *Thoughts*, pp. 128–129.
70. *Liberator*, January 23, 1832.

in the acquisition of property. . . ." In short, they were to turn them, if possible, into paragons of middle-class virtue.[71]

Advice of this kind had a number of implications. First, it demonstrated that for many abolitionists human perfectibility actually meant little more than the attainment of conventional middle-class attributes. It further revealed that abolitionists often acknowledged a kind of *de facto* cultural inferiority that placed most free blacks on a plane lower than most whites. Although this situation was seen as correctible, such a judgment could be used to reinforce the unfavorable free-Negro stereotype that was promulgated by colonizationists and defenders of slavery. Such evaluations also led some abolitionists to make appeals for "equality" that were carefully qualified by middle-class conceptions of social hierarchy. In 1832 another writer in the *Liberator* described the degradation of the free blacks and emphasized that they had to earn their equality: "till they are equal to other people in knowledge and cultivation, they will not and cannot rank as equals."[72] Similar assumptions were often revealed when abolitionists countered the troubling charge that they advocated immediate social equality, including intermarriage. "On the subject of equality," wrote Lydia Maria Child in 1834, "the principles of the abolitionists have been misrepresented. They have not the slightest wish to do violence to the distinctions of society by forcing the rude and illiterate into the presence of the learned and refined." All they were interested in was giving blacks the same rights and opportunities possessed by "the lowest and most ignorant white man in America."[73]

Recognizing that racial discrimination in the North made it more difficult for Negroes to start at the bottom and struggle upward in a competitive society, abolitionists campaigned vigor-

71. Quoted in William H. and Jane H. Pease, "Antislavery Ambivalence: Immediatism, Expediency, and Race," *American Quarterly*, XVII (Winter 1965), 689–690. My conclusions on abolitionist thinking are in general agreement with the findings of Pease and Pease in this excellent article. At times, however, their account of antislavery attitudes toward the blacks seems to confuse specifically *racial* prejudice with the middle-class *social* prejudices that many abolitionists manifested.

72. *Liberator,* January 23, 1832.

73. Lydia Maria Child, ed., *The Oasis* (Boston, 1834), p. ix.

ously against enforced segregation and other discriminatory practices in their own communities. But when they complained that
free Negroes were not doing enough to help themselves, they
revealed that they could go only so far in acknowledging that a
"free" society created conditions that excused what the white
middle class regarded as moral and economic failure. Most of the
abolitionists believed that the capitalistic free-labor system of the
North was healthy at the core, that its arbitrary inequalities were
surface phenomena resulting either from the baneful influence of
the slave South or from the intellectual and institutional remnants of an older and less egalitarian form of society, and that
such inequalities were not sufficiently inhibiting to negate the
general proposition that everyone had a substantial opportunity
for self-improvement. The kinds of disabilities faced by the free
blacks were not regarded as fully condoning their degraded condition, any more than the selfishness of capitalists and the desti-
tution of free white workers condoned the vices of the poor.[74]

Some abolitionists went so far as to contend that the free
Negroes, with all their handicaps, had both the duty and the
capability to behave better than white people who were similarly
or more advantageously placed. "It must not be supposed because I say so much about good conduct," a writer identified as
"S.T.U." wrote in the *Liberator* in 1832, "that I think the
colored people not as good as the whites; for I have no doubt
that they are so, in proportion to their advantages. But in this
case something more than commonly good conduct is needed in
order to overcome the unfortunate prejudice against them." He
went on to recommend that they demonstrate their good qualities by avoiding resentfulness and receiving "with the true

74. Even Garrison, the most radical of major abolitionist leaders, was relatively conservative on questions involving the basic social and economic relationships of Northern society. When confronting English Chartists and other
labor radicals, he made clear his belief that the grievances of workingmen did
not constitute "industrial slavery" and were no cause for replacing individual
"self-help" with new and militant forms of collective action. In the first issue
of the *Liberator*, he denied the existence of conflict between wealth and
property, or between labor and capital, and demonstrated his faith in an
industrial order held together by the benevolence of the rich and the cultivation of Protestant virtues by the poor. Both of Garrison's recent biographers
stress his conservatism on such questions (see Thomas, *The Liberator*, pp.
298–299, and Walter M. Merrill, *Against Wind and Tide: A Biography of
William Lloyd Garrison* [Cambridge, Mass., 1963], pp. 47–48) .

dignity of meekness any treatment arising from the injurious prejudices of people toward them."[75] The blacks' failure to live up to the full expectations of many abolitionists persisted through the antebellum period; as late as 1859, the essential role of Negro improvement and perfect manners in the winning of equality was reasserted by the Reverend James Freeman Clarke. After questioning the efficacy of merely agitating for equal rights, Clarke concluded: "The public opinion in behalf of the colored people is yet to be made. Every colored man who is industrious, virtuous, intelligent and gentlemanly helps to make it. *Prejudice cannot be talked down; it must be lived down.*"[76]

The notion that free-Negro self-help was an indispensable part of the campaign against racial antipathy suggests that the abolitionist concept of prejudice and how to combat it could be more pragmatic and complex than one might gather from their critique of the colonizationists. On one level, of course, prejudice was simply a sinful attitude to be overcome by moral suasion and education. As the Reverend Robert B. Hall told the New England Anti-Slavery Society in 1832: "A prejudice is generated in our youth against the blacks, which grows with our growth and strengthens with our strength, until our eyes are opened to the folly by a more correct feeling. . . ."[77] The abolitionist demand for immediate emancipation was in itself an implicit call for immediate racial brotherhood; if men could be converted to one, they would in effect be converted to the other.[78] But on another level of abolitionist discourse, prejudice was recognized less as a sin than as a sociological fact resulting from slavery and free-Negro degradation. Abolitionists generally made this point when disputing the claim that prejudice was the inevitable result of differences in pigmentation. "It is against *condition, degradation and poverty* that the prejudice lies, and not against the color of the skin," one abolitionist writer affirmed in 1838.[79] And late in his life Garrison made a clear and unequivocal assertion of what had always been his basic position: ". . . the color of the skin,"

75. *Liberator,* February 11, 1832.
76. *Liberator,* March 25, 1859. (The italics are mine.)
77. *Liberator,* April 14, 1832.
78. This point is made in Kraditor, *Means and Ends,* especially pp. 242–243.
79. S. B. Treadwell, *American Liberties and American Slavery* (New York, 1838), p. 242.

he told an English audience after the Civil War, "has nothing to do with prejudice. It is the offspring of slavery, it is not to be found anywhere in the world excepting where slavery has victimized those of the Negro race."[80]

Such an analysis would seem to suggest that the only way to begin to eliminate prejudice was to abolish slavery; but, as abolitionists commonly acknowledged, prejudice itself was a major barrier to emancipation.[81] The abolitionist emphasis on the exemplary possibilities of free-Negro self-help can be seen in part as an effort to break out of this vicious circle. By improving themselves and becoming model citizens, the free blacks would destroy the identification that existed in the public mind between the Negro and the degraded slave. This apparent tactical necessity explains and to some extent justifies the patronizing preachments addressed to free Negroes. But the circle had not in fact been broken, because the free Negro himself was held down by prejudice and was the product of his own background and heritage; hence he was not usually in a position to respond to the abolitionist demand that he "earn" his full equality by becoming an exemplary middle-class American.

In refusing to push an environmentalist interpretation of black "degradation" to its logical outcome by acknowledging that most blacks in the North as well as in the South were so acted upon that there was comparatively little they could do to improve their own situation in the ways that whites recommended, the abolitionists revealed how their underlying commitment to an individualistic philosophy of moral reform prevented them from perceiving the full dimensions of the American race problem. A related failure of perception was their apparent underestimation of the force of color prejudice as a semiautonomous influence on white thought and behavior. There was probably more truth than they were willing to acknowledge in Tocqueville's suggestion that slavery per se did not fully explain white prejudice and black "degradation." In the United States an invidious group identity had been forced on all Negroes not only because they were or had been slaves, but also because of a racial

80. *American Freedman,* II (December, 1867) , 325.
81. See Kraditor, *Means and Ends,* pp. 254–255.

visibility, a palpable physical difference, which made it easy for blacks to be singled out as victims of stigmatization and discrimination whenever social tensions prompted insecure whites to buttress their own self-image at the expense of a noticeably different group. Prejudice would undoubtedly have existed to some extent even if Africans had arrived in North America as free immigrants; when slave background was added to color as a basis of stigmatization, a powerful set of anti-Negro attitudes was created, capable of surviving the formal abolition of slavery and serving the psychological needs of white groups in a competitive free-labor society. In the 1830s and 1840s racial prejudice was becoming more virulent in the North, not only because of popular opposition to abolition and abolitionism but also, one suspects, because the rise of egalitarianism and competitive individualism resulted, as Tocqueville had suggested, in an increase of status anxieties among whites. In turn, these anxieties presumably lent urgency to new efforts to exclude blacks from participation in the community, because one result of anti-Negro action was to call attention to the guaranteed social status of a white skin. It can also be argued that the decline of corporate thinking that undermined colonizationism and helped lay the foundation for the abolitionist emphasis on universal egalitarianism and individual moral reform also helped set in motion more powerful currents running in a different direction—toward an articulate and aggressive racism which excluded the Negro from the society of competing equals without deporting him, by the simple and brutal mechanism of formally defining him as subhuman.

The abolitionist philosophy of social reform through individual self-regeneration, with equivocal and sometimes grudging concessions to the inescapable effects of a repressive environment on the black character, would not prove an adequate response to this challenge. Moral exhortation and example were not powerful enough to persuade very many whites to give up the social and psychological rewards they derived from a sense of their own racial supremacy or to convince most free blacks that it was worth the effort to engage in difficult, frustrating, and perhaps unavailing efforts to prove their worth in the eyes of white Americans by achieving a kind of middle-class perfection that few whites had actually attained. But before we condemn the abolitionists for their failure to convert America to a belief in racial equality by confronting directly the social, economic, and psychological roots of prejudice, it must be acknowledged that no other approach than the one they adopted was really open to them. Their time and place provided them neither the means nor the social philosophy to deal adequately with the ravages of racial prejudice and the growth of racism as an ideology. If they did not succeed in making racial egalitarianism an operative national creed, they did at least contribute eventually to a rise in the intensity of Northern opposition to slavery as an institution. What remains to be explained is the apparently paradoxical fact that the abolitionists could thus gain support for their attack on slavery at the very time a newly systematized doctrine of black inferiority was also triumphing in American thought.

Chapter Two

•

Slavery and Race:
The Southern Dilemma

PRIOR TO THE 1830s, black subordination was the practice of white Americans, and the inferiority of the Negro was undoubtedly a common assumption, but open assertions of *permanent* inferiority were exceedingly rare. It took the assault of the abolitionists to unmask the cant about a theoretical human equality that coexisted with Negro slavery and racial discrimination and to force the practitioners of racial oppression to develop a theory that accorded with their behavior. Well before the rise of radical abolitionism, however, spokesmen for the lower South gave notice that they were prepared to defend slavery as an institution against any kind of attack that might develop. In the 1820s the leadership of the major cotton-producing states made it clear that a national colonization effort was unacceptable because in their view slavery was an essential and Constitutionally protected local institution which was no concern of the Federal government or the nonslaveholding states. These apologists for black servitude characteristically answered the colonizationists by agreeing with them that emancipation on the soil was unthinkable and then proceeding to point out not only that colonization was impractical as a program of Negro removal but also that its very agitation was a danger to the security of a slave society because the expectations it raised among blacks threatened to undermine the discipline of the plantation. A permanent and rigid slave system, it was argued, was both economically necessary in the rice- and cotton-growing areas and vital as a system of control for a potentially dangerous black population. Such a viewpoint soon triumphed in all the slaveholding states. In 1831 and 1832, the Virginia legislature debated a colonization proposal that might have opened the way to gradual emancipation, but its defeat marked the end of a serious search, even in the upper South, for some way to set slavery on the path to extinction.[1]

After the Virginia debate, Professor Thomas R. Dew of William and Mary College, speaking for the victorious proslavery faction, set forth the most thorough and comprehensive justification of the institution that the South had yet produced. Dew's effort should properly be seen as reflecting a transitional stage in the proslavery argument. Since he was refuting the proponents of gradual emancipation and colonization who still thrived in western Virginia and not the new and radical abolitionists of the North, his arguments stressed practicality and expediency and, in a sense, did little more than help bring Virginia in line with the kind of proslavery sentiment already triumphant farther South. Much of his lengthy essay was devoted to showing that colonization was an impossible scheme because the natural increase of the black population would outrun any number that could possibly be colonized. His justification of slavery rested first of all on the contention that servitude had been a necessary stage of human progress and hence could not be regarded as evil in itself. He then went on to argue that the concrete circumstances of Southern life required the institution and that no set of abstract principles should be invoked to obscure the basic fact that the Negro was not prepared for freedom. Although this was fundamentally an extension of the kind of argument that had previously been

1. On proslavery attitudes in the lower South in the 1820s, see William W. Freehling, *Prelude to Civil War: The Nullification Controversy in South Carolina, 1816–1836* (New York, 1966), Chapter III and pp. 122–128; and William Sumner Jenkins, *Pro-Slavery Thought in the Old South* (Chapel Hill, N.C., 1935), pp. 65–79. The best account of the Virginia debate is Joseph Clarke Robert, *The Road from Monticello: A Study of the Virginia Slavery Debate of 1832* (Durham, N.C., 1941).

the basis of the defense of slavery as "a necessary evil," Dew implied that such a practical adjustment to reality had no evil in it, and he raised expediency to the level of conservative principle when he cited Edmund Burke's dictum that "circumstances give in reality to every political principle its distinguishing color and discriminating effect."[2]

In his discussion of Negro character and prospects, Dew did not deviate forthrightly and insistently from traditional quasi-environmentalist assumptions about the nature of most racial differences. Although at the beginning of his essay he described Negroes as "differing from us in color and habits and vastly inferior in the scale of civilization," he did not deal consistently with the question whether this inferiority resulted from innate character or from the "habits" engendered by a long exposure to inhibiting circumstances. In his discussion of "obstacles to emancipation," Dew at one point provided an analysis not incompatible with the conservative environmentalism of the colonizationists. "The blacks," he wrote, "have now all the habits and feelings of slaves, the whites have those of masters; the prejudices are formed, and mere legislation cannot improve them. . . . Declare the Negroes of the South free tomorrow, and vain will be your decree until you have prepared them for it. . . . The law would make them freemen, and custom or prejudice, we care not which you call it, would degrade them to the condition of slaves." Such a prediction, he indicated, was merely an application of the rule that "each one should remain in society in the condition in which he has been born and trained, and not [try] to mount too fast without preparation."[3]

This ultraconservative principle could presumably have been applied to slaves or serfs of any race; and, as if to substantiate this inference, Dew went on to give as an example of premature emancipation the attempt to liberate the Polish peasants in the 1790s. But Dew could also describe black behavior as if it were predetermined by innate racial traits; for he contradicted his

2. "Professor Dew on Slavery," *The Pro-Slavery Argument* (Charleston, 1852), p. 355, and *passim*. Dew's essay was originally published as *Review of the Debate of the Virginia Legislature of 1831 and 1832* (Richmond, 1832).
3. *Ibid.*, pp. 287, 435–436.

suggestion that Negro characteristics were simply acquired habits of servility by arguing, somewhat obscurely, that the supposed indolence of free blacks resulted from "an inherent and intrinsic cause." And when he asserted that "the free black will work *nowhere* except by compulsion," he decisively parted company with the colonizationists.[4] If Dew was a transitional figure in the general defense of slavery because he combined arguments from expediency with hints of a conservative, proslavery theory of society, he was equally transitional as a racial theorist, because of his vacillation between arguments for black inferiority drawn from a perception of the force of "habits," "customs," and "prejudices" and those suggesting that a permanency of racial type justified enslavement.

By the middle of the 1830s the full impact of the abolitionist argument had been felt in the South, and Dew's ambiguous treatment of the racial factor and his contention that slavery was sometimes justified by circumstances no longer provided Southern apologists with what they regarded as a fully adequate defense of the institution. The abolitionists' charge that slavery was inherently sinful was now met increasingly by the unequivocal claim that slavery was "a positive good." Furthermore their practical assertion of racial equality as something to be achieved in the United States and not through colonization inspired proslavery spokesmen to clarify their racial views and to assert, as a major part of their case, the unambiguous concept of inherent Negro inferiority.

South Carolinians led the way. In 1835 Governor George McDuffie told the South Carolina General Assembly that the Negroes were "destined by providence" for slavery and that this was made evident not only by the color of their skin but also by "the intellectual inferiority and natural improvidence of this race." They were, he indicated, "unfit for self-government of any kind," and "in all respects, physical, moral, and political, inferior to millions of the human race." McDuffie professed astonishment that anyone should "suppose it possible to reclaim the African race from their destiny" as slaves or subjects of some

4. *Ibid.*, pp. 437, 429–430. (The italics are mine.)

other form of absolute despotism.[5] The Charleston lawyer William Drayton said much the same thing the following year in a pamphlet attacking the abolitionists: "Personal observation must convince every candid man, that the negro is constitutionally indolent, voluptuous, and prone to vice; that his mind is heavy, dull, and unambitious; and that the doom that has made the African in all ages and countries, a slave—is the natural consequence of the inferiority of his character."[6] In 1837 John C. Calhoun made his famous defense of slavery before the Senate of the United States and showed how important racial doctrines really were in the new and militant defense of servitude which developed in the 1830s. "I hold that in the present state of civilization, where two races of different origin, and distinguished by color, and other physical differences, as well as intellectual, are brought together, the relation now existing in the slaveholding states between the two, is, instead of an evil, a good—a positive good."[7]

It was thus in tandem with the concept of slavery as "a positive good" that the doctrine of permanent black inferiority began its career as a rationale, first for slavery itself and later for post-emancipation forms of racial oppression. The attitudes that underlay the belief that the Negro was doomed by nature itself to perpetual slavishness and subordination to the whites were not new, nor was the doctrine itself if considered as a popular belief that lacked intellectual respectability; but when asserted dogmatically and with an aura of philosophical authority by leading Southern spokesmen and their Northern supporters in the 1830s, it became, for the first time, the basis of a world view, an explicit ideology around which the beneficiaries of white supremacy could organize themselves and their thoughts.

The emergence of racist ideology in the United States was comparable in some respects to the rise of European conservative

5. Speech before the General Assembly of South Carolina, as reprinted in *The Source Book of American History,* ed. Albert Bushnell Hart (New York, 1905), p. 245.

6. William Drayton, *The South Vindicated from the Treason and Fanaticism of the Northern Abolitionists* (Philadelphia, 1836), p. 232.

7. John C. Calhoun, *Works,* ed. Richard K. Crallé (New York, 1853–1857), II, 631.

ideology, as described by Karl Mannheim in his essay on "Conservative Thought." Mannheim made a distinction between "traditionalism"—the emotional and relatively inarticulate tendency to hold on to established and inherited patterns of life—and "conservatism," which he saw as "conscious and reflective from the first, since it arises as a counter movement in conscious opposition to the highly organized, coherent, and systematic 'progressive' movement." This distinction is clearly analogous to one that can be drawn between racial prejudice as an emotional response to an enslaved and physically distinct group and the early form of ideological racism as a "conscious and reflective" attempt to develop, in response to an insistent egalitarianism, a world view based squarely and explicitly on the idea that whites are unalterably superior to blacks. As long as the traditional order was not threatened by radicalism, it required no elaborate theoretical defense. Or, as Gustave de Beaumont, Tocqueville's companion, put it in his novel, *Marie:* "As long as philanthropy on behalf of the Negroes resulted in nothing but useless declamation, the Americans tolerated it without difficulty; it mattered little to them that the equality of the Negroes should be proclaimed in theory, so long as in fact they remained inferior to the whites." But abolitionism, like Jacobinism, forced previously unarticulated assumptions to the level of defensive ideological conscious.[8]

The colonizationists may have stimulated an indirect and pragmatic defense of slavery as a regional necessity, but their occasional expressions of a theoretical racial egalitarianism had not forced their Southern opponents to proclaim vigorously that the Negro was inherently inferior and slavish, for the reason that proponents of colonization had not challenged the necessity or inevitability of black subservience as a fact of life in the United States. The abolitionist contention that Christianity and the Declaration of Independence not only affirmed equality in theory but cried out for its immediate implementation could not go similarly unanswered by the defenders of black subordination.

8. Karl Mannheim, *Essays on Sociology and Social Psychology* (London, 1953) , pp. 99 and 74–164, *passim;* Gustave de Beaumont, *Marie, or Slavery in the United States* (Stanford, Cal., 1958) , p. 11. (First published in 1835.)

In their efforts to justify slavery as a necessary system of race relations, the proslavery theorists of the 1830s and 1840s developed an arsenal of arguments for Negro inferiority which they repeated *ad nauseam*. Heavily emphasized was the historical case against the black man based on his supposed failure to develop a civilized way of life in Africa. As portrayed in proslavery writings, Africa was and always had been the scene of unmitigated savagery, cannibalism, devil worship, and licentiousness. Also advanced was an early form of the biological argument, based on real or imagined physiological and anatomical differences—especially in cranial characteristics and facial angles—which allegedly explained mental and physical inferiority. Finally there was the appeal to deep-seated white fears of widespread miscegenation, as proslavery theorists sought to deepen white anxieties by claiming that the abolition of slavery would lead to intermarriage and the degeneracy of the race. Although all these arguments had appeared earlier in fugitive or embryonic form, there is something startling about the rapidity with which they were brought together and organized in a rigid polemical pattern, once the defenders of slavery found themselves in a propaganda war with the abolitionists.

The basic racist case against the abolitionist assertion of equality sprang full blown—but without the authoritative "scientific" underpinning that would later give it greater respectability—in a pamphlet published in New York in 1833, entitled *Evidence Against the Views of the Abolitionists, Consisting of Physical and Moral Proofs of the Natural Inferiority of the Negroes.* In this extraordinary document a writer named Richard Colfax set forth in rudimentary form all the basic elements of the racist theory of Negro character. Colfax emphasized in particular a whole range of physical differences between whites and blacks which supposedly demonstrated inherent Negro inferiority. The Negro's facial angle, he contended, was "almost to a level with that of the brute"; hence "the acknowledged meanness of the Negro's intellect only coincides with the shape of his head." The lesson to be drawn from such data was that the black man's *"want of capacity to receive a complicated education renders it improper and impolitic that he should be allowed the privileges of citizenship*

in an enlightened country." Since "the Negroes, whether physically or morally considered, are so inferior as to resemble the
brute creation as nearly as they do the white species, . . . *no
alteration of their present social condition would be productive
of the least benefit to them,* inasmuch as no change of their
nature can be expected to result therefrom." This unchangeability of the black character had been demonstrated historically,
according to Colfax, because over a period of three or four thousand years Africans had had many opportunities to benefit from
personal liberty and "their proximity to refined nations," but
they had "never even *attempted* to raise themselves above their
present equivocal station in the great zoological chain."[9]

The only element lacking in Colfax's racist argument was a
full scientific explanation of the underlying *causes* of inequality.
In the century that followed, theorists of racial inferiority would
offer new and ingenious proofs or explanations for Colfax's assertions, but they would add very little to his general thesis.

As part of their effort to gain widespread support for such
views, proslavery polemicists turned their attention to the free
Negroes of the North, whom they presented not so much as a
population degraded by white prejudice and color consciousness
as one demonstrating its natural unfitness for freedom. When the
census of 1840, which later proved to be inaccurate, revealed a
very high rate of insanity among free Negroes as compared with
slaves, they seized upon these statistics as evidence of the Negro's
constitutional inability to function in a free society. In 1844
Calhoun, then Secretary of State, concluded that "the census and

9. Richard H. Colfax, *Evidence Against the Views of the Abolitionists . . .*
(New York, 1833) , pp. 25–26, 30, and *passim.* In the late 1840s and 1850s,
these arguments would be placed in a framework of respectable scientific
theory by the "American School of ethnology" (see Chapter Three below) .
Subsequent to the publication of Colfax's *Evidence Against the Views of the
Abolitionists,* the same historical and biological case against the Negro was
presented, for example, in Drayton's *The South Vindicated* (1836) ; James
Kirke Paulding's *Slavery in the United States* (New York, 1836) ; J. H.
Guenebault's *Natural History of the Negro Race* (Charleston, 1837) ; The
Reverend Josiah Priest's *Slavery, As It Relates to the Negro or African Race*
(Albany, N.Y., 1843) ; Samuel A. Cartwright's *Essays, Being Inductions Drawn
from the Baconian Philosophy . . .* (Vidalia, La., 1843) ; and Matthew Estes,
A Defense of Negro Slavery, As It Exists in the United States (Montgomery,
Ala., 1846) .

other authentic documents show that, in all instances in which the states have changed the former relation between the two races, the African, instead of being improved, has become worse. They have been invariably sunk into vice and pauperism, accompanied by bodily and mental afflictions incident thereto—deafness, insanity and idiocy—to a degree without example. . . ."[10]

II

As the debate progressed, it became evident that Northern opponents of slavery could, if they chose, easily deflect the increasingly vexed question of biological differences by arguing that constitutional Negro deficiencies, even if they existed, provided no justification for slavery. On the contrary, they would only make it more sinful; for what could be more unchristian than exploitation of the weak by the strong? Owen Lovejoy, an abolitionist Congressman from Illinois and brother of the martyred editor Elijah P. Lovejoy, eloquently presented this point of view in 1860: "We may concede it as a matter of fact that [the Negro race] is inferior; but does it follow, therefore, that it is right to enslave a man simply because he is inferior? This, to me, is a most abhorrent doctrine. It could place the weak everywhere at the mercy of the strong; it would place the poor at the mercy of the rich; it would place those who are deficient in intellect at the mercy of those that are gifted in mental endowment. . . ."[11]

Many Southerners were themselves too strongly influenced by

10. John C. Calhoun, *Works*, V, 337. There are excellent discussions of the controversy over the census of 1840 in Leon F. Litwack, *North of Slavery: The Negro in the Free States, 1790–1860* (Chicago, 1961), pp. 40–46, and Norman Dain, *Concepts of Insanity in the United States, 1789–1865* (New Brunswick, N.J., 1964), pp. 104–108.

11. "The principle upon which slaveholding was sought to be justified in this country would, if carried out in the affairs of the universe," Lovejoy added, "transform Jehovah, the supreme, into an infinite juggernaut, rolling the huge wheels of his omnipotence, ankle deep, amid the crushed, and mangled, and bleeding bodies of human beings on the ground that he was infinitely superior, and that they were an inferior race." (Cited in the *Liberator*, April 26, 1860.)

Christian and humanitarian values to let such an indictment stand. Their answer was that the slave was not only unfit for freedom but was ideally suited to slavery; for the Negro found happiness and fulfillment only when he had a white master. As one writer put it, Negro slaves are "the most cheerful and merry people we have among us."[12] Far from the blacks' being "degraded," Southern apologists maintained that they were much better off in slavery than they had been in Africa. According to the South Carolina novelist William Gilmore Simms, the Negro came from a continent where he was "a cannibal, destined . . . to eat his fellow, or be eaten by him." Southern slavery "brought him to a land in which he suffers no risk of life or limb other than that to which his owner is equally subjected," and had increased "his health and strength," improved "his physical symmetry and animal organization," elevated "his mind and morals," and given "him better and more certain food, better clothing, and more kind and valuable attendance when he is sick." It was no wonder, then, that he had developed a happy disposition.[13]

In promulgating the stereotype of the happy and contented bondsman, Southerners were doing more than simply putting out propaganda to counter the abolitionist image of the wretched slave. They were also seeking to put to rest their own nagging fears of slave rebellion. It was no accident that proslavery spokesmen in the Virginia legislature made much of the alleged contentment of the slaves; for the debate took place in the wake of the Nat Turner uprising of 1831, and servitude had come under attack as leading inevitably to black resistance. One of the proslavery members made it clear that the recent rebellion was a bizarre exception to the general pattern of master-slave relationships: "Our slave population is not only a happy one, but it is a contented, peaceful and harmless . . . during all this time [the last sixty years] we have had one insurrection."[14]

12. William A. Smith, *Lectures on the Philosophy and Practice of Slavery* . . . (Nashville, 1856), pp. 223–224.

13. William Gilmore Simms, "The Morals of Slavery," *The Pro-Slavery Argument*, p. 273. (Originally published in *The Southern Literary Messenger* III [November, 1837], 641–657.)

14. From a speech of James Gholson of Brunswick County, in Robert, *Road from Monticello*, p. 67.

The image of black violence and retribution, drawn not only from Nat Turner but from memories of what had occurred in Santo Domingo, continued to haunt the Southern imagination however. Insurrection panics were frequent after 1830, and for men who supposedly ruled over a docile population, Southern slaveowners were extraordinarily careful to maintain absolute control over their "people" and to quarantine them from any kind of outside influence that might inspire dissatisfaction with their condition. In moments of candor, Southerners admitted their suspicion that duplicity, opportunism, and potential rebelliousness lurked behind the mask of Negro affability.[15]

A concept of the duality or instability of Negro character was in fact one of the most important contributions made by Southern proslavery propagandists to the racist imagery that outlasted slavery. In its original protoracist form, this duality was the one set forth by Thomas R. Dew between the savage Negro of Africa and the "civilized" black slave. Dew maintained that no large-scale insurrections were likely "where the blacks are as much civilized as they are in the United States. Savages and Koromantyn slaves can commit such deeds, because their whole life and education have prepared them; but the Negro of the United States has imbibed the principles, sentiments, and the feelings of the whites; in one word, he is civilized. . . ."[16] But Dew's analysis implicitly conceded too much to environment; indeed it made the Negro character seem almost infinitely plastic. What, it might be asked, was to prevent blacks from soon becoming "civilized" up to the level of the whites and claiming equality with them? Later writers often qualified the notion that slavery "civilized" the Negro by asserting that innate racial traits limited his potential development to a more or less tenuous state of "semi-civilization," a conception which provided an unequivocal justification of permanent servitude.

According to this theory, the Negro was by nature a savage brute. Under slavery, however, he was "domesticated" or, to a

15. See Mary Boykin Chesnut, *A Diary from Dixie,* ed. Ben Ames Williams (Boston, 1949) , p. 141, for a classic expression of Southern doubts about slave contentment and docility.

16. *Pro-Slavery Argument,* p. 463.

limited degree, "civilized." Hence docility was not so much his natural character as an artificial creation of slavery. As long as the control of the master was firm and assured, the slave would be happy, loyal, and affectionate; but remove or weaken the authority of the master, and he would revert to type as a blood-thirsty savage. That many Southerners did not believe, even in theory, in Negro docility under *all* conditions came out most vividly in proslavery discussions of emancipation and its probable consequences. Servile war was often seen as the inevitable result of loosening the bonds of servitude. In the words of William Drayton, who drew on the example of Santo Domingo, "the madness which a sudden freedom from restraint begets—the overpowering burst of a long buried passion, the wild frenzy of revenge, and the savage lust for blood, all unite to give the warfare of liberated slaves, traits of cruelty and crime which nothing earthly can equal."[17] Drayton's suggestion that emancipation would bring a reversion to basic savage type was set forth more explicitly by a writer in *De Bow's Review*, who described as follows the consequences of liberating a large black population: ". . . the brutish propensities of the negro now unchecked, there remains no road for their full exercise . . . but in the slaughter of his white master, and through the slaughter, he strides (unless he himself be exterminated) to the full exercise of his *native barbarity and savageness.*"[18] As proof of the Negro's inevitable "reversion to type" when freed, defenders of slavery pointed continually to the alleged "relapse into barbarism" which had taken place in Haiti, the British West Indies, and Liberia, once the domesticating influence of slavery had been removed.[19]

The notion that bestial savagery constituted the basic Negro character and that the loyal "Sambo" figure was a social product of slavery served to channel genuine fears and anxieties by suggesting a program of preventive action, while at the same time

17. Drayton, *The South Vindicated*, p. 246.
18. "L. S. M.," review of John Campbell's *Negromania*, in *The Industrial Resources of the Southern and Western States*, ed. J. D. B. De Bow (New Orleans, 1852) , II, 203. (The italics are mine.)
19. See for example, Thomas R. R. Cobb, *An Inquiry into the Law of Negro Slavery in the United States of America* (Philadelphia, 1858) , pp. cxcvii, ccxxvii.

legitimizing a conditional "affection" for the Negro. As a slave he was lovable, but as a freedman he would be a monster. This duality was expressed in its most extreme form by Dr. Samuel A. Cartwright of Louisiana, who wrote in 1861 that ". . . the negro must, from necessity, be the slave of man or the slave of Satan."[20]

There were, however, ambiguities in the concept of Negro "domestication" or "semi-civilization" under slavery. One involved the question of whether or not, in the far distant future, the slave's savage instincts might entirely disappear as the result of some quasi-Lamarckian process of evolution, a development which would presumably fit the Negro for a change of status. Many writers regarded this question as open and undecided; others fell into blatant self-contradiction when they confronted it. William Gilmore Simms, in setting forth a proslavery theory of human progress, described how the rise of peoples to civilized status had often involved the tutelage of slavery as a stage in their development. "It is possible that a time will come," he wrote, "when, taught by our schools, and made strong by our training, the negroes of the southern states may arrive at freedom." Later in the same paragraph, however, he rudely shut the door that he had tentatively opened: "I do not believe that [the Negro] will ever be other than a slave, or that he was made to be otherwise; but that he is designed as an implement in the hand of civilization always."[21] This view was given authoritative expression from the mid-1840s on by "ethnological" writers like Samuel Cartwright and Josiah Nott. From a narrowly proslavery perspective, however, the whole question was in effect academic, because even those apologists who accepted the possibility that blacks might someday be ready for freedom maintained that additional centuries of servitude would be required to transform the essential Negro character.[22]

A more significant ambiguity, one which led to an important

20. Dr. Samuel Cartwright, "Negro Freedom: An Impossibility under Nature's Laws," *De Bow's Review*, XXX (May–June, 1861), 651.
21. *Pro-Slavery Argument*, pp. 266–268.
22. For an example of the thesis that blacks would be ready "at some distant day" for "the privileges of civil liberty," see W. A. Smith, *Lectures on . . . Slavery* (1856), p. 246 and *passim*. By the time Smith wrote, however, this was clearly not the dominant view among proslavery apologists.

cleavage, resulted from differences over exactly what Negro "domestication" meant in terms of the actual relationships between masters and slaves. One way of suggesting what was at issue is to ask whether the model for the ideal slave was taken from the realm of the subhuman, with the slave as a high type of domesticated animal to serve as the white man's tool like another beast of burden, or from the human family as a "domestic" and domesticating institution, with the slave in the role of a child, responding with human affection to a kindly master. This ambiguity was related to an ambiguity about the nature of the plantation: was it a commercial enterprise with the blacks as a subhuman labor force, or a small patriarchal society?

George Fitzhugh, writing in the 1850s, was the most eloquent spokesman of the familial or paternalist view of slavery. For him, the harsh, exploitative side of slavery disappeared almost entirely; the master became a "parent or guardian," and the slave a child who, on the basis of a "common humanity," was admitted to "the family circle"[23] and subjected to "family government." The view of Negro psychology that sustained such a view was set forth by the Reverend H. N. McTyeire in a typical example of the advice that clergymen of a certain type gave to slaveholders: "The sympathies which have their range within the social system—the emotions which form the ordinary cement of social existence, are found in the negro, and they are to be taken into account, in dealing with him. The master who ignores them and proceeds on brute principles, will vex his own soul and render his servants worthless and wretched. Love and fear, a regard for public opinion, gratitude, shame, the conjugal, parental, and filial feelings, these must all be appealed to and cultivated."[24]

The very fact, however, that such advice had to be given suggests that there was a contrary point of view. Paternalists emphasized the reality of slave "gratitude" as a natural human emotion deriving from kindly treatment; men with a different orientation thought differently. This, for example, is how George S. Sawyer,

23. George Fitzhugh, *Sociology for the South; or, the Failure of Free Society* (Richmond, 1854), pp. 82–83, 105–107; *Cannibals All! or, Slaves Without Masters,* ed. C. Vann Woodward (Cambridge, Mass., 1960), p. 205. (First published in 1857.)

24. H. N. McTyeire, "Plantation Life—Duties and Responsibilities," *De Bow's Review,* XXIX (September, 1860), 361.

a Louisiana slaveholder, described the Negro character: "The very many instances of remarkable fidelity and attachment to their masters, a characteristic quite common among them, are founded not so much upon any high intellectual and refined sentiment of gratitude, as upon instinctive impulse, possessed to an even higher degree by some of the canine species."[25]

It was a short step from such an analogy to the argument that it was more difficult to mistreat Negroes or to overwork them than would be the case with whites; and some Southerners even concluded that for most purposes a master could simply forget about the possibility that his charges had normal human sensibilities. Cartwright, a Louisiana physician who had many years of practice on the plantations of what was then the Southwest, maintained in 1843 that the Negro race "has a peculiar instinct protecting it against the abuses of arbitrary power"; for blacks could not be overworked and were comparatively insensitive to sufferings that would be unbearable to whites. But Cartwright did believe that there was such a thing as "mismanagement" of Negroes. In a later "medical" essay, he described various Negro "diseases" that resulted from it, including drapetomia (running away) and rascality. Since such afflictions stemmed from bad government or imperfect slavery, their source was not in the harshness of servitude but in the unnatural liberty permitted by ineffectual masters.[26] The comforting notion that slaves did not suffer, even from flagrant mistreatment, was given expression by a Southern lady novelist in 1860. She not only argued that Negroes could not be overworked but claimed that it was physically impossible for a master to knock a slave "senseless to the ground"—as he was so often knocked in abolitionist writings— because the Negro skull was so thick that such an effort would bruise or break a white man's fist.[27]

The supposed animal insensitivity of the Negro was also

25. George S. Sawyer, *Southern Institutes; or, an Inquiry into the Origin and Early Prevalence of Slavery and the Slave Trade* (Philadelphia, 1858), p. 197.

26. Samuel A. Cartwright, *Essays*, p. 3, and "Diseases and Peculiarities of the Negro," in De Bow, ed., *Industrial Resources*, II, 318–324. For another expression of the view that the Negro, like the mule, could not be overworked, see Estes, *Defense of Negro Slavery*, pp. 78–80.

27. Mrs. Henry Schoolcraft, *The Black Gauntlet: A Tale of Plantation Life in South Carolina* (Philadelphia, 1860), pp. 49, 61.

invoked as a basis for denying familial affection among slaves and thereby implicitly justifying the breakup of families. According to Thomas R. R. Cobb of Georgia, the Negro's "natural affections are not strong, and consequently he is cruel to his offspring, and suffers little by separation from them."[28] Sawyer went further and asserted that blacks are totally lacking in family feeling and that it is "lust and beastly cruelty" and not "emotions of parental and kindred attachment" that "glow in the negro's bosom."[29] Such opinions suggest that the kind of "hard" racism that manifests itself in the image of "the Negro as beast" did not originate in the era of segregation late in the nineteenth century but had its origins in the antebellum period, when it vied for supremacy in Southern propaganda with the "soft" image of the black slave as beloved child.

III

The South's fundamental conception of itself as a slaveholding society was unstable. In the intellectual context of the time, the notion of the slave as dependent or child implied one kind of social order; the view that he was essentially subhuman suggested another.

Seeing the Negro as basically human despite his inferiority was compatible in theory with his integration into a certain type of human society—one based on a frank and open recognition of a whole range of inequalities. One branch of proslavery thought took this tack—the theoretical defense of a social order in which slavery was part of a larger hierarchy maintained by a sense of mutual obligation between superiors and inferiors. This viewpoint was foreshadowed by Thomas R. Dew's dictum that everyone, white or black, should be content to remain in the social station "in which he has been born and bred," and that consequently it was as ill advised for planters to encourage white overseers to aspire to gentility by giving them access to the

28. Cobb, *Inquiry*, p. 39.
29. Sawyer, *Institutes*, p. 222.

drawing room as it was to invite expectations of freedom from the slaves.[30] In a defense of slavery published in 1838, Chancellor William Harper of the University of South Carolina elaborated on this hierarchical concept when he answered the abolitionist charge that the slave was denied the possibility of intellectual improvement by attacking the very notion of a society based on equality of opportunity. "The slave receives," Harper wrote, "such instruction as qualifies him to discharge the duties of his particular station. The Creator did not intend that every human being should be highly cultivated, morally and intellectually." Then, hitting even more directly at the American egalitarian ideal, he added: ". . . if, as Providence has evidently decreed, there can be but a certain portion of intellectual excellence in any community, it is better that it should be *unequally* divided. It is better that a part should be fully and highly cultivated, and the rest utterly ignorant." As a matter of principle, the lower classes, regardless of race, should be subordinated and kept in ignorance. Following the logic of his argument, Harper contended that the misery and uncertainty of status which seemed endemic to the "laborious poor" of nonslaveholding societies could be readily relieved by the imposition of something like slavery.[31]

Out of this kind of reactionary thinking there evolved by the early 1850s the fully developed thesis that slavery was "a positive good," not only as a system of controlling an inferior race but, more basically, as a way of providing security to the laboring class of any society. George Fitzhugh carried this line of thought to its logical extreme when he attacked the fundamental assumptions of capitalism and democracy by arguing that the working class of advanced industrial countries like Great Britain would be better off under slavery. For Fitzhugh and other Southern defenders of a reactionary seigneurialism, the patriarchal plantation was the best model for society in general, because the cement of all enduring social relationships was the pattern of responsibility and dependence that existed in the family and on the idealized plantation. Their attack on "free society" was based

30. *Pro-Slavery Argument*, p. 436.
31. "Harper on Slavery," *ibid.*, pp. 35–36, 49–50 (originally published as *Memoir on Slavery* [Charleston, 1838]) .

on the claim that a lack of such relationships led inevitably to misery, anarchy, and revolution.[32]

Fitzhugh was aware that his whole reactionary social philosophy would be undermined if slavery were justified principally in terms of racial differences; hence in his writings of the mid-1850s, he was emphatic in his assertion that the South must be willing to defend slavery in general and not just for blacks. "The strongest argument against slavery, and all the prejudice against it," he wrote in 1857, "arise from the too great inferiority of race, which begets cruel and negligent treatment in the masters, who naturally feel little sympathy for ignorant, brutal savages. Inferiority of race is quite as good an argument against slavery as in its favor." "The whole history of the institution," he concluded, "shows that in giving up slavery in the abstract, we take the weakest position of defense that we could possibly select. We admit it to be wrong and then attempt to defend it in that peculiar form that has always been most odious to mankind."[33]

Fitzhugh's concern with this ideological problem suggested that many people in the South had not in fact taken his high ground and were trying to justify slavery on what he considered the narrow and treacherous basis of race alone. And he was right; for the view that slavery was rooted in the peculiar nature of the Negro rather than in ultraconservative concepts of society and government was a popular one. James D. B. De Bow, editor of De Bow's Review, a major source of proslavery doctrine, encouraged Fitzhugh's assault on a free society and liberal ideas, but he also opened his journal to the ethnological school and actively endorsed the views of men like Cartwright, Josiah C. Nott, and John H. Van Evrie who defended slavery almost exclusively on the basis of racist anthropology, arguing that the Negro was so radically inferior to the Caucasian that his destiny in America was either brute servitude or extermination. The Biblical curse of Ham could serve almost as well, and in the hands of writers like Matthew Estes and Josiah Priest, it became a judgment of God

32. Fitzhugh, Sociology for the South and Cannibals All!, passim. See also Henry Hughes, Treatise on Sociology: Theoretical and Practical (Philadelphia, 1854), for a different formulation of the same basic argument.

33. George Fitzhugh, "Southern Thought Again," De Bow's Review, XXIII (November, 1857), 451.

which placed the black man virtually beyond the pale of humanity.[34]

If Fitzhugh envisioned a seigneurial society based on the image of a patriarchal plantation, the militant racists implicitly or explicitly projected a democratic and egalitarian society for whites, denying that the blacks were, in any real sense at all, part of the human community. They were advocates of what the sociologist Pierre L. van den Berghe has called "Herrenvolk democracy." In his comparative study of racism, van den Berghe has contrasted "Herrenvolk democracies"—"regimes like those of the United States or South Africa that are democratic for the master race but tyrannical for the subordinate groups"—with genuinely aristocratic multiracial societies like those of colonial Latin America.[35] The conflict between a developing Herrenvolk ideology and an aristocratic or seigneurial philosophy theoretically incompatible with democracy served to divide the mind of the Old South. To understand this conflict, one must recognize that Southerners could mean two different things when they questioned the applicability of the Declaration of Independence. They could reject the idea of equality in general, like Chancellor Harper and Fitzhugh, or they could reject simply the interpretation of it which included the Negro as a man created equal to the whites. Those who embraced the second option saw themselves as preserving the egalitarian philosophy as a white racial prerogative. This latter view was stated succinctly by the Alabama fire-eater William L. Yancey before a Northern audience in 1860: "Your fathers and my fathers built this government on two ideas: the first is that the white race is the citizen, and the master race, and the white man is the equal of every other white man. The second idea is that the Negro is the inferior race."[36] In the same year, a writer in the *Southern Literary Messenger* made a similar

34. For more on De Bow and the ethnological school see Chapter Three, below. The virulently racist use of the curse of Ham was most strikingly manifested in Josiah Priest's *Slavery, As It Relates to the Negro* (1843), reissued as *Bible Defense of Slavery* . . . (Glasgow, Ky., 1852). See also Estes, *Defense of Negro Slavery.*

35. Pierre L. van den Berghe, *Race and Racism: A Comparative Perspective* (New York, 1967), pp. 17–18.

36. Extracts from a speech of Yancey in Boston, October 12, 1860, in the *Liberator,* October 26, 1860.

point in an historical analysis of slavery. Unlike the paternalists, he condemned ancient slavery and medieval serfdom in principle, because under such systems "races richly endowed by nature, and designed for high and lofty purposes, were kept from rising to their natural level." But all forms of white servitude and subordination had fallen before "the progress of truth, justice, and Christianity." Negro slavery, on the other hand, had persisted because it was not really incompatible with the growth of liberty and equality.[37]

Southerners often went further and contended that Negro slavery was not only compatible with white equality but was the very foundation of it. Governor Henry A. Wise of Virginia contended that true equality could exist among whites only where black servitude existed. "Break down slavery," he argued, "and you would with the same blow destroy the great democratic principle of equality among men."[38] The claim was frequently made that the white South had no recognized social classes; that far from establishing an aristocracy of slaveholders, as the abolitionists claimed, it put all white men, whether they owned slaves or not, on a dead level. Thomas R. R. Cobb described the lower-class whites of the South as having the sense of belonging "to an elevated class": "It matters not that he is no slaveholder; he is not of the inferior race; he is a freeborn citizen. . . . The poorest meets the richest as an equal; sits at the table with him; salutes him as a neighbor; meets him at a public assembly, and stands on the same social platform."[39]

Such observations obviously reflected a social ideal radically at variance with the image of the South as a seigneurial or quasi-feudal society. The proponents of this view made racial consciousness the foundation and cement of Southern society and not an incidental aspect. It was carried to its logical extreme in the writings of Dr. John H. Van Evrie, a proslavery New York physician and editor whose views were widely hailed in the

37. "The Negro Races," the *Southern Literary Messenger*, XXXI (July, 1860), 9–10.
38. Quoted in Jenkins, *Pro-Slavery Thought*, p. 190.
39. Cobb, *Inquiry*, p. 213. This statement of Cobb and those of several other prominent Southern spokesmen who made the same points are quoted in Jenkins, *Pro-Slavery Thought*, pp. 190–194.

South. In the 1853 pamphlet version of his *Negroes and Negro "Slavery,"* which carried on the cover the enthusiastic endorsements of Jefferson Davis, J. D. B. De Bow, and other prominent Southern spokesmen, Van Evrie combined arguments for the biological inequality of the blacks with a vigorous attack on all past or present forms of class privilege and social hierarchy within homogeneous white societies. He denounced with particular emphasis the oppression of British peasants and laborers by an "aristocracy" that was not naturally superior to those it governed. Having condemned all forms of subordination of whites to other whites as "artificial" and unjust, Van Evrie then relegated the blacks to abject and perpetual servitude for one reason alone—because they constituted a permanently inferior biological species. He even attacked those proslavery writers who attempted "to defend Southern institutions by comparing the condition of the Negro with the condition of the British laborer," because "no comparison is allowable or possible":

> The Negro is governed by those *naturally* superior, and is in the *best* condition of any portion or branch of his race, while the British laborer, governed by those *naturally* his equals, and even sometimes his inferiors, is in the *worst* condition of any portion of *his* race. The first is secure in all the rights that nature gives him, the latter is *practically* denied all or nearly all of his—the first is protected and provided for by those the Creator has designed should govern him, the latter is kept in ignorance, brutalized, over worked and plundered by those who it is designed should only *govern themselves—one is a normal condition,* the other an *infamous usurpation.*[40]

The most famous and authoritative statement of the principle that hierarchical subordination should always be strictly reserved for inferior races appeared in Alexander H. Stephens's famous "Cornerstone Speech" of 1861, heralding the foundation of the Confederacy. "Many governments," said the newly elected Vice

40. John H. Van Evrie, pamphlet *Negroes and Negro "Slavery": The First an Inferior Race: The Latter Its Normal Condition* (Baltimore, 1853), pp. 30–31 and *passim.* Van Evrie's doctrines as elaborated in the later book of the same title will be discussed more extensively in Chapter Three as applications of the "scientific" racism that burgeoned in the North as well as in the South during the 1850s.

President of the Confederate States of America, "have been founded on the principles of subordination and serfdom of certain classes of the same race; *such were, and are in violation of the laws of nature*. Our system commits no such violation of nature's laws. With us, all the white race, however high or low, rich or poor, are equal in the eyes of the law. Not so with the Negro. Subordination is his place. He, by nature, or by the curse against Canaan, is fitted for that condition which he occupies in our system." As for the basis of the new Confederate government: "Its foundations are laid, its cornerstone rests upon the great truth that the Negro is not equal to the white man, that slavery—subordination to the superior race—is his natural or normal condition."[41]

IV

Empirically speaking, Southern slavery was *both* an example of slavery in general *and* a form of servitude strictly limited to a single and supposedly inferior race. Two qualities about his laborers were thus bound to impress themselves upon the slave-holder's consciousness—that they were slaves and that they were black. On an unreflective attitudinal level these two aspects of the situation could coexist, reinforcing each other by creating a disposition to defend slavery because it was simultaneously the basis of concrete economic and social privilege for a class of Southerners and the institutional underpinning for a psychologically satisfying sense of racial superiority. But, as we have seen, the attempt to develop a consistent philosophical defense of the institution led inevitably to efforts to derive the argument principally from one facet or the other. Emphasis on slavery per se as an organizing principle of society led to a genuinely reactionary and paternalistic theory of society; but if racial differentiation was seen as the heart of the matter, then the result, in the larger American ideological context, was *"Herrenvolk* democracy" or "egalitarian" racism.

41. Henry Cleveland, *Alexander H. Stephens, In Public and Private; With Letters and Speeches, Before, During, and Since the War* (Philadelphia, 1866) , pp. 722–723, 721. (The italics are mine.)

The elaborate intellectual efforts of writers like Fitzhugh and Henry Hughes (the Mississippi "sociologist") to prove that the "ethnical qualification" in the South's system of labor was "accidental,"[42] can perhaps best be seen as an attempt to articulate the genuinely antidemocratic aspirations of an elite of large planters by legitimizing in the abstract the self-serving principle of aristocratic domination. There is undoubtedly some truth in Eugene Genovese's assertion that the master-slave relationship and the plantation environment tended by their very nature to produce a class with "an aristocratic, antibourgeois spirit with values and mores emphasizing family and status, a strong code of honor, and aspirations to luxury, ease, and accomplishment."[43] Fitzhugh, Hughes, and other aristocratic paternalists with similar if less highly developed views—men like Edmund Ruffin, William J. Grayson, and George Frederick Holmes—probably did express, in some sense, the deeper impulses of the South's upper class, "the logical outcome" of its social thinking.[44]

It is doubtful, however, that these aristocratic proslavery theorists produced a coherent world view that placed the South as a whole on the road to accepting a reactionary class ideology as opposed to a modern type of race ideology. First of all, these thinkers betrayed their own ambivalence by giving greater attention to racial inferiority as a justification of Southern slavery than their general theory actually required. Although Hughes had described the racial factor as an "accidental" element in the Southern labor system, he went on to argue at some length that subordination of the blacks in the South was essential to prevent amalgamation and preserve the purity of the white race;

42. Hughes, *Treatise,* p. 42.
43. Eugene D. Genovese, *The Political Economy of Slavery: Studies in the Economy and Society of the Slave South* (New York, 1965) , p. 28.
44. See Edmund Ruffin, *The Political Economy of Slavery* (1859) ; William J. Grayson, *The Hireling and the Slave* . . . (Charleston, 1856) ; and Robert L. Dabney, *A Defense of Virginia* . . . (New York, 1867) . For a provocative discussion of Fitzhugh's thought as the natural outgrowth of the slaveholder's situation, see Part Two of Eugene Genovese's *The World the Slaveholders Made: Two Essays in Interpretation* (New York, 1969) . For reasons that will become clear, however, I dissent from Genovese's thesis that the reactionary, consistently antidemocratic slaveholder's philosophy was the dominant world view that emerged from the antebellum South.

Edmund Ruffin combined universalist arguments for slavery with a full rendition of the historical thesis that blacks as a race had demonstrated a peculiar intellectual inferiority and incapacity for freedom; even Fitzhugh maintained that the inherent "child-like" character of the Negro was in itself a persuasive argument for his enslavement.[45]

Moreover, it is questionable that even an "ethnically quali-fied" argument for aristocracy and slavery as being good in them-selves won very many adherents outside a circle of slaveholding intellectuals who seemed alienated to some extent from their society and were without a determining influence on Southern politics or the formation of public opinion. Some of these theo-rists severely limited their own influence by openly manifesting aristocratic revulsion to the values and practices that resulted from the extension of democratic procedures and attitudes dur-ing the Jacksonian period. Among the older paternalistic theo-rists, Ruffin and Grayson belonged to the group that William R. Taylor describes as "Southern mugwumps," men who had re-treated from politics in the 1820s and 1830s, partly because of their temperamental and ideological opposition to the changing character of public life. It also is noteworthy that most of the paternalist ideologues were from Virginia and South Carolina, the most conservative Southern states. Their point of view was not so commonly expressed by the proslavery apologists of the newer and increasingly dominant Southwestern states, where a quasi-democratic ethos and a forthright emphasis on *"Herren-volk"* solidarity were made evident.[46]

The overwhelming majority of antebellum Southerners, it should be recalled, either owned no slaves or were farmers who owned only a few. Although many undoubtedly aspired to become planters, there is little indication that they accepted a reaction-ary social philosophy or even understood it. On the contrary,

45. Hughes, *Treatise,* pp. 238–243; Ruffin, *Political Economy,* pp. 10–19; Fitzhugh, *Sociology for the South,* pp. 82–83, and *Cannibals All!,* p. 20.

46. William R. Taylor, *Cavalier and Yankee: The Old South and American National Character* (New York, 1961), pp. 55–65. Edmund Ruffin's eschewal of a public career in the face of "democratic" tendencies that he refused to accept is further documented in Avery O. Craven's *Edmund Ruffin, South-erner* (New York and London, 1932), pp. 39–43.

most signs would suggest that for intraracial purposes they were fiercely democratic in their political and social thinking, strongly opposed to any formal recognition of the principle of aristocracy among whites. The reactionary elements of the planter class could not readily force their values on such a population, because political democracy in the Old South, and particularly in the Southwest, was no sham: universal white manhood suffrage existed in most states during the late antebellum period, and candidates closely identified with a "black belt" or planter interest were sometimes defeated in bitterly contested elections which revealed a vigorous two-party system and a high level of popular interest and participation. The "plain folk," mostly stiff-necked back-country farmers with their own frontier-type traditions, were not, despite their relative poverty, economically or socially dependent, in any full sense, on the planter elite; and with the extension of the suffrage in the 1830s this element acquired a political leverage that required some upper-class accommodation.[47]

47. That the Old South experienced a "democratic revolution" (for whites only) during the Jacksonian period has been argued most effectively by Fletcher M. Green and Charles S. Sydnor (see Green, *Democracy in the Old South and Other Essays*, ed. J. Isaac Copeland [Nashville, 1969], pp. 65–86; and Sydnor, *The Development of Southern Sectionalism 1819–1848* [Baton Rouge, La., 1948], Chapter XII), and has been reiterated in Clement Eaton's *The Growth of Southern Civilization, 1790–1860* (New York, 1961), pp. 172–175, 308–309. These historians recognize that this "democratization" was largely political and did not in the end undermine the social and economic dominance of the planter class, but contend that it did force the elite to adjust to the new order because it impelled them to profess a "democratic" ideology and to work through democratic electoral processes. Green and Sydnor have probably overstated their thesis because they have paid too little attention to persistently conservative and aristocratic facets of Southern life. But recent historians of basically Marxist orientation, such as Eugene Genovese and Barrington Moore, Jr. (see Moore's *Social Origins of Dictatorship and Democracy: Lord and Peasant in the Making in the Modern World* [Boston, 1966], Chapter Three), have gone to the other extreme by overlooking almost entirely the fact that the Old South had even a limited democratic aspect. They seem to imply that the planters ruled pretty much like the hereditary aristocracy of a typical premodern and hierarchical agrarian society. It admittedly strains credulity to describe the Old South as having been in any profound sense democratic or egalitarian. There were immense inequalities not only between masters and slaves but also between rich planters and much of the nonslaveholding population. But it seems clear that the late antebellum Southern oligarchy lacked the aura of unquestioned legitimacy

In the end, therefore, the planter class, whatever its own inner feelings, endeavored to maintain its *de facto* hegemony by making a "democratic" appeal, one which took into account the beliefs, desires, and phobias of an enfranchised nonslaveholding majority. No successful Southern politician, whatever his ties to the "aristocracy," was able to talk like Fitzhugh and give theoretical sanction to the enslavement or subordination of whites. When politicians justified slavery, they almost invariably did so largely in terms of race; the nonslaveholders feared blacks as potential competitors and opposed emancipation as a threat to their own "equal" status as whites. Because of inherent limitations on their ability to rule as they saw fit, the dominant class had to be content with a public defense of slavery that contradicted any consistently aristocratic pretensions they may have had; for they recognized that efforts to sanction white servitude in the abstract might endanger black servitude as a concrete reality. The fundamental insecurity that made such an adjustment mandatory was revealed by the hysterical reaction of Southern conservatives to the publication in 1857 of Hinton Rowan Helper's *The Impending Crisis of the South,* an attack on the slave system from a lower-class white point of view.[48] Not at all sure of the adherence of nonslaveholding whites to slavery itself, much less to a reactionary view of its implications, spokesmen for the planter class were generally willing to gain the necessary support for their concrete interests on any platform that would sanction them, even if it sacrificed their full ideological ambitions. In the last analysis, therefore, *Herrenvolk* egalitarianism was the dominant public ideology of the South, because it was the only one likely to ensure a consensus.

Spokesmen for the class of large planters were able to endorse such a doctrine without blatant hypocrisy because they themselves had never denied that inferiority of race was *one* justification of slavery. It has already been noted that Fitzhugh, who had

that surrounds an established seigneurial class with a privileged status recognized and accepted by the community as a whole.

48. This reaction is discussed in the introduction to Hinton Rowan Helper, *The Impending Crisis of the South: How to Meet It,* ed. George M. Fredrickson (Cambridge, Mass., 1968) , pp. xv–xix.

tried harder than anyone to confine racial differences within an ultraconservative social perspective—as only one example of the manifold inequalities which ought to be reflected in paternalistic institutions—had nevertheless always argued that the inherent characteristics of the Negro race made its enslavement both natural and necessary. And at the very end of the antebellum period, when the sectional conflict was approaching its climax, Fitzhugh himself put an increasing stress on the racial factor and consented to an enlargement of the theoretical gap between the races. Indeed, one of the most dramatic indications that the effort to develop and promulgate a genuinely paternalistic world view was aborted by concessions to racism and Negrophobia can be found in the shifting emphasis in Fitzhugh's writings between 1857 and 1861. In 1857 Fitzhugh had warned against a defense of slavery that relied on "too great inferiority of race." But in his 1859 article "Free Negroes in Hayti," he revealed his own growing interest in racial doctrines. Paying tribute to "ethnology, a study almost neglected fifty years since," which had now "been elevated to the dignity of a science," he went on to describe how Haitian blacks were "relapsing into their former savage state." In support of the view that Haitian "degeneration" revealed basic Negro traits, he cited Count Joseph Arthur de Gobineau, the father of modern European racism, whose book *The Moral and Intellectual Diversity of Races* was published in the United States in 1856. But Fitzhugh still held back from an unequivocal endorsement of Gobineau's assertion that Negroes had an absolutely fixed and unchangeable set of undesirable traits. He acknowledged that the Haitian experience demonstrated the current inability of the Negro to make progress under freedom but intimated that it was still an open question what might eventually be made of him under slavery.[49] In 1861, however, Fitzhugh announced his capitulation to extreme racism. In a review of Van Evrie's *Negroes and Negro "Slavery,"* in book form, Fitzhugh concluded that Van Evrie had provided "demonstrative reasoning, demonstrative proof, that the negro is of a different species, physically, from the white man. He then shows that the

49. George Fitzhugh, "Free Negroes in Hayti," *De Bow's Review,* XXVII (November, 1859) , 527–549.

habitudes, instincts, moral and intellectual qualities and capabilities of all animals are the universal and necessary concomitants
(if not the consequences) of their physical conformation. . . .
We maintain then, that without descending to moral reasoning
or speculation, he has *demonstrated* that the negro is physically,
morally, and intellectually a different being (from necessity)
from the white man, and must ever so remain. . . ." Fitzhugh
concluded that Van Evrie had "a new idea, a new and fruitful
idea."[50]

When he yielded to the pressure of Negrophobic opinion and
to a materialist racism that by his own earlier admission was
incompatible with a paternalist concept of slavery, Fitzhugh
demonstrated that the aristocratic slaveholder's philosophy had
failed to capture the Southern mind. His new racial emphasis
reflected his inability to convert the South to reactionary seigneurialism as an alternative to the extreme racist doctrines that
were growing in popularity as the basis of the proslavery argument during the 1850s. As his own heightened interest in "ethnology" suggests, one of the factors behind this rise in the significance
of anti-Negro thought was the growth, outside the South as
well as within it, of a body of "scientific" opinion which seemed
to give the racial emphasis such intellectual authority that there
was an almost irresistible temptation to make it a principal
weapon against proponents of emancipation and racial equality.

Chapter Three

•

Science, Polygenesis, and the Proslavery Argument

DURING THE 1840s and 1850s the conclusions of scientists on the nature and extent of racial diversity came for the first time to play an important role in the discussion of black servitude.[1] In educated circles in the South as well as in the North, there developed, especially among those who wished to expose the "errors" of their opponents, a growing belief that Jefferson had been right in anticipating that science would eventually decide once and for all whether Negroes were biologically equal to whites or were ever likely to be.

At the time when Garrison first challenged American racial assumptions and forced Southerners and Northern antiabolitionists to examine and articulate their preconceptions, American ethnological thinking was in a state of flux. The dominant

1. On rare occasions the abolitionists of the 1830s did discuss the scientific basis of racial differences by reverting to the eighteenth-century notion that variations in pigmentation were the direct result of climate and custom. But they did not place any practical reliance on the physiological theory that American blacks would eventually turn white. They saw this process as taking a long time, and in the meantime they demanded equality for the Negro—whatever his color—on moral, religious, and ideological grounds. Perhaps the fullest presentation in the abolitionist literature of the 1830s of the thesis that "custom and climate fully account for the diversities of the human form" is the anonymous article "The Diversities of Men," in the *Quarterly Anti-Slavery Magazine*, II (January, 1837), 199–208. See also John Rankin, *Letters on Slavery* (Boston, 1833), pp. 8, 11.

authority in the field was still Samuel Stanhope Smith, who had been dead for more than a decade but whose *Essay on the Causes of the Variety of Complexion and Figure in the Human Species,* originally published in 1787 and republished in an enlarged edition in 1810, still commanded respect. Smith, a Presbyterian minister and president of the College of New Jersey (now Princeton University) from 1795 to 1812, had presented a vigorous defense of "monogenesis"—the dominant view of eighteenth-century science on the origin of racial differences. All the races of man, he argued, were members of the same species and had a common remote ancestry; differences in color, anatomy, intelligence, temperament, and morality could be attributed to differing physical and social environments, especially climate and the contrasting habits of life produced by "savagery" and "civilization." Hence radical changes in environment, of the kind experienced by the American Negro in being transplanted from Africa and of the kind that would occur if slaves were emancipated, could be relied upon to eliminate in a relatively short time all the differences between two races residing in the same territory and subjected to the same external influences. This viewpoint did not make Smith a thoroughgoing racial egalitarian in the twentieth-century sense; like most other eighteenth-century advocates of the unity of the human species, he believed that the white race was the superior race, the original human norm from which other races had degenerated. The Negro, it was suggested, could become equal to the whites, but only by ceasing to be a Negro— i.e., by actually turning white. It was this belief in the possibility of a literal transformation of one race into another through the power of environment that was the central and most vulnerable element in Smith's formulation. Since no one had ever really observed such a racial change, this assertion was seriously questioned even in the eighteenth century: Smith had been obliged in his writings to refute two British theorists, Lord Kames and Charles White, who challenged the dominant opinion of their time by asserting that racial differences were innate and not the product of environment.[2]

2. See William R. Stanton, *The Leopard's Spots: Scientific Attitudes Toward Race in America, 1815–1859* (Chicago, 1960), pp. 3–14; and Samuel

Smith's first important American critic was Dr. Charles Cald-well, a native of North Carolina, who practiced medicine in Philadelphia and later became a founder of two medical schools in Kentucky. Caldwell began to attack Smith's environmentalism as early as 1811 in an anonymous review, but it was not until 1830 that he published his opinions in full detail. Caldwell's book *Thoughts on the Original Unity of the Human Race* was the first extensive and seemingly authoritative answer to Smith, and it presented, with all the appearance of scientific objectivity, the case for "polygenesis," or the separate creation of the races as distinct species.[3] Caldwell, employing the accepted Biblical chronology of Archbishop James Ussher, argued that Negroes were known to have existed 3,445 years ago, or only 743 years after Noah's ark—not enough time for a new race to come into exis-tence through the effects of climate. He also contended that the "vast preëminence of the Caucasian in intellect" was of such an order that it could not be attributed to environment but must be a "gift of nature" that had been withheld from inferior races. Apparently recognizing that such a conclusion might be used to justify Negro slavery and Indian extermination, Caldwell dis-avowed any such application, contending that "inferior beings become the objects of kindness, *because* they are inferior." "The Caucasians," he continued, "are not justified in either enslaving the Africans or destroying the Indians, merely because their supe-riority in intellect and war enable them to do so. Such practices are an abuse of power."[4]

As might have been anticipated, Caldwell's attempt to divorce the argument for innate racial inequality from the defense of slavery fell on deaf ears. In 1833 Richard H. Colfax made the

---

Stanhope Smith, *An Essay on the Causes of the Variety of Complexion and Figure in the Human Species,* ed. Winthrop D. Jordan (Cambridge, Mass., 1965). Jordan's introduction to the latter volume contains an excellent discus-sion of Smith's ideas.

3. Stanton, *Leopard's Spots,* pp. 19–22; [Charles Caldwell,] "An Essay on the Causes of the Variety of Complexion and Figure in the Human Species . . . ," *American Review of History and Politics,* II (1811), 128–166; Charles Caldwell, M.D., *Thoughts on the Original Unity of the Human Race* (New York, 1830).

4. Caldwell, *Thoughts,* 73, 101–102, 134, vi, vii.

idea of separate origins part of his racist attack on the abolitionists, and later scientific advocates of the plurality hypothesis
made no disclaimers which would stand in the way of a proslavery use of ethnology. The South's first important exposure to
the view that the black man was a member of a separate and
permanently inferior species, not simply a savage or semicivilized
member of the same species, probably came in 1837 in Charleston, then the center of proslavery thought. South Carolina's
intelligentsia reacted favorably, it would appear, when an émigré
Frenchman read to the Charleston Literary and Philosophical
Society portions of his translation from a book by J. J. Virey, an
early French proponent of polygenesis.[5]

The new doctrine, however, did not become an accepted view
even in scientific and intellectual circles until the 1840s and
1850s, when the "American school of ethnology" emerged and
affirmed on the basis of new data that the races of mankind had
been separately created as distinct and unequal species. The full
scientific assault on environmentalism came at a time, therefore,
when it was bound to have some influence on the discussion of
slavery and Negro prospects.

The originator of the new scientific ethnology was Dr. Samuel
George Morton of Philadelphia, who published a book in 1839
that promised to bring an end to loose speculation about racial
origins and differences by opening an era of hardheaded empiri-
cism. Morton's *Crania Americana* was the result of years of col-
lecting and examining human skulls. As he gathered and studied
the crania of different types of men, Morton became aware of the
differences between white, Indian, and Negro skulls and of the
fact that the ancient crania from a given race did not seem to
differ from those of their modern descendants. Morton concluded
that the races had always had the same physical characteristics
and, by implication, the same mental qualities. In the 1840s,
Morton collaborated with George R. Gliddon, an Egyptologist,
who provided him with mummy heads and information about

5. Richard H. Colfax, *Evidence Against the Views of the Abolitionists* . . .
(New York, 1833), pp. 7–8; J. H. Guenebault, *Natural History of the Negro
Race* (Charleston, 1837). Only the portions relating to the Negro were trans-
lated by Guenebault from the original work, J. J. Virey's *Histoire Naturel du
Genre Humain* (Paris, 1801).

the racial significance of Egyptian tomb inscriptions. In *Crania Aegyptiaca,* published in 1844, Morton pointed out that both cranial and archaeological evidence showed that the Egyptians were not Negroes—as abolitionists and colonizationists had maintained—and that in fact blacks had been relegated to the same servile position in ancient Egypt as in modern America. All Morton's findings were interpreted as supporting the belief that Negroes were permanently inferior to whites, and eventually he followed the logic of his discoveries to the point of arguing that Negroes had been separately created to inhabit tropical Africa and that only Caucasians were authentic descendants of Adam.[6]

Morton's assertion of the polygenesis of the races was vigorously supported by Dr. Josiah C. Nott of Mobile, Alabama, whose own "researches" had led him to believe that the mulatto was a genuine hybrid, weaker and less fertile than either parent stock. Joining Morton and Gliddon, Nott completed the scientific triumvirate which attempted to convince educated Americans that the Negro was not a blood brother to the whites. Their effort was given invaluable support when Louis Agassiz, the great Swiss biologist who emigrated to America in 1846 and became a professor at Harvard two years later, was converted to the doctrine of the plural origins of mankind, a theory which, as it happened, fitted in perfectly with Agassiz's hypothesis that specific differences within the plant and animal kingdom were the result of separate creations dictated by the environmental demands of differing regions of the earth. Thus a theory was developed—and presented on good scientific authority—which affirmed the permanence of race characteristics within what was then the accepted chronology of human life on the earth, postulated the separate creation of the races within the areas that they now principally inhabited, and maintained that the races constituted distinct species of *genus homo* and not simply varieties of the same species. In order to establish the last point, it was neces-

6. Stanton, *Leopard's Spots,* 24–53, 137–144; Samuel George Morton, *Crania Americana; Or a Comparative View of the Skulls of Various Aboriginal Nations of North and South America, to which is Prefixed an Essay on the Varieties of the Human Species* (Philadelphia, 1839); Morton, *Crania Aegyptiaca, or Observations on Egyptian Ethnography, Derived from Anatomy, History, and the Monuments* (Philadelphia, 1844).

sary to revise the theory of hybridity in order to meet the traditional argument for the unity of the human race based on a belief that all hybrids were sterile and that consequently mulattoes could not be included in this category. Morton and Nott both contributed to such a new view of hybridity by claiming the existence of varying degrees of interspecific sterility which included diminishing reproduction for a few generations before the mixed stock died out.[7]

II

The exact importance for the slavery controversy of the new scientific attitudes toward race—that is, the extent to which the theory was promulgated to serve conscious proslavery purposes or was, in any case, appropriated and used by the defenders of slavery—needs to be re-examined. William Stanton, the historian who has written most fully on the "American school," has argued that its doctrines, which he sees in general as the legitimate product of disinterested scientific inquiry, were peripheral to the defense of slavery. Because pluralist ethnology was propagated under the banner of anticlericalism and because it conflicted with orthodox religious beliefs about human origins, it was, Stanton argues, rejected by Southern opinion.[8] But there is evidence, some of it presented by Stanton himself, to support a somewhat different view.

Unquestionably Morton's original researches reflected legitimate scientific interests. A Quaker by upbringing and a scientist whose interests ranged far and wide—he published articles in medicine, anatomy, geology, and paleontology that bore no relation to race—Morton had nothing in his background to suggest a particular bias in favor of slavery or racism. Since Gliddon was an Englishman who did not even come to the United States until 1837, he likewise had no obvious personal reason for providing a

7. Stanton, *Leopard's Spots*, 65–81, 100–109, 113–121; see also Edward Lurie, *Louis Agassiz: A Life in Science* (Chicago, 1960), pp. 245–255. Much more could be said about the purely scientific basis for these hypotheses, but our main concern is with the uses or misuses of this theory and not with the theory itself as a part of the history of anthropology.

8. For Stanton's conclusions see *Leopard's Spots*, pp. 182–198.

scientific rationalization for American racial policies. Yet it is significant that once they had made discoveries that bore on the question of racial differences, Gliddon and, to a lesser extent, Morton welcomed and even encouraged a proslavery application of them. When *Crania Aegyptiaca* was completed in 1843, Gliddon, who was lecturing in the South, wrote enthusiastically to Morton about the potential Southern reception of a book which would give "powerful support" to slavery and reduce Southern fear of the antislavery "voices of Europe and Northern America." Morton wrote back (in response to a suggestion of Gliddon's) that an advance copy should be sent to John C. Calhoun. In 1844 Gliddon promoted the book in Charleston and wrote that it would soon be "fairly launched down South," where its racial findings "would draw plenty of customers." In the same year there was an important correspondence between Calhoun, then Secretary of State, and Morton and Gliddon, in which the two scientists supplied Calhoun ethnological information to bolster his diplomatic effort to refute British and French objections to the pending annexation of Texas as a slave state.[9]

Morton and Gliddon's gratification over such uses of their ideas suggests that they had a commitment to the new anthropology as an applied science—a commitment which implied a willingness, indeed a desire, to see it used for the conservative and "patriotic" purpose of justifying America's racial *status quo* in the eyes of the world. In *Types of Mankind* (1854), a massive compilation of the opinions of the "American School," the author of a eulogistic memoir of Morton (who had died in 1851) pointed out that ethnology was "eminently a science for American culture," because "three of the five races into which [the German comparative anatomist Johann Friedrich] Blumenbach divided mankind, are brought together to determine the problem of their destiny as they best may." What came next amounted to a scientific apology for Negro slavery and Indian extermination—the American racial practices which Dr. Charles Caldwell, despite his pluralist ethnology, had found abhorrent on humanitarian grounds: "It is manifest that our relation to

9. Stanton, *Leopard's Spots*, pp. 25–26, 45–46, 52–53, 62. On the relationship with Calhoun see also J. C. Nott and George R. Gliddon, eds., *Types of Mankind: Or Ethnological Researches . . .* (Philadelphia, 1854), pp. 50–51.

and management of these people must depend, in great measure, upon their intrinsic race character. While the contact of the white man seems fatal to the Red Indian, whose tribes fall away before the onward march of the frontier-man like snow in the spring (threatening ultimate extinction), the Negro thrives under the shadow of his white master, falls readily into the position assigned him, and exists and multiplies in increased physical well-being."[10]

The most fervent of the scientific apologists for the American system of racial subordination was Dr. Josiah C. Nott, who became the leading exponent of the new ethnology after the death of Morton. Preconceived racial attitudes probably drew him to ethnology in the first place and influenced his inquiries. In 1845 Nott wrote to James Henry Hammond, a vigorously proslavery South Carolina planter and political leader, that his work was designed to confound the abolitionists. "Abolition," he wrote, "is one of those unfortunate questions which presents one face to the philosopher and another to the mass—reason or religion can never decide it—the results of emancipation. I hope that *the grounds I have taken* may do something after a while."[11] In another letter to Hammond in the same year, he confessed that his interests were not so much in races in general as in the Negro in particular and implied that some of his evidence for plural origins was designed to attract attention and add support to an a priori assumption of innate Negro inferiority. "The Negro question was the one I wished to bring out and [I] embalmed it in Egyptian ethnography, etc., to excite a little more interest." His intent, obviously dictated by Southern obsessions, was "to follow out the Negro, moral and physical, in all his ramifications." He liked to describe his field of study as "the nigger business" or "niggerology."[12]

10. Henry S. Patterson, M.D., "Memoir of Samuel George Morton," in Nott and Gliddon, eds., *Types of Mankind*, pp. xxxii–xxxiii.
11. Letter of Josiah C. Nott to James Henry Hammond, July 25, 1852, Hammond Papers, Library of Congress.
12. Nott to Hammond, Aug. 12, 1845, and Sept. 4, 1845, Hammond Papers. See also William Sumner Jenkins, *Pro-Slavery Thought in the Old South* (Chapel Hill, N.C., 1935), pp. 256–257, 259–260.

In 1850 Nott presented his views to the Southern Rights Association in Mobile, by an antiabolition lecture on "The Natural History of Mankind, Viewed in Connection with Negro Slavery."[13] In this address and in many other pronouncements, he openly attempted to put himself and his views at the forefront of the proslavery defense. But Nott's concept of what ethnology had revealed was not limited to its justification of Negro servitude. The full sweep of his racism and how he hoped to see it implemented came out in one of the sections he wrote in *Types of Mankind.* He described the Caucasians as having "in all ages been the rulers"; their destiny therefore is "to conquer and hold every foot of the globe where climate does not interpose an impenetrable barrier. No philanthropy, no legislation, no missionary labors can change this law; it is written in man's nature by the hand of his creator." As for the "inferior races," they would serve their purposes and become extinct.[14] Here, as in other places in his writings, Nott was arguing less from the supposed facts of craniology or Egyptology than from a dogmatic white-racialist view of history, of the kind then coming into fashion all over the Western world as a justification not only for slavery but also for imperial expansion. In 1856 he helped edit a selective American edition of Gobineau's *Essai sur l'inégalité des races humaines,* a work that was short on biology and long on dogmatic assertions about the historical role of the races.[15]

Nott's writings, therefore, would seem to belong at least as much to the history of proslavery and racist propaganda as to the history of science. The fact that Nott was recognized as a leading scientist was perhaps more indicative of the racial preconceptions of his audience than of the quality of his research and theoretical formulations. His "research" consisted primarily of what he thought he had found out about Negroes in the course of practicing medicine in Mobile. Among the most important "facts" gleaned from "experience" upon which he based his conclusions

13. Stanton, *Leopard's Spots,* p. 158. Extracts from the address appeared as "Nature and Destiny of the Negro," *De Bow's Review,* X (1851) , 329–332.

14. Nott and Gliddon, eds., *Types of Mankind,* p. 79.

15. Count Joseph Arthur de Gobineau, *The Moral and Intellectual Diversity of Races, with Particular Reference to Their Respective Influence in the Civil and Political History of Mankind* (Philadelphia, 1856) .

were these two: that mulattoes were less prolific than Negroes and became increasingly so, until a line died out in three or four generations, and that Negroes had reached the highest level of civilization of which they were capable after one or two generations of "domestication" under slavery. His views on hybridity provided a scientific rationale for the long-standing white repugnance to intermarriage—he wrote, for example, that "the superior race must inevitably become deteriorated by any intermixture with the inferior"—and his theory of the limits of "domestication" provided new support for what was already a conventional justification of slavery.[16] If the racist case against emancipation was basic to the proslavery argument, Nott must be considered a major proslavery apologist.[17]

Nott was a firm believer in biological equality, however, when it came to whites. He attacked those supporters of monogenesis who argued that acquired characteristics could be inherited. "It is not to the children of the educated class alone that we look for ruling intellects," he wrote, "but *nature's noblemen,* on the contrary more often spring from the families of the backwoodsmen, or the sturdy mechanic. Not only the cultivation, but the genius of great men, as a general rule dies with them. . . ."[18] He could assert in 1861, without any sense of self-contradiction, that Southern secession was justified by the Declaration of Independence—"the chart by which the Anglo-Saxon race sails" and

16. Stanton, *Leopard's Spots*, 66–68; Nott and Gliddon, eds., *Types of Mankind,* pp. 260, 407.

17. I cannot agree with all the assumptions and implications of Stanton's contention (*Leopard's Spots*, p. 160) that "Nott had no love for slavery. He did not defend it with any of the numerous arguments then fashionable. . . . Nott was simply unable to see any solution other than slavery to the problems presented by two species of men living in the same zoological province." Nott did give the impression in an 1861 interview with the British journalist William Howard Russell that he disliked slavery (Russell, *My Diary North and South* [New York, 1863], p. 88), but he was not alone among major proslavery spokesmen in admitting orally or in private correspondence that slavery had its undesirable aspects. George Fitzhugh himself conceded in a letter of 1855, "I see great evils in slavery, but in a controversial work I ought not to admit them." (Quoted in Harvey Wish, *George Fitzhugh: Propagandist of the Old South* [Baton Rouge, 1943], p. 111.)

18. Josiah C. Nott, *Two Lectures on the Connexion between the Biblical and Physical History of Man* (New York, 1849), p. 45.

a doctrine "repeated in every one of the Southern state constitutions." "The Southern people," he concluded, "will see all the
whites and blacks on the globe slaughtered before they will yield
this point."[19]

The view that Nott was primarily an apostle of science rather
than a direct apologist for Southern racial ideas and practices
rests mainly on the assumption that he defended an anti-Biblical
scientific theory of the origins of man in the face of a generally
hostile Southern public opinion; that, in other words, he was a
courageous combatant in the nineteenth-century war between
science and religion. It was true that Nott's anticlerical predilection led him to argue that on certain questions the public should
pay more attention to men of scientific training than to clergymen and that he engaged in an early form of "higher criticism"
of the Bible in order to advance his views, a tendency which
naturally aroused the clergy against him. Like any theorist he
was fond of his own theories. But he was hardly a martyr to
scientific truth; for his views circulated freely in the South, he
suffered no harassment or personal disadvantage because of
them, and, as we shall see, he eventually gained widespread and
influential support for his most fundamental conceptions.[20]

Most damaging to Nott's image as an embattled apostle of
science are the indications that he was somewhat less attached to
polygenesis as a scientific hypothesis than to the "practical fact"
of inherent Negro inferiority, however it might be explained. In
reviewing a book by a monogenesist critic, Nott noted trium-
phantly that his opponent, by describing the Negroes as a
permanent and inferior variety of the human species, had admitted "the *practical fact* for which we have been contending."[21]
In his introduction to *Types of Mankind,* he made clear again
the essential point he was trying to make: "Whether an original
diversity of races be admitted or not, *the permanence* of existing
physical types will not be questioned by any archaeologist or

19. Quoted in Stanton, *Leopard's Spots,* p. 183.
20. Stanton, *Leopard's Spots, passim;* for a different view on the South's
reception of Nott's theories, see below, this chapter.
21. Josiah C. Nott, "Diversity of the Human Race," *De Bow's Review,* X
(February, 1851), 115.

Naturalist of the present day. Nor . . . can the consequent permanence of moral and intellectual peculiarities of type be denied. The intellectual man is inseparable from the physical man."[22]

After the Civil War, in a pamphlet written in the hope of influencing the racial policy of the victorious North, Nott reiterated all his "practical facts" in support of Negro inferiority and then calmly acknowledged that the new Darwinian doctrine of human evolution over a vast span of time had cast doubt on his own theory of separate creation. But even this school of thought "requires millions of years for their theory, and would not controvert the facts and deductions I have laid down."[23] This apparent receptivity to new scientific theories might have represented, as William Stanton suggests, Nott's unselfish devotion to the progress of scientific truth; but it seems more likely, given its context, that it simply reflected what had been Nott's major concern all along—"the practical fact" of permanent white superiority. From this standpoint it did not matter a great deal whether one contended that Negroes had been created inferior a few thousand years ago or had become inferior through a glacially slow process of evolution. In either case, they were inferior and would remain so in any future that needed to be contemplated by living men.[24]

III

The most dramatic and unambiguous way to make this point of genetic inferiority before the rise of Darwinism was to argue that whites and Negroes had literally been *created* unequal, and in defending this proposition in the 1840s and 1850s, Nott stirred up a controversy in the South. Adherents of the common descent of mankind accused him and his supporters of infidelity for denying the accepted Biblical view of the origin of all races in the progeny of Adam. But the narrow and technical nature of

22. Nott and Gliddon, eds., *Types of Mankind*, p. 50.
23. Josiah C. Nott, *The Negro Race: Its Ethnology and History* (Mobile, 1866), p. 12.
24. For Stanton's interpretation, see *Leopard's Spots*, pp. 186–188.

this controversy, when considered in relation to its immediate and practical consequences, soon became apparent. Leading proponents of "the unity of mankind," such as the Reverend John Bachman of Charleston and Professor J. L. Cabell of the University of Virginia, disagreed fundamentally with Nott only on the question of how the races had originated and not on their present and future place in the racial hierarchy. Nott described the blacks as members of a distinct and inferior species; Bachman and Cabell saw them as "permanent varieties" of a single human species. According to both Bachman and Cabell, the races had diverged as a result of environmental factors, principally climate, but this divergence had now reached the point of irreversibility; therefore Negro inferiority was an unchangeable fact of nature. In a real sense the monogenesist view, as formulated and defended in the antebellum South, was, like the pluralist view, a form of biological racism and not a genuine revival of eighteenth-century environmentalism.[25]

Some proslavery writers readily acknowledged that for their purposes this was an academic controversy. Thomas R. R. Cobb, for example, refused to take a stand on "the much-mooted question of the unity of the human race," pointing out that "whether the negro was originally a different species, or is a degeneration of the same, is a matter indifferent in the inquiry as to his proper status in his present condition."[26] E. N. Elliott, in an introduction to a large compendium of proslavery writings published in 1860, emphasized the common ground on which the defense of slavery rested by noting that it was "well established" that "the negro is *now* an inferior species, or at least variety of the human race." All present authorities agreed "that by himself he was never emerged from barbarism, and even when partly civilized under the control of the white man, he speedily returns to the same state if emancipated. . . ."[27]

25. John Bachman, D.D., *The Doctrine of the Unity of the Human Race Examined on the Principles of Science* (Charleston, 1850), pp. 208–210; J. L. Cabell, M.D., *The Testimony of Modern Science to the Unity of Mankind* (New York, 1859), pp. 23–24.

26. Thomas R. R. Cobb, *An Inquiry into the Law of Negro Slavery in the United States of America* (Philadelphia, 1858), p. 27.

27. E. N. Elliott, ed., *Cotton Is King and Pro-Slavery Arguments* (Augusta, Ga., 1860), p. xiii.

If the question whether Negroes constituted a separate species or a permanent variety did not matter to those who were most narrowly and pragmatically concerned simply with the defense of slavery, it could have great symbolic significance for those pro-slavery writers who were also concerned with defining the South's social identity. George Fitzhugh summed up the paternalist objection to the pluralist theory of racial origins in 1854: "We deplore the doctrine of the 'Types of Mankind,' first, because it is at war with scripture, which teaches us that the whole human race it descended from a common parentage; and secondly, because is encourages and incites brutal masters to treat negroes, not as weak, ignorant and dependent brethren, but as wicked beasts without the pale of humanity."[28] Bachman, the foremost scientific defender of monogenesis, made a similar point when he accused "the advocates of a plurality of the races" of seeking "to degrade their servants below the level of those creatures of God to whom a revelation has been given, and for whose salvation a saviour died. . . ."[29] The spokesmen for *Herrenvolk* egalitarianism, on the other hand, were sometimes attracted by the new doctrine precisely because it provided support for the view that Negroes were creatures set apart who did not have to be conceded any social status at all within an officially homogeneous and egalitarian Southern community. In a sense, therefore, the debate constituted a transfer to the scientific realm of the larger debate over the nature of the Negro and his relation to Southern social ideals. The difference between a variety and a species meant also, in theory at least, the difference between a black man who was inferior to the whites but akin to them, and therefore deserving of affection and a protective social status, and a black man who was more animal than human and could, for most purposes, be treated as such.

Consequently it becomes necessary to go more deeply into the whole question of how the pluralist hypothesis was received in the South, as a way of further testing the importance of extreme racism in antebellum ideology. What is most striking is not that

28. George Fitzhugh, *Sociology for the South: or, the Failure of Free Society* (Richmond, 1854), p. 95.
29. Bachman, *Doctrine*, p. 8.

polygenesis encountered opposition from the spokesmen of conservative Christianity but that, even in its aggressively secular form as put forth by Nott, it won as much acceptance as it did. Nott himself never doubted the popularity of his doctrines. In 1845, after his initial formulation of the concept of Negroes as a separate species, he wrote to Hammond about how his views had been received in Mobile: "The grounds I have taken in my lecture were never for the mass, but they have been much talked of and read here and public opinion has come over to me as I was sure it would *in the South*—the few that hold out admit that it is debatable ground and ought to be investigated." He added that his medical practice had been much enhanced by his identification with the new ethnological theory.[30] The theory was soon heralded and promulgated in *De Bow's Review,* the most important journal of Southern opinion, and by the mid-1850s it had won the adherence of the *Southern Quarterly Review,* the South's second most significant intellectual forum.[31]

The belief of historians that the theory was rejected out of hand has derived in part from Moncure Daniel Conway's recollection in his autobiography of being shouted down at a Virginia lyceum in 1850 for citing scientific authority to support the thesis that the Negro was not a man within the terms of the Declaration of Independence.[32] But in a book that he wrote during the Civil War, Conway, who by then had reversed himself by going North and becoming an abolitionist, described in detail how he had come for a time to accept such views, an account which gives a somewhat different impression of the South's response to pluralism than one derives from the autobiography he published half a century later. In *Testimonies Concerning Slavery,* Conway recalled that a kinsman who was a leading Southern editor—presumably his cousin John M. Daniel of the fire-eating Richmond *Examiner*—became a convert to the viewpoint of the "scientific advocates of the diversity of the races" and made a public state-

30. Letter of Nott to James Henry Hammond, July 25, 1845, Hammond Papers, Library of Congress.

31. Jenkins, *Pro-Slavery Thought,* p. 262; Stanton, *Leopard's Spots,* pp. 155–156.

32. Stanton, *Leopard's Spots,* pp. 110–112; Moncure Daniel Conway, *Autobiography, Memories, and Experiences* (New York, 1904) , I, 87–90.

ment in which he held that "Negroes are not *men,* in the sense in which that term is used by the Declaration of Independence. Were the slaves men, we should be unable to disagree with Wendell Phillips." It was from his cousin that Conway himself learned of the plurality hypothesis and its implications. "He went with me carefully through the subject of races," Conway recalled, "adducing the well-known arguments of Agassiz in favor of their diversity of origin, and the inferiority of the African." Conway was readily convinced, although at this time he was a pious Methodist. Only momentarily disconcerted by the problem of making such opinions compatible with the Scriptures, he quickly concluded that there was "orthodox authority for setting [the Bible] aside on such questions." Later, Conway recalled, he came in contact with "some leading public men," mostly secessionists, who fully accepted the doctrine. In general, his account suggests that whatever initial shock the theory aroused, it rapidly achieved considerable popularity in intellectual and political circles.[33]

Such an impression could explain why the advocates of unity felt themselves on the defensive in the South when *Types of Mankind* appeared in 1854. In a review of the book, Bachman noted that politicians were using the argument for diversity in defense of slavery and that the advocates of unity "were sometimes stigmatized as abolitionists and enemies of the South."[34] At this time, too, Fitzhugh was warning the South against the headlong acceptance of racialist doctrines. The trend in the 1850s, therefore, seemed to be towards the acceptance of polygenesis by those who were seeking to bolster the case for slavery. By 1861 the pressure had become so great and the doctrine so attractive that Fitzhugh himself, as we have seen, capitulated to the idea that the Negro belonged to another species.[35]

The writings of Morton, Nott, and Agassiz were of course accessible directly only to the most highly educated Southerners. Argued on a scientific basis, the theory was abstruse and difficult

33. Moncure Daniel Conway, *Testimonies Concerning Slavery* (London, 1864) , pp. 28–30.
34. Quoted in Stanton, *Leopard's Spots,* p. 72.
35. See the concluding section of Chapter Two, above.

for those without some knowledge of biology. But the basic idea was disseminated by popularizers, who not only simplified the concepts but labored to remove the single objection that carried real weight—the impression that pluralism conflicted with scripture. Among the important popularizers were John H. Van Evrie, George S. Sawyer, and Samuel A. Cartwright. Cartwright, the Louisiana physician and proslavery writer, is of particular significance in the Southern context because of his strenuous efforts to make pluralism jibe with the Bible. Indeed, the main impulse behind all of Cartwright's speculations was the desire to reconcile whatever scientific theory would most denigrate the Negro with a literal reading of Genesis. In 1843, before he was exposed to pluralism, Cartwright wrote a book to show how the anatomical evidence of Negro inferiority could be correlated with the Biblical description of "the curse on Canaan"—God's condemnation of Canaan and his allegedly black descendants to be "servants unto servants." Science and religion came together perfectly, Cartwright concluded, to make an overwhelming case for the servile inferiority of the blacks.[36] In the 1850s, however, Cartwright became a convert to separate origins and willingly gave up the curse on Canaan in its conventional form to adopt what seemed to be a better basis for a racist reconciliation of science and Scripture. In 1860 he set forth in detail a theory that had been in the air for some time, when he argued in *De Bow's Review* that there was no conflict whatever between Genesis and the idea of a separate creation, since the Negro was actually referred to in the Bible as a separately created and inferior creature. His seemingly bizarre conclusion was that Negroes and Indians were created before Adam and Eve and were included among the "living creatures" over which Adam was given dominion. As a clincher, he added that the serpent or "Nachash" who tempted Eve was not a serpent at all but a "negro gardener," basing this ingenious theory on the contention that the Hebrew word "Nachash" meant not only snake but "to be or to become black." These pre-Adamite Negroes, it turned out, were also the inhabitants of the Land of Nod with whom Cain intermarried,

36. Samuel A. Cartwright, *Essays, Being Inductions Drawn from the Baconian Philosophy* . . . (Vidalia, La., 1843) .

making that much-cursed son of Adam the first amalgamationist. "That they were black," Cartwright claimed, "is inferred from the mark they put on Cain. The hybrids were so exceedingly wicked that the Lord determined to destroy them in the flood." Thus miscegenation was the sin for which God had sent the Deluge. Pure blacks, however, were apparently taken on the ark; for Noah's son Ham was not the father of Canaan (Genesis ix), as was erroneously believed, but "the headmaster or overseer of the Nachash race of which Canaan was a member."[37]

These fantastic theories cannot, strange as it may seem, be dismissed as the curious musings of an isolated crackpot. Cartwright's views were respected in the South, probably more than Nott's, and he was chosen to represent the ethnological defense of slavery in E. N. Elliott's anthology *Cotton Is King and Pro-Slavery Arguments,* which summed up the Southern case for servitude in 1860. In less extravagant form, the theory that nonwhite races already existed and inhabited "the Land of Nod" and other outlying regions at the time of Adam and Eve was set forth in 1854 in the staid *Southern Quarterly Review.* In a long and learned discussion of the whole ethnological controversy, an anonymous writer criticized *Types of Mankind* only because it intimated that the "Bible is not an inspired book," and suggested that a more careful reading of Genesis would resolve the dilemma and allow the proslavery South to have its ethnology and its religion too.[38]

Evidence that the theory Cartwright presented in August 1860 had previously won acceptance among influential segments of Southern opinion can be found in a speech delivered by Jefferson Davis to the United States Senate in April of the same year. Speaking in opposition to a proposal to appropriate money for Negro education in the District of Columbia, Davis referred to white men as the naturally equal "members of the Adamic race" and gave his own version of the early history of race relations. He contended that the vast superiority of whites over Negroes was

37. Samuel A. Cartwright, "Unity of the Human Race Disproved by the Hebrew Bible," *De Bow's Review,* XXIX (August, 1860), 129–130, 134.
38. "On the Unity of the Human Race," *Southern Quarterly Review,* XX (October, 1854), 277–278, 281.

"stamped from the beginning, marked in decree and prophecy—the will of God which the puny efforts of man have in vain attempted to subvert—confirmed by history through all its successive stages, until we reach the remote period where it is only to be drawn from the pictorial monuments of the people who then existed." Davis then traced the story of Negro inferiority back beyond the Egyptians: "When Cain, for the commission of the first great crime, was driven from the face of Adam, no longer the fit associate of those who were created to exercise dominion over the earth, he found in the Land of Nod those to whom his crime degraded him to an equality; and when the low and vulgar son of Noah, who laughed at his father's exposure, sunk by debasing himself and his lineage by a connection with an inferior race of men, he doomed his descendants to perpetual slavery." Although Davis's version differed from Cartwright's in detail, with Davis making Ham as well as Cain guilty of miscegenation, it was basically the same Biblical theory of polygenesis.[39]

That the future President of the Confederacy could adopt and expound a version of the new ethnology—one that was extreme in its denigration of the black race but allegedly compatible with a literal interpretation of Scripture—would seem to raise considerable doubt about the proposition that the South found no use for pluralist doctrines and that the scientists who developed them can be considered guiltless of having contributed in any significant way to the proslavery argument. However it may have conflicted with Scripture—and obviously Cartwright's gymnastics did not remove that conflict for genuinely orthodox Christians—pluralism did speak to certain Southern needs. For one thing, it raised prejudice to the level of science; thereby giving it respectability. As a writer in *De Bow's* put it in 1860, the new doctrine of hybridity which postulated "the probable ultimate infertility of the mulatto" meant that so-called prejudice of color was really an *"aversion to hybridity"*; hence white repugnance to "amalgamation" could now be justified on scientific grounds.[40] A second

39. *Jefferson Davis, Constitutionalist: His Letters, Papers and Speeches,* ed. Dunbar Rowland (Jackson, Miss., 1923), IV, 230, 235.
40. W. W. Wright, "Amalgamation," *De Bow's Review,* XXIX (July, 1860), 3, 12–14.

reason for the popularity of pluralism was that it responded to the Southern desire to place the Negro as low as possible on the scale of creation, not only because this was one way to justify slavery but also because it did so in a manner that allowed the whites to retain their belief that all "men"—meaning now all members of the Caucasian "species"—were created equal.

IV

The influence of the new ethnology in giving support to pro-slavery or antiabolitionist sentiment was not limited to the South. A substantial segment of Northern opinion was prepared to welcome the biological theory that the Negro belonged to a separate and inferior species. As in the South, this susceptibility to extreme racist thinking was reinforced, in certain ways, by the rise of democratic and egalitarian aspirations among whites.

The emergence of democratic ideology in the antebellum North was a complex phenomenon which cannot be understood simply with reference to Jacksonianism and the Democratic Party. Nevertheless the Jacksonian movement, in more ways than one an amalgam of what today may seem like contrary tendencies, carried the rhetoric of popular democracy to an extreme almost unparalleled in American political history, while at the same time condoning a form of anti-Negro demagoguery that anticipated the Southern race baiters of a later era. This tendency was particularly evident in New York State, where extreme disparagement of local blacks was often combined with fervent assertions of Jacksonian principle. Even the most radical spokesmen for "the common man," including those associated with workingmen's movements, went out of their way to emphasize that their "democracy" was for whites only.[41] The philosophy of Democratic Negrophobia was set forth in 1836 by James Kirke

41. On the use of the blacks as an important "negative reference group" by New York Democratic politicians and editors, see Lee Benson, *The Concept of Jacksonian Democracy: New York as a Test Case* (New York, 1961), pp. 318–320. On the anti-Negro and antiabolition sentiments of "spokesmen for the Northern workingmen" in New York and elsewhere, see Lorman Ratner, *Powder Keg: Northern Opposition to the Antislavery Movement* (New York, 1968), pp. 62–64.

Paulding, a New York writer and staunch Jacksonian, in a defense of slavery that foreshadowed the arguments of the scientific racists of the 1840s and 1850s. Paulding described the differences between whites and blacks as "equivalent to those which separate various species of animals" and defended racial distinctions in an otherwise egalitarian society because, unlike the odious class divisions of Europe, they were based on the natural inequalities.[42] This conjunction of Northern white egalitarianism and Negro proscription was more than rhetoric: it was put into practice in New York in 1821 and in Pennsylvania in 1838 when constitutional extensions of white suffrage were accompanied by restrictions or (in the case of Pennsylvania) complete denial of the Negro's right to vote.[43] By the 1850s, therefore, there seemed to be an established relationship in the North between democratic ideology and extreme racism; consequently arguments that served to exclude the black man from the community of equals defined by the Declaration of Independence were welcomed by many who claimed to be in the vanguard of the movement to implement the Declaration's egalitarian philosophy. In 1859, two years after the Supreme Court's decision in the Dred Scott case denying American citizenship to all Negroes, Abraham Lincoln noted that some Northern Democrats were now asserting openly that when the Declaration of Independence spoke of "all men" this did not include Negroes. Although a believer in black inferiority, Lincoln was not willing to go so far as to countenance a doctrine that demoted the Negro "from the rank of a man to that of a brute."[44]

With opinions of the kind Lincoln attacked being circulated in the North in the 1850s, it was inevitable that someone would come forth to show in detail how science had now laid a firm foundation for the ideological marriage of intraracial egalitarianism and overt Negrophobia that had long been popular among Northern Democrats. The leading proponent of this

42. James Kirke Paulding, *Slavery in the United States* (New York, 1836), pp. 270–271.
43. See Edward R. Turner, *The Negro in Pennsylvania, 1639–1861* (Washington, 1912), Chapter X; Benson, *Concept*, pp. 7–8; and Leon F. Litwack, *North of Slavery: The Negro in the Free States* (Chicago, 1961), pp. 74–86.
44. Abraham Lincoln, *Collected Works*, ed. Roy P. Basler (New Brunswick, N.J., 1953–1955), III, 423–424.

synthesis was Dr. John H. Van Evrie of New York, who prefaced a pamphlet edition of the Dred Scott decision with the contention that the Supreme Court had now affirmed that the Declaration of Independence applied to whites only; its opinion, which was "in accord with the natural relations of the races," had thus "fixed the *status* of the subordinate race *forever*."[45] Van Evrie, discussed above as a proslavery writer who had an influence on Southern thinking, addressed much of what he wrote primarily to a Northern audience. He had his greatest impact during the Civil War as a major spokesman for racist opposition to emancipation.[46] In a variety of anti-Negro publications that he edited and in *Negroes and Negro "Slavery,"* issued as a pamphlet in 1853 and then enlarged and published as a book in 1861 and 1863, Van Evrie presented the case against emancipation as drawn from the new pluralist ethnology. Not in any sense a scientist himself, he was blatantly and openly an anti-Negro propagandist, perhaps the first professional racist in American history. Van Evrie defended slavery by repeating for popular consumption all the biological arguments for permanent Negro inferiority that had been set forth by Nott and the "American School." He is interesting and significant as a theorist because his attack on the Negro character was accompanied by what appears to be a peculiarly radical conception of white democracy. In *Negroes and Negro "Slavery,"* he attacked all class distinctions among whites, predicted that American ideas of equality would soon overthrow all the despotisms of Europe, and, using the most militant kind of Jacksonian rhetoric, denounced the oppression of the "producing classes" by Northern capitalists and their political allies, protesting that *"those who produce everything enjoy nothing, while those who produce nothing enjoy everything."*[47]

Ultimately, however, Van Evrie was more a deflector of class

45. John H. Van Evrie, *The Dred Scott Decision* (New York, 1860) , p. iii.
46. On Van Evrie's activities during the war, see Forrest G. Wood, *Black Scare: The Racist Response to Emancipation and Reconstruction* (Berkeley and Los Angeles, 1968) , pp. 9, 35–37, 58–68.
47. John H. Van Evrie, *Negroes and Negro "Slavery": The First an Inferior Race: The Latter Its Normal Condition* (New York, 1863) , pp. 20, 280–282, 288–289, 299–302.

antagonisms than a spokesman for them; his concept of white equality was calculated to appeal to socially insecure whites in search of a compensatory foundation for personal pride and status, a sense of identity which could help make the existing social and economic system more tolerable. He appealed to the psychological needs of such whites by asserting that all Caucasians had natural capacities that were literally identical—as did all Negroes, on a much lower level. "God has made the negro an inferior being," he wrote, "not in most cases, but in all cases. . . . There never could be a negro equalling the standard Caucasian in natural ability. The same almighty creator made all white men equal—for idiots, insane people, etc., are not exceptions, they are the result of human vices, crimes, or ignorance, immediate or remote." All white shortcomings, in other words, had environmental explanations, while Negro frailties were inherent.[48]

Van Evrie argued further that American egalitarianism would not have developed in the first place without the presence of an inferior race, and that slavery and racial discrimination therefore constituted the real bedrock and preservative of the national democracy. The settlers of colonial Virginia had been English "Cavaliers," imbued with reverence for class distinctions and the idea that some white men were better than others. But their contact with the radically inferior Negro, a creature of another species, had made them see how alike and naturally superior all white men really were. This consciousness of the insignificance of differences among whites, when compared to the gulf that yawned between the races, produced the Virginia "democrats" of the Revolutionary era, who had laid the foundation of egalitarian ideas and practices in the United States. "The presence of the negro," Van Evrie wrote, ". . . was and always must be a test that shows the insignificance and indeed nothingness of those artificial distinctions which elsewhere govern the world, and constitute the basis of the political as well as social order." He maintained that "the happiest conjunction that ever occurred in human affairs" was the presence of the Negro in America, because his obvious inferiority had permitted the building of a

48. Van Evrie, *Negroes and Negro "Slavery,"* p. 221.

social and political order built on the "natural" distinctions of
race and not the artificial differences of class; for what had resulted was *"a new civilization based on foundations of everlast-
ing truth—the legal and political equality of the race, or of all
those whom the almighty creator has himself made equal."*
Elsewhere in the book, however, he indicated that this new
civilization was now being threatened not only by Northern
capitalists but by the abolitionists, whom he described as agents
of a monarchist plot, originating in England, to impose the
European class idea in place of the American race idea.[49]

There was perhaps a crazy kind of half-truth in Van Evrie's
theory of the racial character of American democracy. He himself
was living proof that it was possible, in a certain sense, to be an
ultrademocrat and a virulent racist at the same time, and the
wartime public for his diatribes against emancipation probably
had a similar combination of beliefs. His weekly paper, the New
York *Day Book,* was directed in part at the poverty-stricken Irish
immigrants, Democrats to a man, who rioted in large numbers in
1863 against being drafted to "fight for the niggers," venting
their rage against a defenseless local black population.[50] His
ideology undoubtedly had an appeal not only to the Southern
advocates of *Herrenvolk* egalitarianism but also to frustrated and
deprived groups in the North who were seeking a way to maintain, against all evidence to the contrary, an image of themselves
as equal participants in American society. He may have hit
obliquely on a sociological truth when he asserted that citizenship for Negroes was conceivable in Latin America, because,
unlike in the United States, its society was based primarily on
"artificial" distinctions of class and not on "natural" distinctions
of race.[51]

One does not have to accept the view that racial distinctions
are "natural" to see some kind of reciprocal relationship between
American white egalitarianism and racial consciousness. But it
was not the *fact* of white equality that encouraged racial prejudice, but rather an ideology of equality maintained in the face of

49. *Ibid.,* pp. 271–282, 283, 292, 17–32.
50. Wood, *Black Scare,* pp. 23–24.
51. Van Evrie, *Negroes and Negro "Slavery,"* pp. 317–318.

real inequalities. In mid-nineteenth-century America the traditional categories of status had almost disappeared, but differences in the wealth and power of individuals and groups persisted or even in some cases increased—the Northern groups to whom Van Evrie appealed during the war tended to be socially unequal in reality, if not in theory, to most middle- and upper-class Northerners. But the prevailing ideology of social and political equality meant that such differentials were difficult to face squarely, because the rewards of wealth and success were supposedly available to all citizens. The assertion that such advantages were a product of "monopoly" and undemocratic privilege was one answer; another was to take refuge in the consolations of that great overriding equality allegedly guaranteed by race. The frustrations of low or uncertain status in a supposedly egalitarian society were, therefore, apt to encourage efforts to define the blacks as a different and lower species. Many "poor whites" in both the North and the South were ready to respond violently to apparent threats to the social value of their single claim to status—the white skin that guaranteed that they were better than somebody and not at the rock bottom of society.[52]

It was to such feelings that Van Evrie appealed. Had equality existed in fact and not simply as ideology, or, alternatively, had

52. A cogent analysis of the anxieties resulting from the American social pattern that crystallized in the nineteenth century appears in Chapter IV of David M. Potter's *People of Plenty: Economic Abundance and the American Character* (Chicago, 1954). Relying on the work of recent sociologists, Potter contends that actual social mobility in the United States has been accompanied by a myth of equal opportunity that goes beyond the facts and makes it seem that "every man is the architect of his own destiny" (p. 97). This ideal encourages high expectations, and "in so far as these expectations fail of realization, social and personal tensions result" (p. 99). Not only did the American social and economic system fail to produce the "classless society" that was promised, but it also "destroyed the one value which seemed inherent in the traditional class society—namely, that sense of the organic, organized relationship between the individual and the community which was defined by the individual's status" (p. 103). This public denial of organic status, however, has not removed "a deep psychological craving for the certitudes it offers. . . . At times the appetite for the assurances which status gives has taken a pathological turn" (p. 106). Potter does not relate this psychosocial complex directly to racism or racial prejudice, but his model of American attitudes helps explain the pathological white tendency to seize upon racial identity as a foundation for status.

the kind of acknowledged class hierarchy that Van Evrie perceived as blunting the edges of racial consciousness in Latin America existed also in the United States, then presumably there would have been less inducement to view the Negro as beyond the pale of humanity and outside the American community.[53]

53. In Latin America, color has traditionally been far from irrelevant as a criterion for social classification, but it has not been the only or even the most important basis upon which generally accepted social distinctions could be made. The color line has characteristically been adjusted to some extent to class lines which followed their own logic; for despite the fact that a kind of racial hierarchy was recognized in theory, it could be obscured at least at the margins of the racial categories by a sense of social hierarchy that was at least as strong. See, for example, Marvin Harris's discussion of the Brazilian pattern in *Patterns of Race in the Americas* (New York, 1964), pp. 60–64.

Chapter Four

•

Uncle Tom
and the Anglo-Saxons:
Romantic Racialism
in the North

IN LITERATURE and historical writing, as in science, there was a
new stress in mid-nineteenth-century American thought on the
peculiarities of diverse peoples and national "stocks," which
approached, if it did not actually proclaim, a racialist explanation of society and culture. In Europe, intellectuals associated
with the romantic movement in thought and literature were
turning away from the universalism of the Enlightenment and
embracing, at least implicitly, concepts of inbred national character and genius that could readily be transmuted into concepts
of "racial" superiority. Initially, however, the romantic contem-
plation of how human psychology and behavior varied by nation
or latitude did not always lead to ethnic chauvinism; there was
in fact some tendency to celebrate diversity, as showing the rich-
ness and plenitude of the human spirit. The original exponent of
an apparently cosmopolitan approach to the varieties of national
genius was Johann Gottfried von Herder, a late-eighteenth-
century German philosopher who was an important source of
nineteenth-century cultural nationalism. Denying the rigid hierarchical division of mankind into four or five biological races,
Herder attempted to deal impartially with a variety of cultural
or national groups, each allegedly with special gifts manifested in
the course of its historical development. In fulfilling its unique
cultural or spiritual heritage, each *Volk* was bringing to fruition

a single and laudable aspect of human character which no other people could express as well. The philosopher could contemplate these differences without making invidious comparisons, much as he appreciated diverse beauties of nature. Although nineteenth-century historians of the romantic nationalist school tended to emphasize the innate virtues of their own nation at the expense of others, Herder's willingness to see the good qualities of other peoples provided an example for those Europeans and Americans who sensed some spiritual inadequacies in their own heritage and looked to peoples "differently constituted" for the flowering of neglected human virtues.[1]

In the United States, the romantic fascination with differences in the character of nations and peoples was manifested around mid-century in the writings of William H. Prescott, Francis Parkman, and John Lothrop Motley—three great American practitioners of romantic historiography. In his histories of the Spanish conquest of Mexico and Peru, Prescott generalized about the Spanish character in comparison with that of both the Indians they conquered and the "Anglo-Saxon races" who settled to the North; Parkman compared the natural characteristics of the Anglo-Saxons and the "Celtic" French in the course of describing the struggle between the French and the English for the control of North America; and Motley in *The Rise of the Dutch Republic* invoked a Germanic-Celtic contrast in differentiating the two stocks that comprised the Dutch nation. From such descriptions of contacts between peoples of supposedly contrasting innate characteristics emerged a celebration of the Anglo-Saxon, or Germanic, stock at the expense of the Celtic or Iberian. The Anglo-Saxon was represented as carrying in his blood a love of liberty, a spirit of individual enterprise and resourcefulness, and a capacity for practical and reasonable behavior, none of which his rivals possessed.[2]

1. See Théophile Simar, *Étude Critique sur la Doctrine des Races au XVIIIe Siècle et Son Expansion au XIXe Siècle* (Brussels, 1922), pp. 91–94 and Chapter III, *passim;* and Johann Gottfried von Herder, *Reflections on the Philosophy of the History of Mankind*, ed. Frank E. Manuel (Chicago and London, 1968), *passim.* Professor Manuel's introduction contains an excellent analysis of Herder's romantic variety of cultural relativism.
2. Thomas F. Gossett discusses the "Anglo-Saxonism" of Prescott, Parkman,

Such were the beginnings of a nationalistic glorification of the dominant stock, a tendency to make America's virtues racial rather than historical or environmental in origin. But antebellum "Anglo-Saxonism" can be distinguished from the late-nineteenth-century variety by its lack of exclusiveness, as reflected in a general unwillingness to acknowledge significant and enduring ethnic divisions among white Americans. The Know-Nothing movement of the 1850s, the principal prewar manifestation of antiimmigrant feeling, placed very little reliance on a quasi-racial contrast between Celts and Anglo-Saxons, despite the fact that the Irish were its principal targets. Its central theme was anti-Catholicism. It was clearly implied, as a rule, that all whites in the United States could readily be assimilated by the dominant stock without altering basic national characteristics, though Democratic politicians with their large Irish and Scotch-Irish followings had to be wary in discussing this subject. To make this perspective absolutely clear, Senator Thomas Hart Benton of Missouri said in 1846 that the mission of the composite "Celtic–Anglo-Saxon" vanguard of the Caucasian race was to dominate both North and South America.[3]

Notions of white or Anglo-Saxon superiority were common even among critics of the slave system. Francis Lieber, a German-born political theorist who remained unsympathetic to slaveholding despite a long residence in the South, wrote in the 1850s of "Anglican liberty," that marvelous combination of individual freedom with the capacity for national unity and cooperative action which was "common to the whole Anglican race" and which had been "evolved first and chiefly by this race." It was on

and Motley in *Race: The History of an Idea in America* (Dallas, 1963), pp. 89–96. On Parkman's racial comparisons see also Edward N. Saveth, *American Historians and European Immigrants, 1875–1925* (New York, 1948), pp. 103–104.

3. Cited in Edward McNall Burns, *The American Idea of Mission: Concepts of National Purpose and Destiny* (New Brunswick, N.J., 1957), pp. 199–200. See also Gossett, *Race*, p. 97; and Ray Allen Billington, *The Protestant Crusade: 1800–1860* (New York, 1938). For a typical expression of antebellum Anglo-Saxonism, with its emphasis on the ability of Anglo-Saxons to assimilate other Caucasian groups without losing their innate characteristics, see "The Anglo-Saxon Race," *North American Review*, LXXII (July, 1851), 34–71.

this ethnic and historical basis that the United States, according to Lieber, had developed its Republican institutions.[4]

Theodore Parker, liberal Unitarian minister and militant abolitionist, went even further. The early settlers of Massachusetts Bay, he announced in 1854, "had in them the ethnologic idiosyncrasy of the Anglo-Saxon—his restless disposition to invade and conquer other lands; his haughty contempt of humbler tribes which leads him to subvert, enslave, kill, and exterminate; his fondness for material things, preferring these to beauty; his love of personal liberty, yet coupled with most profound respect for peaceful and established law; his inborn skill to organize things to a mill, men to a company, a community, tribes to a federated state; and his slow, solemn, inflexible, industrious, and unconquerable will." Only in America, he continued, did "the peculiar characteristics of the Anglo-Saxon" come to full development.[5] As a humanitarian and an antislavery radical, Parker was not entirely happy with the harshly exploitative and genocidal side of the Anglo-Saxon character, but he concluded in another address of the same year that "the Anglo-Saxon," as "the Caucasian's best," was "a good hardy stock for national welfare to grow on,"[6] and in a letter to an English friend in 1857 he wrote: "I look with great pride on this Anglo-Saxon people. It has many faults, but I think it is the best specimen of mankind which has ever attained great power in the world."[7]

The American "ethnologic" self-image, whether described as Anglican, Anglo-Saxon, Celtic–Anglo-Saxon, or simply Caucasian, was being formulated and popularized at the very time when the slavery controversy focused interest on the Negro character. No longer were Americans in general being characterized primarily by their adherence to a set of political and social ideals allegedly representing the universal aspirations of all

4. Francis Lieber, *On Civil Liberty and Self-Government*, Enlarged Edition (Philadelphia, 1859), pp. 53–57.

5. Theodore Parker, "The Nebraska Question," sermon of Feb. 12, 1854, *Collected Works*, ed. Francis P. Cobbe (London, 1863–1870), V, 250.

6. Theodore Parker, "Dangers Which Threaten the Rights of Man in America," sermon of July 2, 1854, *ibid.*, VI, 117.

7. Letter to Miss Cobbe, Dec. 4, 1857, in John Weiss, *Life and Correspondence of Theodore Parker* (New York, 1864), I, 463.

humanity, but democracy itself was beginning to be defined as racial in origin and thus realizable perhaps only by people with certain hereditary traits. The heightened consciousness of what were supposed to be white racial characteristics undoubtedly helped make it easy for many, on both sides of the sectional debate over slavery, to accept a stereotype of the Negro which made him a kind of anti-Caucasian.

In fact, the growing popularity of racialist thinking, with its emphasis on contrasting stereotypes, seems to have led to a change in the character of the debate over Negro personality and prospects. The discussion of the 1830s had been largely a dialogue between environmentalist defenders of a single human nature and proponents of deep-seated racial differences; the dialogue of the 1840s and 1850s tended increasingly to start from a common assumption that the races differed fundamentally. The biological school saw the Negro as a pathetically inept creature who was a slave to his emotions, incapable of progressive development and self-government because he lacked the white man's enterprise and intellect. But those who ascribed to the priority of feeling over intellect sanctioned both by romanticism and evangelical religion could come up with a strikingly different concept of Negro "differences." Whereas scientists and other "practical" men saw only weakness, others discovered redeeming virtues and even evidences of black superiority.

This comparatively benign view of black "peculiarities" has been neglected by historians, who have had difficulty distinguishing it from the mainstream of racist thought, but it is impossible to understand the antebellum discussion of Negro character and prospects without acknowledging its existence as a separate tradition, a body of thought and imagery about black-white differences that meshed at some points with scientific racial determinism, but which had, in the minds of its adherents at least, very different implications. This doctrine—which we shall call romantic racialism—resembled Herder's relativism more than Gobineau's hierarchical racism, and was widely espoused by Northern humanitarians who were more or less antislavery. Although romantic racialists acknowledged that blacks were different from whites and probably always would be, they pro-

jected an image of the Negro that could be construed as flattering or laudatory in the context of some currently accepted ideals
of human behavior and sensibility. At its most tentative, the
romantic racialist view simply endorsed the "child" stereotype of
the most sentimental school of proslavery paternalists and plantation romancers and then rejected slavery itself because it took
unfair advantage of the Negro's innocence and good nature. The
Reverend Orville Dewey, pastor of the Unitarian Church of the
Messiah in New York City, hinted at the antislavery potentialities of racial romanticism when he contended in 1844 that the
"inferiority" of the Negro meant simply "that he has not brought
within the pale of civilization the rough, fierce Northern energies
to rend and tear to pieces; that his nature is singularly childlike,
affectionate, docile, and patient. . . ." Such "inferiority," Dewey
argued, was "but an increased appeal to pity and generosity." "Is
it," he asked, "the part of a chivalrous and Christian people to
oppress the weak, to crush the helpless?"[8] A further development
of the romantic racialist position was to deny unequivocally that
these traits constituted inferiority, and its logical extreme was to
argue, as Methodist Bishop Gilbert Haven did during the Civil
War, that the Negro was the superior race—"the choice blood of
America"—because his docility constituted the ultimate in Christian virtue.[9]

II

As previously suggested, one of the sources of this romantic conception of the Negro was the stereotype slave depicted in the
proslavery plantation romances of the 1820s and 1830s. Along
with more grotesque specimens of black humanity, the novels of
George Tucker, William Gilmore Simms, James Kirke Paulding,
John Pendleton Kennedy, and Nathaniel Beverley Tucker presented slaves who were, in the words of William R. Taylor, "re-
sponsive to kindness, loyal, affectionate, and co-operative." And,

8. Orville Dewey, *A Discourse on Slavery and the Annexation of Texas*
(New York, 1844) , p. 10.
9. Gilbert Haven, *National Sermons* (Boston, 1869) , p. 358.

as Taylor has pointed out, proslavery novelists thus unwittingly opened the door to an antislavery use of the same stereotype: "To attribute to someone the simplicity of a child . . . especially in the middle of the nineteenth century, was a compliment of the first order, and dangerous, too, if the child were to be mistreated and sympathy was not the response sought for."[10]

One of the earliest uses of the stereotype by a moderate antislavery writer occurred in William Ellery Channing's 1835 essay *Slavery*. After asking how some slaves had escaped the moral degradation that seemed an inevitable consequence of their condition, Channing suggested a racial explanation: "The African is so affectionate, imitative, and docile that in favorable circumstances he catches much that is good; and accordingly the influence of a wise and kind master will be seen in the very countenance of his slaves."[11] In 1836 Charles Stuart, a British-born abolitionist, wrote an article for the *Quarterly Anti-Slavery Magazine,* in which he praised the black slaves for being so "eminently gentle, submissive, affectionate and grateful." "It is," he added, "almost impossible to excite them to revenge." "In making the best of their miserable lot," the blacks were "exhibiting better qualities, than probably any other people on earth would exhibit under similar provocation." Stuart concluded that the "virtuous" behavior of the slaves, far from showing how well adapted they were to their condition, showed how ready they were for emancipation and how criminal it was to take advantage of their naturally amiable qualities by keeping them in servitude.[12]

Although Channing and Stuart conveyed the rudiments of the romantic racialist image, there was an important step that remained to be taken—the obvious one of identifying the alleged Negro virtues with Christianity. The idea that the Negro was a natural Christian was set forth in detail, with many of the implications inherent in such a notion, in a series of lectures given in

10. William R. Taylor, *Cavalier and Yankee: The Old South and American National Character* (New York, 1961) , pp. 304–305, and Chapter IX, *passim.*
11. William Ellery Channing, *Works* (Boston, 1849) , II, 95.
12. Charles Stuart, "On the Colored People of the United States," *Quarterly Anti-Slavery Magazine,* II (October, 1836) , 12–14.

Cincinnati in 1837 and 1838 by Alexander Kinmont, a leading Midwestern exponent of Swedenborgianism. Kinmont, who conducted a school where scientific education was harmonized with classical literature and divine revelation, sought in his *Twelve Lectures on Man* to combine ethnology and religion in a new system. His efforts, it appears, excited great interest in Cincinnati, then the center of Western intellectual life. In response to the widespread praise for his ideas, Kinmont prepared his lectures for publication but died before they appeared in print in 1839.[13]

Kinmont began from premises not unlike those of the scientific racists, contending that Negroes, in both "their physical and mental condition, . . . are naturally and originally distinct" from whites. He maintained further that it was "the effect of a particular providence, or, to speak in the dialect of science, an express law of nature, that each peculiar race of men should occupy those limits, which have been assigned and none other." Thus the enslavement and forced migration of the blacks was not only a violation of Christian morality but also a "sad error" that went in the teeth of natural law. But unlike the scientific proponents of polygenesis, Kinmont did not accept the notion that blacks constituted a lower order of beings. Although the "original" differences between the races were not caused by "any combination of causes, natural or artificial, with which we are acquainted," and were in fact "*obscure*," they were nevertheless compatible with the religious doctrine of the unity and fraternity of the human race. Whites and blacks manifested different traits because this was part of what Kinmont saw as God's plan for the gradual fulfillment of man's intellectual, moral, and spiritual

13. Alexander Kinmont, *Twelve Lectures on the Natural History of Man* (Cincinnati, 1839). Kinmont was born in 1799 in Scotland and attended the University of Edinburgh. After emigrating to America in 1823, he served for a time as the principal of an academy in Bedford, Pennsylvania, and became a convert to Swedenborgianism, a complex and mystical faith whose impact on nineteenth-century American intellectual history was greater than the number of its adherents would suggest. Going to Cincinnati in 1839, he opened a school which emphasized scientific education within a Swedenborgian religious framework. A man of broad scholarly interests, he gave his first set of public lectures in 1833–1834, taking as his subject "The Physical and Intellectual History of Man." (See *Twelve Lectures*, pp. 1–16.)

potentialities. The present epoch, he indicated, was obviously that of the Caucasians, a race which excelled all others in "intellectual expansion"; and it was the divinely appointed mission of the whites to develop the arts and sciences. But such intellectual advancement was not the last word in human aspiration. Negroes, even in their present unfulfilled state, possessed some very desirable traits sadly lacking in Caucasians—"light-heartedness," a "natural talent for music" and, above all, "willingness to *serve,* the most beautiful trait of humanity, which we, from our innate love of dominion, and in defiance of the Christian religion, brand with the name of *servility,* and abuse not less to our own dishonor than to their injury." The fact was that the Caucasian, with all his gifts, was almost constitutionally unable to be a true Christian: "All the sweeter graces of the Christian religion appear almost too tropical and tender plants to grow in the Caucasian mind; they require a character of human nature which you can see in the rude lineaments of the Ethiopian."[14]

It followed that the African race had a glorious future. Kinmont foresaw the eventual emergence in "the Peninsula of Africa" of a great civilization which would reflect the peculiarities of the Negro character. "Who can doubt," he asked, "that here, also, humanity in its more advanced and millennial state will reflect, under a sweet and mellow light, the softer attributes of the Divine beneficence?" If the Caucasians were destined to reflect "the Divine science," was it not probable that the Negro would develop "a later but far nobler civilization," which would "return the splendor of the Divine attributes of mercy and benevolence in the practice and exhibition of the milder and gentler virtues?" In Kinmont's scheme, therefore, it was the blacks and not the whites who would first achieve millennial perfection.[15]

While Kinmont was expounding such views in Cincinnati, Channing was developing a similar conception in Boston. In his 1840 essay on "Emancipation," he took note of Kinmont's lectures and contended that he had arrived independently at a similar view of black potentialities. Channing's formulation was

14. *Ibid.,* pp. 188–193, 198, 218.
15. *Ibid.,* p. 91.

less striking in that it lacked the visionary, prophetic quality that Kinmont, as a Swedenborgian, had been able to supply. But in the more cautious tones of liberal Unitarianism, Channing said much the same thing. As he put it, "We are holding in bondage one of the best races of the human family. The negro is among the mildest and gentlest of men." Since the Negro's nature was "affectionate, easily touched," he was peculiarly susceptible to religious experience, more so than the white man, who excelled in "courage, enterprise, and invention" but was inferior to the black when it came to "the dispositions which Christianity particularly honors." Indeed, Channing concluded, it was "remarkable" that Christianity had ever taken root at all among Europeans, given the fact that they had so many "qualities opposed to Christianity," as manifested, for example, in the "law of honor" that the Christian message had been unable to repeal. The African, on the other hand, was a better natural candidate for Christian perfection because he "carries within him, much more than we, the germs of a meek, long-suffering, loving virtue." Like Charles Stuart, Channing employed such a stereotype to counter the argument that emancipation would be dangerous. "There is no reason for holding such a race in chains," he wrote; "they need no chains to make them harmless."[16]

By 1843 the theories of Kinmont and Channing had attracted international attention. A writer in the British *Westminster Review* quoted both of them at length on the peculiar virtues and exalted destiny of the Negro and affirmed in his own words that "the spirit of Christianity is at variance with the whole tone and elements of the European character;—it is in unison with many of the innate qualities of the African race."[17] Later the same year, portions of this article were reprinted as a contribution to the abolitionist cause by the *National Anti-Slavery Standard,* the official journal of the American Anti-Slavery Society.[18] The *Standard's* receptivity to such views reflected a new willingness on the part of at least some abolitionists to entertain views which were essentially racialist but which did not seem to deni-

16. Channing, *Works,* VI, 88–89, 51–52.
17. "W.R.G.," "Dr. Arnold," *Westminster Review,* XXXIX (1834), 8–12.
18. *National Anti-Slavery Standard,* April 27, 1843.

grate the blacks. In 1842 Lydia Maria Child, the editor of the *Standard*, had aired her own speculations on racial diversity and had concluded that "the races of mankind are different, spiritually as well as physically." She denied, however, that such differences had always existed; they were rather the "effects of spiritual influences, long operating on character, and in their turn becoming *causes*." In any case, she saw no reason to expect or even desire that the races would evolve in the same direction and eventually become identical. But the impossibility of wiping out the effects of a long history of separate development gave the whites no license to claim an innate superiority or tyrannize over others. The proper response to racial differences was a brotherly pluralism, "variety without inferiority"; for "flutes on different keys . . . will harmonize the better."[19]

Thus by the early 1840s the antislavery movement itself provided fertile soil for romantic racialism, a doctrine which acknowledged permanent racial differences but rejected the notion of a clearly defined racial hierarchy. In the Unitarian clergyman James Freeman Clarke's characteristic formulation of 1842 it meant that "in some faculties [the Negro] probably *is* inferior—in others superior," and that his superiority was found largely in "a strong religious tendency, and that strength of attachment which is capable of any kind of self-denial and self-sacrifice."[20] In 1845 James Russell Lowell, then a Garrisonian abolitionist as well as an emerging literary figure, advocated an immediate and radical application of Kinmont's concepts. "We have never had any doubt," he wrote, "that the African race was intended to introduce a new element of civilization, and that the Caucasian would be benefited greatly by an infusion of its gentler and less selfish qualities. The Caucasian mind, which seeks always to govern at whatever cost, can never come to so beautiful or Christian a height of civilization, as with a mixture of those seemingly humbler but truly more noble qualities which teach it to obey." Lowell did not spell out exactly how this mixture would take place, but he made it clear that if Kinmont and others were right

19. *Ibid.*, January 5, 1842.
20. James Freeman Clarke, *Slavery in the United States: A Sermon Delivered on Thanksgiving Day, 1842* (Boston, 1843) , p. 24.

about the Negro character, it would not do to wait for a distant African millennium; Caucasians who genuinely believed in encouraging "the gentler and less selfish qualities" were duty bound to allow the Negro the fullest scope for exercising a corrective, mollifying influence on white civilization, and this meant not only emancipation but the elimination of "every barrier of invidious distinction" between the races.[21]

The growth of romantic racialism in antislavery circles can be accounted for in several ways. It was, first of all, a reflection of the general trend of thought away from racial environmentalism and toward an acceptance of inherent diversity; more precisely, it was a way of adjusting to this compelling idea that was apparently compatible with Christian humanitarianism and opposition to slavery. It seemed to add strength to the antislavery argument to contend that slavery constituted the oppression of "one of the best races of the human family." But there was more to it than this. For romantic racialists, the Negro was a symbol of something that seemed tragically lacking in white American civilization. For those who resolutely adhered to Christian morality and idealized standards of gentility, the national spectacle during this period was far from edifying. With the "log cabin and hard cider" campaign of 1840, politics had seemingly degenerated into an unprincipled and demagogic scramble for office. The economic growth of the country appeared to bring nothing but a gross materialism, a willingness to sacrifice anything for personal wealth. Worst of all, in the eyes of peaceable humanitarians, was the crude national expansionism, justified as "manifest destiny," that led to the annexation of Texas as a vast new slave territory and finally to an unjust war with Mexico. Some who were disturbed by such tendencies were attracted to the prevailing racial stereotypes as symbols of their discontent. If this was the way Caucasians behaved—and the proponents of slavery and expansionism were openly celebrating the aggressive, warlike, and domineering character of the Caucasian or Anglo-Saxon—then it was possible that something was wrong with the race. The idealized Negro was a convenient symbol to point up

21. James Russell Lowell, *Anti-Slavery Papers* (Boston and New York, 1902), I, 21–22.

the deficiencies, not so much perhaps of the white race itself as of the racial self-image it seemed in danger of accepting.

In an age when traditional religious and moral values seemed to be losing their hold on whites, many could be consoled by contemplating a people supposedly free of a lust for wealth and power and therefore immune to desires that led Anglo-Saxons to expand their domain by enslaving or exterminating other peoples. Similarly, in an age of bad manners and vulgar materialism, there was something attractive about the idea that the black race possessed, in the words of James Freeman Clarke, "a native courtesy, a civility like that from which the word 'gentleman' has its etymological meaning, and a capacity for the highest refinement of character."[22] Hence benevolent reformers tended to see the Negro more as a symbol than as a person, more as a vehicle for romantic social criticism than as a human being with the normal range of virtues and vices. A critical observer might also wonder how deeply and unequivocally white humanitarians really identified themselves with the stereotype of the submissive black. Meekness might be a virtue, but was it in fact the only virtue or even the cardinal one for those who celebrated its presence in the Negro?

Of course the whole conception would have been impossible if the slaves had risen up in large numbers and rebelled against their masters. Romantic racialism was facilitated by the fact that no massive insurrections took place in the South after the Nat Turner rebellion of 1831. This apparent quiescence was widely interpreted in the North as reflecting a natural black docility. Senator Charles Sumner of Massachusetts confidently asserted in 1862 that a Northern act of emancipation, which he was then advocating, would not lead, as some critics of the measure had charged, to a bloody slave rebellion in the unconquered areas of the South. "This whole objection," he told a Faneuil Hall audience, "proceeds on a mistaken idea of the African slave. . . . The African is not cruel, vindictive, or harsh, but gentle, forgiving, and kind."[23]

22. Clarke, *Slavery*, p. 24.
23. Charles Sumner, *Works* (Boston, 1874) , VII, 226.

III

The image of the Negro as natural Christian received its fullest treatment and most influential expression in Harriet Beecher Stowe's *Uncle Tom's Cabin*. This immensely popular novel, which more than any other published work served to crystallize antislavery feeling in the North in the 1850s, was also the classic expression of romantic racialism. Little is known of the precise sources of Mrs. Stowe's racial views, which were, in any case, commonplace by 1851, when *Uncle Tom's Cabin* began to appear serially in a moderate antislavery journal, the *National Era*. But there is a strong possibility that she was drawn initially to the romantic-religious concept of racial differences by the lectures of Alexander Kinmont. She was living in Cincinnati at the time Kinmont was lecturing; and little of a religious or cultural nature which could be provided by "the Athens of the West" escaped her attention as the member of a family that was at the center of Cincinnati's intellectual and spiritual life. If she failed to hear Kinmont, she almost certainly read him in the beautifully bound memorial edition which was a major publishing event in Cincinnati in 1839. Whatever the circumstances of her first encounter with Kinmont's ideas and whatever influence they may have had at the time, their presence in *Uncle Tom's Cabin* seems indisputable.[24]

The opening paragraph of the preface presents her essential position. "The scenes of this story," she wrote, "lie among . . . an exotic race, whose ancestors, born beneath a tropic sun, brought with them, and perpetuated to their descendants, a character so essentially unlike the hard and dominant Anglo-Saxon race, as for many years to have won from it only misunderstanding and contempt." Elsewhere in the novel she described the millennial future of Africa in language strikingly like Kin-

24. Mrs. Stowe's Cincinnati years (1832–1850) are described in detail in Forrest Wilson, *Crusader in Crinoline: The Life of Harriet Beecher Stowe* (Philadelphia, 1941), pp. 99–234. Unfortunately, we learn little from this source about what she read or what lectures she heard during this period.

mont's. When Africa awoke, she predicted, it would develop a rich and luxuriant civilization; "and the negro race . . . will perhaps show forth some of the latest and most magnificent revelations of human life. Certainly they will, in their gentleness, their lowly docility of heart, their aptitude to repose on a superior mind and rest on a higher power, their childlike simplicity of affection, and facility of forgiveness. In all these they will exhibit the highest form of the peculiarly Christian life. . . ."[25]

These black potentialities are manifested in the character of Uncle Tom; although not a typical slave, he embodies that perfect "gentleness" and "facility of forgiveness" which are supposedly latent in the Negro and which will come to flower under favorable circumstances. When arguing for the plausibility of this character in *A Key to Uncle Tom's Cabin*, Mrs. Stowe cited several examples of blacks who had revealed a perfect Christian character. Since Negroes were "confessedly more simple, docile, child-like and affectionate, than other races," it followed that "the divine graces of love and faith, when in-breathed by the Holy Spirit, find in their natural temperament a more congenial atmosphere."[26] In the novel, Uncle Tom speaks for this simple, childlike religious faith; and in this he is abetted by the angel-child, Little Eva, who manifests an identical simplicity. When Tom attempts to convert his educated, sophisticated, and jaded master Augustine St. Clare, the "heart" of the Negro is pitted against the worldly intellectuality of the white man. "It seems to be given to children, and poor, honest fellows, like you, to see what we can't," St. Clare confesses to Tom; and the pious slave replies in Biblical language: "Thou hast hid from the wise and prudent, and revealed unto babes . . . even so, Father, for so it seemed good in thy sight."[27] Here Tom is not simply a Negro but a spokesman for the evangelical "religion of the heart" which

25. Harriet Beecher Stowe, *Uncle Tom's Cabin; or, Life Among the Lowly*, ed. Kenneth S. Lynn (Cambridge, Mass., 1962), pp. 1, 185. (Originally published in 1852.)

26. Harriet Beecher Stowe, *A Key to Uncle Tom's Cabin* (Boston and Cincinnati, 1853), p. 25.

27. Stowe, *Uncle Tom*, pp. 307–310.

Harriet Beecher Stowe was recommending as the only path to salvation for those whose cultivation and intellectuality led them to doubt the redeeming power of Christ. Behind this affirmation, as some of her later novels would make clear, was a struggle with Calvinist theology with its "system" and its hard, logical barriers to simple faith. Thus Harriet Beecher Stowe was not only a romantic but also a proponent of a childlike evangelical piety, and Uncle Tom served as a weapon in her war against the doubting intellect.[28]

In her second antislavery novel, *Dred,* published in 1856, Mrs. Stowe attempted to deal with a different kind of black man, a rebel modeled after Nat Turner. She was, to say the least, hindered in this effort by her assumptions about the Negro character and her basic revulsion to the idea of black retaliation against whites. The novel features a female Uncle Tom, named Milly, who attempts to talk Dred out of his bloody project. Confused by theological hairsplitting, Milly finds refuge in a simple and emotional faith, and exercises a good influence on some of the white characters; but she is unable to reach Dred, who refuses to accept her view that vengeance belongs to the Lord. Dred himself is portrayed as literally insane, or very close to it—presumably only madness would drive a Negro to violence—and his derangement derives primarily from his long periods of solitude in the savage swamps where he had subsisted as a runaway. In describing how contact with the natural "sublime" in its most fearsome shapes warps the mind of a man with a powerful imagination, Mrs. Stowe was describing a typical romantic situation; she was in fact making Dred a kind of black Byron. Slavery receives part of the blame for his state of mind, however, for Dred sees the "weird, fantastic forms" of the swamp as natural growths "hindered by unnatural pressures," which are symbolic of the effects of slavery. Under the kind of "fearful pressure" to which Dred has been subjected, "souls whose energy, well directed, might have blessed mankind start out in preternatural and fearful developments, whose strength is only a portent of dred." To

28. There is an excellent discussion of Mrs. Stowe's religious beliefs in Alice Crozier, *The Novels of Harriet Beecher Stowe* (New York, 1969); see especially pp. 17–23.

Harriet Beecher Stowe a black rebel was clearly a warped and deviant personality, forced by "unnatural pressures" to depart from the racial type of the "natural" Negro; under more favorable circumstances, Dred might have been an Uncle Tom.[29]

The Minister's Wooing (1859), Mrs. Stowe's third novel, was not centrally concerned with slavery and the black personality, but it did contain a Negro character, who again represented the religion of the heart, this time in direct conflict with an intellectualized Calvinist doctrine. In this story, which takes place in eighteenth-century Newport, a woman, who supposes her son to have died at sea without being in a state of grace, is comforted by Candace, her black servant, who asks her to disregard the subtleties of Calvinist theology and "look right at Jesus," forgetting everything except the love for all men that He showed on the cross. Like Uncle Tom and Milly, Candace speaks for a sentimental Christianity that answers the needs of the human heart better than Calvinism. But the principal exponent of post-Calvinist piety in the novel is not Candace but the white heroine, Mary, one of the most impossibly good characters in all nineteenth-century fiction, who ends up playing a redemptive role not unlike that of Uncle Tom. Uncle Tom, as a naturally Christian black man, had sought to show brutal or sophisticated whites the way to a pure and simple faith; Mary, as a woman, performs much the same function for members of what Mrs. Stowe called "the coarser sex." It becomes clear from this novel, therefore, that women and Negroes are almost interchangeable when it comes to their natural virtues. According to Mrs. Stowe, "women are burdened with fealty, faith, and reverence, more than they know what to do with," and hence they can serve as mediators between the overly intellectual male and a God who responds to simple devotion. In comparing Mary to the Congregational theologian Samuel Hopkins, who appears as a character in the novel, Mrs. Stowe indicates that Hopkins, for all his virtues, is excessively prone to "subtle mental analysis." Mary, on the other hand, "had the blessed gift of womanhood, that vivid

29. Harriet Beecher Stowe, *Dred, A Tale of the Great Dismal Swamp* (Boston and New York, 1895), p. 522, and *passim*.

life in the soul and sentiment which resists the chill of analysis, as a healthful human heart resists cold." All of which gives substance to the conclusion of Helen Papashvily that Uncle Tom might have been a woman.[30]

There was, in fact, a general acknowledgment among romantic racialists that women and Negroes were alike in the gifts they brought to the world. Kinmont himself had maintained that the black race was "more feminine and tenderminded" than the white.[31] Women and Negroes were also linked in the minds of many because they allegedly suffered similar repressions; it is not surprising, therefore, that there was a close relationship between feminism and abolitionism. The tyranny of slaveholders over affectionate and forgiving blacks seemed to be matched only by the brutality of males who took advantage of feminine tenderness and devotion; and the romantic reformist concept of female "superiority" that developed during this period was very similar to the notion of the moral and spiritual pre-eminence of the Negro.[32]

Such conceptions led some antislavery exponents of romantic racialism to espouse an equally romantic feminism. James Russell Lowell, for example, combined his reform interests in this way.[33] So did Theodore Tilton, who was not only a leading male feminist but also one of the most eloquent of those who praised Negroes for their "feminine" characteristics. During the Civil War, Tilton, who was then the editor of the New York *Independent,* provided a clear and unequivocal expression of this Negrophile-feminist viewpoint: "In all the intellectual activities which take their strange quickening from the moral faculties—which we call instincts, intuitions—the negro is superior to the white

30. Harriet Beecher Stowe, *The Minister's Wooing* (Boston and New York, 1910), pp. 253–254, 134, 211. Helen Papashvily, *All the Happy Endings: A Study of the Domestic Novel in America, the Women Who Wrote It, the Women Who Read It, in the Nineteenth Century* (New York, 1956), p. 73.

31. Kinmont, *Lectures,* p. 218.

32. For expressions of a romantic-feminist view of female superiority, see Robert E. Riegel, *American Feminists* (Lawrence, Kans., 1963), pp. 56, 110–111, 195.

33. See Martin B. Duberman, *James Russell Lowell* (Boston, 1966), pp. 79–80.

man—equal to the white woman. It is sometimes said . . . that the negro race is the feminine race of the world. This is not only because of his social and affectionate nature, but because he possesses that strange moral, instinctive insight that belongs more to women than to men."[34]

The romantic and "feminine" conception of the Negro character, as popularized by Harriet Beecher Stowe, was one of the factors that contributed to a revived interest in black expatriation or colonization in the 1850s.[35] The Kinmont-Stowe image of Africa as the future home of a peculiarly Christian and "feminine" civilization implied that American blacks should return to the environment where their special potentialities could be most fully realized. In the conclusion to *Uncle Tom's Cabin*, Mrs. Stowe made her colonizationist sentiments very clear, not only by suggesting that the romantic racialist vision of the Negro future could be attained only in Africa but also by explicitly describing how Negroes would be prepared for the transatlantic refuge that God had provided for them. In speaking of the fugitives who were then arriving in the North, she gave what in effect was her blueprint for emancipation and colonization: "Let the Church of the North receive these poor sufferers in the spirit of Christ; receive them to the educating advantages of Christian republican society and schools, until they have attained to somewhat of a moral and intellectual maturity, and then assist them in their passage to those shores [Africa], where they may put into practice the lessons they have learned in America."[36] In the same year that *Uncle Tom's Cabin* began to appear in the *National Era*, Harriet's equally famous brother, the Reverend Henry Ward Beecher, made exactly the same kind of endorsement of colonization. "I am for Colonization," he said. ". . . for the sake of the continent of Africa, Colonization is the true scheme." But, such an aim did not free white Americans from a kind of paternal responsibility. "Do your duty first to the colored people

34. Theodore Tilton, *The Negro: A Speech at Cooper Institute, New York, May 12, 1863* (New York, 1863), pp. 11–12.

35. For a discussion of some of the other factors responsible for the revival of colonizationism in the 1850s, see Chapter Five, below.

36. Stowe, *Uncle Tom*, p. 458.

here, educate them, Christianize them, and *then* colonize them."[37]

Such antislavery colonizationist thinking was fairly common in the 1850s, which saw a general resurgence in Northern humanitarian circles of an interest in the repatriation of American blacks to Africa. *Uncle Tom's Cabin* was only one of several antislavery novels of the period which ended up advocating colonization as the long-range solution to the race problem.[38] By adding drama and significance to the long-standing colonizationist hope for "Africa's redemption," romantic racialism contributed significantly to this trend of thought. Conservative colonizationists like William Henry Ruffner, a leading Presbyterian minister of Philadelphia, were now able to provide new fuel for an old cause by grounding their expectations for the African future on "features in the negro character of peculiar interest." Ruffner's hopes were sustained by his belief that "of all others," the Negro "is the kindest, brightest, gayest, and most inclined to religion. He has eloquence, grace, and a gorgeous fancy and a most touching pathos."[39] The fullest exposition of romantic racialism as an argument for colonization appeared in a book published during the war by Hollis Read, a New York minister and former missionary to Africa. In *The Negro Problem Solved,* Read described Africa as "reserved for the development of a higher civilization and a better type of Christianity than the world has yet seen." Citing Kinmont and the *Westminster Review* on the destiny of the Negro as a better Christian than the European, Read saw "the peculiar religious instincts of the people, and the facility with which they receive religious teachings" as giving substance to his prediction. But despite his professed admiration for such qualities in the black race, Read

37. Henry Ward Beecher, *Patriotic Addresses in America and England,* . . . ed. John R. Howard (New York, 1887) , p. 186.

38. After reviewing this literature, Lorenzo Dow Turner concluded: "Most of the advocates of immediate emancipation . . . so far as American literature is concerned favored colonization after the Negroes should be freed and educated." (*Anti-Slavery Sentiment in American Literature Prior to 1865* [Washington, D.C., 1929], p. 103.) Other examples of such antislavery colonizationist novels are Elizabeth A. Roe, *Aunt Leanna* (1855) , and Hezekiah L. Hosmer, *Adela, the Octoroon* (1860) .

39. William Henry Ruffner, *Africa's Redemption: A Discourse on African Colonization* (Philadelphia, 1852) , pp. 8, 9.

reverted to the conventional colonizationist argument that white prejudice was ineradicable, and went on to maintain that the only black fulfillment was in Africa.[40] Those neocolonizationists —like Harriet Beecher Stowe and Henry Ward Beecher—who were part of the antislavery movement of the 1850s generally avoided making such statements and professed to be interested simply in benefiting the blacks, not in removing them because they were objectionable to whites. But by arguing—like George Harris, Mrs. Stowe's mulatto spokesman for colonization in *Uncle Tom's Cabin*—that the American Negro craved "an African *nationality*," they were implying that American nationality could never really include the blacks.[41]

IV

The romantic conception of racial differences was also useful in explaining the supposed consequences of race mixture. It is clear that the mulatto George Harris has a psyche quite different from that of a pure black like Uncle Tom: "From one of the proudest families of Kentucky [Harris] had inherited a set of fine European features and a high, indomitable spirit." Throughout the novel he displays this high spirit by refusing to adhere to the nonresistant philosophy of Uncle Tom. Indeed all the mulatto characters—George, his wife Eliza, and Simon Legree's female victims Cassy and Emmelene—are clearly distinguished from the full-blooded Negroes in that they alone run away or otherwise actively resist slavery. Uncle Tom, of course, also resists, but only passively, in refusing to carry out orders that violate his Christian conscience. Mrs. Stowe's own opinion on the probable effects of an infusion of white blood into Southern slaves is suggested in the novel by a comment of Augustine St. Clare. If large-scale rebellion ever breaks out in the South, St. Clare predicts, "Anglo-Saxon blood will lead on the day. Sons of white fathers, with all

40. The Reverend Hollis Read, *The Negro Problem Solved; Or, Africa As She Was, As She Is, And As She Shall Be* (New York, 1864), pp. 33, 347–348, 374, 316–320.
41. Stowe, *Uncle Tom*, p. 444.

our haughty feelings burning in their veins, will not always be bought and sold and traded."[42]

Another popular antislavery novel, Metta V. Victor's *Maum Guinea, and Her Plantation "Children,"* published in 1861, had a similar cast of docile blacks and restive browns. In this crude but vivid literary indictment of slavery, all the characters with real sufferings and sensibilities are described as light-skinned mulattoes, while the pure-blooded Negroes are simple souls who can endure anything with a smile. Maum Guinea herself is a mulatto woman of serious demeanor, who possesses "a strange look in her eyes which might be sadness or hate or both"; her smoldering feelings eventually come to the surface when, in a bold and striking scene, she curses the entire white race. The docile Scipio, on the other hand, manifests the contentment of the pure black; he rebounds cheerfully from bad treatment on the theory that "it's better to laugh dan cry," adding that "trouble don't hurt me. It rolls off my min' like water off a duck's back."[43]

Since the restive and rebellious mulattoes who appear in romantic racialist novels like *Uncle Tom's Cabin* and *Maum Guinea* are treated sympathetically, their characterization brings to the fore a serious question about the totality of the commitment, on the part of the white authors, to the submissive virtues attributed to the full-blooded Negro. When he reviewed *Uncle Tom's Cabin* in the *Liberator* in 1852, William Lloyd Garrison, himself a dedicated believer in "Christian non-resistance" for all races, raised the possibility that Mrs. Stowe might have a double standard. "We are curious to know," he asked, "whether Mrs. Stowe is a believer in the duty of non-resistance for the white man, under all possible outrage and peril, as well as for the black man. . . ." He went on to point out that there was a tendency to ask Negroes to live up to Christian commandments that the white man (and he might have added the near-white man as well) was not required to obey.[44]

42. *Ibid.*, 114, 274, and *passim*.
43. Mrs. Metta V. Victor, *Maum Guinea, and Her Plantation "Children"* (New York, 1861) , pp. 11, 72–73, 49–53.
44. *The Liberator*, March 26, 1852.

There was opposition to this apparently equivocal glorification of Negro docility, not only from genuine "non-resistants" who suspected a double standard, but also from their antislavery opposites, those who in the 1850s began to encourage slave resistance and other forceful methods of destroying slavery. Thomas Wentworth Higginson and Theodore Parker, militant Unitarian reformers and financial backers of John Brown, who favored forceful action against "the slave power," contended that slave docility, if a fact, was a legitimate source of white contempt. ". . . if the Truth were told," Higginson wrote in 1861, "it would be that the Anglo-Saxon despises the Negro because he is *not* an insurgent, for the Anglo-Saxon would certainly be one in his place." There was, he contended, "more spontaneous sympathy with Nat Turner than with Uncle Tom."[45] Elsewhere, however, Higginson indicated that he himself was not convinced that the popular view of innate black passivity was fully justified. He wrote in an essay on "Physical Courage" that in "desperate emergencies" the black slave "seems to pass at one bound, as women do, from cowering pusillanimity to the topmost height of daring. The giddy laugh vanishes, the idle chatter is hushed, and the buffoon becomes a hero. Nothing in history surpasses the bravery of the Maroons of Surinam, . . . or those of Jamaica. . . . Agents of the 'Underground Railroad' report that the incidents which daily come to their knowledge are beyond all Greek, all Roman fame."[46]

Theodore Parker, on the other hand, accepted the stereotype more completely. This was one reason that he indulged occasionally in a disparagement of the Negro character which added a discordant note to his militant abolitionism. "If the African be so low that the condition of slavery is tolerable in his eyes, and he can dance in chains," Parker had said in a sermon of 1841, "then it is all the more a sin in the cultivated and strong, in the Christian, to tyrannize over the feeble and defenseless."[47] But

45. Thomas Wentworth Higginson, "The Ordeal by Battle," *Atlantic Monthly*, VIII (July, 1861), 94.
46. *Atlantic Monthly*, II (November, 1858), 94.
47. Theodore Parker, "A Sermon on Slavery," *Works*, V, 4. There is obviously a need for a further and more detailed explanation of the paradox

Parker did not rule out entirely the prospect of black insurrection. In a letter written in defense of John Brown, he acknowledged that "the African race is greatly inferior to the Caucasian in general intellectual power, and also in that instinct for liberty which is so strong in the Teutonic family." Blacks even lacked a "desire for vengeance—the lowest form of justice." But, he continued, Santo Domingo had demonstrated that *"there is a limit even to the Negro's forbearance."*[48]

Parker of course did not believe the Anglo-Saxon perfect either, despite his undeniable superiority over other races. In his addresses of 1854 and 1855 Parker criticized the dominant race and suggested how it might be improved. He confessed that in America since the Revolution, "some of the least lovely qualities of the Anglo-Saxon tribe have become dreadfully apparent. We have exterminated the Indians. . . . We have taken a feeble tribe of men and made them slaves. . . . The American treats his African victims with the intensest scorn." Although he believed that it was a good thing, in the main, that the national stock was predominantly Anglo-Saxon, Parker apparently thought that this "strong, real, Anglo-Saxon blood" needed to be mixed with that of the other American races, including the Negroes and the Indians, "just enough to temper [it]," and "furnish a new composite tribe, far better I trust than the old."[49] Parker could not specify what the Negro in particular would

---

presented by Parker's tendency to be an extreme racist when he discussed black capabilities in the abstract and a militant egalitarian on questions of racial policy. Although willing to countenance, or even recommend, miscegenation, Parker had a very low opinion of the "ethnologic" characteristics of the blacks. In a letter of 1857, for example, Parker wrote: "The African has the largest organs of generation in the world, the most exotic heat: he is the most polygamous of men. The Negro girls of Boston are only *chaste* in the sense of being *run after*. After their first menstruation they invariably take a man—so say such who know." (Parker to D. A. Wasson, Dec. 12, 1857, Parker Papers, Massachusetts Historical Society.) In 1856 Parker indicated that the blacks suffered from a "regressive tendency"—"an ethnological misfortune"— and, as a result, "have advanced the least of any of the races" (*Works*, VI, 249) ; and in a letter of 1859 he described the Negro as "slow—a loose-jointed sort of animal, a great child" (John Weiss, *Life and Correspondence of Theodore Parker* [New York, 1864], II, 176) .

48. Weiss, *Parker*, II, 174.

49. Parker, *Works*, V, 270; VI, 42–43, 159.

contribute to this new blend, but he had, whether he realized it or not, opened the way for a romantic racialist concept of the mulatto character that would challenge the fundamental white supremacist belief in the evils of intermarriage.

Praise of the mulatto as a superior human type was occasionally forthcoming in antislavery writings of the 1850s. C. G. Parsons, for example, wrote in *Inside Slavery* (which had a flattering introduction by Mrs. Stowe): "The mulattoes . . . are the best specimens of manhood found in the South. The African mothers have given them a good physical system, and the Anglo-Saxon fathers a good mental constitution."[50] But it was not until wartime emancipation raised the specter of widespread miscegenation in the minds of Northern Negrophobes that a pair of deadly serious romantic racialists actually carried the doctrine to its logical extreme and openly defended intermarriage as a way of taking the rough edges off the overly aggressive Anglo-Saxons. One was Moncure Daniel Conway, an abolitionist of Southern origin who emigrated to England during the Civil War, partly because he was disgusted with the mixed motives and equivocation with which the North had approached the slavery question.[51] Writing to a British audience in 1864, Conway argued that "each race is stronger in some direction than all others but for that strength it has suffered loss in other directions." The European was distinguished for his "intellect and energy" but deficient in "simple goodliness, kindliness, and affectionateness"; and it was precisely here that the Negro excelled. In considering the desirability of miscegenation, therefore, Conway was led to conclude that "the mixture of the blacks and whites is good; that the person so produced is, under ordinarily favourable circumstances, healthy, handsome, and intelligent. Under the best circumstances, I believe that such a combination would evolve a more complete character than the unmitigated Anglo-Saxon." And it was inevitable, in his opinion, that such a mixture would take place in America; for the nation

50. C. G. Parsons, M.D., *Inside Slavery, or a Tour among the Planters* (Boston, 1855) , pp. 65–66.
51. George M. Fredrickson, *The Inner Civil War: Northern Intellectuals and the Crisis of the Union* (New York, 1965) , pp. 123–127.

was "bound by Fate" to "rear a new race" which would also be a better one.[52]

The other outspoken amalgamationist was Gilbert Haven, Methodist Bishop of Massachusetts, who openly asserted at the end of the Civil War that the Negro was superior to the Caucasian. He found in the Southern freedman's apparent lack of rancor against his former master evidences of "where the sweetest fountains of grace are in this land." Of all the American races and national groups, the Negro "has the most of Christ. He is the nearest to God. . . . He shall season our worldliness, selfishness, and irreligion with his heavenly salt." Haven was openly enthusiastic about the prospect of intermarriage with such a race, maintaining that God had "emancipated them in order that He may thus reunite all mankind in one blessed brotherhood of blood and love," and adding further, as if to make his point unmistakably clear, that "The daughters of those haughty Southerners, who have shrank from their touch as leprous, shall gratefully accept the offers of the sons of their fathers' slaves."[53]

Views on amalgamation as bold and forthright as those of Conway and Haven represented an extreme position, even among abolitionists. Antislavery radicals who addressed themselves to this question during the war were usually more tentative in their evaluation of race mixing. Their characteristic response to the charge that emancipation would lead to wholesale amalgamation was that they did not advocate intermarriage as a deliberate policy and felt that short-run miscegenation would actually decrease once the slavemaster lost control over his black concubines. But they were opposed to legal prohibitions on intermarriage, believing that such alliances should be a matter of personal choice, and they held out the possibility that in the course of centuries, the Negro blood would be absorbed by the white.[54] Some antislavery spokesmen, however, actually shared

52. Moncure Daniel Conway, *Testimonies Concerning Slavery* (London, 1864), pp. 73–77.

53. Gilbert Haven, *National Sermons* (Boston, 1869), pp. 548–549.

54. See the New York *Independent*, Feb. 25, 1864, and the *National Anti-Slavery Standard*, Jan. 30, 1864, for typical abolitionist comments on miscegenation. See Chapter Six, below, for a general discussion of the miscegenation controversy of 1864.

the strong aversion to intermarriage characteristic of Northern opinion in general and were receptive to the views of the American school of ethnology on the dire consequences of racial mixture.[55] Even fervent adherents of a romantic view of the Negro could shrink back from the prospect of amalgamation. Mrs. A. M. French—one of the humanitarians who went to Port Royal, South Carolina, to teach the ex-slaves who fell under Union control after the capture of some of the Sea Islands in late 1861—was impressed from the beginning by the religious sensibilities of the blacks. "In some of the deep things of God we may learn from some of them," she wrote; for "They have religious experience deep in the heart. . . ." But she opposed amalgamation on the ground that "there is not in the Caucasian the warmth of soul to adapt him to the African. There is not the colored adaptation to him." *"It is far better that the races are distinct,"* she concluded, and added that the pure Negro was unquestionably superior to the mulatto.[56]

Romantic racialists who accepted the idea that the races were sexually incompatible and that the mulatto was a degenerate type, and who were also opposed to colonization, were likely to end up advocating a limited kind of *cultural* amalgamation in which the blacks, although remaining forever a distinct race, would somehow add a touch of softness to a national character that currently manifested too much Anglo-Saxon toughness and insensitivity. The Reverend Increase Niles Tarbox of West Newton, Massachusetts, in a book on the Negro published in 1864 by the American Tract Society, wrote that he was opposed to expatriation of the Negro because "We want them, that our harsh and grasping spirit, as a race, may be tempered by the sight of their more simple-hearted and forgiving natures. We want them that our anxious and never-resting lust for gain may be shamed and softened by their more joyous and holiday feeling." He concluded that the blacks, as "a politer and more genial

55. It was, for example, the view of Samuel Gridley Howe and his Freedmen's Inquiry Commission that race mixing was biologically disastrous. See Chapters Five and Six, below.

56. Mrs. A. M. French, *Slavery in South Carolina and the Ex-Slaves; or, The Port Royal Mission* (New York, 1862) , pp. 29, 135–136.

race," might well "give some lighter and more delicate touches to our civilization and our Christianity."[57]

The most authoritative and complete presentation of the romantic racialist concept of cultural amalgamation appeared in 1864 in the Final Report of the American Freedmen's Inquiry Commission, a three-man body set up by President Lincoln to recommend policy affecting the newly emancipated slaves. The commission specifically ruled out intermarriage as undesirable on biological grounds, but in a section written by Robert Dale Owen, the Indiana reformer, and later reprinted in his *The Wrong of Slavery,* it promulgated a comparison of whites and blacks which heralded the potential black contribution to American civilization.

> The Anglo-Saxon race, with its great force of character, much mental activity, an unflagging spirit of enterprise, has a certain hardness, a stubborn will, only moderate geniality, a lack of habitual cheerfulness. Its intellectual powers are stronger than its social instincts. The head predominates over the heart. There is little that is emotional in its religion. . . . It is a race more calculated to call forth respect than love, better fitted to do than to enjoy. The African race is in many respects the reverse of this. Genial, lively, docile, emotional, the affections rule; the social instincts maintain the ascendent except under cruel repression, its cheerfulness and love of mirth overflow with the exuberance of childhood. It is devotional by feeling. It is a knowing rather than a thinking race. . . . As regards the virtues of humility, loving-kindness, resignation under adversity, reliance on Divine Providence, this race exhibits these, as a general rule, in a more marked manner than does the Anglo-Saxon. . . . With time, as Civilization advances, these Christian graces of meekness and long-suffering will be rated higher than the world rates them now. With time, if we but treat these people in a Christian fashion, we shall have our reward. The softening influence of their genial spirit, diffused throughout the community, will make itself felt as an element of improvement in the national character.[58]

57. Increase Niles Tarbox, *The Curse; or, The Position in the World's History Occupied by the Race of Ham* (Boston, 1864), pp. 157–158.

58. "Final Report of the American Freedmen's Inquiry Commission to the Secretary of War, May 15, 1864," *The War of the Rebellion: Official Records*

V

The romantic racialist view of the Negro and his role in American society, popular and even influential by 1864, occupies a curious and anomalous position in the history of American racial thinking. It was benevolent in intent and, generally speaking, not linked to an unequivocal theory of white supremacy. When most generous and sincere, it came close to the kind of pluralist perception of distinct racial "gifts" that was expounded by black writers like W. E. B. Du Bois and Kelly Miller around 1900.[59] As characteristically put forth by whites, however, it often revealed a mixture of cant, condescension, and sentimentality, not unlike the popular nineteenth-century view of womanly virtue, which it so closely resembled. It sometimes reflected little more than a nagging sense, on the part of "tender-minded" reformers, that their culture had its harsh and unattractive side and that white Americans lacked the disposition to conform fully to their own "spiritual" values. It was never suggested that whites become literally like the black stereotype and sacrifice their alleged superiority in intellect and energy.

Hence it was a racial philosophy that could easily be transmuted into an overt doctrine of Negro inferiority, distinguished from harsher forms of racism only by a certain flavor of humanitarian paternalism. In its relation to the larger trend of white racial thinking, it was one aspect of the retreat from environmentalism and the Enlightenment view of a common human nature. Despite its pretensions to being a Christian doctrine, it

of the Union and Confederate Armies, Series III, Vol. IV (Washington, 1900), 378–379; Robert Dale Owen, The Wrong of Slavery; the Right of Emancipation; and the Future of the African Race in the United States (Philadelphia, 1864), p. 195.

59. See W. E. B. Du Bois, The Conservation of Races (Washington, D.C., 1897), passim; and Kelly Miller, Race Adjustment: Essays on the Negro in America (New York and Washington, 1908), pp. 144–151. Miller's views in particular were very close to those of mid-century romantic racialists: he glorified the Negro's natural "meekness" and aptitude for Christianity and contrasted such qualities with the overly aggressive and domineering qualities of the "haughty Caucasian."

also verged on a heretical departure from the traditional Christian concept of a common spiritual nature for all men, although in this respect romantic racialism appeared to celebrate the black character at the expense of the white. Perhaps its most insidious quality was its tendency to provide an implicit excuse for Anglo-Saxon aggressiveness, including its mistreatment of other races; for if such a tendency was "in the blood," it would inevitably find outlets, however morally objectionable some of the consequences might be. In effect, it logically tended to undermine the notion of white moral responsibility and capability, upon which the abolitionist movement had originally placed such heavy reliance. It also implicitly deprived the Negro of the inherent ability to compete on equal terms with the ruggedly aggressive Anglo-Saxons, for he was denied the very qualities necessary in such a competition. Hence it indirectly encouraged a fatalistic attitude toward any failure of freed Negroes to rise to white levels of practical competence and worldly success.

Sensing these implications, perhaps, some of the original leaders of the abolitionist movement—men like Garrison, Theodore Weld, and Wendell Phillips—never, as far as can be determined, succumbed openly to the romantic theory of racial differences. They continued during the 1850s and through the Civil War to speak and act on the assumption that all men had the same basic psychology, possessed identical moral capabilities, and were likely to react in similar ways to common conditions. But these persistent environmentalists made few explicit efforts during this period to combat the growing belief in innate racial differences, except insofar as they objected to those extremist uses of the notion which justified slavery and discrimination on the theory that the Negro was so radically inferior that he was not even akin to the whites. Perhaps they were unsure of their own ground—hardly surprising, considering the verdict of both American science and American romanticism. What was clear, however, was that they regarded slavery and racial discrimination as morally objectionable. To them, equality was a moral concept and not one to be decided or even influenced by scientific or romantic speculations on the differing characteristics of whites and blacks. Unfortunately, however, they convinced relatively few—even among those who by the time of the Civil War had joined the broadened antislavery crusade—that a sense of racial difference should in no way determine the status of American Negroes. The inability of the abolitionists to ground their case for the black man on a forthright and intellectually convincing argument for the basic identity in the moral and intellectual aptitudes of all races weakened their "struggle for equality" and helps explain the persistence of racist doctrines after emancipation.[60]

Although romantic racialism reflected a movement away from the environmentalist explanation of racial differences that abolitionists and, for that matter, colonizationists, had originally espoused, there was one interesting attempt to combine the "Uncle Tom" stereotype with a kind of cultural determinism. In 1861 Mary Lowell Putnam, elder sister of James Russell Lowell, published anonymously a novel called *Record of an Obscure Man* in which she developed the theory that the peculiar virtues of the Negro could be attributed in large part to a cultural inheritance from Africa. The usual romantic description of the black character was provided: the Negro allegedly excels in "a sense of beauty and harmony," "rude eloquence," and, above all,

60. The racial beliefs of abolitionists are discussed by James M. McPherson in *The Struggle for Equality: Abolitionists and the Negro in the Civil War and Reconstruction* (Princeton, 1964), Chapter VI. McPherson acknowledges that some abolitionists had racialist views but concludes that on the whole the movement threw its weight on the side of racial equality. In my opinion, he somewhat exaggerates the egalitarianism of the abolitionists. His discussion, for example, of abolitionist advocacy of intermarriage (p. 148) gives a misleading impression because it consists mainly of statements from the relatively few abolitionists who took a strong and unequivocal stand on this issue; similarly, his discussion of Samuel Gridley Howe's influential analysis of Negro prospects (pp. 145-147) fails to plumb the depths and extent of Howe's racism. (See Chapter Five, below.) Also questionable is his assertion (p. 137) that "several abolitionists made intensive studies of the question of race" in order to refute the ethnology of "the American School." He cites only one example of such an effort, the review in an antislavery journal of the work of a French exponent of monogenesis. My own research has uncovered little of this nature, and I have concluded that the abolitionists were on the defensive on this question and preferred to avoid the whole subject. Despite these points of difference, I would agree in general with McPherson's conclusion that "in the final analysis, argued abolitionists, the question was not of race but of human rights" (p. 153).

"in the love that seeketh not its own, that suffereth long and is kind." Many stories follow which illustrate the kind of extraordinary loyalty and devotion which slaves can render to white masters, and one of the characters is led to conclude that "the eminence of the negro race in the Christian virtues has almost brought them into discredit in our time." The root of these qualities was traced to African civilization, where slavery existed as a genuinely familial system. "The slavery of African to Africa," Mrs. Putnam wrote, "is, in truth, the mildest form of serfdom. It is not unusual for the slave to call the master 'my father'!" Without being aware of it, the American master was often the undeserving beneficiary of this form of servitude: "The unquestioning acquiescence of the slave in his lot, his absorption in the family on which he depends, and identification of its interests with his own, are parts of a very old creed. The self-devotion which has more the spirit of clanship than of servility, and which the master himself must love and wonder at, is traditional. . . . Where they have been met by anything like a corresponding sense of duty on the part of the master, above all, where they have been fostered by a true Christian love, they have even struck new and deeper roots. The most unworthy master still has his share of the old traditional affection."[61]

Although intended to be an antislavery tract, sympathetic to the Negro and to African civilization, *Record of an Obscure Man* came dangerously close to justifying a genuinely paternalistic system of slavery. Because Southern slavery contained such evils as the domestic slave trade with its violence to familial bonds, the slave was reputed to feel a deep sense of grievance, stemming ultimately from the fact that African servitude allowed him certain "rights" that were denied by American slavery. If this was true, then a "reformed" version of Southern slavery, such as that proposed by some Southern paternalists, ought to have been acceptable in theory. In addition, the African "cultural" traits which Mrs. Putnam attributed to the blacks seemed to have some of the tenacity of biological traits, since they were not radically affected by a completely different form of servitude in America.

61. [Mary Lowell Putnam,] *Record of an Obscure Man* (Boston, 1861), pp. 81–88, 163–164.

Justly praised by historians for its favorable view of African civilization, *Record of an Obscure Man* nevertheless was hardly a protomodern environmentalist classic; in essence it presented a slightly heterodox version of the romantic racialism of the mid-nineteenth century.[62]

62. *Ibid.*, pp. 164–165. See also McPherson, *Struggle for Equality*, pp. 140–141; and Duberman, *Lowell*, pp. 12–13.

Chapter Five

•

White Nationalism: "Free Soil" and the Ideal of Racial Homogeneity

MID-CENTURY ROMANTIC racialists, it has been suggested, were of two minds on the question of the American Negro's ultimate destiny. Those most radical in their abolitionism saw the blacks as permanent Americans who would make a special and valuable contribution to national life and character; the more conservative admirers of the Negro's "natural" Christianity believed that his only fulfillment would take place in Africa, and they therefore supported colonization as both necessary and desirable. This latter strain of romantic racialist thinking gained momentum in the 1850s, as part of the growing segment of Northern opinion that opposed slavery but resisted the radical abolitionist demand that the black population be accepted after emancipation as a permanent and participating element in American society. Supporters of this broader antislavery consensus often harbored the image of a future America that would be all white, or nearly so. But most who cherished such a vision had no romantic expectations about a black millennium in Africa; they were mainly or even exclusively concerned with the national "purification" and homogeneity that allegedly would result from the narrow localization or complete disappearance of an "inferior" and undesirable Negro population.

Some perspective on the overtly Negrophobic or exclusionist

facet of the antislavery or "free soil" consciousness can perhaps be gained by recognizing it from the outset as an open manifestation of a deep-seated and long-existing desire on the part of many white Americans for a racially homogeneous society. H. Hoetink, a Dutch sociologist and student of comparative race relations, has contended that every distinct racial group in a "segmented society"—one in which race is a determinant of social position—harbors a desire for "homogenization," which can mean either intermarriage or the actual or symbolic elimination of the other racial segment or segments. He attributes the desire for homogenization partly to the fact "that the different segments derive from homogeneous societies." This "psycho-social force" is an indication of the "pathological" nature of racially hierarchical societies, and is inevitably "reflected in the minds of those who speculate on the fate of their society." The hope for racial uniformity seems to have taken a form in New World "segmented societies" of Northwest European origin different from that which it has manifested in Latin America. According to Hoetink, homogenization through intermarriage has become both an aspiration and a long-range possibility in the societies of Iberian origin but has been traditionally ruled out in English, Dutch, and French colonies. If this is true, one would expect that in English North America the white desire for homogeneity would be reflected most dramatically in expectations of Negro removal or elimination.[1]

It may be objected, however, that slaveholders and other

1. Harmannus Hoetink, *The Two Variants in Caribbean Race Relations: A Contribution to the Sociology of Segmented Societies* (London, 1967), pp. 106–110, and *passim*. My own findings on the racial thinking of the nineteenth century bear out Hoetink's implication that a hope for homogeneity by some means other than intermarriage has been an important element in white racial speculation throughout all or most of American history. But he may place too much stress on original and permanent "somatic norm images" as a cause of the differing expectations in societies of West European as opposed to Iberian derivation. That English settlers had complexions that really did contrast more sharply with those of Negroes than was the case with the more swarthy Spanish and Portuguese colonials may be of some significance, but it is impossible to know how much weight to give to the psychological effects of color per se until a further comparative analysis is made of purely sociological factors such as demography, class structure, and patterns of settlement.

Americans who exploited the Negro economically or socially had no desire to get rid of the black population. Hoetink says that those whose economic or social position necessitates a subservient racial group, or groups, achieve a kind of "pseudo-homogeneity" by regarding "the other segments" as "foreign bodies, outsiders, even aliens." In the nineteenth-century South, as we have seen, the presence of an egalitarian ethos seemed to require that the Negro be regarded, not merely as an alien, but as a creature not quite human.[2]

In nineteenth-century America, North and South, the equivalent of Hoetink's "pseudo-homogeneity" was often affirmed in the context of opposition to "amalgamation," or intermarriage. In the United States the racial ideal was of course lily-white, and legal barriers to intermarriage certified black exclusion from the "real" community, within which men and women were free to marry by choice. As James Kirke Paulding put it in 1836, amalgamation of the races would "destroy the homogeneous character of the people of the United States, on which is founded our union, and from which results nearly all those ties which constitute the cement of social life."[3] It never occurred to Paulding that the mere presence of the Negro as a slave in the South and a social pariah in the North in any way contradicted the notion that Americans were racially homogeneous. With the development in the 1840s and 1850s of scientific race theory and a new sense of Caucasian or Anglo-Saxon racial pride, it became possible to articulate such a concern for continued "homogeneity" with greater authority. In 1857 J. Aitken Meigs, professor at the Philadelphia College of Medicine and a leading disciple of Samuel George Morton, gave a scientist's view of the danger to the nation that would result from the fusing of diverse races. "As long as the blood of one citizen . . . differs from that of another," he asserted, "diverse and probably long forgotten forms would crop out . . . as indications of the past, and obstacles to the assumption of that perfectly homogeneous character which belongs to pure stocks alone." Meigs went on to cite Gobineau on

2. *Ibid.*, p. 110. See also Chapters Two and Three, above.
3. James Kirke Paulding, *Slavery in the United States* (New York, 1836), p. 64.

the national degeneracy that inevitably sets in when a people fails to preserve its "leading ethnical principle" and concluded that Americans needed to "provide intelligently for the amelioration of that disease whose seeds were planted when the Declaration of Independence was proclaimed and whose deadly influences threaten, sooner or later, like the Lianes of a tropical forest, to suffocate the national tree over which they are silently spreading."[4]

The "pseudo-homogeneity" that could be attained by the exclusion of the Negro from the community of citizens, through enslavement, patterns of discrimination, and ultimately through the absolute prohibition of intermarriage, did not satisfy all segments of anti-Negro opinion in the pre-Civil War period. Aberrant Southerners like J. J. Flournoy and Hinton Rowan Helper objected openly to the physical presence of blacks, however lowly and subordinate they might be, and advocated deportation of the entire race.[5] Such thinking was much more common in the North, which lacked a direct dependence on Negro labor and consequently manifested a tendency to look on the free blacks as superfluous population. Negro exclusionist sentiments were particularly strong in the Midwest, where there were various efforts in the 1840s and 1850s to prevent Negro immigration and to remove the blacks who were already there. In 1851 Indiana prohibited all Negroes from entering the state, and Illinois followed suit in 1853. At about this same time, the Midwest saw an upsurge of the kind of colonizationist activity

4. J. C. Nott and George R. Gliddon, eds., *Indigenous Races of the Earth* (Philadelphia, 1857), pp. 251–252. Meigs's reference to the Declaration of Independence is a little obscure, but presumably he was referring to its claim that "all men are created equal"—a doctrine which, if literally applied, might threaten what Meigs conceived of as the racial integrity of the nation.

5. See E. Merton Coulter, *John Jacobus Flournoy: Champion of the Common Man in the Antebellum South* (Savannah, 1942); and Hinton Rowan Helper, *The Impending Crisis of the South: How to Meet It*, ed. George M. Fredrickson (Cambridge, Mass., 1968), pp. xxxi, 97, 182. Flournoy, a Georgian who published his views in pamphlet form in the 1830s, was a half-mad local eccentric whose theories were hardly noticed in the South. Helper's expulsionism is more significant because his doctrines attracted great attention and may have expressed the otherwise unarticulated desires of many nonslaveholding whites. But Helper's greatest visible impact was on Northern freesoil enthusiasts.

that was openly and explicitly concerned with simply getting rid of the local free Negroes by sending them anywhere outside the United States.[6]

A leading Midwestern intellectual who articulated his section's desire to be all-white was Dr. Daniel Drake, physician, scientist, and central figure of Cincinnati's literary and cultural life. In a series of letters written to the *National Intelligencer* in 1851 Drake offered the following proposition: "The free States should not hereafter permit negroes, or their descendants of mixed blood, citizens of Liberia excepted, to reside in, pass through, or even visit them; and the slave States should forbid emancipation, except a guaranty be given that the liberated should not seek the free states." He made this proposal, Drake explained, because of his belief "that we do not *need* an African population. That these people whether bond or free, are, in every part of the United States, a serving people, parasitic to the white man in propensity, and devoted to his menial employments." The influx of European immigrants, he pointed out, had removed the need for blacks as servants, and there was in fact nothing else they could do. The Negroes who lived in the Northern states were troublesome and thoroughly disliked, and therefore responsible for provoking whites to violence and disorder; they had no hope of attaining a position that was "either elevated or secure." Drake's long-range answer to the race problem was colonization or deportation, and if the North refused to absorb the South's excess black population, such a solution would eventually be forced on the Southern states. In the meantime, however, the best policy was "not only to leave all *slaves*, but all *negroes* (those now in the North excepted) to the management of the South."[7]

Drake spoke for many in his region in expressing the fear that, unless something were done, the Midwestern states might at some point be indundated by a flood of Negroes pouring across the Ohio River. This sense of a black peril, building up in the South

6. See Eugene H. Berwanger, *The Frontier Against Slavery: Western Anti-Negro Prejudice and the Slavery Extension Controversy* (Urbana, Ill.,1967), pp. 44–59.

7. Dr. Daniel Drake, *Letters on Slavery to John C. Warren of Boston, Reprinted from the National Intelligencer, April 3, 5, 7, 1851* (New York, 1940), pp. 29, 31, 32, 34, 37, 54–67.

as slavery reached what were supposed to be its natural limits of expansion, haunted the popular imagination of the Midwest and reached panic proportions when the Civil War brought the prospect of emancipation.[8] The characteristic Midwestern view of race relations was set forth in a relatively temperate manner in the late 1850s by Whitelaw Reid, editor of the Xenia, Ohio, *News* and later the successor to Horace Greeley as editor of the New York *Tribune*. "Where Negroes reside in any great numbers among the whites," Reid wrote, ". . . both parties are the worse for it, and it is to the interest of both that a separation should be made as soon as practicable."[9]

This, of course, was what proponents of colonization from all sections had been saying since the late eighteenth century, when Jefferson described slavery, or any conceivable biracial situation that might replace it, as inherently dangerous and unstable. Colonizationists had always implied that a complete separation of the races was the only satisfactory answer, the only way to fulfill safely and adequately the popular desire for racial homogeneity that was assumed to exist. But something new was added in the 1840s and 1850s, giving greater impetus to the hope for homogenization through the removal or elimination of the Negro. Only in connection with larger historical developments can one understand why speculations which denied Negroes a continued existence in the United States were so frequently ventured and so widely accepted in the North during a period of sectional conflict climaxed by a somewhat reluctant acceptance of Negro emancipation.

One such development was the rise of a new sense of American nationalism that had clear racial overtones. The early promulgation of a concept of white or Anglo-Saxon character that was supposedly synonymous with the American national character has been described above. But the full significance of this growing tendency to identify race and nationality, as well as the kind of applications that were likely to be made of such a correlation

8. Drake, *Letters*, pp. 66–67; V. Jacque Voegeli, *Free but Not Equal: The Midwest and the Negro during the Civil War* (Chicago, 1967) , pp. 17–18.
9. Quoted in Royal Cortissoz, *The Life of Whitelaw Reid* (New York, 1921) , I, 41.

from mid-century on, can best be seen in the public debate that took place between 1846 and 1848 on the question of whether the United States should follow up its victory in the Mexican War by annexing all of Mexico. As the historian Frederick Merk describes this debate, much of it hinged on whether American institutions reflected the needs and capabilities of all men or merely expressed the genius of a particular race, a question which arose because the Mexican population was largely of Indian or "mixed blood." The proponents of "All Mexico" were expansionists who did not believe in colonial dependence. and they argued that American democratic institutions were capable of incorporating and "regenerating" nonwhite races, a thesis that reflected the universalist concept of a democratic future for all mankind up to this time widely accepted as an abstract proposition even though it conflicted with actual American racial practices. The opponents of annexation, on the other hand, arguing that American interests would be well served only if acquisitions were limited to thinly populated areas contiguous to the United States, objected to the incorporation of all Mexico on ethnic grounds.[10]

This latter point of view was presented in classic form by John C. Calhoun in his Senate speech of January 4, 1848. Calhoun, like some other proslavery spokesmen, saw no future for the "peculiar institution" in such an arid country, and he opposed annexation because he regarded Mexicans as an inferior breed. The United States, he pointed out, had never "incorporated into the Union any but the Caucasian race. . . . Ours is a government of the white man. . . . in the whole history of man . . . there is no instance whatever of any civilized colored race, of any shade, being found equal to the establishment and maintenance of free government."[11] Many other opponents of annexation, Northern as well as Southern, expressed the same point of view. They carried the day, because the "All Mexico"

10. Frederick Merk, *Manifest Destiny and Mission in American History* (New York, 1963) , Chapters VII and VIII, *passim.*
11. From John C. Calhoun's Senate speech against the annexation of Mexico, Jan. 4, 1848, in John C. Calhoun, *Works,* ed. Richard K. Crallé (New York, 1853–1857) , IV, 410–411.

slogan failed to rally enough popular support to win its objective. Frederick Merk, who describes the basic position of Calhoun and his supporters as affirming "that the American type of government is a white man's affair," concludes that "the disintegration of the All Mexico crusade seemed to mean that the Southerner and his ideas had triumphed," and that the extremists of Manifest Destiny—those who saw no limit to the areas and populations which the United States and its form of government might incorporate—had suffered a defeat from which they would never fully recover.[12] For the next fifty years, in any case, one of the principal barriers to American expansionism into tropical areas was a reluctance to have anything whatever to do with the "inferior races" that inhabited them. Such a consensus was bound to affect the prospects of American Negroes because it implicitly defined the racial basis of American citizenship in a way that was incompatible with their assimilation into American life.[13]

Reinforcing such racial limitations on the kind of people who could be incorporated was the concept of a clearly delineated climatic zone suitable for *white* habitation and dominance. When Louis Agassiz, after his arrival in the United States in 1846, applied his theory of "zoölogical provinces" to the races of man, he immediately won wide support for the general concept, even among those who were unwilling to accept the idea that separate human creations had literally occurred in each zone. As he stated his theory in its most general form in 1854, it meant that *"the boundaries, within which the different natural combinations of animals are known to be circumscribed upon the surface of our earth, coincide with the natural ranges of distinct types of man."*[14] Another scientific writer, who restated the theory in 1860, took it as meaning that the races of mankind "vary in physical and mental structure, in accord with the diverse conditions of the earth's great sections, each constituted to

12. Merk, *Manifest Destiny*, p. 192.
13. *Ibid.*, Chapter XI; see also Chapter Ten, below.
14. Louis Agassiz, "Sketch of the Natural Provinces of the Animal World and Their Relation to the Different Types of Man," in J. C. Nott and George R. Gliddon, eds., *Types of Mankind: Or Ethnological Researches* . . . (Philadelphia, 1854) , p. lvii.

flourish best in a climate akin to its native one."[15] What this
meant in practical terms was that the Caucasian could have
unlimited sway over the temperate regions—an idea which appealed to American racial nationalists who could look upon most
of North America as a great Caucasian preserve—but he should
be wary of efforts to expand into the tropics, the natural habitat
of races differently constituted. The Negro, of course, was seen as
the tropical race par excellence. According to John H. Van Evrie,
writing in 1853: "The negro is as much a product of the tropics
as the orange or the banana, or any other form of existence
originally created within these latitudes, and the instinct of his
nature prompts, as well as urges, him onward to his original and
final home."[16] The identification of the Negro with the tropics,
of course, raised questions about his destiny in the United States
and provided a theoretical framework within which the "psycho-
social" wish for homogeneity could express itself.

II

The immediate political context which made hopes or expectations for a total separation of the races seem tremendously
relevant and significant was the controversy over the future of
slavery in the territories, a struggle which began in 1846 with the
effort in Congress to enact the Wilmot Proviso, a measure
prohibiting slavery in all areas acquired in the Mexican War.
This great political conflict was temporarily dampened by the
Compromise of 1850, but it broke out anew with the Kansas-
Nebraska Act of 1854 and thereafter increased in intensity until
the election of Lincoln and the secession of the South in 1860
and 1861. Primarily this was a struggle over what kind of institutions—slave or free—would triumph in the Western territories
and ultimately in the nation as a whole. In the minds of many
Northerners, however, it was also a contest to decide whether

15. Thomas Ewbank, *Inorganic Forces Ordained to Supersede Human
Slavery* (New York, 1860) , p. 16.
16. John H. Van Evrie, "Slavery Extension," *De Bow's Review*, XV (July,
1853) , 6.

white or black populations would predominate in the new areas.

On the precise question that often seemed to be at issue— whether Negro slaves or free white men were destined in the long run to provide the labor for the existing territories—the climatic racialist theory of nationality seemed to provide a clear and unequivocal answer. Van Evrie, who popularized the current scientific race theories as the basis of his defense of slavery as the Negro's "natural condition," held no hope in 1853 for black servitude on a large scale in places like Kansas and Nebraska. In an article for *De Bow's Review*, he acknowledged that laws of population, not the Northwest Ordinance, had kept blacks out of the region north of the Ohio River, an area which possessed a climate "utterly uncongenial to the negro constitution." What was more, he predicted that the northern tier of slave states was destined to be free, as white labor from the North pushed down upon it and drove the blacks southward and closer to their natural habitat. But the prospect of this pressure from a growing white population—fed as it was by immigration from Europe— led Van Evrie to conclude that the South must have "an outlet" for its excess black population. This outlet was to be found in the American tropics and could be provided only by the exten- sion of slavery into those areas; for the Negro supposedly would not work unless enslaved to whites, and the world needed the tropical staples which his labor alone could provide. As Van Evrie envisioned a Caribbean slave empire, the whites would reside in the highlands, while the Negroes occupied "the fertile regions of the coast," where no Caucasians could live perma- nently but where they could appear often enough to exercise the necessary "control and guidance." He concluded by emphasizing the importance of Cuba, which Southern expansionists were then seeking to have annexed by the United States, and demanded that this fertile island be seized before the British forced the Spanish colonial authorities to emancipate the slaves, an action that would allegedly make the whole Caribbean barbarous and unproductive, a threat to "the subordination of blacks in the Gulf States."[17] Many of the same points were made in 1855 by an anonymous proslavery writer in the *Southern Literary Mes-*

17. *Ibid.*, pp. 5–13.

senger, who also argued that slavery was receding southward and would eventually disappear in states like Virginia, Kentucky, and Tennessee. The future of American slavery, as he saw it, included not only expansion into the Caribbean but well beyond it, with the greatest future field for "our Anglo-American race with their auxiliaries" being South America, especially the valley of the Amazon.[18]

Despite the fact that intellectual proponents of the expansion of slavery tended to look southward rather than westward, the political opportunities and exigencies of the late antebellum period impelled Southern leaders to make an issue of the status of slavery in areas that they themselves often acknowledged were not very promising as plantation regions. The militant defense of "Southern rights" in the Western territories was probably more than a symbolic gesture, emanating from a defensive preoccupation with regional honor. Some Southerners perceived that the kind of influence over national policy that was required to protect American slavery where it already existed and to provide for its future expansion into Latin America necessitated efforts to maintain a balance of power between slave and free states by gaining political hegemony in the territories. Thus the South was drawn, somewhat reluctantly, into a contest for the control of regions that the North had come to regard as set aside by nature for white men and free labor.

The political free-soil movement, which developed out of Northern anxieties about Southern expansionism and the extension of slavery, combined principled opposition to slavery as an institution with a considerable amount of antipathy to the presence of Negroes on any basis whatever. Representative David Wilmot of Pennsylvania, whose historic proviso of 1846 opened the Northern free-soil campaign, made this conjunction clear when he pleaded "the cause and rights of white freemen," and announced that he "would preserve to free white labor a fair country, a rich inheritance, where the sons of toil, of my own race and own color, can live without the disgrace which association with negro slavery brings upon free labor."[19] When the Repub-

18. "The Black Race in America," *Southern Literary Messenger,* XXI (November, 1855), 676–681.
19. Quoted in Berwanger, *Frontier Against Slavery,* pp. 125–126.

lican Party came into existence as a vehicle for the free-soil impulse, some Republican leaders not only disavowed any belief in racial equality but asserted openly that theirs was "the white man's party," solely and exclusively concerned with the interests of the Caucasian race.[20] In attacking the proslavery Lecompton Constitution of Kansas in 1858, Senator William H. Seward, the most important Republican spokesman before the election of Lincoln in 1860, warned against "the error which thrusts [slavery] forward to oppose and resist the destiny not more of the African than that of the white races." "The white man," he continued, "needs this continent to labor upon. His head is strong, and his necessities are fixed. He must and will have it."[21] Where this left the Negro was revealed in a Republican campaign speech Seward delivered in Detroit in September, 1860: "The great fact is now fully realized that the African race here is a foreign and feeble element, like the Indians incapable of assimilation . . . and it is a pitiful exotic unnecessarily transplanted into our fields, and which it is unprofitable to cultivate at the cost of the desolation of the native vineyard."[22]

Seward's political statements reveal something about the general drift of racial thinking, because they demonstrate familiarity with the ethnological and climatic theories used to support the notion that all of the United States, or a large part of it, was intended by Providence for the exclusive habitation of the white race. The implications of this point of view were worked out more fully by those free-soil writers and theorists who attempted to envision more precisely the destiny of the American Negro. All of them agreed that blacks had no future in the North, unless artificially introduced as slaves, but they could not quite agree, as it turned out, on what in the long run was likely to happen to them in the South.

One point of view was expressed by ultraconservative Northerners who may have been repelled by some aspects of Southern slavery but had no objection to Negro servitude per se and accepted the racial justification of it. These men were drawn to the

20. *Ibid.*, pp. 124–132.
21. *Congressional Globe*, 35 Cong., 2 Sess., I, 944.
22. William H. Seward, *Works*, ed. George E. Boker (Boston, 1884), IV, 317.

free-soil movement or Republicanism solely because they opposed the apparent Southern effort in the 1850s to overthrow the tradition of sectional compromise by demanding the unlimited extension of slavery. In October, 1856, George Templeton Strong, an aristocratic New York lawyer and diarist, recorded his support of John Charles Frémont, the Republican Presidential candidate, but added that "party feeling has not changed my views about the abstract right and wrong of the institution of slavery. I still firmly believe that the relation of master and slave violates no moral law. I can imagine a state of society in South Carolina itself that would make the servile condition infinitely better for the black race than any other, especially if you leave out the doubtful possibility of higher development of that race in the future and look merely to their present welfare and happiness."[23]

Another conservative and aristocratic lawyer from the Middle Atlantic states, Sidney George Fisher of Philadelphia, made the fullest exposition of this point of view in his pamphlet *The Laws of Race, as Connected with Slavery*, published anonymously in 1860. Fisher argued that Negroes, as members of an inferior species, were naturally suited to be slaves of white masters wherever the races were in direct contact. He nevertheless went on to oppose any extension of slavery into the territories. As he saw it, the widespread Northern opposition to the South's assertion of a right to carry slave property into newly opened Western areas was based primarily on a belief that "these negroes are not property but men, and bring with them human influences not of the highest order"; furthermore, "whether property or not, they will occupy the land and consume its produce all of which [the Northern white] wants for his own race." Fisher also opposed slavery extension into the tropics on ethnological grounds, arguing that the white man could not effectively colonize an area so unsuited to his physical nature; he would merely degenerate as the Spanish had allegedly done in Latin America. His solution, if it can be called that, was based on the assumption that the deep South had a climate conducive to the maintenance of a black

23. George Templeton Strong, *Diary*, ed. Allan Nevins and Milton H. Thomas (New York, 1952) , II, 304.

population; so long as the whites attempted to rule in that area, slavery must be maintained. His long-range expectation, however, amounted to a willingness to write off "the extreme South" as a region for white habitation. Where climate gave the Negro "a permanent foothold," he would multiply faster than the whites: "All facts, all tendencies, all causes, therefore point in one direction—the ultimate ascendency of the black race in that country favorable to its nature." The deep South was, in fact, already well on its way to becoming a "new Africa." Contending that the history of nations overrun by barbarian races showed the need "to check the extension of Africa in our country," Fisher ended up advocating a drastic containment of slavery to localize "this mass of barbarism" and preserve the rest of the United States for Anglo-Saxon civilization.[24]

An argument with a slightly different twist was advanced in another pamphlet of 1860. In *Inorganic Forces Ordained to Supersede Human Slavery,* Thomas Ewbank, scientist, inventor, and former United States Commissioner of Patents, wrote that some type of Negro servitude was not only the natural consequence of biological inferiority but also a requirement for the cultivation of tropical staples; until, that is, an anticipated technological revolution rendered servile labor unnecessary. But Ewbank objected on unspecified grounds to the particular institutional form slavery had taken in the South and was adamant in his opposition to the extension of slavery into the territories. Lamenting the fact that the Kansas-Nebraska Act and the Dred Scott decision had abrogated the Missouri Compromise line between slave and free territories, he charged that it was "a weak point in the slaveholder's code to claim the right to carry the system deep into the temperate zones, since their occupants have an equal right, at least, to say they shall not; otherwise, it would depend on the will of the former whether any part of the earth shall be reserved for white labor—that is, for the perfect development of the white race."[25]

Because men like Strong, Fisher, and Ewbank justified in the

24. [Sidney George Fisher,] *The Laws of Race, as Connected with Slavery* (Philadelphia, 1860), pp. 8–15, 18, 40–41, 27–31.

25. Ewbank, *Inorganic Forces,* p. 14, and *passim.*

abstract some localized form of Negro slavery, they did not express the ideological revulsion to slavery in any clime which was characteristic of many free-soilers. But even those who had come to regard slavery per se as an evil could present a similar argument against "the extension of Africa." In reviewing Fisher's pamphlet, Charles Eliot Norton, a Boston man of letters and close friend of James Russell Lowell, objected to Fisher's description of slavery as the inevitable condition of the Negro but went on to endorse in full his demand for racial containment. Expansion of slavery must be resisted, Norton agreed, because it constituted spreading the influence of an inferior race and enlarging the "transatlantic Africa" which the South had become. He was willing to concede that the South was already lost to white civilization, but the question remained whether the rest of the country "shall be occupied a century hence by a civilized or a barbarous race." For him as for Fisher, the essence of the Northern free-soil position was a demand that the Negro be confined at all costs within the deep South.[26]

Norton, writing in the *Atlantic Monthly*, addressed himself to the prejudices of a portion of the Northern intelligentsia. James Shepherd Pike, a correspondent for Horace Greeley's popular and influential New York *Tribune*, presented substantially the same case for Negro containment to a wider audience and in conjunction with both a more militant antislavery doctrine and a more visceral kind of anti-Negro sentiment. There was no question about Pike's hatred of slavery as an institution and his hope for its destruction; but he also believed that Negroes were unfit to associate with whites and could never be granted civil equality. Since Negro "fecundity" in the Gulf States meant they could never be "rooted out" of that area, the best policy would be to make sure that they remained there and only there. "The slaveholder is claiming to spread the negro everywhere," Pike wrote in March, 1860, "and the Popular Sovereignty men stand coolly by, and say, 'Let him do it wherever he can.' We say the Free States should say, confine the negro to the smallest possible area. Hem him in. Coop him up. Slough him off. Preserve just so much of North America as is possible to the white man, and to free institutions." The ultimate result, Pike hoped, would be not only the

26. *Atlantic Monthly*, VII (February, 1861), 252–254.

death of slavery but also a total geographical separation of the races.[27]

After the outbreak of the Civil War, some Northerners who were willing to concede a slice of the United States for exclusive Negro occupancy became convinced that emancipation would lead naturally to such a result and might even narrow the existing zone of black population. Joseph Henry Allen, a New England clergyman and editor, wrote in a Unitarian journal in April, 1862, on the future of "Africans in America" and concluded that "natural laws" would solve the race question: after emancipation the races would distribute themselves in accordance with "the ethnological laws" discovered by Professor Agassiz. This meant that Negroes would then be concentrated in "a belt of population of purely African type, fringing the gulfcoasts, the low, hot valleys, and semi-tropical marshlands of the South." Since the natural instincts of the Negroes would lead them to abandon higher and cooler regions into which they had been artificially introduced by slavery, large areas of the South would be open to settlement by Northern whites who would redeem these areas from barbarism by introducing "free industry and free intelligence."[28]

III

Predictions that the containment and eventual disappearance of slavery would bring about a welcome division of the United States into a vast white region and a severely restricted "African belt" were not the ultimate expressions of Northern racial nationalism. The full white-nationalist position, the logical outcome of the desire for racial and institutional homogeneity, was more radical: it pointed ahead to the elimination of the Negro as an element in the population, through planned colonization, unplanned migration, or extermination through "natural" processes. Those unwilling to concede the black man his "foothold"

27. Robert Franklin Durden, *James Shepherd Pike: Republicanism and the American Negro, 1850–1882* (Durham, N.C., 1957), pp. 31–35; New York *Tribune*, Mar. 12, 1860, as quoted in Durden, p. 33.

28. Joseph Henry Allen, "Africans in America," *Christian Examiner,* CCXXXII (April, 1862), 110–112, 121–122.

in the Gulf States argued from a strict interpretation of the climatic theory of race, which made him seem out of place even there. This line of argument was popular in the 1850s among antislavery spokesmen with roots in the Southern and border states. Hinton Rowan Helper, the North Carolinian whose anti-slavery book of 1857, *The Impending Crisis*, set off a national controversy, wrote: "Instead of its being too hot in the South for white men, it is too cold for negroes, and we long to see the day arrive when the latter shall have entirely receded from their uncongenial homes in America and given full and undivided place to the former."[29] Similarly, Francis P. Blair, Jr., Republican leader in Missouri in the late 1850s, made it clear in an 1859 speech that the idea that there were parts of the South where white men could not work was pure myth. "Our whole country is in the temperate, not the torrid zone . . .," he pointed out as part of his rationale for Negro expatriation.[30]

The belief that the entire nation, and not just the major portion of it, was set aside by laws of ethnology for the exclusive use of the white race was clearly implied in Seward's statement of 1858 that the white man "needs this continent" and in his 1860 description of the Negro as "a foreign and feeble element . . . a pitiful exotic, unnecessarily transplanted into our fields, and which it is unprofitable to cultivate . . ." The Civil War brought authoritative statements of white continentalism that were even more explicit. In 1862, a Republican-dominated House committee concerned with emancipation and colonization concluded in its official report "that the highest interests of the white race, whether Anglo-Saxon, Celt, or Scandinavian, require that the whole country should be held and occupied by these races alone"; for "The Anglo-American looks upon every acre of our present domain as intended for him and not for the negro."[31] Significant in Republican and free-soil thinking of the

29. Helper, *Impending Crisis*, p. 299.
30. Frank [Francis] P. Blair, Jr., *The Destiny of the Races of This Continent. An Address Delivered before the Mercantile Library Association of Boston . . .* (Washington, D.C., 1859) , p. 27.
31. *Report on Emancipation and Colonization*, 37 Cong., 2 Sess., House Exec. Doc. No. 148, 13–14, 16, as quoted in Robert H. Zoellner, "Negro Colonization: The Climate of Opinion Surrounding Lincoln, 1860–1865," *Mid America*, XLII (July, 1960) , 134.

late 1850s and well into the Civil War, it appears, was a militant racial nationalism, an expectation of white expansion into every corner of the nation, with the disappearance of the Negro as the inevitable corollary.

The new climatic racial determinism was one factor in reviving interest in various emigration and colonization schemes for Negroes during the 1850s, as was the effect of romantic racialism in reviving interest in Africa. In addition, a small amount of support for emigration resulted from the frustration and pessimism of abolitionists, who were responding to the 1850 Fugitive Slave Law and subsequent judicial decisions which appeared to undermine the legal rights and personal safety of Northern free Negroes. In 1851 James G. Birney, a leading abolitionist, reluctantly recommended to Negroes that they emigrate, pointing out that hopes for equality in the United States seemed to be receding.[32] The decade that followed saw a growth of interest in voluntary expatriation among Negro leaders who had given up on the abolitionist promise of American equality. But many free blacks refused to be turned aside from their campaign for full rights as American citizens.[33] For maintaining this antiemigrationist point of view, they were sometimes chided by the free-soil press, which found a lamentable lack of realism and practical initiative in Negro rejection of colonization. In an 1853 editorial in the New York *Tribune,* Horace Greeley, who represented a militant wing of the burgeoning free-soil movement, defended colonization on the grounds that the Negro race must prove itself abroad before it could expect its claims for equality to be recognized in America. ". . . the blacks," he wrote, "will never attain the position they aspire to in this country until they have nobly achieved a like position out of it."[34] In 1860 the Springfield *Republican,* another leading Republican journal, made an even harsher indictment of American blacks for their failure to prove themselves by establishing successful colonies outside the United

32. James G. Birney, *Examination of the Decision of the Supreme Court of the United States in the Case of Strader, Gorman and Armstrong* vs. *Christopher Graham, . . . Concluding with an Address to the Free Colored People, Advising Them to Remove to Liberia* (Cincinnati, 1852) .

33. See Benjamin Quarles, *Black Abolitionists* (New York, 1969) , pp. 215–222.

34. New York *Tribune,* May 31, 1853.

States: "When the negro himself shall demonstrate to the world the spirit, enterprise, and power necessary for founding and governing and establishing a thrifty colony, the first step will have been taken toward the Universal emancipation of the African race."[35]

Such endorsements of colonization did not close the door entirely on future black equality in America, although they seemed to postpone it to a remote day. It was otherwise with the late antebellum movement dedicated to developing a government-sponsored colonization program. In 1858 a group of Congressional Republicans, led by Representative Francis P. Blair, Jr., of Missouri and Senator James R. Doolittle of Wisconsin, introduced legislation to subsidize Negro colonization in Central America. To some extent this was a political maneuver designed to help the Republican Party counter the charge that it was pro-Negro. But there is no reason to believe that the supporters of the measure were insincere in their belief that colonization was the best policy that the government could follow in regard to the black population.[36] The proposal was explained and defended by Blair in a speech in Boston in 1859. He made his basic attitude unmistakably clear by describing "that sable race, bred in the pestilence of Africa," as "a blot on the fair prospect of our country." Negro inferiority, he argued, did not justify slavery, but it was "a conclusive argument against blending the two races then in the same community, to deteriorate the superior by admixture or contact with the inferior races. . . ." His solution, he pointed out, was in accordance with the doctrine that "the marked distinctions between the races indicate [an] adaptability to various climates of our earth, as plainly and conclusively as the vegetable life of each zone proclaims the climate which produced it." In his opinion, colonization of blacks in Latin America would restore them to a congenial climate that was more accessible than Africa, and, more importantly, make the United States a unified and homogeneous nation: "Deliverance

35. Reprinted in the *Liberator*, April 31, 1863.
36. See Leon F. Litwack, *North of Slavery: The Negro in the Free States, 1790–1860* (Chicago, 1961), pp. 272–273; and Berwanger, *Frontier Against Slavery*, pp. 131–132.

. . . from a people who cannot assimilate with our people, the subjects of an institution utterly abhorrent to our free institutions, is the natural and easy mode of restoring symmetry to our political system, and equality among the people and States of the Union"; it would guarantee the "homogeneous institutions" needed "to make our Union perpetual." To Blair and his supporters the mere presence of the Negro constituted a threat to American nationality.[37]

Blair's proposal and the reasoning behind it were endorsed by several prominent Republicans, including Senator Lyman Trumbull of Illinois, who said in a speech supporting the scheme that the Republicans, as "the white man's party," wished "to settle the territories with free white men" and believed that the blacks "should not be among us," that "it would be better for them to go elsewhere." Blair's general proposition even gained the tentative approval of radical antislavery spokesmen like Gerrit Smith and Theodore Parker, who wanted to be sure, however, that emigration would be completely voluntary. In 1860 Senator Benjamin F. Wade of Ohio, a leader of the radical wing of the Republican Party, endorsed negotiations to gain the permission of Central American states to settle blacks from the United States within their borders. Such a policy, he argued, would open up "vast tracts of the most fertile land, in a climate perfectly congenial to that class of men, where the negro will be predominant." He rejoiced in the prospect of a vast black migration: ". . . they will go of themselves and relieve us of the burden. They will be so far removed from us that they cannot form a disturbing element in our political economy."[38]

The belief that the American race problem could be solved by establishing black colonies in Central America or the Caribbean did not die with the outbreak of the Civil War and the expectation of slavery's demise, but was advocated with new urgency as a necessary part of the emancipation process by President Lincoln and other leading Republicans. Lincoln had long been partial to

37. Frank [Francis] P. Blair, Jr., *Destiny of the Races*, pp. 21–22, 4.
38. *Ibid.*, pp. 29, 32–33; *The Radical Republicans and Reconstruction, 1861–1870,* ed. Harold M. Hyman (Indianapolis and New York, 1967), pp. 14–15.

colonization; in 1854 and again in 1857, he had endorsed black expatriation as the response to the race question that best reconciled the "self-interest" and "moral sense" of the white population. It was the only policy that promised freedom and independence for the blacks, while at the same time coming to grips with what Lincoln regarded as the unalterable facts of American race relations. As he indicated in a debate with Stephen A. Douglas in 1858, "political and social equality between the white and the black races" was impossible. "There is a physical difference between the two," he explained, "which in my judgment will forbid their living together on the footing of perfect equality . . ."[39]

During the first two years of the Civil War, Lincoln labored to combine hesitant steps toward emancipation with a workable plan of colonization. He negotiated for a tract of land in Panama, made an arrangement with the government of Haiti to accept an American Negro colony, asked Congress to appropriate money for colonization, and in December, 1862, called for a series of Constitutional amendments relating to slavery, one of which authorized a government-supported program of colonization.[40] His justification for such a policy remained what it had been before the war. As he told a delegation of Negro leaders in August, 1862, separation was best for both whites and Negroes: "You and we are different races. We have between us a broader difference than exists between almost any other two races. . . . this physical difference is a great disadvantage to us both, as I think your race suffer very greatly, many of them by living among us, while ours suffer from your presence." He recommended colonization in Central America, "especially because of the similarity of climate with your native land—[it] thus being suited to your physical condition."[41] Lincoln had apparently

39. Abraham Lincoln, *Collected Works*, ed. Roy P. Basler (New Brunswick, N.J., 1953–1955) , II, 255–256, 409; III, 16.

40. Benjamin Quarles, *Lincoln and the Negro* (New York, 1962) , pp. 108–123; Zoellner, "Negro Colonization," Paul J. Scheips, "Lincoln and the Chiriquí Colonization Project," *Journal of Negro History*, XXXVII (1952) , 418–453; Walter A. Payne, "Lincoln's Caribbean Colonization Plan," *Pacific Historian*, VII (1963) , 65–72; Voegeli, *Free but Not Equal*, pp. 43–45, 66, 97–98.

41. Lincoln, *Works*, V, 371–373.

absorbed two of the basic principles of Northern white nationalism: that whites and blacks could not live together in equality and that each was biologically suited to inhabit a different region. That colonization proved impracticable, making it necessary after 1863 to seek other means of establishing a racial *modus vivendi,* does not obviate the fact that it was the preferred solution of Lincoln and other Northern leaders.[42]

Implicit in the statements of Republican colonizationists was the notion that the kind of American nationality for which the North was fighting in the Civil War could be fully achieved only by the removal of the Negro. This was made clear in the 1862 House *Report on Emancipation and Colonization,* which advocated colonization on the grounds that "the highest interests of the white race" required that they have sole possession of "every acre of our present domain." In a pamphlet published in 1863, Captain Edward Bissell Hunt, U.S. Army Corps of Engineers, made a more abstract and theoretical correlation between Civil War nationalism and Caucasian territorial rights. Hunt, who was a well-known scientist, sought to describe the physical foundations of the Union; or, as he put it in his subtitle, "American Nationality as a Fact of Science." After showing that the nation was a physiographic entity, he went on to discuss the recommendations of science on its future racial composition. He began with the following axiom: "As each animal species has its own limits of habitation on the earth's surface beyond which it cannot flourish, so have the varieties of the human race." The logical deduction was that the United States "is not a natural home for the negro, and he is only here on compulsion. He belongs within the tropics whence he came." But despite the Negro's supposed inability to acclimate, he was very prolific under slavery, which functioned as a kind of domestic breeding system; hence the blacks in the slave states showed "a truly threatening rate of increase," making it a question as to whether "these states shall be hopelessly Africanized" or "reclaimed for the sole use of the white man." Hunt believed that half of the country was at stake and

42. Zoellner, "Negro Colonization"; Voegeli, *Free but Not Equal,* pp. 160, 169, and *passim.*

that "energetic *deportation*" of the blacks was necessary if white America was to fulfill its racial and geographic destiny.[43]

IV

Hunt's policy recommendations did not necessarily follow from his "facts of science." If Negroes had been artificially introduced into the South and had been made prolific there only as a result of "the superior sagacity of white men, stimulated by the base profits of slave-breeding and slave labor," then the abolition of slavery, by removing the motives for white nurture, would by itself undermine the continued increase—perhaps even the very presence—of the Southern black population, thereby making "deportation" less urgent or even unnecessary.[44] Another school of "free-soil" or antislavery racial theorists believed that planned colonization, while possibly desirable, was not really essential for the achievement of an all-white America; they placed their primary reliance on natural processes. These men tended to be more radical on the slavery issue than the free-soil colonizationists; some openly advocated emancipation in the South during the 1850s, a time when most Republican leaders were strongly disavowing any intention of interfering with slavery where it already existed. They also tended to argue that the government should take no official colonizationist role, because such action would single out Negroes and constitute a departure from the egalitarian tradition that all Americans should be equal in the eyes of the law and its enforcers. In 1862 Gerrit Smith, an upstate New York abolitionist, spoke for men of this persuasion when he came out against Republican proposals for government-sponsored emigration on the grounds that such matters were

43. Captain E. B. Hunt, *Union Foundations: A Study of American Nationality, as a Fact of Science* (New York, 1863), pp. 48–53. Hunt, who became chief engineer of the Department of the Shenandoah in 1862, was killed in October, 1863. He was a member of several scientific associations and had contributed a number of articles to literary and scientific periodicals. (See George W. Cullum, *Biographical Register of the Officers and Graduates of the U.S. Military Academy* [Boston and New York, 1891], II, 209.)

44. *Ibid.*, 50.

none of the government's concern. "I confess," he wrote in an open letter to Montgomery Blair, Lincoln's Postmaster General and a leading proponent of colonization, "that I am among those who believe that, were Government to allow full play to the law of nature, the blacks would move toward and the whites from the Equator. But government is not to act nor so much as take knowledge of these theories. Its work is to protect those who *for the time being* are its subjects."[45]

Smith's belief that emancipation would inevitably lead to the southward migration of the blacks and presumably to an eventual separation of the races—all without discriminatory action on the part of the government—had long been an article of faith among political abolitionists and free-soil radicals. As early as 1849, Gamaliel Bailey, editor of the *National Era,* a moderate antislavery organ, had justified his advocacy of emancipation on the soil as follows: "We have no doubt that the creator has ordained laws . . . for the distribution of men over the face of the earth. . . . Were slavery abolished today, . . . these laws would begin to operate, and different races of men would seek the latitudes congenial to their constitutions and habitudes. . . ." As a result, "without any violent disturbance or compulsory colonization," the blacks would migrate to the tropics, leaving the whites to occupy the more temperate regions.[46] This belief in a natural and inevitable separation of the races was shared by Salmon P. Chase, the militant free-soil Senator from Ohio, who wrote to the Negro lecturer and writer Frederick Douglass in 1850 that he was opposed to discrimination against blacks but "looked forward to the separation of the races," on the theory that they were "adapted to different latitudes and countries." He thought it likely that "the islands of the West Indies & portions of South America" would be the future home of American Negroes.[47] In the same year another Ohioan, the Reverend Charles Elliott, a leading Methodist clergyman and a proponent

45. *Gerrit Smith to Montgomery Blair* (Peterboro, N.Y., 1862), 3-page broadside. (The italics are mine.)

46. *National Era,* March 22, 1849.

47. Quoted in Hans L. Trefousse, *The Radical Republicans: Lincoln's Vanguard for Racial Justice* (New York, 1969), p. 29.

of gradual emancipation, published a book on *The Sinfulness of American Slavery*, in which he made the same prediction. "A climate farther South is the object of earnest desire to the colored man," he wrote; and thence he would go if released from thralldom, partly because of his natural instincts and partly out of a recognition that he could never achieve in the United States the full equality that could be provided only by white acceptance of intermarriage. Although Elliott denied that color was an "excuse for injustice or wrong of any kind," he felt that white repugnance to genuine "social equality" ran too deep to be removed.[48]

If humanitarians like Smith, Bailey, Chase, and Elliott envisioned the eventual whitening of America as coming through an amicable and painless process of voluntary migration allegedly beneficial to both races, another group of free-soil theorists manifested a more callous attitude toward the future of the blacks. In their opinion the United States would become racially homogeneous through a competitive process which would see the white man pushing his inferior black rival to the wall. Before the Civil War brought the prospect of emancipation as an act of military necessity, spokesmen for this point of view saw emancipation itself as resulting from such competitive pressures and predicted that freedom would be accompanied by the disappearance of the Negro, not so much because he would be happy to move southward but because he would be pushed out or otherwise eliminated in an unequal economic struggle. As the free-soil economist George M. Weston put it in 1857: "When the white artisans and farmers want the room which the African occupies, they will take it not by rude force, but by gentle and gradual and peaceful processes. The Negro will disappear, perhaps to regions more congenial to him, perhaps to regions where his labors can be made more useful, perhaps by some process of colonization we may yet devise; but at all events he will disappear." Weston compared the fate of the Negro to that of the Indians, who were then expected to become extinct shortly, and denied that the

48. The Rev. Charles Elliott, D.D., *The Sinfulness of American Slavery* . . . (Cincinnati, 1857), pp. 214–215. Elliott was presiding elder of the Dayton, Ohio, district of the Northern Methodist Episcopal Church in 1851, when *Sinfulness of American Slavery* was first published. He was also a leader of the antislavery element within Methodism.

disappearance of inferior races in the presence of more vigorous stocks was a catastrophe; it was rather the beneficent result of "laws which nature manifests throughout not only the animal but the vegetable world." The only thing that now prevented Negro "extinction" was the artificial protection provided by the institution of slavery, which was "no scheme of 'nature' but a violation of all moral and natural laws."[49]

Weston's predictions suggest that the "Darwinian" concept of a struggle for existence between the races antedated Darwin, whose *Origin of Species* was not published until 1859. Proslavery writers, of course, had often argued that Negro extermination was the inevitable consequence of emancipation and had used this prediction to make a case for slavery on pseudohumanitarian grounds.[50] They had not anticipated, however, that some Northerners would accept their argument on the results of freeing the slaves and then boldly reply that nature should be allowed to take its course. As early as 1839, Horace Bushnell, a Congregational clergyman and the North's most distinguished theologian, had predicted that the black race would not survive emancipation because it would then be placed in direct competition with the whites. Within fifty years, he predicted, "vices which taint the blood and cut down life" might well "penetrate the whole stock, and begin to hurry them off, in a process of premature extinction; as we know to be the case with another barbarous people, [the Indians] now fast yielding to the infection of death." Bushnell believed that the day of emancipation would be "glorious," especially for the whites: " . . . as to the poor herd who may yet be doomed to spin their brutish existence downward into extinction, it will be a relief to know, that a first day of conscious liberty made them one bright spot, in the compass of a sad and defrauded immortality."[51] In 1860, in a sermon on "The Census and Slavery," he returned to this happy theme and en-

49. George M. Weston, *The Progress of Slavery in the United States* (Washington, D.C., 1857) , pp. 33, 131.

50. See, for example, Paulding, *Slavery in the United States,* pp. 59–60; and Josiah C. Nott, *Two Lectures on the Connexion between the Biblical and Physical History of Man* (New York, 1849) , p. 18.

51. Horace Bushnell, *A Discourse on the Slavery Question, Delivered in the North Church, Hartford, Conn., January 10, 1839* (Hartford, 1839), pp. 12, 14.

visioned the free white population of the North pushing down on the South and setting off a Malthusian struggle for existence which would end in the disappearance of the blacks. "I know of no example in human history," Bushnell told his congregation, "where an inferior and far less cultivated stock has been able, freely intermixed with a superior, to hold its ground. . . . it will always be seen that the superior lives the other down, and finally quite lives it away. And indeed, since we must all die, why should it grieve us, that a stock thousands of years behind, in the scale of culture, should die with few and still fewer children to succeed, till finally the whole succession remains in the more cultivated race?"[52]

The full intellectual underpinning of Bushnell's prophecy of black extinction was revealed in the 1860 edition of *Christian Nurture*, his classic work on religious education. In a newly added chapter on "The Out-Populating Power of the Christian Stock"—a discussion that was to become an important source for Christian racists and imperialists of the late nineteenth century—he maintained that such acquired characteristics as "good principles and habits, intellectual culture, domestic virtue, industry, order, law, faith" could be transferred biologically from one generation to the next. Once such traits were acquired by a people, they "become thoroughly inbred in the stock"—even specifically religious qualities could become part of the hereditary make-up of a people. "The populating power of any race, or stock," he concluded, "is increased according to the degree of personal and religious character to which it has attained." Hence "any people that is physiologically advanced in culture" is "sure to live down and finally live out its inferior." An inherited capacity for Christian civilization therefore guaranteed the survival of the white race, and the lack of it condemned the Negro to extinction. American racism and American Christianity had at last been thoroughly reconciled![53]

52. Horace Bushnell, *The Census and Slavery* (Hartford, 1860) , p. 12.
53. Horace Bushnell, *Christian Nurture* (New York, 1871) , pp. 202, 204–205, 207. (This was a reprinting of the revised edition of 1860.) Bushnell's arguments had an acknowledged influence on the views of the Reverend Josiah Strong, the principal religious proponent of Anglo-Saxon expansionism

Strange as it may seem, Bushnell's basic views on the future of the American Negro were shared by Theodore Parker. Although he was willing to fight for Negro freedom, Parker was unwilling to concede a permanent Negro future in America. Unlike Bushnell, he kept such opinions largely to himself, revealing them only in private correspondence; but his public depiction of the destiny of Anglo-Saxons to expand their domain at the expense of inferior races implied that the blacks would have a difficult time after emancipation.[54] His full view of the matter came out in a letter of 1858 to an English correspondent. In illustrating that "curious law of nature" which dictates that "the strong replaces the weak," Parker described how one kind of New England grass invariably drives out another. "Thus," he continued, moving easily to another sphere of natural competition, "the white man kills out the red man and the black man. When slavery is abolished the African population will decline in the United States, and die out of the South as out of Northampton and Lexington." He also wrote in 1857: "There are inferior races of men which have always born the same ignoble relation to the rest of man and *always will*. For two generations, what a change there will be in the condition and character of the Irish in New England! But in twenty generations, the negroes will stand just where they are now; that is if they have not disappeared."[55]

Elsewhere Parker suggested that black blood might be absorbed into the Anglo-Saxon amalgam through intermarriage. But whether it was miscegenation or merely competitive failure that would lead to the Negro's disappearance as a distinct American race, he was fairly certain he would vanish. And, given his negative view of the essential Negro character, there is no reason to believe that he shed any tears over the prospect, how-

---

in the late nineteenth century. When maintaining in 1886 that the Anglo-Saxons were destined to triumph in the coming struggle of the world's races for dominance and survival, Strong quoted Bushnell at length on how an advanced people was "sure to live down and finally live out its inferior." (See Strong, *Our Country*, ed. Jurgen Herbst [Cambridge, Mass., 1963], p. 214.)

54. See Theodore Parker, *Collected Works*, ed. Francis P. Cobbe (London, 1863–1870), VI, 328.

55. Octavius Brooks Frothingham, *Theodore Parker: A Biography* (Boston, 1874), pp. 472–473, 467.

ever outraged he may have been by the immorality of slavery.[56]

Predictions of Negro extinction as an acceptable, even desirable, consequence of emancipation continued to be made during the Civil War by men who rejoiced at the impending annihilation of the slave system. In 1862 Charles Francis Adams, Jr., who was in the Army in South Carolina, wrote to his father that, in his opinion, the black race "will be destroyed the moment the world realizes what a field for white emigration the South affords. The inferior will disappear . . . before the more vigorous race."[57]

The following year, the Reverend J. M. Sturtevant, president of Illinois College, wrote in the *Continental Monthly* on "The Destiny of the African Race in the United States," and explained in detail exactly how black extinction would occur. Sturtevant, who was probably influenced by Bushnell, began by conceding that the white prejudice against black equality was insurmountable. Although most Americans believed that slavery was "economically, socially, politically, and morally wrong," the fear of a growing and assertive Negro population was a barrier to general acceptance of the government's emancipation policy. Sturtevant assured those who could not decide which they disliked more, slavery or the Negro, that emancipation would be a safe and easy way to dispose of both. He concluded, "with a high degree of assurance," that "the result of emancipation must be, not the amalgamation of the races, not an internecine war between them, but the inevitable extinction of the weaker race by the competition of the stronger." After citing statistics to show that the American Negro population had never increased except in slavery, he went on to demonstrate why this was so, and why emancipated blacks could be expected to die out. There was always, he pointed out, a "lower stratum" of the population that did not earn enough to support a family; this situation was irremediable because it reflected the operation of "a necessary and beneficient law," which ordained that only "the strongest,

56. See Chapter Four, above, for a discussion of Parker's other racial views.
57. Charles Francis Adams, Jr., to his father, Mar. 11, 1862, *A Cycle of Adams Letters 1861–1865*, ed. Worthington Ford (Boston and New York, 1920) , I, 118.

most vigorous, and noblest specimens of the race" would propagate and, conversely, that "the weak, the vicious, the degraded the broken down classes" would be weeded out. After emancipation, the Negro would enter into direct competition with the whites and, because of the superiority of the latter, would be pushed into that "lower stratum." "The consequence is inevitable. He will either never marry, or he will, in the attempt to support a family, struggle in vain against the laws of nature, and his children, many of them at least, die in infancy. . . . Like his brother the Indian of the forest, he must melt away and disappear forever from the midst of us."[58]

Sturtevant's racial Malthusianism anticipated the Darwinian notion of a struggle for existence between the races as well as the "social Darwinist" justification of a *laissez-faire* economy as the arena for a biological competition resulting in the "survival of the fittest." In terms of the racial aspirations of many mid-century American whites, his prediction was an explicit and extreme expression of the ideal of racial homogeneity that was brought to the surface by the sectional conflict. For antislavery racists like Weston, Bushnell, and Sturtevant, this desire for homogeneity led logically to a defense of emancipation as a step toward genocide by natural causes.

V

The war and the impending collapse of slavery naturally prompted a good deal of speculation on what would happen to the Negro after emancipation. Much of this discussion had an immediate practical significance. Sturtevant's article, for example, was directed at racist opponents of emancipation. Given the respectable intellectual genealogy of his proto-Darwinist view of Negro prospects, there is no reason to doubt his sincerity; but his opinions had propagandistic value for those who were seeking to convince a strongly anti-Negro public opinion that emancipa-

58. J. M. Sturtevant, "The Destiny of the African Race in the United States," *Continental Monthly*, II (May, 1863), 602, 605, 608–609.

tion would not challenge white hegemony in the North. North-ern fears of a black inundation had to be countered by proponents of emancipation. Since the race-climate theory was ideal for this purpose, throughout the war antislavery politicians, clergymen, and intellectuals asserted over and over again that the abolition of slavery would not mean a black migration to the North. The ex-slaves would remain in the more congenial Southern climate, and, what was more, free Negroes now in the North would go south, drawn by their natural instincts once the threat of enslave-ment was completely removed. Hence, in the short run, emanci-pation and natural processes would whiten the North, and in the long run they might whiten all or most of the South as well.[59]

Many spokesmen were so sure that such predictions would be fulfilled that they saw no need to inquire into the subject very deeply. But not Dr. Samuel Gridley Howe, the famous New England physician, philanthropist, and reformer, who in 1863 was appointed by the President to the three-man American Freedmen's Inquiry Commission, a body which was instructed to examine the condition of the newly freed blacks and recommend policy in regard to their future treatment. Howe was a radical antislavery man and supporter of John Brown; in his efforts to combine humanitarian moralism with a hardheaded acceptance of scientific conclusions on racial differences, he manifested the same kind of ambivalence shown by Theodore Parker. After his appointment to the commission, he sought to find out the full "facts" in regard to Negro prospects in America. He was ready to allow science to answer the empirical questions because he be-lieved that whatever the future might hold for the black man, such determinations would not obviate the moral imperative to accord him fair treatment.[60]

59. For examples of this point of view see William Aikman, *The Future of the Colored Race in America* (New York, 1862), pp. 25–26; The Reverend Frederick Starr, *What Shall Be Done with the People of Color in the United States?* (Albany, 1862), p. 25; E. H. Derby, "Resources of the South," *Atlantic Monthly*, X (October, 1862), 508–509. See also Voegeli, *Free but Not Equal*, pp. 20–29.

60. For biographical information on Howe, see Harold Schwartz, *Samuel Gridley Howe: Social Reformer, 1801–1876* (Cambridge, Mass., 1956). Howe's work with the Freedmen's Inquiry Commission is described in James M. McPherson's *The Struggle for Equality: Abolitionists and the Negro in the Civil War and Reconstruction* (Princeton, 1964), pp. 182–187.

As part of his inquiry, Howe directed in writing a series of questions to Agassiz. Of these questions, the one that Howe confessed "occupies me most now" was whether "the African race . . . will be a persistent race in this country? or will it be absorbed, diluted, and finally effaced by the white race . . . ?" He asked further if it was true that the "mulatto is unfertile, leaving but few children, and those mainly lymphatic and scrofulous?" Agassiz's answer to the first query was in harmony with the "permanent foothold" hypothesis; he saw no reason why a population of full-blooded Negroes—he estimated their present number at two million—could not "perpetuate their race *ad infinitum*" in the warmer portions of the South. In reply to the second question, Agassiz not unexpectedly described the mulattoes as a degenerate, sterile, and short-lived breed which would quickly disappear from the population if amalgamation with the whites was arrested. The likely result of emancipation as far as the North was concerned, he concluded, was that "the colored people in whom the negro nature prevails will tend toward the South, while the weaker and lighter ones will remain and die out among us."[61]

Howe was clearly impressed with Agassiz's arguments, which presumably bore out his own suspicions. Although he replied by announcing his intention to defend the legitimate rights of Negroes "though the heavens fall," he had in fact come to the conclusion that sound racial policy and opposition to slavery were perfectly reconcilable. Slavery, Howe pointed out in reply to Agassiz, had "fostered and multiplied a vigorous black race, and engendered a feeble mulatto breed." Many of both types had drifted northward, "in the teeth of thermal laws," to escape servitude; but the complete destruction of slavery would "remove all these disturbing forces and allow fair play to natural laws, by the operation of which, it seems to me, the colored population will disappear from the Northern and Middle States, if not from the continent, before the more vigorous and prolific race." He went so far as to suggest that it would be "the duty of statesmen to favor, by wise measures, the operation of these laws and the

61. Howe to Agassiz, Aug. 3, 1863, and Agassiz to Howe, Aug. 9 and 10, 1863, in Elizabeth Cary Agassiz, *Louis Agassiz: His Life and Correspondence* (Boston and New York, 1890), pp. 592–593, 595, 596–601.

purification and elevation of the national blood." More specifically, he recommended that "mulattoism," which was the same as "hybridism," ought "to be met and lessened as far as may be by wise statesmanship and by enlightenment of public opinion."[62]

Howe's suggestion that the free operation of "natural laws" might lead to the extinction of the Negro in the entire continent as well as in the North implied that he was not entirely convinced of "the permanent foothold" doctrine as put forth by Agassiz, and thought it quite possible that the United States was destined to be all white. In his report published in 1864 describing his personal investigation of the Negro refugee population of Canada—the result of a trip in the summer of 1863—Howe took up this question again. He began by describing the blacks in Canada as a representative sample of the black population of North America; then he noted that most of them were in fact mulattoes and explained this circumstance as the natural consequence of rampant miscegenation on the plantations of the South. For Howe, this mixture of blood was clearly one of the principal evils of the slave system, and he believed that mulattoism had gone so far as to be "widespread among the whole population of the United States," which meant that it had already impaired "the purity of the national blood taken as a whole." His observations of mulattoes seemed to bear out Agassiz's theories; they appeared highly susceptible to disease and relatively infertile: ". . . without the continuance of mulatto breeding, in the South, and fresh accessions of population from that quarter," he contended, "mulattoes would soon diminish in Canada; and moreover, . . . Mulattoism would fade out from the blood of the Northern states." In Canada, he pointed out, intermarriage was rare, and he assured Northern readers that the newly emancipated blacks were not likely to marry outside their own race. "With freedom and protection of their legal rights; with an open field for industry, and opportunities for mental and moral culture, colored people will not seek relationship with whites, but will follow their natural affinity, and marry among themselves." Once given the right "of choosing the soil and

62. Howe to Agassiz, Aug. 18, 1863, *ibid.*, pp. 614–616.

climate most congenial to their nature," those in the North would migrate to the South, where they had a curious fate in store for them: "Drawn by natural attractions to warmer regions, they will co-operate powerfully with whites from the North in re-organizing the industry of the South; *but they will dwindle and gradually disappear from the peoples of this continent.* But surely, history will record their blameless life as a people; their patient endurance of suffering and of wrong; and their sublime return of good for evil to the race of their oppressors."[63]

In Howe's opinion, therefore, most of the Negro population, perhaps all of it, was doomed to disappear because of inherited weaknesses that would put them at a disadvantage in the inevi-table competition. The touch of romantic racialism appended to his prediction of Negro extinction—his reference to the blacks' "patient endurance of suffering and of wrong"—suggested how little the "natural" Christian virtues attributed to blacks would actually avail them in the long run. His condescending accep-tance of the romantic racialist stereotype also came out in his description of the Canadian fugitives as "a little effeminate, as though a portion of the *grit* had been left out of their composi-tion." ". . . with their African blood," he maintained, "they may have inherited more of womanly than of manful disposi-tions; for Africans have more of womanly virtues than fiercer

63. S. G. Howe, *The Refugees from Slavery in Canada West, Report to the Freedmen's Inquiry Commission* (Boston, 1864), pp. 18, 26, 33. (The italics are mine.) Howe indicated (p. 83) that he had not been discussing the Negro race as one of the great subdivisions of mankind but only the mulatto "breed" that had developed in the United States as a result of miscegenation on the plantations of the South. Hence his generalizations do not necessarily apply to pure blacks. But he described the Canadian Negroes as "fair representatives of our colored people" with "about the same proportion of pure Africans, half-breeds, quarter-breeds, octoroons, and of others in whom the dark shade grows fainter and fainter . . ." (p. 1), and then discussed the experience of this predominantly mulatto population as indicative of how *Southern* freedmen were likely to respond to emancipation. Howe apparently believed that most American Negroes, in the South as elsewhere, were of mixed blood and suffered from the constitutional weaknesses of such "breeds." Hence the Negro population was likely to diminish after emancipation whatever the fate of a pure black minority of uncertain proportions. Furthermore, it was possible that genuine blacks would go down to extinction with the rest because of the further diffusion of "mulattoism" that would result from future unions be-tween pure-blooded Africans and mulattoes.

people have. Indeed, it may be said that, among the races, Africa is like a gentle sister in a family of fierce brothers." Romantic racialism had in fact helped set the black man up for the kill, in a sense, by denying him the very qualities he would need to survive.[64]

With Howe the racial thinking of an advanced and liberal segment of Northern white opinion received its fullest expression. The limitations of such "egalitarianism" were painfully obvious. Howe was an enemy of slavery and a proponent of legal equality for blacks, but he regarded intermarriage as disastrous, without apparently realizing that such a judgment legitimized a white prejudice that acted as a fundamental barrier to meaningful equality. Furthermore, like so many other whites who stood with him against slavery, he was unable to visualize a permanent future for Negroes in America. His ideal America was all white; he was quite willing to see the Negroes diminish and even disappear after they had served their purpose in Reconstruction. Such friends as these might help free black Americans from slavery, but they could hardly promise full equality. They themselves did not really regard Negroes as potential brothers; they saw them rather as temporary and inferior sojourners in a white America, to be granted "rights," perhaps, but not the deeper acceptance reserved for members of "the more vigorous and prolific race."

64. *Ibid.,* p. 101.

Chapter Six

•

Race and
Reconstruction

ONCE FREED, the black population of the South constituted a new element that had to be incorporated somehow into the American social and political structure. Some Radical Republicans and veterans of the antislavery crusade regarded justice and equality for the freedmen as a fulfillment of national ideals and a desirable end in itself. For a larger number of loyal Northerners the question of Negro rights was, from first to last, clearly subordinate to the more fundamental aim of ensuring national hegemony for Northern political, social, and economic institutions. But even those who lacked an ideological commitment to black equality could not avoid the necessity of shaping a new status for the Southern blacks; for there they were in large numbers, capable of being either a help or a hindrance to the North's effort to restore the Union and secure the fruits of victory.

Before 1863 and 1864, Northern leaders had been able to discuss with full seriousness the possibility of abolishing slavery while at the same time avoiding the perplexing and politically dangerous task of incorporating the freed blacks into the life of the nation. President Lincoln and other moderate or conservative Republicans, feeling the pulse of a racist public opinion, had looked to the reduction or elimination of the black population through colonization or emigration as a way of approaching the racial homogeneity which they associated with guaranteed national unity and progress. By itself the Emancipation Proclamation had not destroyed such hopes, but events soon made the colonization schemes irrelevant and inappropriate. There was, first of all, the obvious but important fact that the concrete colonization projects of the Lincoln administration had come to nothing. Efforts to establish black colonies in Chiriquí (Panama) and Haiti were dismal failures. Secondly, it became apparent that even if such colonies could be established they could drain off only a small portion of the millions of blacks who were suddenly being freed from servitude by the necessities of war. Lincoln had hoped for a gradual emancipation that would be tied to continuing colonization efforts but had been forced by the exigencies of the war and the pressure of Radicals in his party to choose what amounted to immediate emancipation on the soil. Whatever the long-range destiny of the blacks, it became apparent that their immediate future was to remain in the United States in some status other than chattel slavery.[1]

The history of colonizationist thinking reveals that the dream of separation through black emigration or deportation could thrive as a long-range hope even when there were no practical or immediate prospects for its realization. But after 1863 even the speculative and theoretical colonizationism that had been an important element in Northern race-thinking since the early nineteenth century markedly declined. One reason for the eclipse of the colonizationist dream was the fact that the dreaded influx of Southern blacks into the North, which had long been feared as a consequence of emancipation on the soil, failed to materialize in 1863 and 1864. For some, the willingness of ex-slaves to remain in the South simply confirmed the climatic theory of racial distribution. What had really happened, however, was that the Lincoln administration had adopted a deliberate policy designed to keep the freedmen in the South. V. Jacque Voegeli has demonstrated that the failure of colonization was followed by a political

1. See Chapter Five, above, on wartime colonizationism. For an excellent analysis of the failure and abandonment of deportationist schemes see V. Jacque Voegeli, *Free but Not Equal: The Midwest and the Negro during the Civil War* (Chicago, 1967), *passim.*

decision to do the next best thing as far as Northern opinion was concerned, namely, to institute a policy of "employing and caring for the blacks in the South"—a program of organized work and relief, supervised by military commanders, which "effectually sealed the vast majority of them in the region." This was done in clear rejection of another live option—the emigration of large numbers of blacks to the Midwest, where there was an acute wartime labor shortage. In the calculations of Northern politicians, the racial animosities of their white constituents apparently weighed more heavily than local manpower needs.[2]

One aspect of the administration's program of racial containment was the recruitment and use of black troops in the South. But there was an even more pressing reason to enlist ex-slaves as soldiers: the military manpower shortage, acute by 1863, was only partially relieved by a conscription policy that was controversial and difficult to implement. Although the "blacks in blue" were used initially for military labor behind the lines or for foraging, they eventually went into heroic combat against such objectives as Fort Wagner in Charleston Harbor and Port Hudson on the Mississippi near Baton Rouge.[3]

Whatever the original motivation for the decision to enlist blacks in the Union Army, its effect was to mitigate Northern racial prejudice and to dispel rather dramatically any lingering sentiment in favor of government-sponsored colonization. It was difficult to ask a man to fight for a nation without recognizing his right to live in it. Orestes A. Brownson, a Catholic publicist who spoke for the most conservative kind of Northern antislavery opinion, made this point in 1864. Two years previously Brownson had defended emancipation as a war measure but had also argued, as a confirmed Negrophobe, for the absolute necessity of colonization, maintaining that a "voluntary" separation, such as Lincoln envisioned, would probably work but strongly implying that the blacks should be compelled to leave the United States if

2. Voegeli, *Free but Not Equal*, pp. 105–112 and *passim*.
3. *Ibid.*, pp. 101–106; see Dudley Taylor Cornish, *The Sable Arm: Negro Troops in the Union Army, 1861–1865* (New York, London, and Toronto, 1956), for a full account of the recruitment, employment, and military contribution of black troops during the Civil War.

this became necessary. In 1864, however, Brownson conceded that the use of Negroes as soldiers had put "forced colonization out of the question": "The Negro, having shed his blood in defense of the country, has the right to regard it as his country."[4]

The general effect of the performance of black troops was suggested with greater eloquence by Lincoln himself. "When the war is won," the President wrote in a public letter of August, 1863, "there will be some black men who can remember that, with silent tongue, and clenched teeth, and steady eye, and well-poised bayonet, they have helped mankind on to this great consummation."[5] In 1864 Robert Dale Owen, a member of the Freedmen's Inquiry Commission, pointed to the shift of opinion in the Negro's favor which had resulted from his record as a soldier. At the end of the conflict, George William Curtis, a well-known writer and orator, summed up the effect of the Negro's military contribution on prejudiced Northerners who were also supporters of the Union cause: "Five years ago," Curtis recalled in his 1865 lecture "The Good Fight," "there were good men among us who said, if white hands can't win this fight let it be lost. I have seen the same men agreeing that black hands had even more stake than we, giving them muskets, bidding them godspeed in the Good Fight, and welcoming them with honor as they returned."[6]

But it would be a mistake to assume that the old stereotype of the docile and inferior "Sambo" was now replaced by a radically new image of self-reliant and intelligent blacks in uniform. The Sambo image, rather than being abolished with slavery, was merely modified. The traditional view of innate Negro docility had actually been reinforced in the early stages of the war by the failure of the slaves to engage in massive rebellion once their

4. *The Works of Orestes A. Brownson*, ed. Henry F. Brownson (Detroit, 1882–1907), XVII, 256–268, 552–553. (From *Brownson's Quarterly Review* for April, 1862, and April, 1864.)

5. Abraham Lincoln, *Collected Works*, ed. Roy P. Basler (New Brunswick, N.J., 1953–1955), VI, 410.

6. Robert Dale Owen, *The Wrong of Slavery; the Right of Emancipation; and the Future of the African Race in the United States* (Philadelphia, 1864), pp. 195–198; *Orations and Addresses of George William Curtis*, ed. Charles Eliot Norton (New York, 1894), I, 174.

masters had gone off to fight the Yankees. In 1862 the Reverend Joseph Henry Allen of Massachusetts had described the blacks as "a race that takes kindly to domestication, and receives its crumbs of a higher culture with grateful submissiveness." As evidence of such traits, he pointed to their passivity, docility, and "non-resistance" following the outbreak of the war. Submissiveness, he concluded, "was one of those characteristics of the race, on the right understanding of which our whole solution rests."[7] Charles Sumner, as previously indicated, made a similar point in a more flattering way in October, 1862, when he argued that an emancipation proclamation would not lead to rebellion because "the African is not cruel, vindictive, or harsh, but gentle, forgiving, and kind."[8]

This image of innate black docility and inoffensiveness was, as it turned out, too deeply rooted to be demolished by the emergence of the Negro as a soldier. In fact, the potential or actual successes of black troops were often seen as the *result* of their submissiveness—which in a military context could mean the same thing as susceptibility to discipline. Since their units were officered by whites, the alleged willingness of blacks to submit to military rule could also be interpreted as an instinctive sense of racial subordination. In February, 1863, Jacob D. Cox, a Union general of antislavery background who later became Republican Governor of Ohio, endorsed the use of black troops by arguing "that blacks make excellent troops when well officered and disciplined, *that they are most easily ruled.*"[9] The Freedmen's Inquiry Commission came to a similar conclusion in its *Preliminary Report,* noting that the effectiveness of Negro troops depended to a large extent on the caliber of their white officers: ". . . colored regiments badly officered would be more liable to give way than badly officered regiments of the more self-reliant white race." To support this point of view, the commission quoted Colonel Thomas Wentworth Higginson, a fiery New England abolitionist

7. Joseph Henry Allen, "Africans in America and Their New Guardians," *Christian Examiner,* CCXXXII (July, 1862) , 114–116.

8. Charles Sumner, *Works* (Boston, 1874) , VII, 226.

9. Letter to Aaron F. Perry, February 9, 1863, Cox Papers, Oberlin College Library. (The italics are mine.)

and commander of the First South Carolina Volunteers, the earliest black regiment to be recruited in the South. In Higginson's view, Negro troops "will depend more upon their officers than white troops, and be more influenced by their conduct. If their officers are intimidated they will be; and if their officers stand their ground so will they. If they lose their officers the effect will be worse on them than upon white troops, not because they are timid, but because they are less accustomed to entire self-reliance."[10]

This paternalistic and condescending attitude toward blacks, who, it was claimed, knew how to follow orders but lacked Anglo-Saxon self-reliance, was reflected even more dramatically and with clearer racial overtones in Colonel Higginson's camp diary and journal of 1862 and 1863. Higginson, who described himself as having "a constitutional affinity for undeveloped races," professed to find the blacks attractive and was delighted to find no mulattoes among his recruits—"all looked as thoroughly black as the most faithful philanthropist could desire." He was also readily impressed with their aptitude for military drill: "To learn the drill, one does not want a set of college professors; one wants a set of eager, active, pliant schoolboys; and the more childlike these pupils are the better." He therefore predicted at the outset that blacks, whom he described as "simple, docile, and affectionate almost to the point of absurdity," would "surpass whites" in military drill. Further association did not change Higginson's opinion that his charges were "the world's perpetual children, docile, gay, and loveable," and he reveled in a sense of his absolute power over them. "They could be made fanatics if I chose," he noted; "but I do not choose. The whole mood is essentially Mohammedan, perhaps, in its strength and its weakness; and I feel the same degree of sympathy that I should if I had a Turkish command,—that is, a sort of sympathetic admiration, not tending towards agreement, but towards co-operation."[11]

10. *Preliminary Report . . . to the Secretary of War, by the Freedmen's Inquiry Commission, June 30, 1863* (New York, 1863), pp. 17–18.
11. *Letters and Journals of Thomas Wentworth Higginson*, ed. Mary Thacher Higginson (Boston and New York, 1921), p. 213; Thomas Wentworth Higginson, *Army Life in a Black Regiment* (Boston, 1870), pp. 7, 10, 29, 54.

Higginson, it would appear, had a kind of sahib complex, suggestive of the pleasure derived during the same period by British officers in command of native troops in India and elsewhere. Indeed, an aura of pseudocolonial paternalism surrounded the "Negro soldier cause" in New England, where the endeavor had its greatest popularity. *Noblesse oblige* was the characteristic note struck in New England's glorification of white "aristocrats" who officered black regiments—men like Higginson and the martyr Robert Gould Shaw, who led the ill-fated assault of black troops on Fort Wagner—and a prevalent attitude toward the loyal black followers was summed up by Charles Eliot Norton, man of letters and wartime propagandist, when he recommended Negro troops as "American Sepoys without any disposition to treachery."[12] Hence it was possible to advocate the use of Negro troops and glorify their achievements without giving up the cherished stereotype of black submissiveness and docility in the presence of "superior" whites.

II

If emancipation and the black contribution to the war effort had led to a thoroughgoing transformation of racial attitudes resulting in a new commitment to the concept of full equality, such a development would have been reflected in a tendency to revise traditional attitudes toward the highly sensitive area of interracial marriage or "amalgamation." But a controversy which erupted in 1864 demonstrated clearly that the deeply rooted belief in the need to preserve the purity of the "white race" remained unaltered. This controversy was the artificial creation of two Democratic journalists, David Goodman Croly and George Wakeman of the New York *World,* who perpetrated an ingenious hoax designed to discredit the Republican Party in the

12. See George M. Fredrickson, *The Inner Civil War: Northern Intellectuals and the Crisis of the Union* (New York, 1965), Chapter X; Charles Eliot Norton is quoted in George Winston, "Broadsides for Freedom: Civil War Propaganda in New England," *New England Quarterly,* XXI (September, 1948), 303.

election of 1864. Recent historical research has revealed that Croly and Wakeman were the authors of a famous anonymous pamphlet, entitled *Miscegenation,* which appeared at the end of 1863. *Miscegenation,* which added a new word to the language, was written from what purported to be the point of view of a Radical Republican or abolitionist. In an open assault on prevailing notions, it argued that mixed races were superior to pure ones and that racial amalgamation was the inevitable and desirable result of Republican doctrines. It ended by quoting statements of Wendell Phillips and Theodore Tilton which seemed to support the new philosophy of "miscegenation."[13]

The pamphlet, which was generally accepted as the actual work of a radical abolitionist, created an immediate sensation. It was widely noticed and violently condemned in the press, although Horace Greeley's New York *Tribune* and the *National Anti-Slavery Standard* gave cautious endorsement to some of its arguments.[14] The most thoughtful abolitionist response appeared in the *Independent,* then edited by Tilton. In an editorial of February 25, 1864, he took issue with the pamphlet's argument that the Civil War had been caused by racial prejudice rather than by slavery and denied that future racial peace and equality depended on a mixture of blood and the obliteration of distinctions of race. The editorial, drawing on the romantic racialist tradition, contended that "the Negro is naturally more peaceable than either Saxon or Celt. It is not half so necessary to American stability that we should absorb the Negro . . . as that we should melt down and remold his master according to a better model man." The *Independent* also criticized the pamphlet's recommendation that abolitionists should advocate intermarriage as a political cause, arguing rather that marriage must be a matter of individual choice and that interracial unions should

13. [David Goodman Croly and George Wakeman,] *Miscegenation: The Theory of the Blending of the Races, Applied to the American White Man and Negro* (New York, 1863; dated 1864). For descriptions of the controversy and evidence of *Miscegenation's* true authorship, see Julius Marcus Bloch, *Miscegenation, Melaleukation, and Mr. Lincoln's Dog* (New York, 1958); and Forrest G. Wood, *Black Scare: The Racist Response to Emancipation and Reconstruction* (Berkeley and Los Angeles, 1968), Chapter Four.

14. Bloch, *Miscegenation,* pp. 5–6.

take place only in those presumably rare cases where there was "a natural affinity between individuals." Basically, the editorial concluded, the real issue was not intermarriage but equality of right; but Tilton ventured the long-range prediction that "intermingling," which was "forced and frequent" under slavery, would now continue on a "voluntary and infrequent" basis, leading in the course of many centuries to a whitening of the Negro.[15]

Tilton's qualified defense of intermarriage as something allowable but not to be recommended represented the outer limits of what, under the circumstances, was a viable abolitionist position. More enthusiastic endorsements of miscegenation came only from isolated and iconoclastic individuals like Gilbert Haven or Moncure Daniel Conway, who carried the logic of romantic racialism farther than was generally acceptable even in the most radical circles. To the right of Tilton were influential antislavery men like Samuel Gridley Howe who fully accepted the current scientific doctrine on the undesirability of race mixture and argued that miscegenation should be positively discouraged.[16] Howe's views were given a semiofficial status in the final report of the Freedmen's Inquiry Commission which came out in May, 1864, while the "miscegenation" controversy was still raging. The report concluded that amalgamation was neither inevitable nor desirable, because "the mixed race is inferior, in physical power and in health, to the pure race black or white."[17] Here was evidence that "practical" antislavery men were repudiating the arguments of *Miscegenation* and basing their work with the freedmen on a belief in the value of "racial purity." In September, 1865, the *Freedman's Record,* the official organ of the New England Freedmen's Aid Society—an important organization for the relief and education of Southern blacks—affirmed that "mixture of blood diminishes vitality and force, and shortens life. What is gained in cerebral development is lost in the tendency to

15. "The Union of Races," New York *Independent,* February 25, 1864.

16. See Chapters Four and Five, above.

17. "Final Report of the American Freedmen's Inquiry Commission to the Secretary of War, May 15, 1864," *The War of the Rebellion: Official Records of the Union and Confederate Armies,* Series III, Vol. IV (Washington, 1900), 375.

scrofula and other diseases. . . . 'Miscegenation' is the last measure to be recommended for the elevation of the negro race,
whether morally or physically."[18]

If the issue raised by the Croly-Wakeman pamphlet revealed
some abolitionist reservations about how far to push the concept
of racial equality, it elicited a more direct and unequivocal response from official spokesmen for the Republican Party, who
were of course the principal targets of the hoax. In February
1864, Representative Samuel S. "Sunset" Cox of Ohio, a leading
Democratic Negrophobe, gave a speech in Congress made up
mostly of excerpts from *Miscegenation* and ended by accusing the
Republicans of endorsing its doctrines. Republican Congressmen
rose without hesitation to deny unequivocally that they had any
sympathy whatever for racial amalgamation. Republican newspapers took the same line, often pointing out that the real source
of mulattoism in the United States had been the institution of
slavery.[19] In the end the Democrats failed to make "miscegenation" into a successful campaign issue partly because, as one
historian has concluded, "the whole miscegenation issue was just
too fantastic"; the voting public was not gullible enough to
believe that the Republicans would countenance anything so
repugnant as the intermarriage of the races.[20]

The controversy is significant, not because of its political
impact—which was negligible—but because it further reveals the
extent to which Northerners approached Reconstruction with
their basic racial prejudices largely intact. The Negro was appreciated as an amiable being with some good qualities, whose
innate submissiveness had served—and might continue to serve—
Northern purposes. But he was expected to remain in his "place,"
defined in a double sense as being, first of all, *in the South,* and
secondly on his own side of the line allegedly established by God
and science to ensure that the white race would not be contami-
nated by an infusion of Negro blood.

18. Quoted in Tilden G. Edelstein, *Strange Enthusiasm: A Life of Thomas
Wentworth Higginson* (New Haven and London, 1968) , p. 328.
19. *Congressional Globe*, 38 Cong., 1 Sess., Pt. I, 708–713; for a collection of
excerpts from Republican papers, see the *Liberator*, April 8, 1864.
20. Wood, *Black Scare*, p. 75.

III

Shortly after the surrender of the Confederacy, Horace Greeley summed up the Northern belief, firmly established by that time, that the Negro would remain in his present location as a permanently distinct race: "*One* bugbear has already vanished—that which held up to view four millions of vagabond Negroes, overspreading the entire area of the Free States, begging, stealing and smelling. . . . scarcely a handful have left the South. There they were born; there they have lived; there they mean to live and die."[21] This much now seemed clear; but what would be the status of the blacks in the South and their relation to the white majority of that region?

One possible approach was discussed briefly during the summer of 1865 and then rejected. The idea was perhaps suggested by General William T. Sherman's famous Special Field Order Number 15, issued on January 16, 1865, which set aside the Sea Islands of South Carolina and Georgia and a coastal area for thirty miles inland for exclusive settlement by Negroes, who were given temporary "possessory" titles to the land.[22] If Sherman's order had been carried out on a permanent basis and if the area had been enlarged or the concept applied to other regions, the resulting separation of the black and white populations in the South would have drastically altered, for better or worse, the future history of the region. Fantastic as the idea may seem in retrospect, there was actually some support in 1865 for the notion that the North should seize its opportunity to remake the South by effecting a thoroughgoing geographical separation of the races. The principal exponent of this policy was the moderate Republican General Jacob D. Cox, who was running for Governor of Ohio. In a letter of July 9, 1865, Cox argued that Northern policy toward the freedmen should combine a respect for "the rights of man in the fullest and most literal sense" with a realistic

21. New York *Tribune*, May 25, 1865.
22. *The War of the Rebellion: Official Records*, Series I, Vol. XLVII, Part II (Washington, 1895), 60–62.

recognition of "the real conflict of races." Accepting in principle the Radical Republican view that the Negro should be given political rights, Cox nevertheless said that "co-partnership in political privileges between races that will not amalgamate, only intensifies the strife between them, and invariably ends in a war which either exterminates, extirpates, or subjugates the weaker." His solution was separation of the races *within* the South, giving to the blacks the coasts of South Carolina and Georgia and the entire state of Florida, as an area in which they could enjoy political rights and all the other benefits of "a separate corporate existence." Cox reasserted his proposal in a public letter to a group at Oberlin College, more fully describing the racial antagonism that made separation necessary. On the basis of his own observations, Cox contended that the war had not only embittered the relations of the races in the South but had also brought to the surface "a rooted antagonism which makes their permanent fusion in one political community impossible." The whites despised the blacks and the blacks utterly distrusted the whites, Cox said, affirming "the permanence and durability" of "such prejudices and enmities of race" as then existed in the South.[23]

Cox's views received considerable attention in the Republican press. A fairly typical comment was that of the Springfield *Republican,* which accepted "the facts upon which General Cox bases his argument for the local separation" but argued that the scheme was impracticable because the government lacked the power to force the redistribution of population that Cox advocated. Even if the plan could be carried out, the *Republican* contended, racial antipathy would simply crop up in a new form when representatives from the new black states attempted to take their seats in Congress.[24] The Chicago *Tribune,* a leading Radical organ, was more sympathetic to Cox's proposal; but

23. Letters to William Dennison, July 9, 1865, and to E. H. Fairchild, et al., July 25, 1865, Cox Papers, Oberlin College Library.
24. Springfield *Republican,* August 12, 1865; clipping in the Cox Papers, Oberlin College Library. The *Republican* misinterpreted Cox's plan; he did not propose admission of black-dominated areas to statehood but suggested rather that they be governed as territories.

Horace Greeley's New York *Tribune,* also considered a Radical paper, rejected it out of hand as "utterly impracticable" and as based on an exaggerated notion of the strength of racial feelings.[25]

Greeley's response in the *Tribune* might have been anticipated. The previous January he had objected to Sherman's special order for black settlement in the Sea Island area because he believed it would deprive the ex-slaves of the elevating association with whites that was a necessary part of their tutelage. Southern blacks, he affirmed, "must, like their fellows at the North, take their chance as a part of the whole people, free from the wrongs and disabilities of slavery, and aided by contact with white civilization to become good citizens and enlightened men."[26] Although Senator Doolittle of Wisconsin made a proposal similar to Cox's in the fall of 1865, Greeley's approach triumphed in Republican thinking.[27] Southern resettlement on racial lines was rejected because it required a coercive power greater than the government was thought to possess, smacked too much of the now discredited doctrines of the colonizationists, and did violence to the deep-seated belief that the black man could make little progress on his own. An important additional consideration was raised in a letter to Cox from Postmaster General William Dennison, who warned him that his proposal would be unacceptable to the Radicals "not only because they believe the negro is fitted to exercise all the rights of the citizen where he is, but that his remaining and exercizing such rights, even to the extent of voting, is necessary to make the Southern states loyal and desirable members of the Union."[28]

Having rejected colonization, migration to the North, and racial separation within the South, concerned Northerners were left with the problem of how to influence the face-to-face relationship of the freedmen and their former masters in such a way

25. Undated clippings in the Cox Papers, Oberlin College Library.
26. New York *Tribune,* January 30, 1865.
27. Lawanda and John H. Cox, *Politics, Principle, and Prejudice: Dilemma of Reconstruction America* (Glencoe, Ill., 1963) , p. 215.
28. William Dennison to Cox, July 19, 1865, Cox Papers, Oberlin College Library.

as to prevent the *de facto* re-enslavement of the blacks, something which according to many observers was a real possibility in 1865 and 1866. The Northern racial policy that took shape was most often described as an attempt to implement "equality before the law" or "equal rights." Among Republicans, all but the most conservative—those who sided with President Johnson in the struggle that soon developed between Congress and the President—came to the conclusion in the months after the war that the government should guarantee some sort of fundamental equality to Southern Negroes, and a growing number were beginning to say that this should include the right of suffrage. Behind the complex events that led to Radical Reconstruction, one of the underlying factors was this strong conviction on the part of an apparent majority in the North that the freedmen must be granted certain rights and protected in their exercise, in order to preserve the fruits of victory and pay the debt owed the Negro for his aid in saving the Union.

It should be recognized from the outset, however, that this commitment to equality was often limited or conditioned by an underlying set of values that were not consistently egalitarian. "Equality before the law" was compatible in theory with a very conservative kind of society; in England it had been formally guaranteed for centuries without conflicting with an institutional pattern which sanctioned flagrant forms of political and social inequality.[29] In October, 1865, the *Nation,* edited by the transplanted Englishman E. L. Godkin, described Northern Reconstruction aims in the following terms: "What we do seek for the negro is equality before the law, such as prevails between a Parisian water-carrier and the Duc de Rohan, or between a London cabman and the earl of Derby. This accomplished, we propose to leave him to make his own social position."[30] The *Nation* was obviously thinking in terms of a concept of equality that did not rule out vast disparities in the wealth, power, and status of individuals or groups. The statement was also in harmony with current *laissez-faire* concepts of the role of govern-

29. See W. R. Brock, *An American Crisis: Congress and Reconstruction,* 1865–1867 (London, 1963) , p. 289.
30. *Nation,* I (October 19, 1865) , 491.

ment and clearly implied that it was not the function of public agencies to elevate any group by extending aid and advantages that were not available to others and which went beyond the mere recognition of legal equality.

Such influential attitudes tended to place a priori limitations on what could be done to improve the situation of Southern blacks. A minority of humanitarians had argued from the beginning of their work among the freedmen during the war that a long period of special care and guardianship would be required before their charges could be expected to compete economically with the whites, but their views were out of tune with the dominant *laissez-faire* ideology.[31] In the course of providing an influential blueprint for Reconstruction measures, the Freedman's Inquiry Commission recommended the setting up of a Freedmen's Bureau to extend special help to the ex-slaves, but concluded that "all aid given to these people should be regarded as a temporary necessity. . . . The sooner they shall stand alone and make their own unaided way, the better both for our race and theirs." The best response to Southern white efforts to treat the freedmen in "an unjust and tyrannical manner" was not "special laws or a special organization for the protection of the colored people, but the safeguard of general laws, applicable to all against fraud and oppression." The commission predicted that once the Negro was given his basic rights he "will somewhere find, and will maintain, his own appropriate social position."[32]

The constant use of the singular to describe the Negro's future "position" suggested that Negroes *as a group* would inevitably find a definite social niche, rather than being fully integrated and dispersed as individuals up and down an interracial status hierarchy. Some representatives of Northern benevolence strongly implied or openly predicted that this "natural" group situation would be at or near the bottom of society. The Reverend Jared Bell Waterbury, writing for the American Tract

31. For an illuminating discussion of the conflict among wartime humanitarians on the question of special assistance for blacks vs. a strict laissez-faire approach, see Willie Lee Rose, *Rehearsal for Reconstruction: The Port Royal Experiment* (Indianapolis, 1964) , Chapter Eight.

32. *War of the Rebellion: Official Records,* Series II, Vol. IV, 382, 370.

Society, opined that "the two races are, it seems probable, to dwell side by side for years to come," noted that "amalgamation is not desirable," and concluded that "it may seem best they should dwell together in the relation generally of proprietors and laborers." Of course it would be the whites who would generally be the employers and "the blacks the employed." "Hence . . . even with strenuous efforts for their improvement the African must still acknowledge the superiority of the Saxon race."[33] The Reverend Horace James, Superintendent of Negro Affairs in North Carolina in 1864, maintained in 1865 that the blacks were "a nation of servants," who would "always make the most faithful, pliable, obedient, devoted servants that can enter our dwellings." "In the successive orders or ranks of industrial pursuits," James pointed out, "those who have the least intelligence must needs perform the more menial services, without respect to color or birth. Give the colored man equality, not of social condition, but equality before the law, and if he proves himself the superior of the Anglo-Saxon, who can hinder it? If he falls below him, who can help it?"[34]

James's approach to the Southern Negroes amounted to a willingness to see them find their natural level, which, it was strongly suggested, was that of a servant class. Thus "equality before the law" could readily be translated as *de facto* inequality in a "naturally" stratified social system. Such a view was common even among those Northerners who seemed most favorably disposed to the cause of Negro rights. Many, however, avoided the positive implication of racial inferiority made by Waterbury and James and spoke merely of equal rights as a fair "test" of racial differences. In 1866 the *American Freedman,* organ of the Freedmen's and Union Commission (another major endeavor for relief and education of Southern blacks), candidly described such a relationship between equality of opportunity and possible differences in racial capacity: "The wisest and best friends of the freedmen do not aver that the African race is equal to the Anglo-

33. The Reverend Jared Bell Waterbury, D.D., *Southern Planters and the Freedman* (New York, n.d. [probably 1865]) , pp. 41–42.
34. Reverend Horace James, *Annual Report of the Superintendent of Negro Affairs in North Carolina* (Boston, 1865) , p. 46.

Saxon. Neither do they admit any racial inferiority. They simply assert that the negro must be accorded an opportunity for development before his capacity for development can be known." Until such time "as both races shall enjoy the same rights, immunities, and opportunities . . . the white man's claim to superiority rests on a very shadowy foundation." The only fair way to determine the social position of the Southern blacks, the *American Freedman* concluded, was "untrammeled development of their native character" to "determine their place in society. Their specific gravity will fix their true level."[35]

Such thinking was characteristic of those committed to work among the freedmen and also part of the intellectual rationale for Congressional Radicalism. In February, 1866, Representative Ignatius Donnelly of Minnesota, then a militant Radical Republican, gave a speech on Negro rights in which he acknowledged the likelihood of the Negro's inferiority and inability to compete successfully with whites: "If he is, as it is claimed, an inferior being and unable to compete with the white man on terms of equality, surely you will not add to the injustice of nature by casting him beneath the feet of the white man." If, after a fair trial, the Negro "proves himself an unworthy savage and brutal wretch, condemn him, but not till then."[36] The following year, Thaddeus Stevens, the most powerful and dedicated of the Radicals in the House of Representatives, threw down the gauntlet before white supremacists in a somewhat similar fashion. After defending absolute equality of rights, Stevens advised "any who are afraid of the rivalry of the black man in office or in business" to "try to beat their competitor in knowledge or in business capacity, and there is no danger that his white neighbors will prefer his African rival to himself."[37]

Such statements suggested that some of the most egalitarian

35. *American Freedman,* I (April, 1866) , 3.
36. *Congressional Globe,* 39 Cong., 1 Sess., Pt. I, 589. In a speech given in the preceding Congress, Donnelly had indicated that he believed that Negroes were indeed inferior. After arguing that blacks deserved a chance of achieving "the fullest development of which they are capable," he added that he would not "rate them above or even equal to our proud, illustrious, and dominant race" (quoted in Voegeli, *Free but Not Equal,* p. 178) .
37. *Congressional Globe,* 39 Cong., 2 Sess., Pt. I, 252.

Northerners were willing to surrender the Southern blacks to a *laissez-faire* competitive process without ensuring that the freedmen had any real prospect of reaping the same rewards as the whites. It is not fair, perhaps, to include Stevens among this group, because in 1865 he proposed the confiscation of land and its distribution among the ex-slaves; but little support developed, even among Radicals, for this proposal—it was too obviously a violation of "the rights of property" and a departure from the competitive ideal.[38] The operative Northern concept of equality was in fact doubly flawed in its application to the Negro: it gave prior sanction to social and economic inequalities which were likely to result from what was in fact—if not in theory—an unfair competition; and, in addition, it was compatible with a residual or hypothetical belief in racial inequality. The idea that equal rights led to equal opportunities was obviously not applicable to a people just released from slavery, but the prevailing belief in the probability of racial inferiority provided an ideological escape valve, a ready explanation for future Negro failures which would not call the bourgeois ideology of "self-help" and "equal opportunity" into question.

Some of the callousness implicit in the notion that a race degraded by slavery and suspected to be biologically inferior should simply be given its formal rights and then forced to compete in a capitalistic free-labor society was manifested in the postwar comments of Horace Greeley, who became known as a principal advocate of "the root hog or die" approach to the Negro problem. "Freedom and opportunity—these are all that the best Government can secure to White or Black," Greeley wrote. "Give every one a chance, and let his behavior control his fate. If negroes will not work, they must starve or steal; and if they steal, they must be shut up like other thieves. If there be any among them who fancy that they, being free, can live in comfort without work, they have entered a school in which they will certainly and speedily be taught better." Greeley ended by indicating that all that needed to be done was to "clear away the

38. On the fate of Stevens's confiscation proposal see Hans L. Trefousse, *The Radical Republicans: Lincoln's Vanguard for Racial Justice* (New York, 1969) , pp. 320, 322, 369.

wreck of slavery, dispel the lingering fear of a return to it, and we may soon break up our Freedmen's Bureaus and all manner of coddling devices and let negroes take care of themselves."[39]

Such an ideology helped shape Northern Reconstruction policy, as it developed in 1866 and 1867, by establishing limits beyond which the North was unwilling to go in its effort to aid and protect the Southern blacks. The Freedmen's Bureau was gradually weakened and phased out after 1866 and was replaced by "the safeguard of general laws," as provided by the Civil Rights Act of 1866 and the Fourteenth Amendment. But attempts to guarantee the Negro's equality before the law by Congressional action or amendments to the Constitution proved insufficient to protect him from the threat of oppression by Southern whites. Basic to the decision to go beyond such measures to a Reconstruction based on Negro suffrage was the growing conviction that Negroes must be given the vote to protect them against the extralegal efforts of "disloyal" whites to deny them the benefits of equality.

Negro suffrage came about despite the fact that only a small minority in the North had been in favor of such a step before 1866. Few Northern states at that time allowed Negroes to vote. Some leading Republicans still accepted the traditional belief that there was a distinction between such basic "rights" as the right to acquire property, receive equal treatment in the courts, and have free access to the professions, and "the privilege" of suffrage, which was supposedly given or withheld in accordance with the interests of the community.[40] Arguments against Negro suffrage could range from the blatantly racist claim that blacks were inherently unfit for self-government to the more reasonable argument that a people recently freed from bondage and almost entirely illiterate was not yet prepared for the responsibilities of full citizenship. What made Negro suffrage in the South acceptable to the North by 1867 was not a profound belief in the black man's capacity for intelligent citizenship but the political necessities of restructuring the Union under Northern or Republican hegemony. More precisely, it was the refusal of Southern whites

39. New York *Tribune*, May 25, 1865.
40. See Brock, *American Crisis*, pp. 112, 291–292.

to submit fully and in the proper spirit to minimal Northern demands which gave vital impetus to the movement to extend voting rights to the blacks.

Although there had been some disposition at the end of the war to give the ex-rebels a chance to show their loyalty to the Union, the behavior of the new Southern state governments in taking advantage of the vacillating and permissive Reconstruction policy of President Johnson to enact "black codes"—which, in the opinion of many Northerners, virtually re-established slavery—and to elect ex-Confederate leaders to state and national office, conveyed to the North the impression that the overwhelming majority of Southern whites remained hostile to the Union.[41] The Negro, on the other hand, whatever his shortcomings, was at least "loyal." Increasingly persuasive as a guide to policy was the view that Representative George S. Boutwell of Massachusetts put forth in July, 1865: "Under all circumstances, a majority, a confessed majority of the South have shown themselves the enemies of this country. . . . On the other hand, the black man, despised, down-trodden, with no reason to cheer or bless the flag of the Republic, has led and guided and cheered the soldier, has enlisted in the armies of the Republic, has fought for the integrity of the nation and the safety of freedom."[42] In January, 1866, Representative Josiah Grinnell of Iowa echoed the sentiments of most Republicans when he said, "I will never prefer a white traitor to a loyalist black."[43] But it was Carl Schurz who provided what was perhaps the fullest and most eloquent statement of the basic argument that would soon become overpowering when he recommended Negro suffrage to President Johnson in the fall of 1865:

In all questions concerning the Union, the National debt, and the future social organization of the South, the feelings of the

41. See Eric L. McKitrick, *Andrew Johnson and Reconstruction* (Chicago, 1960), for a full discussion of the South's failure to meet Northern expectations of how defeated rebels should behave. McKitrick places a great deal of blame for this revival of Southern intransigence squarely on Andrew Johnson, who, he contends, misled the South about Northern attitudes.

42. Address reprinted in the *Liberator*, August 4, 1865.

43. *Congressional Globe,* 39 Cong., 1 Sess., Pt. I, 223.

colored man are naturally in sympathy with the views and aims of the National Government. While the Southern white fought against the Union, the negro did all he could to aid it; while the Southern white sees in the national government his conqueror, the negro sees in it his protector; while the white owes to the National debt his defeat, the negro owes to it his deliverance; while the white considers himself robbed and ruined by the emancipation of the slaves, the negro finds in it the assurance of future prosperity and happiness. In all the important issues the negro would be led by natural impulse to forward the ends of the government, and by making his influence, as part of the voting body, tell upon the legislation of the states, render the interference of the National authority less necessary."[44]

Many Republicans who came to endorse Negro suffrage on such grounds did so with obvious misgivings. After a tour in the South in which he found much evidence of white intransigency and little disposition to give the freedmen even their most obvious rights, the journalist Whitelaw Reid argued that black suffrage was a necessity even though the Negroes are "not such material as, under ordinary circumstances, one would now choose for the duties of American citizenship."[45] Representative James A. Garfield of Ohio, who eventually supported Negro suffrage for pragmatic reasons, confessed privately in July, 1865, that he had "a strong feeling of repugnance when I think of the negro being made our political equal and I would be glad if they could be colonized, sent to heaven, or got rid of in any decent way. . . . But colonization has proved a hopeless failure everywhere."[46]

There were of course Republican Radicals like Charles Sumner who sincerely welcomed Negro suffrage because they saw it as fulfilling the egalitarian philosophy of the Declaration of Independence, but it is significant that at the time of the passage of

44. Carl Schurz, "Report on the Condition of the South," in *Speeches, Correspondence, and Political Papers,* ed. Frederic Bancroft (New York and London, 1913), I, 365–366.

45. Whitelaw Reid, *After the War: A Southern Tour, May 1, 1865, to May 1, 1866* (Cincinnati and New York, 1866), p. 580.

46. Garfield to Jacob D. Cox, July 26, 1865, Cox Papers, Oberlin College Library.

the Reconstruction Act only six Northern states allowed blacks to vote. Between 1865 and 1868 there were a number of state referenda on black suffrage, most of which were decisively rejected by Northern voters. Understandably, then, some Republican politicians who advocated Negro suffrage in the South hesitated to commit their party to a campaign to give ballots to Negroes in all the Northern states. This double standard was embodied in the Republican platform of 1868, which made a distinction between the necessity of federally imposed black voting in the South and the right of Northern states to determine their own suffrage requirements. After the election the Republicans took a bolder position and secured the passage of the Fifteenth Amendment, which effectively enfranchised Northern blacks. But a recent study of the origins of the Fifteenth Amendment suggests that its enactment resulted more from hardheaded political calculation than from ideological fervor. It would appear that Republicans anticipated a real political advantage from the black vote in states that generally saw a close contest with the Democrats.[47] It seems likely, therefore, that the decisive factor which provided the necessary support for black enfranchisement was not a popular commitment to racial equality but a belief that Republican hegemony and the restoration of the Union on a safe and satisfactory basis could be accomplished only by subordinating racial prejudices to political necessities.

47. See C. Vann Woodward, "Seeds of Failure in Radical Race Policy," *New Frontiers of American Reconstruction*, ed. Harold M. Hyman (Urbana, Ill., 1966), pp. 137–143; and William Gillette, *The Right to Vote: Politics and the Passage of the Fifteenth Amendment* (Baltimore, 1965), *passim*. Gillette contends that a principal reason the Republican leaders determined after the election of 1868 to enact the Fifteenth Amendment was that they sought to garner a Northern black vote that might be decisive in close elections. This thesis has been disputed by Lawanda and John H. Cox in their article "Negro Suffrage and Republican Politics: The Problem of Motivation in Reconstruction Historiography," *Journal of Southern History*, XXXIII (August, 1967), 303–330. The Coxes base their argument for Republican idealism, as opposed to political expediency, largely on the fact that the Republicans did not, as it turned out, benefit much from the new black vote. But this result does not actually refute Gillette's well-supported contention that many Republican leaders advocated the amendment because they *anticipated*, rightly or wrongly in the perspective of historical hindsight, that Negro suffrage would give them a vital political advantage.

IV

Whatever the motivation of Radical Reconstruction and however inadequate its programs, it was a serious effort, the first in American history, to incorporate Negroes into the body politic. As such, it inevitably called forth bitter opposition from hardcore racists, who attempted to discredit radical measures by using many of the same arguments developed as part of the proslavery argument in the prewar period.

The new cause was defined as "white supremacy"—which in practice allowed Southern whites to reduce the freedmen to an inferior caste, as they had attempted to do by enacting the "Black Codes" of 1865. To further this cause in 1868, Van Evrie simply reissued his book *Negroes and Negro "Slavery"* with a topical introduction and under the new title *White Supremacy and Negro Subordination.*[48] Nott also entered the Reconstruction controversy. In an 1866 pamphlet he reasserted the "scientific" case for inherent black inferiority as part of an attack on the Freedmen's Bureau and other Northern efforts to deal with the Southern race question. "If the whites and blacks be left alone face to face," he wrote, "they will soon learn to understand each other, and come to proper terms under the law of necessity."[49]

Edward A. Pollard, a Richmond journalist and prewar fire-eater, also attacked Northern Reconstruction proposals on racial grounds. His book *The Lost Cause Regained,* published in 1868, contended that "the permanent, natural inferiority of the Negro was the true and *only* defense of slavery" and lamented the fact that the South had wasted its intellectual energy on other arguments. Before the war, Pollard had advocated a revival of the slave trade because it would deflate the pretensions of uppity house servants and town Negroes by submerging them in a flood

48. John H. Van Evrie, *White Supremacy and Negro Subordination* (New York, 1868).
49. Josiah C. Nott, *The Negro Race: Its Ethnology and History* (Mobile, 1866), p. 27.

of humble primitives; he now endorsed Van Evrie's thesis that white democracy depended on absolute black subordination, and concluded his discussion of Negro racial characteristics by asserting that the established "fact" of inferiority dictated "the true *status* of the Negro."[50] Other propagandists of white supremacy, North and South, joined the fray. A writer named Lindley Spring attacked Radical Reconstruction in 1868 with a lengthy discourse on the benighted and savage record of blacks in Africa; and a Dr. J. R. Hayes excoriated the proposed Fifteenth Amendment in 1869 with a rehash of all the biological "evidence" for Negro incapacity.[51]

Inevitably, the pre-Adamite theory of Dr. Samuel A. Cartwright and Jefferson Davis was trotted out. In 1866 Governor Benjamin F. Perry of South Carolina made it the basis of a defense of white supremacy; and in 1867 a Nashville publisher named Buckner Payne, writing under the pseudonym "Ariel," revived a controversy among racists by expounding the doctrine at some length in a pamphlet entitled *The Negro: What Is His Ethnological Status?*[52] Payne not only asserted that the Negro was "created before Adam and Eve" as "a *separate* and *distinct* species of *the genus homo,*" but also argued that it was because some of the sons of Adam intermarried with this inferior species, related, as it was, to the "higher orders of the monkey," that God had sent the flood as a punishment for human wrongdoing. Like almost all the racist respondents to Reconstruction, he contended that Negro equality would lead inevitably to amalgamation, and that miscegenation, in addition to resulting in the debasement of the white race, would bring on catastrophic divine intervention: "The states and people that favor this equality and amalgamation of the white and black races, *God will exterminate.* . . . A

50. E. A. Pollard, *The Lost Cause Regained* (New York, 1868), pp. 114–115, 128; and *The Southern Spy, or Curiosities of Negro Slavery in the South* (Washington, 1859), pp. 37–40.

51. Lindley Spring, *The Negro at Home* (New York, 1868); Dr. J. R. Hayes, *Negrophobia on the Brain, in White Men . . .* (Washington, D.C., 1869).

52. John W. De Forest, *A Union Officer in the Reconstruction,* ed. James H. Croushore and David M. Potter (New Haven, 1948), p. 117; "Ariel" [Buckner H. Payne], *The Negro: What Is His Ethnological Status?* (Cincinnati, 1867); see also Wood, *Black Scare,* pp. 6–7.

man can not commit so great an offense against his race, against his country, against his God, . . . as to give his daughter in marriage to a negro—a *beast*. . . ."[53]

Most of the propagandists who attacked Radical measures on extreme racist grounds had a prewar record as apologists for slavery, but Hinton Rowan Helper attracted the greatest attention because of his fame or notoriety as an antebellum critic of slavery. As we have seen, Helper had never concealed his anti-Negro sentiments. A letter of 1861 summed up his philosophy: "A trio of unmitigated and demoralizing nuisances, constituting in the aggregate, a most foul and formidable obstacle to our high and mighty civilization in America are Negroes, Slavery, and Slaveholders. . . .

> Death to Slavery!
> Down with the Slaveholders!
> Away with the Negroes!"[54]

Having done justice to the first two imperatives in *The Impending Crisis*, Helper turned after the war to the third. His *Nojoque*, published in 1867, may have been the most virulent racist diatribe ever published in the United States. It contemplated with relish the time when "the negroes, and all the other swarthy races of mankind," have been "completely fossilized." To speed up the divinely ordained process of racial extermination, Helper proposed as immediate steps the denial of all rights to Negroes and their complete separation from the whites. All this of course went in the teeth of the emerging Reconstruction policies of what had been Helper's own party, and throughout the book he excoriated "the Black Republicans" for departing from the attitudes of the prewar period, a time when Republicans had billed themselves as "the white man's party." His heroes were "White Republicans" like Secretary of State Seward and those few Republicans in the House and Senate who had remained loyal to President Johnson and joined the Democrats in

53. "Ariel," *The Negro*, pp. 21–22, 23, 26–27, 47–48.
54. Letter to "W," June 5, 1861, printed in Helper, *Nojoque; A Question for a Continent* (New York, 1867) , pp. 252–253.

efforts to prevent Federal action on behalf of Negro equality.[55]

The active politicians—mostly Democrats—who opposed Radical Reconstruction were quite willing to resort to racist demagoguery, although they generally avoided the excesses of polemicists like Payne and Helper. President Johnson, for example, played subtly but unmistakably on racial fears in his veto messages of 1866; and later, in his third annual message to Congress, he put his views squarely on the line: ". . . it must be acknowledged that in the progress of nations negroes have shown less capacity for self-government than any other race of people. No independent government of any form has ever been successful in their hands. On the contrary whenever they have been left to their own devices they have shown an instant tendency to relapse into barbarism. . . . The great difference between the two races in physical, mental, and moral characteristics will prevent an amalgamation or fusion of them together in one homogeneous mass. . . . Of all the dangers which our nation has yet encountered, none are equal to those which must result from the success of the effort now making to Africanize the [Southern] half of our country."[56] Equally blatant were the Northern Democratic Congressmen who made speeches against Radical measures which appealed directly to the prejudices of white workingmen. As Representative John W. Chanler of New York put it, in attacking an 1866 proposal to give the vote to Negroes in the District of Columbia: "White democracy makes war on every class, caste, and race which assails its sovereignty or would undermine the mastery of the white working man, be he ignorant or learned, strong or weak. Black democracy does not exist. The black race have never asserted and maintained their inalienable right to be a people, anywhere, or at any time."[57]

In addition to such crude appeals to "white democracy," Democratic spokesmen in Congress provided detailed and pretentious discourses on the "ethnological" status of the Negro,

55. Helper, *Nojoque*, pp. 207, 236, 298–299, and Chapter V, *passim*.

56. Cox and Cox, *Politics, Principle, and Prejudice*, p. 213; quotation from Kenneth Stampp, *The Era of Reconstruction, 1865–1867* (New York, 1965), p. 87.

57. *Congressional Globe*, 39 Cong., 1 Sess., Pt. I, 217.

drawn from writers like Nott and Van Evrie. The most notable of such efforts was the speech Representative James Brooks of New York delivered on December 18, 1867, in opposition to the First Reconstruction Act. "You have deliberately framed a bill," he accused the Radicals, "to overthrow this white man's government of our fathers and to erect an African Government in its stead. . . . The negro is not the equal of the white man, much less his master; and this I can demonstrate anatomically, physiologically and psychologically too, if necessary. Volumes of scientific authority establish the fact. . . ." Brooks then proceeded "in the fewest words possible to set forth scientific facts." He discoursed at length on "the hair or wool of the negro," on "the skull, the brain, the neck, the foot, etc.," and on the perils of miscegenation. In considering the last topic, he conceded that "the mulatto with white blood in his veins often has the intelligence and capacity of a white man," but added that he could not consent to suffrage for mulattoes because to do so would violate the divine decree "that all are to be punished who indulge in a criminal admixture of races, so that beyond the third or fourth generation there could be no further mulatto progeny." Having covered black and brown physiology, Brooks went on in standard racist fashion to portray Negro history as a great emptiness.[58]

In general such anti-Negro arguments were simply ignored by the proponents of Radical Reconstruction, who, by and large, tried to avoid the whole question of basic racial characteristics. But Brooks's speech, perhaps the most thorough presentation of the racist creed ever offered in Congress, could not go unanswered. In a brief reply, Thaddeus Stevens dismissed Brooks's views as contradicting the Biblical doctrine of the unity of mankind. Resorting to sarcasm and impugning Brooks's loyalty, Stevens agreed that Negroes were indeed "barbarians," because they had "with their own right hands, in defense of liberty, stricken down thousands of the friends of the gentleman who has been enlightening us today." Disregarding Brooks's point about the "intelligence and capacity of mulattoes," Stevens proposed to match Frederick Douglass against Brooks in an oratorical con-

58. *Congressional Globe*, 40 Cong., 2 Sess., Pt. V, 70–71.

test.[59] A more serious and extended reply to Brooks was made from the Republican side of the aisle by John D. Baldwin of Massachusetts. Baldwin's speech is significant because it clearly reveals both the strengths and weaknesses of the Radical position on race as a factor in Reconstruction.

In the first place, Baldwin contended, Brooks's argument was largely a *non sequitur;* for "the question presented in these discussions is not a question concerning the equality or the inequality of human races . . . it is a question concerning human rights. It calls on us to decide whether men shall be equal before the law and have equality in their relations to the Government of their country." Races, like individuals, might indeed differ in their capacities, but this should not affect their fundamental rights. In reply to Brooks's claim that miscegenation would result from equality, Baldwin suggested that it was much more likely to result from degradation such as had occurred under slavery, a system which provided a "fatal facility" for "the mixture of races." As for Brooks's position on political rights, it meant in effect that all Negroes should be excluded from suffrage while "even the most ignorant and brutal white man" should be allowed to vote: "If he should propose to guard the ballot by some exclusion of ignorance or baseness, made without regard to race or class, candid men would listen to him and discuss that proposition." But Brooks was propounding, according to Baldwin, a concept of white privilege and "divine right" completely incompatible with the American egalitarian philosophy. Eventually Baldwin touched gingerly on the question of inherent racial differences and conceded the point that the races were not alike, but argued that "it is quite possible that we shall find it necessary to revise our conception of what constitutes the superiority of race." The prevailing conception, he noted, had resulted from an admiration for the ability to conquer and dominate; but were such aggressive qualities "really the highest, the most admirable development of human nature?" Pointing to the recent rise of a higher regard for the gentler, more peaceable virtues, Baldwin suggested "that each race and each distinct family of mankind

59. *Ibid.,* Pt. I, 267.

has some peculiar gift of its own in which it is superior to others; and that an all-wise Creator may have designed that each race and family shall bring its own peculiar contribution to the final completeness of civilization. . . ." Although he did not discuss directly how the racial character of whites and Negroes differed, he was clearly invoking the romantic racialist conceptions that had long been popular among Radicals and abolitionists.[60]

At first glance it would appear that Baldwin's speech constituted an adequate response to the racist critique of Radical Reconstruction, despite his avoidance of Brooks's specific physiological, anatomical, and historical arguments. It was indeed "rights" that the Radicals were attempting to legislate and not the identity of the races. But if, as Baldwin conceded, the races had differing "gifts"—with the whites holding a monopoly of the kind of qualities that led to dominance and conquest—then the competitive "test" of racial capabilities that the Radicals envisioned as resulting from their program would, to follow their own logic, lead inevitably to white domination, even without the support of discriminatory laws. Furthermore, their tendency to accept the concept of innate racial differences and their apparent repulsion to intermarriage were invitations to prejudice and discrimination on the part of those whites—presumably the overwhelming majority of Americans—who were less likely to respond to romantic appeals to racial benevolence than to draw traditional white-supremacist conclusions from any Radical admissions that blacks were "different" and, in some sense, unassimilable.

V

A few Radicals and abolitionists had early and serious doubts about the efficacy and underlying assumptions of the Reconstruction Acts of 1867 and 1868. They suspected that quick readmission of Southern states into the Union under constitutions providing for Negro suffrage and the disfranchisement of prominent ex-Confederates would not by itself give blacks a reasonable

60. *Ibid.*, Pt. I, 456–458.

opportunity to develop their full capacities and establish a position of genuine equality. Some understanding of this problem had been reflected in the land confiscation proposals of men like Thaddeus Stevens and Wendell Phillips. But it was the Radicals who worked for extended periods among the freedmen in the South who gained the fullest awareness of what needed to be done beyond what most Congressional proponents of Radical Reconstruction thought was necessary. Charles Stearns, an abolitionist who attempted to establish a co-operative plantation in Georgia as a step toward Negro landownership, attacked the notion that legal and political rights were all that was required to give the black man a fair, competitive position. In *The Black Man of the South and the Rebels,* published in 1872, Stearns denounced Greeley's philosophy of "root hog or die," arguing that even a hog could not root without a snout. In his view, provisions for land and education, far beyond anything that was then available to the blacks, were absolutely essential. Arguing that "the black man possesses all the natural powers that we possess," he pointed out that the blacks had not yet recovered from the degrading effects of slavery and were unable, even under Radical Reconstruction, to compete successfully or maintain their rights in the face of a bitterly hostile Southern white population.[61]

Albion W. Tourgée, an idealistic "carpetbagger" who settled in North Carolina and became a judge under its Radical regime, was an eloquent and persistent spokesman for the same point of view. Tourgée, who eventually made his experiences and perceptions the basis of a series of novels, sensed from the beginning that the Radical program, as it finally emerged from Congress, constituted a halfhearted commitment to Negro equality which was doomed to fail in the long run. In a letter to the *National Anti-Slavery Standard* in October, 1867, he announced his opposition to the "Plan of Congress" that was taking shape. "No law, no constitution, no matter how cunningly framed," he wrote, "can shield the poor man of the South from the domination of that very aristocracy from which rebellion sprang, when once

61. Charles Stearns, *The Black Man of the South and the Rebels* (New York, 1872), p. 16, and *passim.*

states are established here. Anarchy or oligarchy are the inevitable results of reconstruction. Serfdom or bloodshed must necessarily follow. The 'Plan of Congress,' so called, if adopted, would deliver the free men of the South, bound hand and foot to their old-time, natural enemies." The Southern Republican Party, Tourgée was saying, was composed largely of impoverished blacks and lower-class whites. Even if assured of temporary political dominance by the disfranchisement of ex-Confederates, these men would soon find themselves at the mercy of the large landowners, who were in a position to apply economic pressure and undo the reforms of Reconstruction. With rare realism, Tourgée argued in effect that political power could not be maintained on the basis of suffrage alone but must be bolstered by adequate economic and social power—and this was precisely what Southern Republicans lacked.[62]

Tourgée's predictions of course came true. As the North looked on, manifesting an increasing reluctance to interfere—a growing desire to wash its hands of the whole matter—Southern white "redeemers" toppled one Radical government after another between 1870 and 1877 and established white-supremacist regimes. Southern Radicalism, supported largely by black votes and ruling through shifting and unstable alliances of Northern "carpetbaggers," Southern white "scalawags," and emergent black spokesmen, had no chance of withstanding the economic, political, and paramilitary opposition of the white majority. In his 1879 Reconstruction novel, *A Fool's Errand*, Tourgée provided an acute assessment of what the Northern leadership had done and why it failed to achieve its original objectives:

After having forced a proud people to yield what they had for more than two centuries considered a right,—the right to hold the African race in bondage,—they proceeded to outrage a feeling as deep and fervent as the zeal of Islam or the exclusiveness of the Hindoo caste, by giving the ignorant, the unskilled and dependent race—a race which could not have lived a week

62. *National Anti-Slavery Standard*, October 19, 1867 (letter signed "Wenckar"). For an excellent account of Tourgée's career see Otto H. Olsen, *Carpetbagger's Crusade: The Life of Albion Winegar Tourgée* (Baltimore, 1965).

without the support or charity of the dominant one—equality of political right. Not content with this, they went farther, and by erecting the rebellious territory into self-regulating and sovereign states, they abandoned these parties to fight out the question of predominance without the possibility of national interference, they said to the colored man in the language of one of the pseudo-philosophers of that day, 'Root, hog, or die!'[63]

The Negro never had a chance in this struggle, as the entire novel makes clear. His ignorance and poverty made him no match for the white conservative forces.

What Tourgée and a few others—notably Representative George W. Julian of Indiana—would have preferred as a plan of reconstruction was a comparatively long-term military occupation or territorial rule of the South, which would have guaranteed "Regeneration before Reconstruction." This "territorial tutelage" would have lasted for an indeterminate period, perhaps as long as twenty or thirty years—long enough to give the North a chance to prepare the freedmen for citizenship through extensive programs of education and guidance, presumably including some form of economic assistance, while at the same time working for a diminution of the racial prejudice and "disloyalty" of the whites.[64] But such an approach was rendered impossible both by pressures which impelled Republican politicians to seek readmission of loyalist-dominated Southern states to the Union in time for the election of 1868 and by the underlying social and racial attitudes that have been described. According to the dominant "self-help" ideology, no one, regardless of his antecedents, had a claim on society for economic security or special protection, or was entitled to a social status that he had not

63. Albion W. Tourgée, *A Fool's Errand*, ed. John Hope Franklin (Cambridge, Mass., 1961), p. 137.
64. See Tourgée's defense of this approach in the *Anti-Slavery Standard*, Oct. 19, 1867. See also George W. Julian's House speech of January 28, 1867, on "Regeneration before Reconstruction," in his *Speeches on Political Questions* (New York, 1872), pp. 348–360; and Brock, *American Crisis*, pp. 188–190. Julian's proposal for military rule of course became one element in the compromise plan that was actually put into effect, but its basic purpose was vitiated by the haste with which the Southern states were readmitted to the Union under new constitutions providing for Negro suffrage.

earned through independent struggle and hard work; the just penalty for laziness, inefficiency, or vice was severe social and economic deprivation, and it was becoming an open question at this time whether society's most abysmal "failures" should even retain their full right to participate in the political process. Having been provided with Federal laws and Constitutional amendments which supposedly guaranteed his legal equality, the black man was expected to make his own way and find his "true level" with a minimum of interference and direct assistance. When the Reconstruction governments foundered, many in the North were quick to say that the blacks had had their fair chance, had demonstrated their present incapacity for self-government, and could justifiably be relegated, for the time being at least, to an inferior status.[65]

Tourgée probably understood better than anyone how tenuous and conditional the Northern commitment to Negro equality had been. His book *An Appeal to Caesar,* published in 1884, contended that the Northern people "have always reflected the Southern idea of the negro in everything except as to his natural right to be free and to exercise the rights of the freedman. From the first [the North] seems to have been animated by the sneaking notion that after having used the negro to fight its battles, freed him as the natural result of a rebellion based on slavery, and enfranchised him to constitute a political foil to the ambition and disloyalty of his former master, it could at any time unload him upon the states where he chanced to dwell, wash its hands of all further responsibility in the matter, and leave him to live or die as chance might determine."[66]

65. The promulgation of such views in the North during the 1870s is described in Victor P. De Santis, *Republicans Face the Southern Question—The New Departure Years, 1877–1897* (Baltimore, 1959), pp. 44–45, 49–52.
66. Albion W. Tourgée, *An Appeal to Caesar* (New York, 1884), p. 127.

Chapter Seven

•

The New South
and the New Paternalism,
1877–1890

WHEN THE LAST Federal occupation troops were withdrawn from the South in 1877, Northern Republicans took comfort from the fact that spokesmen for the triumphant Southern conservatives disclaimed any intention of depriving blacks of their recently won rights as citizens. The best example of the kind of "redeemer" who could put Northern consciences at ease was Governor Wade Hampton of South Carolina. In his 1876 campaign against the Republican administration of Governor Daniel Henry Chamberlain, Hampton promised: *"Not one single right enjoyed by the colored people shall be taken from them. They shall be the equals, under the law, of any man in South Carolina. And I further pledge that we will give better facilities in education than they ever had before."*[1]

As the candidate of the white supremacists, Hampton was of course committed to drastically reducing the Negro role in the governing of South Carolina. Nevertheless, he was apparently sincere in his belief that conservative white hegemony was compatible with preservation of the formal rights gained by blacks during Reconstruction.[2] Although a representative of one of

1. Quoted in George B. Tindall, *South Carolina Negroes, 1877–1900* (Columbia, S.C., 1952), p. 12.
2. *Ibid.*, pp. 19–21. See also Hampton M. Jarrell, *Wade Hampton and the Negro: The Road Not Taken* (Columbia, S.C., 1950), *passim*; and William J.

South Carolina's most aristocratic families and a celebrated Confederate war hero, he had already demonstrated that he was not a doctrinaire defender of the old order. Shortly after Appomattox, he had proposed that South Carolina, on its own initiative, institute a partial suffrage for blacks.[3] After his efforts to get his state to take a more conciliatory and forward-looking approach in the early stages of Reconstruction failed, Hampton had joined the "straight-out" opposition to the Radicals and emerged as leader of the conservative forces. It became clear during the political campaign for white supremacy, however, that Hampton remained a moderate on the question of how best to deal with the black electorate. In contrast to a faction advocating terror and violence, led by Martin W. Gary, Hampton emphasized efforts to persuade the black voters that defeat of the Radicals would lead to racial accommodation and harmony. As governor, Hampton tried to keep his pledges as he understood them, although this was difficult in the face of the clamor and pressure from Gary and other racist militants. His election to the Senate in 1878 decreased his influence on state affairs and permitted the development of more blatantly discriminatory policies.[4]

Hampton set forth his position on the central post-Reconstruc-

---

Cooper, Jr., *The Conservative Regime: South Carolina, 1877–1890* (Baltimore, 1968), Chapter III. From one point of view, however, both Jarrell and Cooper are too uncritical of Hampton's professed commitment to civil and political rights for blacks. Joel Williamson in *After Slavery: The Negro in South Carolina During Reconstruction, 1861–1877* (Chapel Hill, 1965) provides a useful corrective by emphasizing the fact that Hampton "actually offered the Negroes only the privilege of voting for himself and his followers" and that he "steadfastly refused to recognize the Negro's political equality by joining with him in any political partnership" (p. 406). One's evaluation of Hampton's "moderate" philosophy depends to a great extent on whether it is contrasted with Radicalism, with its full commitment to black equality, or with Tillmanism, with its blatant appeal to race hate. If Hampton is contrasted with his Radical Republican predecessors, the limitations of his doctrine become readily apparent; if he is judged in comparison with his demagogic successors, the comparatively benevolent aspects of his approach tend to stand out.

3. A good discussion of Hampton's conciliatory position on Negro rights at the end of the war can be found in Eric L. McKitrick, *Andrew Johnson and Reconstruction* (Chicago, 1960), pp. 243–246.

4. Tindall, *South Carolina Negroes*, pp. 11–38; Jarrell, *Wade Hampton*, pp. 41–163.

tion issue of Negro suffrage in an 1879 *North American Review* symposium. He argued that it had been a mistake to disfranchise the blacks "at the time and in the manner in which it was done," but disavowed any intention of turning back the clock and undoing the work of the Radicals. The South did not desire disfranchisement, he said, because the black vote was ceasing to be a menace: "As the negro becomes more intelligent, he naturally allies himself with the more conservative whites, for his observation and experience both show him that his interests are identified with those of the white race here." Further, the Negro's growing conservatism was a result of the fact that he was "now acquiring education and property" and hence was ready "to assist in the establishment and maintenance of good government."[5]

Although Hampton clearly exaggerated the tendency of blacks to desert the Republicans and fall in line behind white Democratic conservatives—and this is one of the reasons why his program for interracial political "co-operation" ultimately failed —his basic approach set the tone and suggested the content for a moderate white-supremacist philosophy of race relations. As a white supremacist, Hampton did not offer the blacks any meaningful participation in the decision-making of society; all he was actually conceding was respect for the formal aspects of black citizenship in return for Negro acceptance of the kind of conservative leadership he represented. In recommending such a program, Hampton and other Southern white conservatives who hoped to control the Negro vote were presumably keeping one eye on the North, which might still resort to Federal intervention if Southern repression of the Negro became too flagrant, and the other on opposing white political groups in the South, against whom the black vote might be used.

The Hampton racial philosophy was welcomed in the North as providing a rationale for a "hands-off" policy toward the South, one compatible with a belief that the blacks were not simply being abandoned to their worst enemies. In 1878 Thomas Went-

5. "Ought the Negro to be Defranchised? Ought He to Have Been Enfranchised?" *North American Review*, CLXVIII (March, 1879), 241–243.

worth Higginson, once noted as an abolitionist and supporter of John Brown, visited South Carolina and provided the readers of the *Atlantic Monthly* with a glowing report of race relations under Hampton. Higginson found the blacks making progress in a tolerant atmosphere, saw no evidence of a plot or "covert plan for crushing or reenslaving the colored race," and concluded that further "Federal interference" in the South was unnecessary and undesirable.[6] In 1881 another writer in the *Atlantic* gave a similar report on Southern conditions in an article entitled "The End of the War" and, like Higginson, rejoiced in the spectacle of Hampton's reviewing the colored militia.[7]

Nevertheless the charge that Southern blacks were oppressed was soon revived. Sporadic efforts to win Southern white conservatives to the Republican Party got nowhere, and it soon became obvious to many Northerners that a "controlled" black suffrage meant in practice not a voluntary submission to the political leadership of men like Hampton but a pattern of violence, fraud, intimidation, and obstruction that was drastically reducing the Negro (and Republican) vote. New calls for Federal action to ensure the right of suffrage came, mostly from Republican politicians understandably chagrined at the precipitous decline of the party's Southern constituency. But with the defeat of Representative Henry Cabot Lodge's "Force Bill" in 1890, efforts for Federal control of Southern elections came to an end; and, after a temporary revival of Negro voting in some states as a result of the political divisions of the 1890s, informal methods of limiting the Negro vote were replaced by new state constitutional provisions effectively disfranchising blacks. The late 1870s and 1880s constituted a transitional period in the history of Negro voting between the full suffrage of the Reconstruction era and the total disfranchisement of the end of the century. This was a period when blacks continued, despite increasing

6. Thomas Wentworth Higginson, "Some War Scenes Revisited," *Atlantic Monthly*, XLII (July, 1878), 2–9. See also Tilden G. Edelstein, *Strange Enthusiasm: A Life of Thomas Wentworth Higginson* (New Haven and London, 1968), pp. 331–335.

7. Theodore Bacon, "The End of the War," *Atlantic Monthly*, XLVII (March, 1881), 391–400.

difficulties, to vote in certain localities, encouraged to some extent by white leaders who sought to benefit from their ballots.[8]

In *The Strange Career of Jim Crow*, C. Vann Woodward has argued that this was a transitional period in Southern race policy, in social practices and intellectual responses as well as in politics. According to Woodward, the full pattern of segregation had not yet been established and there was still open discussion of what would soon become "forgotten alternatives" in black-white relations. Although it is clear that for most "social" purposes the races were already separated in the 1880s, Woodward presents evidence to show that kinds of public association later unthinkable were tolerated in some parts of the South, especially in the larger towns of the seaboard states.[9]

Perhaps this phenomenon can best be understood by linking up Woodward's description of the incomplete character of segregation with his analysis of the conservative capitalist oligarchy that ruled the South during this period.[10] If "white supremacy,"

8. See Vincent P. De Santis, *Republicans Face the Southern Question—The New Departure Years, 1877–1897* (Baltimore, 1959) , and Stanley P. Hirshon, *Farewell to the Bloody Shirt: Northern Republicans and the Southern Negro, 1877–1893* (Bloomington, Ind., 1962) , for accounts of the vacillating Republican policy toward the Negro before 1890 and the subsequent abandonment of all efforts to maintain political equality in the South. On the transitional period of black voting in two states with relatively large black populations see Tindall, *South Carolina Negroes,* Chapter 4; and Vernon L. Wharton, *The Negro in Mississippi, 1865–1890* (Chapel Hill, 1947) , pp. 199–206.

9. C. Vann Woodward, *The Strange Career of Jim Crow,* Second Revised Edition (New York, 1966) , Chapters I and II. It has become fashionable to attack the Woodward thesis on the grounds that it puts too much stress on laws *per se* and not enough on patterns of *de facto* segregation that already existed in the South in the 1880s. Woodward may have pushed his thesis too hard, especially in his early formulations of it, but his critics are in danger of going to an opposite, and untenable, extreme by implying that nothing really changed in Southern race relations between the 1870s and 1900. August Meier and Elliott Rudwick have recently attempted to reconcile Woodward and his critics by suggesting that the pattern of segregation that existed in the period immediately before and after the Civil War, as perceived by Richard Wade (*Slavery in the Cities* [New York, 1964], pp. 264–70) and Joel Williamson (*After Slavery,* Chapter X) , may have become less rigid and inclusive in the 1870s, only to be fully re-established around 1900. (See "A Strange Chapter in the Career of 'Jim Crow,'" in *The Making of Black America,* ed. August Meier and Elliott Rudwick [New York, 1969], II, 14–19.) Obviously more work needs to be done on this problem.

10. See C. Vann Woodward, *The Origins of the New South 1877–1913* (Baton Rouge, La., 1951) , *passim.*

as understood by the conservative elements that dominated state governments in the "redeemer" era, did not necessarily mean systematic and rigid segregation, it was probably because these leaders were more concerned with the substance of white power than with its full symbolic expression. Of greater importance to them than separation of all black and white passengers on the railroads were sources of economic control, such as the laws and customs putting black sharecroppers at the mercy of white landlords or convict-lease arrangements making cheap black labor available to white capitalists and planters under a system more brutal than slavery. So long as blacks were readily exploitable and cut off from sources of real power, the "Bourbons" could see little danger to white domination from occasional and peripheral irregularities in the color line. By 1890, however, they were made aware of the political risks resulting from their failure to push white supremacy to its logical extreme. By that time lower-class whites had become restive, not only because they were sometimes denied the full racial exclusiveness many craved but also because the characteristic practices which kept the blacks in subservience during the "Bourbon" era—such as the crop lien, verbal contracts between croppers and landlords, the convict lease system— were not strictly racial policies; poor whites could be caught in the meshes of the same exploitative system. Indeed, one of the things that made "the New South" new was the direct exploitation and dependent status of the kind of whites who had been poor but independent landowning farmers under the old regime. Before political pressures from below forced a re-emphasis on white solidarity, the social thought of the South's leadership veered in the direction of a generalized doctrine of minority privilege prescribing paternalistic treatment of lower-class whites as well as blacks. During this period, for example, the promoters and owners of cotton mills employing only whites freely appropriated the rhetoric and even some of the methods of plantation paternalism. When Henry W. Grady, the leading prophet of the "New South," defended white supremacy as an exercise in "the right of character, intelligence and property to rule," he enunciated an elitist doctrine which implicitly excluded a large number of whites from the governing of society and thus went against the full logic of the South's traditional *"Herrenvolk* democracy."

Southern racial doctrines of the transitional period from Reconstruction to the 1890s cannot be understood in isolation but take
on their full significance only in relation to larger social aspirations of a dominant group.[11]

I I

During the 1880s the South's leading intellectual exponent of an
accommodationist and paternalistic attitude toward the Negro
was the Reverend Atticus G. Haygood of Georgia, a prominent
Methodist editor and educator who was president of Emory
College from 1875 to 1884. In his book *Our Brother in Black*
(1881) and in numerous speeches between 1882 and 1890 as
agent of the Slater Fund, a Northern-based philanthropy to aid
Southern Negro education, Haygood proposed a doctrine of
Negro "uplift" under the guidance of benevolent Southern
whites that won the support of some influential and respectable
elements in the "New South." Although he was occasionally
accused of being a Negrophile by extreme racists, he was no
radical; unlike the novelist George W. Cable, whose thoroughgoing defense of Negro rights set off a bitter controversy, he
endorsed racial segregation and made it clear that his program
for Negro advancement constituted no threat to white supremacy. Haygood's support of a conservative Democratic regime in
Georgia, his reluctance to attack the vicious convict-labor system,
and his enthusiastic endorsement of the "New South" creed of
businessmen and industrial promoters all suggest that his racial
philosophy was compatible with the basic values and aspirations
of the new Southern leadership of the 1880s.[12]

Like other proponents of a "New South," Haygood rejoiced
openly at the demise of slavery, at the same time looking back
nostalgically on the old South and the interracial relationships of
the plantation. Recalling his childhood feelings about his

11. Joel Chandler Harris, *Life of Henry W. Grady, Including His Writings
and Speeches* (New York, 1890), p. 305; Woodward, *Origins*, especially Chapters VII and VIII.
12. Harold W. Mann, *Atticus Greene Haygood: Methodist Bishop, Editor
and Educator* (Athens, Ga., 1965), pp. 108, 126–136, 182–183, 194, and *passim*.

father's slaves, he said that they "loved me and I loved them." He claimed that "the great majority of the slaves did truly love the white people," and that "Negroes got all the good of slavery"; for they obtained "the habit of labor, the English language, some knowledge of the institutions of a Christian republic, and, as to thousands of them, the religion of Jesus Christ." But despite the fact that slavery was an idyllic relationship and a source of benefit to the blacks, emancipation was an act of Providence good not only for the Negro but "better for the white people of the South" and "for our industries and our business," in that it had given dignity to labor and made the whites more productive. Under the new ground rules of a capitalistic free-labor society, whites should manifest the benevolent attitude toward blacks that was a legitimate legacy of slavery by working in various ways for the uplift of the freedmen. In arguing that the Negro must be "elevated," Haygood pointed out that this does not mean that he would rise above the whites. *"That cannot be done unless you get below him,"* he told his white readers; for "intelligence, industry, and integrity" would continue to rule society as before.[13]

A recent biography of Haygood reveals that the most important influence on his thinking about the South and its problems in the late 1870s and in the early 1880s was Henry W. Grady's Atlanta *Constitution*. Haygood found himself in perfect agreement with the *Constitution's* advocacy of Southern industrialization and "reunion" with the capitalistic North, and also with its encouragement of blacks in their efforts to improve their situation in ways that did not threaten white political domination.[14] The *Constitution's* seemingly benevolent attitude toward the Negro was most apparent in the editorials written by Joel Chandler Harris, the author of the "Uncle Remus" stories.[15] Henry W. Grady, the *Constitution's* editor and the great popu-

13. Atticus G. Haygood, *Our Brother in Black: His Freedom and His Future* (New York, 1881), pp. 44, 129; *Pleas for Progress* (Cincinnati, 1889), pp. 28, 132; *The New South: Gratitude, Amendment, and Hope* (Oxford, Ga., 1880), p. 12.

14. Mann, *Haygood*, pp. 109, 126–136.

15. See Julia C. Harris, *Joel Chandler Harris, Editor and Essayist* (Chapel Hill, N.C., 1931), pp. 99–103.

larizer of the vision of the "New South," was not so often identified with the cause of Negro uplift. Like Haygood and Harris, he
was essentially a moderate white supremacist despite his willingness to propagandize vigorously against those who threatened
"necessary" segregation and "home rule" for the South. In 1883
Grady argued against "social equality," but conceded that "the
negro is entitled to his freedom, his franchise, to full and equal
basic rights, and to such a share in its administration as his integrity and intelligence will justify. This he ought to have and
must have."[16] Toward the end of the decade his alarm at the
prospect of renewed Federal intervention in the South led him to
place heavy stress on the necessity of white political domination,
but he also called attention to the significance and durability of
benevolent racial attitudes. "The Northern man, dealing with
casual servants," Grady wrote in his book *The New South*, ". . .
can hardly comprehend the friendliness that existed between the
master and slave." He went on to argue that this kindly relationship still existed: "It has survived war, and strife, and political
campaigns. . . . It is the glory of our past in the South. It is the
answer to abuse and slander. It is the hope of our future."[17]

To sustain their view that there was a durable affection
between the races, spokesmen for the new paternalism popularized a perspective on the Negro's behavior during the Civil War
and Reconstruction that clashed with that presented by extreme
Negrophobes. In the course of attacking another clergyman's
contention that blacks had retrograded since emancipation, the
Reverend C. K. Marshall of Vicksburg, Mississippi, maintained
in 1883 that the Negro's record of fidelity during the Civil War
proved him to be essentially "kindly, temperate, and trust-
worthy"; consequently he should be forgiven for having been
hoodwinked by the Radicals during Reconstruction.[18] Haygood
also described the Negro's behavior during the war as submissive.
In view of the Negro's lack of preparation for the suffrage, he

16. Quoted in Raymond W. Nixon, *Henry W. Grady: Spokesman of the
New South* (New York, 1943), p. 214.

17. Henry W. Grady, *The New South* (New York, 1890), pp. 146, 152.

18. The Reverend Charles K. Marshall, *The Colored Race Weighed in the
Balance* (Nashville, 1883), pp. 57, 60.

argued, the amazing thing about Reconstruction was not that there was occasional disorder but that Negro voting did not bring "utter chaos."[19] The heights of such romanticizing were undoubtedly reached by Grady: "I want no truer soul," he said in an 1887 address, "than that which moved the trusty slave, who for four years while my father fought with the armies that barred his freedom, slept every night at my mother's chamber door, holding her and her children as safe as if her husband stood guard, and ready to lay down his humble life on her threshold. History has no parallel to the faith kept by the negro in the South during the war."[20] On the question of how the "loyal" slave of the war years had become the "disloyal" freedman of Reconstruction, Grady provided an explanation as early as 1876 when he was a reporter covering the election campaign that "redeemed" South Carolina. "I am convinced," he wrote in the New York *Herald*, "that the great masses of negroes in South Carolina, as well as elsewhere, are perfectly peaceable and harmless. It is only when their leadership stir their passions and appeal to their prejudices that they are vicious and dangerous."[21]

In addition to praising the Negro's wartime loyalty and excusing his "misbehavior" during Reconstruction, the Southern racial moderates of the late 1870s and the 1880s promulgated a favorable view of the black man's educational and economic progress since emancipation. In his writing for the Atlanta *Constitution*, Joel Chandler Harris supplemented his famous "Uncle Remus" sketches glorifying "the old time darky" of the slave era with glowing accounts of the black man's accomplishments in the New South, contending that the condition of the Negro was rapidly improving and that blacks were "becoming thrifty and economical."[22] The Reverend C. K. Marshall met charges of black retrogression with facts demonstrating progress in land-ownership and in education.[23] In *Our Brother in Black*, Hay-

19. Haygood, *Pleas for Progress*, pp. 27–28; *Our Brother in Black*, p. 79.
20. Harris, *Grady*, p. 97.
21. New York *Herald*, October 11, 1876, clipping in the Grady Papers, Emory University Library.
22. Harris, *Harris*, pp. 101–103.
23. Marshall, *The Colored Race, passim*.

good devoted an entire chapter to the "work good people are doing" in the field of Negro education; and in an address he gave in 1883 he concluded: "The Negro in the South does make true progress. He is more of man than he was twenty years ago. The elements of Christian civilization are more pronounced in character than before. They are beginning to get them humble homes that are their own." He then went on to cite figures showing that blacks were beginning to accumulate property.[24] In his Boston speech of 1889, Grady made similar claims as part of a defense against Northern charges that blacks did not have a fair chance in the South, pointing out that Georgia Negroes owned ten million dollars' worth of assessed property: "Does not that record honor [the Negro] . . . ? What people, penniless, illiterate, has done so well?"[25]

The claim that the Negro was now making progress with the help and encouragement of Southern whites and that this process constituted a continuation of the harmony and racial development of the slave era was, as Grady's use of it suggests, aimed partly at the North, where there were still lingering doubts about Southern racial policy. But many in the North were quite ready by 1890 to be persuaded that the South's new "paternalism" was the answer to the Negro problem. The romantic image of the old South, popularized at this time by Southern writers like Thomas Nelson Page and Harris, was erasing the memory of slavery as portrayed by the abolitionists, and Northerners tended to listen with approval every time a prominent Southerner spoke of the blacks in a spirit of tolerant benevolence that seemed to hark back to the happy days on the old plantation.[26]

In 1890, the Reverend Henry M. Field, a prominent Presbyterian minister and member of a peculiarly distinguished Northern family, revealed, after a trip through the South, that he had been fully converted to the viewpoint of the Southern moderates. Reflecting on slavery, Field contended that the abolitionist de-

24. Haygood, *Our Brother in Black,* Chapter XIV; *Pleas for Progress,* p. 50.
25. Harris, *Grady,* p. 187.
26. See Paul Buck, *The Road to Reunion, 1865 to 1900* (Boston, 1937), Chapters VIII and IX.

scription of it, as presented, for example, in *Uncle Tom's Cabin*, was "very different from the milder form of servitude known to most of the Southern people, to whom it was a part of their domestic life. The relations of the two races were the closest. . . . Though [the Negroes] stood in the relation of servants to their white masters, yet they 'belonged to the family,' and were the objects of a degree of family affection." Field described the plantation as easygoing and indulgent, a mirthful place in which singing and dancing were the principal activities. Slaves responded to their kindly treatment with "gratitude and devotion," as the alleged faithfulness of slaves during the war demonstrated. The subsequent transition from slavery to freedom would have been easy, he suggested, had it not been for the "suicidal folly" of the North in imposing Negro suffrage during Reconstruction. But despite their false start during Reconstruction, the blacks had made progress since emancipation: they had learned to work on their own, had accumulated some property, and had gone to school in large numbers. On the subject of relations between the races, Field argued that the best hope lay in a revived paternalism, which would give the Negroes the kind of guidance from whites that they had received from good masters under slavery. ". . . in time," he predicted, "unfailing kindness will do its work, by bringing the old masters and their former slaves into a mutual understanding and good feeling that will be for the prosperity and happiness of both."[27]

Field concluded his book, nevertheless, with some direct advice to Negroes which suggests that paternalism was inevitably a tenuous and limited concept in a society devoted to laissez-faire individualism. Having advised Southern whites to be kind to blacks and to cultivate the spirit of *noblesse oblige* in helping to raise their weaker black brothers, he counseled Negroes to elevate themselves by their own efforts without relying on white assistance. "Your fate is in your own hands," he said, prescribing the familiar self-help precepts of the Protestant ethic—hard work,

27. Henry M. Field, *Bright Skies and Dark Shadows* (New York, 1890), pp. 109–111, 120–121, 165–168, Chapter IV (*passim*), 186. Field was the brother of Cyrus W., David Dudley, and Justice Stephen Field.

frugality, and a refusal to look to politics and government for aid in the struggle for existence.[28]

Southern "paternalistic" writers offered similar advice. Haygood warned that it was more dangerous to help the Negro too much than too little, that an excess of philanthropy would reduce him to a status lower than slavery, and that in the end he must make his own way.[29] All that such spokesmen even pretended to offer in the economic sphere was "a fair chance" for blacks to earn their living in a competitive capitalistic setting. According to Grady, the freedmen might at times have a certain natural advantage over whites in such a competition: "Often the blacks crowd the whites from work, or lower wages by their greater need or simpler habits, and yet are permitted because we want to bar them from no avenue in which their feet are fitted to tread."[30] But this offer of a chance to compete with the dregs of the white laboring class hardly constituted a kind of paternalism that the aristocracy of the Old South would have recognized. At the root of the new racial philosophy were social and economic assumptions diametrically opposed to traditional paternalistic concepts. The "paternalists" of the New South did not, despite their claims, really attempt to re-establish anything resembling the plantation relationship or the way of thinking about the dependency it sometimes engendered. Central to the paternalistic side of the proslavery argument had been an emphasis on protecting the worker from the insecurity and starvation threatening free labor in a capitalistic society. The theorists of the new "paternalism" offered no such protection; for they themselves were spokesmen of a new order that denied all the socioeconomic premises supportive of such a concept of benevolent guardianship. Their program for Negro uplift amounted, in the last analysis, to moral guidance and a willingness to provide certain educational facilities, especially industrial education. At best it was an effort to prepare the blacks more adequately for scratching out a living at the lower levels of a capitalist society; at its

28. *Ibid.*, pp. 188, 191–205.
29. Haygood, *Pleas for Progress*, p. 135.
30. Harris, *Grady*, p. 188.

worst it openly capitulated to racial discrimination to such an extent that even this modest goal was endangered.

The difference between the old and new paternalism was symbolized by the two guises of Uncle Remus in Harris's first volume of tales and sketches, published with great national acclaim in 1880. In his more familiar role, Uncle Remus is the kindly and humble plantation figure, living in happy security and telling tales of Br'er Rabbit to his master's young son. But he also appears as a black migrant in postwar Atlanta, who comments on the situation and prospects of the former slaves in their new situation. In this role, he is severely critical of those blacks who refuse to work hard and expect to live on charity or anticipate a new dispensation of plantation permissiveness. "Hit's agin de mor'l law fer niggers fer ter eat when dy don't wuk," he says on one occasion; and on another he argues that Negro improvement will come only with the ending of all special indulgences: "You slap de law onter a nigger a time or two, an' larn 'im dat he's got fer to look atter his own rashuns an' keep out'n udder foke's chick'n coops, an' sorter coax 'im ter feed 'is own chilluns, an' I be blessed ef you ain't got 'm on risin' ground!"[31] If the Negro could make progress only by responding to the stern law of necessity, it followed that the highest form of white charity might well consist of withholding special favors and handouts and that the way to be "a friend of the Negro" in the New South was to emancipate oneself from the specific practices that had characterized the old paternalism. When men like Harris suggested that an idealized master-slave relationship was a model for race relations, all they really meant to say was that whites should continue to do what, under the circumstances, was best for the blacks. One suspects that their real concern was what was best for the whites. In the 1880s it presumably suited important elements of the white South to be free of personal obligations to the blacks in order to treat them more readily as a flexible and exploitable labor force.

In some respects the new paternalism was akin to the nineteenth-century concept of charity which allowed the upper levels

31. Joel Chandler Harris, *Uncle Remus: His Songs and His Sayings* (New York, 1895), pp. 224, 232.

of bourgeois society in the North and Great Britain to express benevolent intentions toward the poor of their own race without doing anything that interfered with the impersonal workings of a competitive, capitalistic society. Post-Civil War Northern philanthropists and charity workers, for example, often used the rhetoric of paternalism and *noblesse oblige* in their efforts for the elevation of "the dangerous classes" in the cities. In practice such paternalism meant the preaching of a severe doctrine of "self-help" and a campaign to eliminate the vestiges of the traditional and allegedly demoralizing forms of charity, such as public "outdoor" relief and indiscriminate giving of "alms" to the "unworthy poor." Although at times they employed an anachronistic rhetoric reminiscent of the sense of mutual obligation between rich and poor that was characteristic of precapitalist society, spokesmen for the new benevolence were in fact basing their policies on the bourgeois assumption that nobody owed anybody anything and that those who refused to work had no right to live. This bourgeois pseudopaternalism was conservative, not in the sense that it denied the economic and social premises of a "liberal" and atomistic society, but only in its opposition to government action to relieve the misery of the unfortunate and in its fear of the ballot in the hands of the poor and the ignorant. The only major responsibility imposed on public agencies was for education, which was seen as a means of inculcating principles conducive to social peace. In the campaign for public education in the North, both before and after the Civil War, middle-class reformers constantly emphasized that only education of the right sort would limit the possibility of class conflict and disorder and mitigate the evils of universal suffrage. By the 1880s a new campaign for educational reform was under way, supported by a substantial segment of the business community, which betrayed assumptions even more obviously anti-egalitarian. This was the new emphasis on industrial education and manual training as a way of fitting the children of the working classes more efficiently for their destined role in society.[32]

32. See George M. Fredrickson, *The Inner Civil War: Northern Intellectuals and the Crisis of the Union* (New York, 1965), pp. 213–215; Merle Curti, *The Social Ideas of American Educators* (Paterson, N.J.), 1959, Chap-

The benevolent philosophy of white supremacy, as put forth in the 1880s by men like Haygood and Harris, resembled the bourgeois paternalism of a Northern elite more than the aristocratic paternalism of the Old South. It reflected a half-conscious desire to replace patterns of dependency with the impersonal relationships of a capitalistic society and to substitute bourgeois concepts of social class for the traditional Southern stress on racial caste. But such an approach was not consistently developed or maintained. This effort to work out and implement an ideology transcending race was doomed to failure because its exponents could not fully emancipate themselves from the assumptions of Southern biracialism.

The new paternalists sounded most like conservative Northern philanthropists confronting "the dangerous classes" when they advocated Negro education, their favorite cause and the backbone of their program. Grady saw the improvement of Negro education as "the chief problem which confronts the white people of the South": only by solving it could the South avoid "political chaos and demoralization."[33] In *Our Brother in Black,* Haygood wrote that Negro suffrage might have been a mistake, but it was a *fait accompli;* and since, in his opinion, the blacks could never be disfranchised, they must be educated so that they could use the ballot intelligently and in harmony with Southern whites. "An ignorant voter, of whatever color he may be, is a constant menace," he wrote.[34] As agent for the Slater Fund, the grant of a Connecticut textile manufacturer to aid Negro higher education in the South, Haygood anticipated the educational philosophy of Booker T. Washington by using the money largely to support the kind of industrial education that would prepare blacks for positions as farmers and artisans, while denying help to liberal-arts institutions of the kind that had been favored by Northern philanthropy during Reconstruction.[35]

---

ter VI, and *passim;* Edward C. Kirkland, *Dream and Thought in the Business Community, 1860–1900* (Ithaca, 1956) , pp. 80–81.

33. Quoted in Nixon, *Grady,* p. 213.

34. Haygood, *Our Brother in Black,* pp. 80, 81, 134.

35. Mann, *Haygood,* pp. 184–187. See also August Meier, *Negro Thought in America, 1880–1915* (Ann Arbor, 1963) , pp. 92–93.

Another prominent Southern champion of Negro education was J. L. M. Curry, a prewar Alabama Congressman who during the 1880s was agent for the Peabody Fund (another effort of Northern philanthropy to aid Southern education) and later Haygood's successor as agent of the Slater Fund. Curry constantly argued that the conservative interests of the South could best be protected by educating the Negro voter.[36] An illiterate Negro was much more dangerous than one who was educated: "Such a mass of illiteracy as we have is worse than a foreign invasion, incites domestic violence, gives supremacy to bad appetites, and is a perpetual menace to the life and well-being of Republican institutions."[37] The potentialities of expanded public instruction as a mechanism of social control and a basis for the political domestication of the masses led Curry and other Southern moderates of the 1880s to put aside their states'-rights principles and defend New Hampshire Senator Henry W. Blair's plan for Federal aid to education, a proposal designed to benefit the South more than any other region. But the bill encountered serious opposition in the South and elsewhere and failed to receive Congressional approval.[38]

Such emphasis on Negro "elevation" can perhaps best be seen as a by-product of the "New South" ideology and the class interests that lay behind it. As C. Vann Woodward's work has revealed, the period after Reconstruction saw the beginnings of Southern industrial development under the aegis of conservative regimes markedly friendly to business interests. In this era, the South's political and economic leaders launched campaigns to promote Northern investment in Southern enterprise and promulgated the values of industrial capitalism in a society that had previously rejected them. Behind these developments was the rise to prominence of a new middle class and the corresponding decline of those remnants of the old planter aristocracy

36. Jessie Pearl Rice, *J. L. M. Curry: Southerner, Statesman and Educator* (New York, 1949), p. 107, and *passim.*
37. Quoted in Curti, *Social Ideas of American Educators,* p. 271.
38. Rice, *Curry,* 116–119; Woodward, *Origins,* pp. 63–64; Claude H. Nolen, *The Negro's Image in the South: The Anatomy of White Supremacy* (Lexington, Ky., 1967), pp. 136–137.

unwilling to accommodate to the changing order. The transition was obscured and made more palatable by sentimental homage to the Old South; "paternalist" racial rhetoric was part of a sleight of hand which concealed the new in the trappings of the old.[39]

Despite sentimental allusions to the plantation relationship, the major exponents of this doctrine clearly belonged to the new order. Haygood, Grady, and Harris, prominent advocates of the New South, reflected backgrounds typical of the new leadership. None stemmed from the antebellum planter aristocracy. Grady was the son and grandson of merchants who ran general stores in antebellum towns; Haygood's father was a representative of the rudimentary urban middle class of the Old South, a Whig lawyer with commercial interests who moved his family to Atlanta when Atticus was thirteen and involved himself in the development of Georgia's fastest-growing city; and Harris was the illegitimate son of a white servant girl and grew up around the fringes of plantation society.[40] Without much stake in the old order, these men were ready and willing to identify themselves, in one way or another, with the emerging middle class of the post-bellum South. Harris's respect for at least some aspects of the plantation ethos was probably authentic, but it is significant that his writings about antebellum times do not romanticize the white planter. Indeed, as the journalist Walter Hines Page noted after meeting Harris in 1881, "he hardly conceals his scorn for the old aristocracy. You can find here and there in Uncle Remus's sayings a sly thrust at the pompous life of the Old South."[41]

If "paternalistic" racial benevolence was part of the "New South" ideology of an emergent middle class, there must have been some hardheaded and practical reasons for its popularity. The most obvious was its congeniality with the economic boosterism of the 1880s. When Grady pointed to the Negro's progress

39. See Woodward, *Origins*, Chapters V and VI, especially pp. 150–154.
40. Nixon, *Grady*, pp. 27–28; Mann, *Haygood*, pp. 8–13; Paul M. Cousins, *Joel Chandler Harris: A Biography* (Baton Rouge, 1968), Chapters 1 and 2.
41. Burton J. Hendrick, *The Training of an American: The Earlier Life and Letters of Walter H. Page, 1855–1913* (Boston and New York, 1928), p. 152.

with optimistic pronouncements about race relations, he was plainly contributing to the image of a South that was peaceful, progressive, and endowed with a dependable labor force, an image that would appeal to Northern investors while appeasing Northern humanitarians. Such rhetoric was part of the effort of Southern spokesmen to create a spirit of intersectional harmony based on a working agreement between the commercial and industrial leadership of the two regions.

In a different sphere, men like Haygood and Curry worked to convince the representatives of Northern philanthropy, who were also in many cases businessmen with an interest in Southern investments, that their money would contribute to sectional harmony and mutual prosperity if used to support work for Negro "elevation" under the direction and control of benevolent Southerners. The recommended program of industrial education for blacks won support because it was anticipated that blacks would make a more effective contribution to general prosperity and individual white profit making if they were taught useful skills. The industrial concept, long propounded by General S. C. Armstrong at Hampton Institute in Virginia and boosted tremendously by Booker T. Washington's advocacy and example, was genuinely popular among the spokesmen for the New South. Few people seemed to realize at the time, however, that Negroes at Hampton and Tuskegee were being taught preindustrial skills of comparatively little value in the emerging economy.[42]

III

The optimistic neopaternalist school of Southern thought was attacked during the 1880s from two sides. At one extreme were the pessimists and die-hard racists who denied the possibility of black progress, except under slavery, and who favored a more openly repressive system. At the other extreme were lonely spokesmen—most notably the novelist George W. Cable—who argued in effect that the "New South" advocates could not

42. See August Meier's excellent discussion of "The Rise of Industrial Education in Negro Schools," *Negro Thought,* Chapter VI.

realize their own professed goal of a prosperous and progressive region unless they implemented a policy of genuine public equality. These differences were brought into focus during a controversy in the mid-1880s over segregation. The point of departure was Cable's address, "The Freedman's Case in Equity," given before the American Social Science Association in September, 1884, and published in the *Century Magazine* for January, 1885. It was a forthright attack on segregation and discrimination because they denied the black man his fundamental rights and the opportunity to benefit from his freedom. Cable noted that "the letter of the laws, with a few exceptions recognizes him as entitled to every right of an American citizen," and charged that "there is scarcely one public relation of life in the South where he is not arbitrarily and unlawfully compelled to hold toward the white man the attitude of an alien, a menial, and a probable reprobate, by reason of his race and color." Writing before segregation in all areas was enforced by law, he was describing a pattern of extralegal community practice and custom that often achieved substantially the same result. As he analyzed it, freedom was a mockery when combined with segregation; for such a system "acknowledges in constitutions and statutes [the Negro's] title to an American's freedom and aspirations, and then in daily practice heaps upon him in every public place the most odious distinctions, without giving ear to the humblest pleas concerning moral or mental character." This unjust and hypocritical arrangement denied self-respect to the blacks and stifled their legitimate ambitions; as a result the entire South suffered from the effects of Negro demoralization. To remedy this situation, he proposed that all public places and institutions, including schools, be opened to blacks on an equal and unsegregated basis.[43]

Cable's genuinely radical proposals were clearly inconsistent with the thinking of respectable Southern proponents of interracial benevolence. Haygood, for example, went further than

43. George W. Cable, *The Silent South, Together with the Freedman's Case in Equity and the Convict Lease System* (New York, 1885), pp. 16–17, and 1–38, *passim*. For biographical information on Cable see Arlin Turner, *George W. Cable: A Biography* (Durham, N.C., 1956).

most of them but nevertheless strongly supported segregation. On the question of separate churches, Haygood argued that they existed because the Negroes themselves wanted them; their "race instincts" led them to desire separation. He defended separate schools on the same grounds. The race instinct, he wrote, "will never be satisfied till it realizes itself in complete separation. Whether we of the white race approve or disapprove matters little."[44]

The trend toward "complete separation," however, created a problem for those who gave more than lip service to paternalistic ideals; for it seemingly undercut the possibility of significant white guidance and supervision of the freedmen. How could whites stimulate Negro improvement by good example and up-lifting advice if they had less and less contact with the black community?

One clergyman who worried about this problem was Episcopal Bishop Thomas U. Dudley of Kentucky, who published an article in the *Century* a few months after Cable's bold statement had appeared, deploring segregation as incompatible with pater-nalistic goals. "The separation of the negro race from the white," Dudley wrote, "means for the negro continued and increasing degradation and decay. His hope for salvation must come from association with that people among whom he dwells, but from whose natural guidance and care he has been separated largely by the machinations of unscrupulous demagogues." He specifically decried the separation of the churches because it deprived the Negro of a major source of white direction and control.[45]

In his own way, Dudley was almost as much of a heretic as Cable, because, according to the dominant view of the "New South" leadership, racial separation and the improvement of the blacks under white hegemony were compatible aims. In an "official" Southern rejoinder to Cable in the *Century*, Grady argued that neither race wanted "social intermingling." Separa-tion was a product of basic racial "instincts," a manifestation of

44. Haygood, *Our Brother in Black*, p. 235; *Pleas for Progress*, p. 40.
45. Bishop Thomas U. Dudley, "How Shall We Help the Negro?" *Century Magazine*, XXX (June, 1885) , 278, 273–280.

the desire of each people to preserve its purity and essential character. Forcing them together would arouse antagonism and open the way to miscegenation and race war. Grady justified segregation on the basis of what was to become a standard apology for the system, arguing that "the assortment of races is wise and proper, and stands on the platform of equal accommodation for each race but separate."[46]

Grady's response to Cable's address was comparatively mild and temperate in comparison to the reaction in certain other quarters. The comments of some of the surviving intellectual and literary figures of the Old South suggested that they not only rejected Cable's egalitarianism but also had grave doubts about Grady's relatively sanguine view of Southern race relations. The Reverend Robert L. Dabney of Virginia, who attacked Cable in the *Southern Historical Society Papers,* was one of the staunchest defenders of the Old South against the "New South" ideology and everything it represented. Stonewall Jackson's chief of staff and a proslavery writer in the Christian paternalist vein, Dabney had refused to abandon his belief that disaster was the inevitable consequence of emancipation; consequently he had no toleration for what he regarded as the futile attempt to make something out of the freedmen. As a forthright opponent of Negro education at public expense, he had, in 1876, countered the argument for schooling to fit blacks for the suffrage by declaring that the right to vote would soon have to be withdrawn.[47] For paternalists of the Old South to become the antipaternalists of the New South was logical, because men like Dabney had contended that slavery alone could provide blacks with a benevolent guardianship and a civilizing "education."[48] In his reply to Cable, Dabney avoided discussing Cable's racial philosophy directly,

46. Harris, *Grady,* pp. 289–290. (The original article, entitled "In Plain Black and White," appeared in *Century Magazine* for April, 1885.)

47. On Dabney's reactionary stand in the post-Reconstruction era, see Woodward, *Origins,* pp. 173–174; William B. Hasseltine, *Confederate Leaders in the New South* (Baton Rouge, 1950) , pp. 70–76; and Thomas Cary Johnson, *Life and Letters of Robert Lewis Dabney* (Richmond, 1903) , pp. 396 ff. and *passim.*

48. See Dabney's *Defence of Virginia* (New York, 1867) , apparently the only thoroughgoing defense of slavery published *after* the war.

probably because he considered it unworthy of serious consideration, and limited himself to a vitriolic attack on Cable's antislavery interpretation of the Civil War. While Grady, like other
proponents of "the New South," was unwilling to justify slavery
in the abstract and was even ready to concede that the North
had, in a sense, done the South a service by removing the burden
of "the peculiar institution," the unreconstructed Dabney boldly
defended slavery and the Confederate cause. He attacked Cable
personally as a traitor to the South who had sold out to the
North for "a liberal recompense."[49]

Another unreconstructed "cavalier," Charles Gayarré, octo-
genarian historian and representative of the Creole aristocracy of
New Orleans, also denounced Cable on grounds Grady would
have found unacceptable. Gayarré's basic views on the race question were set forth in 1877 in the *North American Review*. Taking a pessimistic look at the prospects for racial harmony and
black development, he maintained that history showed "the in-
terminable conflict of races when they attempt to settle in the
same country, as long as the weaker does not merge into the
stronger, or consents to be subservient to its interests and prejudices. . . ." Emancipation had set the races in fundamental antagonism, with an irrevocable rupture of the intimate ties of the
slave system; "the white race and black race are drawing farther
apart every day, notwithstanding the time-serving asseverations
of politicians to the contrary." He saw no reason to expect that
the end of Reconstruction would change this situation and predicted that the Negro would probably "die out in the end . . .
of weak lungs and from the want of congenial air in the more
elevated regions to which he has been raised, and to which he
cannot be acclimated . . ."[50]

Gayarré's opinion of Negro prospects was obviously antitheti-
cal to that of the new paternalists, and it is not surprising that
his answer to Cable, appearing in the New Orleans *Times-
Democrat*, differed in emphasis from Grady's. Grady had tried to

49. R. L. Dabney, "George W. Cable in the Century Magazine," *Southern
Historical Society Papers*, XIII (1885) , 148–153.
50. Charles Gayarré, "The Southern Question," *North American Review*,
CCXXV (November–December, 1877) , 485, 493, 495.

play down the seriousness of the Southern racial problem; Gayarré magnified it to horrendous proportions, contending that "the existence in the same country of two races, as different as day and night in their physical and spiritual endowments and apparently incapable of fusing into a homogeneous whole, is the most dreadful calamity that ever could befall a community."[51] Gayarré was disgusted by the mild and "colorless" quality of Grady's article and agreed completely with the comments of the poet Paul Hamilton Hayne, another literary survivor from the Old South. Grady had conceded too much to the North, Hayne wrote to Gayarré, when he admitted that the abolition of slavery had been justified: "On other points he shows himself wretchedly superficial. For instance, this dreadful problem touching the Negro, and his relations to the whites of the South, Mr. Grady dismisses after a somewhat airy *insouciant* fashion." In particular, Hayne took Grady to task for maintaining that "the Negro has no desire whatever toward social communion & amalgamation; that the Inferior Race desires to keep itself apart from the Whites &c. . . ." Such a view, Hayne concluded, was "a mere sotticism."[52]

Men like Dabney, Gayarré, and Hayne preferred a harsher doctrine of white supremacy to the one promulgated by spokesmen for the New South. For them, the Negro was now what the proslavery writers had predicted he would become after emancipation—a positive menace who must be forcibly contained. Such thinking presaged the extreme racism of the 1890s and constituted part of a submerged link between the antebellum hostility to free Negroes and the Negrophobia which triumphed at the end of the century. To these representatives of the old aristocracy, segregation was not a happy voluntary arrangement providing "separate but equal" facilities; it was, or should be, a deliberately repressive mechanism to hold the Negro in a permanently inferior position. Any other policy, they believed, would threaten the whites with biological contamination or race war.

51. Quoted in Charles R. Anderson, "Charles Gayarré and Paul Hayne: The Last Literary Cavaliers," *American Studies in Honor of William Kenneth Boyd* (Durham, N.C., 1940) , p. 230.
52. *Ibid.*, pp. 235–236.

The fact that some of the most articulate of the unreconstructed defenders of the old order expressed such an attitude casts further doubt on the existence of a vital connection between the aristocratic traditions of the Old South and the new paternalism of the 1880s.

IV

From Cable's point of view, there was more rhetoric than substance in the disagreement between the Grady-style moderates and the hard-line apologists for slavery and repression. He complained in effect that the benevolent and optimistic approach to race relations concealed a perspective little different from the position advocated by extreme racists. In his analysis of Southern thought and conditions, Cable exposed the limitations of middle-class "paternalism" by pointing out that its acceptance of segregation undermined its own professed goals. His vain attempt to convert the South to a consistent application of nineteenth-century liberal values was repudiated by Southerners because it was genuinely "color blind" in its policy implications and not the unstable amalgam of middle-class social ideals and traditional racist assumptions respectable in the 1880s.[53]

Cable did agree with some of the values of the optimistic

53. Cable's support of an egalitarian policy did not signify a belief in the biological equality of the races. His position in fact was similar to that of those Northern Radicals of the Civil War era who accepted the idea of biological inequality but then denied that this necessitated social and political inequality. In 1875, in one of his earliest attacks on segregation, Cable wrote: "If the race is inferior we can the better afford to give them an even start. . . . Yes, the black race is inferior to the white. The Almighty has established inequality as a principle in nature. But the lesson it teaches is magnanimity not scorn." (George W. Cable, *The Negro Question: A Selection of Writings on Civil Rights in the South,* ed. Arlin Turner [New York, 1958], p. 29.) Although he later became less dogmatic in his assertion of inequality, Cable's basic views did not change substantially. In *The Negro Question* (New York, 1888), Cable described his position as follows: "For all that is known the black is 'an inferior race,' though how, or how permanently inferior, remains unproved. But the core of the colored man's grievance is that the individual, in matters of right that do not justly go by race, is treated, whether man or child, without regard to person, dress, behavior, character or aspirations, in public and by law, as though the African tincture, much or little, were itself stupidity, squalor and vice" (pp. 6–7) .

boosters of a progressive South. He referred explicitly to the "New South" idea and indicated his sympathy for its announced aim of capitalistic development and general prosperity. In his earliest utterance on the subject, however, he made clear his dislike for the term itself. In a commencement address at the University of Mississippi in 1882, he boldly announced that this popular expression was "a term fit only to indicate a transitory condition. What we want—what we ought to have in view—is the No South! Does the word sound like annihilation? It is the farthest from it. It is enlargement. It is growth. It is a higher life."[54]

After he had begun to speak out openly on the race question in the middle 1880s, Cable became more specific in his criticism of the "New South" doctrine. In an 1888 essay on "The Negro Question," he described the "remarkable development of material wealth . . . now going on in several parts of the South." Although he was happy to see the South prosper, he hoped "to see wealth built upon public provisions for securing through it that general beneficence without which it is not really wealth." But "despite the assurances of a host of well-meaning flatterers that a New South is laying the foundations of a permanent prosperity," Cable saw only a crudely exploitative system designed to benefit the few at the expense of the many. Much of what was described as industrial progress was simply "the Old South readapting the old plantation idea to a peasant labor and mineral products." Northern businessmen would never suffer from Southern competition until the South built its economy upon a more widely "disseminated wealth," and this would not happen "without a disseminated education," which in turn could "not be brought to any high value without liberty, responsibility, private inequality, public equality, self-regard, virtue, aspirations, and their rewards."[55]

These preconditions for "permanent prosperity" were of course precisely the values and practices Cable described as incompatible with racial segregation. As he wrote elsewhere, the implementation of full civil rights for blacks—which would

54. Turner, ed., *The Negro Question*, p. 44.
55. Cable, *The Negro Question*, pp. 28–29. (This essay was originally published in the British *Contemporary Review* for March, 1888.)

include equal access to all public facilities—would arouse in the freedmen a "new hope and desire toward the prizes of industry, frugality, and a higher cultivation," and by making the black man "a factor in the material and moral progress of the whole land" would bring more "wealth and prosperity" than "all the crops our sun-loved South can yield" and "all the metals and minerals that are under the soil."[56]

What might be called the liberal economic argument for desegregation was stressed even more strongly by Lewis H. Blair, an iconoclastic Richmond businessman, in his book attacking segregation. In *A Southern Prophecy: The Prosperity of the South Dependent upon the Elevation of the Negro,* Blair contended that the promise of a "New South" would remain unfulfilled as long as the blacks were demoralized by the invidious distinctions of a segregated society. The claims made for a prosperous New South were grossly overstated, and the region's economic shortcomings were to be attributed to the degradation of black labor. Under existing conditions the black man was free only to be lazy and inefficient; for the whites lacked the slave-owner's power to compel labor, while the blacks lacked the incentive to hard work that comes from hope of reward and advancement. "But if the Negro is to become an intelligent voter, is to be a citizen capable of taking a sensible part in the affairs of his community, and to be a valuable co-worker in adding to the wealth of the state, then we have a vast deal to do in order to elevate him. To make him *our* assistant in the production of wealth, the Negro must be made to work, or he must be induced by ambition, by the hope of enjoying in full the fruits of his labors, to work steadily and intelligently." Since there was little prospect of reinstituting slavery or anything like it, the latter course was the only one open to the South; and its pursuit, Blair argued, necessitated giving up segregation, including separate schools, in order to inculcate ambition and industrial morale in the black laboring population.[57]

56. Cable, *The Silent South,* pp. 98–99. (From the title essay, originally published in the *Century Magazine* for September, 1885.)

57. Lewis H. Blair, *A Southern Prophecy: The Prosperity of the South Dependent upon the Elevation of the Negro,* ed. C. Vann Woodward (Boston

As consistent proponents of liberal capitalist values, Blair and Cable were telling the South that it could industrialize effectively only if it gave up its obsession with racial distinctions and learned to regard Negroes principally as members of a "free" labor force, extending to them the same opportunities for self-improvement that enlightened Northern capitalists allegedly offered their workers. Such a point of view may have made them egalitarians in regard to racial policy, but it hardly made them social radicals or advocates of equality as the governing principle of society. Cable in particular reflected some of the special kind of middle-class elitism then evident among "genteel reformers" of the North. In a sense, he simply carried to its logical outcome the same concept of *bourgeoisie oblige* that had been present in rudimentary form in the ambivalent thinking of the racial moderates and conventional proponents of the "New South."

Cable's genteel elitism came to the surface when he listed "private inequality" as one of the prerequisites of "a lasting prosperity." In explaining why the rise of a wealthy Southern bourgeoisie would not by itself bring social and economic health to the region, he described as unfortunate "the community whose intelligent few do not make the mass's elevation by public education and equal public liberty the cornerstone of a projected wealth," clearly implying that he himself favored such a benevolent role for the elite.[58] Like the genteel reformers and philanthropists of the North, who spoke during this period of "the duties of educated men" and the need for a refined minority to provide moral leadership for masses, Cable thought naturally in terms of a process of "uplift" and "elevation," supervised by "the best people." At the time he was condemning racial segregation, he was leading the campaign for "home culture clubs," designed to bring people of diverse social backgrounds together for reading and discussion. As he conceived of them, the clubs were a way

and Toronto, 1964), p. 49 and *passim*. See Woodward's discussion of Blair's thought and career in his introduction to this edition and also Charles E. Wynes's "Lewis Harvie Blair, Virginia Reformer: The Uplift of the Negro and Southern Prosperity," *Virginia Magazine of History and Biography*, LXXII (January, 1964), 3–18.
58. Cable, *The Negro Question*, pp. 29–30.

of reaching and "elevating the masses," without "any disturbance of necessary social distinctions and divergencies (and many are highly necessary) ."[59]

Cable's concern for "elevating the masses" without disturbing "necessary social distinctions" was reflected in his attack on segregation. In "The Freedman's Case in Equity," he turned the tables on critics who accused him of advocating "social equality" by arguing that "the color line points straight in the direction of social equality by tending toward the equalization of all whites on one side of the line and of all blacks on the other." Segregation put such an emphasis on racial distinctions that legitimate and "necessary" social distinctions tended to be obscured. In "The Silent South," a reply to critics of "The Freedman's Case in Equity," Cable said that those who raised the bugbear of "social equality" were "themselves thrusting arbitrary and cheap artificial distinctions into the delicate mechanism of society's self-distribution as it revolves by the power of our natural impulses, and of morality, personal interest, and personal preferences." The South's most flagrant violation of a "natural" social hierarchy was its refusal to grant "the rights of gentility" to well-educated and well-behaved Negroes by denying them access to places where they deserved to be "by the simple act of being genteel." Every time a cultivated and well-dressed Negro was forced to associate with "the common herd of clowns and ragamuffins" in a second-class railway car, the idea of a proper social hierarchy was negated.[60]

Cable's attack on segregation was, therefore, also a conscious attack on the Southern tradition of *Herrenvolk* egalitarianism. To preserve proper distinctions among whites, blacks had to be integrated in a social hierarchy which recognized the rewards of gentility. In his novel *The Grandissimes,* Cable had used the case of two brothers in early nineteenth-century New Orleans to illustrate the absurdity and injustice of a caste line. Equally wealthy, cultivated, and "genteel," one was a leader of the community and the other a social outcast because he had Negro blood in his

59. Quoted in Turner, *George W. Cable,* p. 282.
60. Cable, *The Silent South,* pp. 34, 52, 61.

veins.[61] There was nothing wrong, Cable indicated in one of his addresses, with "questions of *social rank*," which could never be avoided, because they were "healthful and ever-vital questions." But caste concepts which violated the principles of a social stratification based on middle-class standards of "gentility" were to be condemned. There was also nothing abstractly wrong, in his view, with what Grady called "the right of character, intelligence and property to rule." Cable himself argued that majority rule was a chimera and that a minority of the wealthy and intelligent could legitimately hold the reins of society if it ruled "by equity," devoting itself to the maintenance of public rights, thereby earning the confidence and support of the common people. What he found abhorrent was the idea that a man could be an aristocrat, for some purposes, simply because his skin was white.[62]

By fearlessly carrying the half-formed ideology of an emergent Southern middle class to its logical extreme, Cable exposed the fatal compromises made by the respectable advocates of Negro "elevation." Like the aristocratic paternalism of the Old South, the middle-class quasi paternalism of the New South could not be consistently conceptualized or fully implemented by the South's leadership because of the region's popular commitment to biracialism. Here, once again, racial considerations warped the South's efforts to envision itself in terms of a social ideology appropriate to communities that lacked a central tradition of slavery and caste.

61. George W. Cable, *The Grandissimes* (New York, 1880).

62. Turner, ed., *The Negro Question*, p. 39; Cable, *The Silent South*, pp. 78–79; Cable, *The Negro Question*, pp. 22–24.

Chapter Eight

•

The Vanishing Negro:
Darwinism and the Conflict
of the Races

SOME INTERPRETERS of the late nineteenth-century racial situation emphatically rejected the comforting vision of benevolent white supremacy and interracial harmony promulgated by middle-class "paternalists" as part of their campaign for a New South and a reunion of the sections. Spokesmen who claimed to represent an unsentimental and tough-minded perception of racial reality denied the prospect of gradual black "progress" in an atmosphere of mutual accommodation, projecting instead a future of increasing interracial antagonism. This grim view of black-white relations was not limited to die-hard intellectual survivors of the Old South like Gayarré and Hayne but was echoed in the 1880s by some influential men of the new order. In an 1884 *North American Review* symposium on "The Future of the Negro," Senator John T. Morgan of Alabama argued that an increase in black wealth, intelligence, and capacity for industrial, commercial, and political activity was inevitable but potentially disastrous, because it could lead only to an increasingly bitter competition with whites. "The greater their personal success may be," he wrote of the Negroes, "the more they will feel the pressure of caste, and their advancement in enterprises which may bring them personal honor and wealth will be checked by the jealousy of caste, so that race prejudice will forever remain as an incubus on all their individual or aggregated efforts." The only way that

Negroes could hope to advance would be to flee from white competition and antagonism by emigrating to Africa.[1]

The same point of view was developed in greater detail at about the same time by Edward W. Gilliam, a Baltimore physician and novelist, in two widely discussed articles on the future of the Negro. He conceded that the blacks, although greatly inferior to the whites, were "an improving race" with a quickening "throb of aspiration," but there were dangers inherent in this situation. His argument was a standard one among those racists who conceded some capacity to blacks but emphasized the inviolability of racial barriers. Individual Negroes, he contended, would advance to the threshold of equality but would then be turned back because of the instinctive white antipathy arising from a necessary and legitimate fear of miscegenation. This rejection would force the blacks to develop racial solidarity and engage in collective efforts to win equal rights, a strategy which would bring Negroes into violent collision with the white population: "The advancement of the blacks," Gilliam concluded, ". . . becomes a menace to the whites. No two free races, remaining distinctly apart, can advance side by side, without a struggle for supremacy." To avoid such a struggle, Gilliam, like Morgan, proposed the removal of the black population.[2]

The notion that a racial "struggle for supremacy" was inevitable so long as blacks and whites tried to inhabit the same soil in a state of freedom was, of course, an old one. Tocqueville, the proslavery writers, and some of the free-soil theorists had seen such a struggle as the unavoidable consequence of emancipation. Estimates of how violent such a competition would be had varied in accordance with a spectrum of views on how much of a fight the blacks would be able to put up. The proslavery alarmists dwelt on the horrors of Santo Domingo, while some ethnologists and free-soilers foresaw the peaceful disappearance of a race of "feeble exotics": the blacks would quietly fade away in the face of white competition because of racial weaknesses that were

1. "The Future of the Negro," *North American Review*, CXXXIX (July, 1884) , 83–84.
2. E. W. Gilliam, "The African in the United States," *Popular Science Monthly*, XXII (February, 1883) , 438–440; see also "The African Problem," *North American Review*, CXXXLX (October, 1884) , 417–430.

accentuated by climatic factors.[3] Although the act of emancipation did not result either in race war or in a decline in the black
population, prophecies of extermination did not cease with the
coming of the postwar era. In fact they were given new impetus
and greater respectability by the intellectual currents set in
motion by the publication of Charles Darwin's *On the Origin of
Species* in 1859.

I I

One of the implications of Darwinism for racial thinking was
suggested by the subtitle of *The Origin of Species*—"The Preservation of Favoured Races in the Struggle for Life." The theory
that evolution toward higher forms of life stemmed primarily
from the conflict and competition of varieties and species, with
the resulting "survival of the fittest" and disappearance of the
unfit, had obvious attraction for those who believed that some
human races had a more exalted destiny than others. Darwin
himself, although not vitally interested in such questions, could
not avoid applying his doctrine to human "varieties." In a letter
written in 1881, he contended that "natural selection"—the
mechanism by which the environment selected some biological
variations and rejected others—had done much for "the progress
of Civilization." He argued that the Turks had failed to conquer
Europe because the "more civilized so-called Caucasian races
have beaten the Turkish hollow in the struggle for existence,"
and he added prophetically: "Looking at the world at no very
distant date, what an endless number of lower races will be
eliminated by the higher civilized races throughout the world."
This final comment echoed a prediction he had made in *The
Descent of Man*, in 1871: "At some future period, not very distant as measured by centuries, the civilized races of man will
almost certainly exterminate and replace the savage races
throughout the world."[4]

3. See Chapter Five, above.
4. These quotations from Darwin, along with information about their context and significance, are found in Gertrude Himmelfarb, *Darwin and the*

Darwin's application of the concept of a "struggle for existence" to human types was natural and inevitable; he recognized no distinction between the factors which made for human survival, development, and differentiation, and those which accounted for "the preservation of favoured races" in the rest of animate nature. As a matter of fact, the evolutionary importance of nature's apparently cruel and wasteful destruction of a large proportion of organisms was suggested to Darwin in the first place by the writings of Thomas R. Malthus, who back in 1798 had attacked Utopian expectations of human betterment by claiming that in the end population would always outrun the means of subsistence, and that starvation, disease, and vice were—and would remain—necessary means for checking a high birth rate and restoring the balance between man and his resources. Darwin applied a similar principle to all living things, and also succeeded in reconciling this originally pessimistic notion with the dominant nineteenth-century belief in progress. He contended that those who lost out in the struggle for existence were apt to be inferior specimens, poorly adapted to their environment, which made the survivors the basis for an improved stock.[5] Antebellum American theorists who had anticipated a Darwinian view of racial competition also started from Malthusian principles. Focusing on the question of what would happen if "higher" and "lower" races were allowed to compete freely for limited resources, they made a direct and simplistic connection between Malthusianism and concepts of racial inferiority. The inferior race, in their view, would be driven to the wall.[6] Like Malthus himself, however, they lacked a framework of ideas to demonstrate convincingly that the survival of one group of people over another was part of a cosmic plan of progressive development. The contribution of Darwinism, therefore, in its implication of cosmic advantages in the disappearance of "lower races" in the struggle for existence, was to make the

Darwinian Revolution (London, 1959), p. 343; and George W. Stocking, *Race, Culture, and Evolution: Essays in the History of Anthropology* (New York, 1968), p. 113.

5. Himmelfarb, *Darwin,* pp. 134–136.
6. See Chapter Five, above.

prospect of Negro extinction under freedom more palatable than if it were considered an unavoidable tragedy, a regrettable necessity, or at best, a convenient solution to the American race problem.

The principal barrier to the acceptance of Darwinian principles by the theorists of American racialism stemmed from differences of opinion about the origins of the races. The polygenist views of the American school of ethnology were, strictly speaking, incompatible with the Darwinian "developmental hypothesis," because the latter derived contemporary human races from a common ancestor. But if Darwinism undermined the theory that blacks were at a competitive disadvantage because they were created a few thousand years ago as a permanently inferior species, it did not foreclose the possibility that they had evolved through a process of natural selection, over hundreds of thousands or even millions of years, into a variety of the genus homo which stood as far below the whites in capacities necessary for survival and progress as any adherent of the American School could have wished. Darwinism was not even logically incompatible with the basic polygenist notion that Negroes were—or were in the process of becoming—a separate species. By denying the permanence of species, Darwinism made it possible to argue that blacks and whites had diverged in their evolution to such an extent that their differences could now be considered specific. Few went this far, however; a more popular and plausible approach was to argue that blacks were an "incipient species." By such devices, the essence of polygenist thinking about race was preserved in a Darwinian framework. Hence all the deductions from comparative anatomy and physiology supporting the biological basis of polygenist racialism were still valid; one simply altered the explanation for these differences in accordance with natural selection and a longer time span. It was not even necessary to sacrifice the fundamental antebellum concept of the persistence of Negro inferiority through all recorded history; for according to the Darwinian theory, a few thousand years would not be enough to bring about basic changes in racial character.[7]

7. See George Stocking's illuminating discussion of "The Persistence of Polygenist Thought in Post-Darwinian Anthropology," in *Race, Culture,*

In 1866 Josiah C. Nott, high priest of the American School of ethnology, affirmed this potential compatibility between Darwinism and much of the polygenist case for Negro inferiority. "It is true," he wrote, "that Lamarck, Geoffroy Saint-Hilaire, Darwin and other naturalists, have contended for the gradual change or development of organic forms from physical causes, yet even this school requires millions of years for their theory, and would not controvert the facts and deductions I have laid down." He went on to argue that the extension of the time for human life on earth had in no way weakened the case for the unchangeability of the Negro during the historical era. "Sir Charles Lyell, who opposed me strongly a few years ago," he wrote, had now accepted the view "that man must have been on earth, not as commonly supposed six thousand years, *but something like one hundred thousand.* . . . This opinion is now the generally received one in Europe. Granting this antiquity for man, we know nothing beyond his *modern* history." The known, modern history of the Negro, Nott reiterated, revealed no racial progress or intellectual development, and thus, for all practical purposes, permanent black inferiority remained the dominant scientific hypothesis. In the course of reaffirming the case for biological racism in a somewhat altered intellectual setting, Nott repeated his prewar prediction that emancipation would lead to Negro extermination.[8]

Nott's concession to the rising tide of evolutionary thought was not the first indication of an American effort to apply Darwin's principles to ethnological questions. Three years earlier, in the midst of the Civil War, Charles Loring Brace, a New York philanthropist, had published an impressive book entitled *The Races of the Old World: A Manual of Ethnology.* Brace, a wartime emancipationist, believed that Darwin had provided the ammunition that would rout the advocates of plural origins and destroy the ethnological argument for slavery. But after present-

---

and Evolution, pp. 42–68. For Darwinist descriptions of human races as "incipient species," see Joseph Le Conte, "The Race Problem in the South" in *Man and the State: Studies in Applied Sociology* (New York, 1892) , p. 372; and Charles E. Woodruff, *The Expansion of Races* (New York, 1909) , p. 7.

8. Josiah C. Nott, *The Negro Race: Its Ethnology and History* (Mobile, 1866) , pp. 12–13, 24.

ing the Darwinian case for the differentiation of the races by natural selection, Brace ended up with a view of racial differences which was far from egalitarian in its implications. Branches of the original human stock, he argued, had migrated from a common center into varying climatic regions. After a long period, "each variety becomes adapted to its country, and climate, and pursuits: and all the spaces for human varieties are filled up. Thus the principle of inheritance comes to make the variety permanent." As a result, the human races had become *"Permanent Types"*—"unchanged in the historical period, each with its own features, its habits, its peculiar diseases." Although he did not rule out the possibility of *"changes of type,"* or even the eventual emergence of a single human variety, he regarded such changes as unlikely in the near future. Rather, he saw "each group" as having for the time being "its peculiar office and duty in the world's development."[9]

Perhaps the clearest indication of how little practical difference there was between Brace's Darwinism and the polygenism he was attacking came out in his discussion of racial mixture. He acknowledged that there would be "a difficulty in two very diverse types crossing at first with permanent fertility" but denied that this problem should be described as one of "hybridity," or the crossing of species. "If individuals of two very different races intermarried," he contended, "their mutual differences and varying constitutions would naturally render the surviving of the first offspring somewhat doubtful. . . . Each parent is adapted to a different and peculiar condition of temperature, soil, and climate. The offspring, if it shares these adaptations equally, must be in so far unadapted to its climate and circumstances. That is, a half-blood mulatto in our Northern states, in so far as he has a negro constitution, is unfitted for our climate; in the Southern, he is equally unadapted, from his white blood, to the climate there, and it may be centuries before he becomes suited to either." Surely this was as good an argument against miscegenation as one derived, strictly speaking, from con-

9. Charles L. Brace, *The Races of the Old World: A Manual of Ethnology* (New York, 1870), pp. 502–503, 511–512, and *passim*. (Originally published in 1863.)

cepts of hybridity; and in assessing the future of the mulatto, Brace conceded that he "may die out, as the Indian dies out, from the wear and tear and contact with a different and grasping race." He concluded in general that "there is nothing in the gradual diminution and destruction of a savage or inferior race in contact with a more civilized and powerful which is 'mysterious' . . . or which has anything to do with the subject of hybridity. The first gifts of civilization are naturally fatal to a barbarous people, from the fact that their constitution and habits have been formed under entirely different circumstances. . . ."[10]

Brace's pioneering effort to develop a Darwinist ethnology in opposition to the American School, although animated to some degree by antislavery humanitarianism, had demonstrated that most of the hierarchical assumptions of the polygenists could be justified just as well, if not better, in Darwinian terms.

III

The potentialities of Darwinism as a rationale for American racist attitudes were soon apparent. In an essay published at the end of the Civil War, Thomas H. Huxley, Darwin's foremost British disciple and defender, addressed himself directly to the evolutionary meaning of emancipation in the United States. He questioned what he took to be the radical abolitionist claim that blacks were equal or superior to whites, and maintained that "no rational man, cognizant of the facts," could deny that the Negro was inherently inferior. Consequently, "it is simply incredible that, when all his disabilities are removed, and our prognathous relative has a fair field and no favor, as well as no oppressor, he will be able to compete successfully with his bigger-brained and smaller-jawed rival, in a contest which is to be carried on by thoughts and not by bites." But the natural inability of the blacks to reach the "highest places in the hierarchy of civilization" was no argument against emancipation: ". . . whatever

10. *Ibid.*, p. 490.

the position of stable equilibrium into which the laws of social gravitation may bring the negro, all responsibility for the result will henceforward lie between Nature and him. The white man may wash his hands of it, and the Caucasian conscience be void of reproach for evermore."[11] If this can be taken as the Darwinist evaluation of Negro prospects after emancipation, then it is clear that the new evolutionary theories fitted in perfectly with the disposition of many Northerners to remove the black man's "disabilities" and give him a competitive chance, not because of a firm conviction that equal opportunity would lead to a demonstration of biological equality, but merely with the expectation that it would permit him to find his "natural level," wherever it might be.[12]

Although Darwinism was now available to buttress prevailing American assumptions about racial hierarchy and the consequence of interracial competition, the beginning of the Reconstruction period was characterized by something resembling a brief moratorium on explicit and systematic efforts to apply ethnological theories to the discussion of long-range Negro prospects. The crude belief that blacks would quickly die out after emancipation because they would not work without compulsion was often expressed by white Southerners in 1865 and 1866, but such expectations obviously failed to jibe with reality and tended to be forgotten in the political struggle which soon developed over the Negro's immediate status.[13] Many Northerners, as we have already seen, also entered the postwar era with a strong suspicion that the blacks would not survive emancipation. In his post-mortem assessment of the thinking behind Northern Reconstruction policy, Albion W. Tourgée referred to the persistence

11. Thomas H. Huxley, "Emancipation—Black and White [1865]," in *Science and Education* (New York, 1896) , pp. 66–67.

12. See Chapter Six, above.

13. John Richard Dennett, a Northern journalist who traveled in the South in 1865–1866, found many white Southerners who professed to believe that the blacks would soon become extinct. (See *The South As It Is, 1865–1866*, ed. Henry M. Christman [New York, 1965], pp. 6, 15, 103, 191, 366.) Southern predictions of the impending disappearance of the Negro are also described in Vernon L. Wharton, *The Negro in Mississippi, 1865–1890* (Chapel Hill, 1947) , pp. 53–55; and Joel Williamson, *After Slavery: The Negro in South Carolina During Reconstruction, 1861–1877* (Chapel Hill, 1965) , pp. 247–248.

of "the belief in the Northern mind that the Negro would disappear beneath the glare of civilization," and added that there was "a half unconscious feeling that such a disappearance would be a very simple and easy solution to a troubling question."[14] Here again, however, the pressure of immediate problems—such as how to help the blacks in ways that would ensure the loyalty of the South—tended to force such speculations into the background.

A few Northern or pro-Northern observers in the late 1860s attempted to predict the ultimate destiny of the American Negro in Darwinist terms. Two of the most interesting speculations of this kind were made by visiting French liberals who strongly sympathized with Radical Republicanism. Auguste Laugel, a geologist who made a trip to the United States during the war, flatly predicted in an 1866 book that the Negro race was "destined to disappear in the South," but still he argued in favor of a Constitutional amendment to give blacks equality before the law. "Since the days of the black race are numbered, and fatal laws condemn it to die out, or rather be transformed," he wrote, "it should be spared at least from new outrages and new injustices."[15]

In 1869 Georges Clemenceau, then a journalist reporting on American affairs, defended Radical Reconstruction as a sound application of Darwinian principles. Now that the Negro rights had been written into the Constitution, the blacks "must gird up their loins and struggle for their existence, in Darwin's phrase, for their physical as well as their moral existence. In a word they must become men." He was not at all certain they would succeed: "In this ruthless struggle for existence carried on by human society, those who are weaker physically, intellectually, and morally must in the end yield to the stronger. . . . If then the black man cannot successfully compete with the white man, he is fated to be the victim of that natural selection which is constantly operating under our eyes in spite of everything, and he

14. Albion W. Tourgée, *An Appeal to Caesar* (New York, 1884) , p. 127.
15. Auguste Laugel, *The United States During the Civil War,* ed. Allan Nevins (Bloomington, Ind., 1961) , pp. 296–297.

must eventually go under, in the more or less distant future."[16]

One of the first Americans to discuss the freedmen's prospect for survival in explicitly Darwinian language was the novelist John W. De Forest, who served as a Freedmen's Bureau officer in South Carolina from 1866 to 1868. Convinced that "the Negro as he is, no matter how well educated, is not the mental equal of the European," he saw the "low down Negro" as passing "into sure and deserved oblivion." The superior Negro, however, "will struggle longer with the law of natural selection; and he may eventually hold a portion of this continent against the vigorous and terrible Caucasian race; that portion being probably those lowlands where the white can not or will not labor."[17]

The question whether the blacks were likely to survive "the struggle for existence" that had been inaugurated by emancipation could be decided—or so many people thought—by reference to statistics from the United States census. But the 1870 census, the first after emancipation, did not provide conclusive results. Since it appeared to demonstrate that the black population had grown in the previous decade at a rate slower than during the slave era and at less than half the rate of the whites, its findings might have signified the beginning of a trend that would accelerate until it led to a positive decrease in the number of Negroes. But there were obvious imponderables; it was possible that the Negro population would grow more slowly under freedom, but at a steady rate, or that the special vicissitudes of emancipation had taken a toll among blacks that would not be repeated in subsequent decades.[18]

There was, however, some effort on the part of Southern opponents of Radical Reconstruction to buttress their case with data

16. Georges Clemenceau, *American Reconstruction*, . . . (New York, 1928), pp. 297–298.

17. John W. De Forest, *A Union Officer in the Reconstruction*, ed. James H. Croushore and David M. Potter (New Haven, 1948), pp. 117, 131.

18. According to Tourgée (*Appeal to Caesar*, p. 128), the census of 1870 left "the matter [of the Negro's ultimate survival] in doubt." The census showed that the white population had increased approximately 25 per cent in the decade 1860–1870, as compared to a black increase of only about 10 per cent. It was later determined, however, that approximately half a million blacks had been overlooked by the census takers. (See S. J. Holmes, *The Negro's Struggle for Survival: A Study in Human Ecology* [Berkeley, 1937], pp. 14 and 288 [table].)

from the census. A writer in the *Southern Review,* a journal of unreconstructed pro-Southern opinion, argued in 1874 that the post-emancipation behavior of the Negro had established a trend to extinction that could be reversed only if blacks ceased to press for equality and put themselves under the domination of Southern whites. Although the census continued to show "some annual gross increase of the Africans, the *rate* of increase, always less than that of the whites, has steadily declined." If blacks did not mend their ways, the writer warned, "the rate of increase will lessen until it changes to a growing rate of decrease," with the result that "the African race will go on to extinction."[19] Three years later, at the end of Reconstruction, Charles Gayarré likewise contended that the disappearance of the Negro was the probable result of current trends, and indicated that such an eventuality would not be surprising given "the mysterious law of providence which seems to compel certain races to move from their cradles . . . to hunt as it were after other races which providence had originally placed at a long distance, and which in the end it brings together, in order that one should wipe the other out of existence."[20] Still, it is significant that neither Gayarré nor the writer in the *Southern Review* complacently assumed, like some Northern prophets of extinction, that the Negro would be "wiped out of existence" gradually and through "natural" causes. Both thought it possible that Negro assertiveness would lead to a violent race war long before such a trend had run its course, which meant that the process might be radically foreshortened.[21]

All predictions that the black population would quietly fade away were thrown into a cocked hat when the census of 1880 appeared to demonstrate that the rate of increase of Southern Negroes was substantially greater than that of the whites.[22] This

19. "The African in the United States," *Southern Review,* XV (January, 1874) , 134, and *passim.*
20. Charles Gayarré, "The Southern Question," *North American Review,* CXXV (November–December, 1877) , 485.
21. "The African in the United States," 148; Gayarré, "Southern Question," 497.
22. According to the census, the white population in the Southern states increased by only 29 per cent from 1870 to 1880, while the black population increased 34 per cent. Since the accuracy of the census count, particularly of

astonishing and alarming situation led Dr. Edward W. Gilliam to write in *Popular Science Monthly* in 1883 that the nation was facing a racial cataclysm. After compensating for probable errors in the census of 1870, he estimated that the black population had grown approximately thirty per cent in a single decade. He projected the current rate of increase and foresaw a Negro population of 192 million by 1980. That the blacks with all their deficiencies and disadvantages should have increased so rapidly could be accounted for only by "the remarkable fecundity of the African." Here indeed was an ominous note for racial Darwinists, because fecundity was one of the most important characteristics which decided the struggle for existence in the animal kingdom. Was it possible that the blacks with all their alleged individual weaknesses would overcome the whites, at least in the South, because of a greater reproductive capacity? Gilliam's prediction was that a rise in the black proportion of the Southern population would lead Negroes to demand equality but that the whites would use all the repressive power at their command to hold them in subservience. This effort would succeed for a time, but there would eventually come "a point at which mere numbers must prevail over wealth, intelligence, and prestige combined." "This dark, swelling, muttering mass along the social horizon, gathering strength with education, and ambitious to rise, will grow increasingly restless and sullen under repression, until at length, conscious through numbers of superior power, it will assert that power destructively, and, bursting forth like an angry furious crowd, avenge in tumult and disorder, the social law broken against them." The only way to avert such a catastrophe, Gilliam insisted, was to embark immediately on a massive program to colonize blacks abroad.[23]

The following year a writer in the *North American Review* took note of the same facts, but he ruled out the possibility of colonization and argued calmly that white Americans would simply have to reconcile themselves, not only to the prospect of

blacks, is open to serious question for both 1870 and 1880, such figures are historically significant mainly because of the polemical uses to which they were put by racial theorists and propagandists.

23. Gilliam, "The African in the United States," 433–436, 441, 443.

eventual black domination in the deep South, but also to the ultimate absorption of the whites who remained in that area through amalgamation.[24] Such detachment was rare, however, because most people who accepted Gilliam's analysis of the situation believed that whites would never consent to amalgamation and that black rule could come only through victory in a bloody war of the races. One of those who regarded the prospect with foreboding was the Reverend J. Benson Hamilton, pastor of the Cornell Memorial Methodist Church of New York City. Hamilton, a leading exponent of racial separation within the Northern Methodist Church, was doing battle in the late 1880s with a declining Radical faction that favored Bishop Gilbert Haven's policy of mixed congregations in the South. In the course of his argument for the legitimacy of racial prejudice among Christians, Hamilton pointed to the danger that Southern whites would be overwhelmed by the growing Negro population unless they maintained all barriers against mixing of the races. Using Gilliam's figures, Hamilton predicted that within seventy years Southern blacks would number fifty million. Since this was an illiterate, licentious, and intemperate population, was it any wonder that "race preference and prejudice has built a wall between the two races in the South" that was bound to be strengthened in the future? But even though Hamilton defended racial discrimination, he did not believe that such a policy could guarantee white supremacy for very long. "The whites," he predicted, "will be outnumbered in a constantly increasing majority, if the black vote is counted; if uncounted or suppressed a bloody war of the races will inevitably result."[25]

Another observer who took Gilliam's prognostications seriously was Albion W. Tourgée. In *An Appeal to Caesar,* published in 1884, Tourgée summarized Gilliam's case for the likelihood of race war in the South and reluctantly agreed with it. He then

24. Charles Gardiner in "The Future of the Negro," 78–81. I have been unable to find out anything about Gardiner and am not even sure that he was white (the symposium had contributors from both races). On the basis of internal evidence, however, I suspect that he was a peculiarly dispassionate white observer.

25. J. Benson Hamilton, *Common Sense and the Color Problem* (New York, n.d.), pp. 11–12.

pointed to the comparatively short-range prospect that by 1900 *"each of the states lying between Maryland and Texas will have a colored majority within its borders; and we shall have eight minor republics of the Union in which either the colored race will rule or a majority will be disfranchised!"* As a militant egalitarian, Tourgée could not reconcile himself to the second possibility, but he was fully aware that any attempt to give full rights to incipient black majorities was liable to provoke the adamant and violent resistance of Southern whites; for Tourgée's bitter experiences during Reconstruction had led him to draw pessimistic conclusions about the strength and durability of racial prejudice. He referred in *An Appeal to Caesar* to "the almost ineradicable belief of the white people of the South that the Negro is an inferior species of the human family and not fit or capable to exercise joint-sovereignty with the white race." Leaping from this particular case to the apparently universal phenomenon of racial conflict, he contended that virulent antipathy had always existed "in history when two races, separated by an insurmountable barrier, have occupied the same territory, neither being subject to the other." He was uncertain whether prejudice was "a natural instinct or an acquired habit of mind," but he was convinced of its tenacity. He quoted Gilliam's description of the indomitable sentiment which prevented intermarriage and social equality in the South, and he sadly admitted that there was nothing here with which he could quarrel. "Race prejudice, if it be possible to overcome it at all . . . ," he concluded, "will only disappear after the lapse not of years but of generations and centuries. At present it is not likely to diminish perceptibly in strength and influence." If the North's leading white exponent of racial egalitarianism could come to such despairing conclusions in the 1880s, it seems reasonable to conclude that the abolitionist dream of racial fraternity had by this time lost most of its power and plausibility.[26]

Still, Tourgée was unwilling to give up his long struggle for equality. He acknowledged that the growth of the black population, when combined with the powerful prejudices of the whites,

26. Tourgée, *Appeal to Caesar*, pp. 135, 79, 89, 91–92, 98.

made race war almost inevitable. "If . . . the existing influences and forces which govern and control Southern life shall continue in their present relation," he wrote, "the point of general conflict must be reached sooner or later." But he held out one last hope of averting an interracial blood bath—Federal aid to education, nationally administered. He did not anticipate an end to all racial antagonism once the landscape south of the Potomac was dotted with schoolhouses, but he contended that the South's only hope was "through the channel of universal intelligence." Education would not eradicate racial antipathies, at least not for a long time, but it might convince Southerners of both races "of the mutual danger, peril, disaster, that must attend continued oppression or sudden uprising." In other words, Southerners would learn to keep their prejudices in check if their newly cultivated rational faculties told them that their own safety and survival depended on restraint.[27]

An Appeal to Caesar was probably the most profound discussion of the American racial situation to appear in the 1880s; certainly it was the most valuable fruit of the speculation provoked by the census of 1880. But in the final analysis its argument did not quite hang together. Either its assessment of the problem made the situation appear more hopeless than it really was or the recommended cure was obviously inadequate. Tourgée was clearly of two minds on the prospects for racial justice and harmony. As a realist who had seen Southern prejudice in action, he understood that the whites would resist equality for blacks unless positively coerced into accepting it; but as an optimistic humanitarian, he clung to the hope that somehow education alone would convince racists that they must behave in a decent and rational way.[28]

A belief that the Southern black population was growing more

27. *Ibid.*, pp. 106, 283.
28. Tourgée eventually became disillusioned with education as a solution to the race problem. At the end of his life he wrote President Theodore Roosevelt that his earlier faith in education "was a genuine fool's notion. I sincerely believed at the time that education and Christianity were infallible solvents of all the evils that have resulted from the white man's claim of individual superiority. Today I am ashamed to have been that sort of fool." (Quoted in Roy F. Dibble, *Albion W. Tourgée* [New York, 1921], p. 126.)

rapidly than the white continued to color discussion of future race relations until the end of the decade. In 1889 Philip Alexander Bruce, a Virginia historian and son of a planter who had owned five hundred slaves, published an influential study, *The Plantation Negro as a Freeman,* in which he tried to reconcile his basic argument that the Negro had degenerated since emancipation with the prevailing notion of a rapid increase in the black population. Bruce maintained that despite a decline in their moral character and productive capacity, blacks for the time being were saved from the extinction they deserved by the continued surplus of fertile land in the South. "For half a century at least," he wrote, "the blacks of the South will continue to expand numerically at an alarming rate, because, during that period of time, the soil must remain comparatively cheap and abundant, and the negro be in sufficient demand as a laborer to supply him with all that is necessary to his existence." Ultimately, however, the growth in the black population would be checked: Bruce discerned a tendency to divide up the land into small holdings cultivated exclusively by the white owners, and when this new agricultural economy matured, "a strong pressure would be brought to bear to force the masses of the [black] race back upon the poorest land where it would be so difficult to earn a subsistence that the growth of the black population would not only cease, but a decline in numerical strength would even set in." In the meantime the blacks would constitute a grave social danger and a blight on Southern prosperity. Even given the South's present dependence on black labor it would be much better if the Negro population were suddenly "withdrawn." "It would be better, indeed, for that entire section to be relegated to its primeval condition with a view to its being settled again exclusively by a white population, just as if it were a virgin territory, than for it to maintain its present position through the manual exertions of the blacks, but with individuals of that race increasing so rapidly as to threaten the extinction in the end of every element of prosperity, with no hope of subsequent revival."[29]

29. Philip A. Bruce, *The Plantation Negro as a Freeman* (New York and London, 1889) , pp. 254–255, 261–262.

Bruce's theories presented racists with a serviceable reconciliation between the traditional notion that blacks could not survive under freedom and the statistical evidence that they were increasing. They also provided a way of sharply distinguishing between population increase and moral and industrial progress. Gilliam had conceded so much to the black capacity for self-improvement that he had made white prejudice seem somehow unjust and irrational, despite his contention that it was "instinctive" and ineradicable. Bruce had clearly put the case for a "black peril" in the South on a firmer foundation.

IV

A new census soon altered the basis of discussion and made Bruce's concept of black degeneracy and "reversion to type" seem more relevant than his analysis of population trends. In 1891, General Francis A. Walker, a leading Northern economist and a former superintendent of the United States census, used the latest figures on the black population to demonstrate that the racial nightmares of men like Gilliam were pure fantasy. The 1890 census, Walker pointed out in an article, revealed that the blacks were in fact increasing at a rate substantially below that of the whites and were concentrating in a diminishing area of the deep South. These figures indicated "that the anticipation which so many Americans have formed . . . , regarding a large continuous increase of that element, up to some ultimate very high point, have little foundation in recent experience." The apparent increase between 1870 and 1880, he contended, had been due to the fact that the census takers had overlooked many blacks in 1870. Not only was it true that the blacks were biologically unsuited to all but the most tropical regions of the United States, but "there is much reason to believe that a race that is limited in its range becomes, by that very fact, subject also to important restrictions on its capabilities of sustained increase within that range." He foresaw an increasing concentration of Negroes in the deep South and no very rapid growth there; indeed he held out the prospect of a tendency toward rapid extinction if economic or social developments should for any reason bring a fall in a "very high birth rate" then maintaining a precarious edge over "a very high death rate." Significantly, Walker did not even consider the possibility that somehow the death rate might be lowered.[30]

Further comfort for Americans who were frightened by the black-population peril was provided by James Bryce, a distinguished British student of American institutions (*The American Commonwealth,* 1888) and a thoroughgoing racist of the imperial school. "In proving that the colored population grows more slowly than the white," Bryce wrote in the *North American Review,* "the census just taken relieves . . . a source of anxiety. It is now clear that the negro, regarded as a factor in the whole community, is becoming far weaker; nor is the prospect likely to be arrested . . ." Soon there would be little need for Southerners to suppress the Negro vote because there would not be enough Negroes to constitute a serious political force.[31]

The 1890 census coincided with the full triumph of Darwinism in American thought, and thus the statistical evidence that blacks were failing to hold their own readily fitted into a thesis of "the survival of the fittest" in an inevitable "struggle for existence" among human races. As a result, the 1890s saw an unparalleled outburst of racist speculation on the impending disappearance of the American Negro. From the most reputable

30. Francis A. Walker, "The Colored Race in the United States," *Forum,* XI (July, 1891) , 506–507. Frederick J. Brown soon demonstrated statistically that Walker and others who maintained that the tendency of Negro migration was southward were misreading the census. Brown showed in *The Northward Migration of the Colored Population: A Statistical Study* (Baltimore, 1897) that the direction of movement was actually to the North and that blacks were being drawn from the deep South by the greater economic and educational opportunities that existed elsewhere. Walker was correct, however, in his contention that the 1890 census showed a Negro rate of population gain that was below that of the whites. But the census figures of 13.9 per cent increase for the blacks as compared to 24.86 per cent for the entire population (which Walker cited) are misleading, not only because the rate of gain for the entire population included a large number of immigrants, but also because, as in the case of the census of 1870, later studies revealed a probable undercount of blacks, this time of about 275,000. (See Holmes, *The Negro's Struggle for Survival,* p. 228.)

31. James Bryce, "Thoughts on the Negro Problem," *North American Review,* CLIII (December, 1891) , 659.

sources came confident predictions of black extinction through natural processes, and few who thus consigned an entire race to oblivion could conceal their satisfaction.

In a study of "the ethnological aspects" of "The Race Problem in the South," published in 1892, Joseph Le Conte, whose contributions to geology and biology had made him the South's most distinguished natural scientist, presented probably the decade's most sophisticated application of Darwinian theory to the American race problem. Le Conte affirmed that the "laws determining the effects of contact of species, races, varieties, etc., among animals," which "may be summed up under the formula, 'The struggle for life and the survival of the fittest,'" were "applicable to the races of men also." The destiny of weaker varieties was either "extinction . . . or else . . . relegation to a subordinate place in the economy of nature; the weaker is either destroyed or seeks safety by avoiding competition." A long discussion of how races improved themselves and why the mixture of such diverse types as whites and Negroes was contrary to the laws of nature followed; then Le Conte concluded: "For the lower races everywhere (leaving out slavery) there is eventually but one of two alternatives—viz., either extermination or mixture. But if mixture makes a feeble race, then this also is only a slower process of extermination." Was there then no "way of escape" for the lower races? The only way out, according to Le Conte, was through a special kind of amalgamation—not between pure specimens of such extreme types as the "Teuton" and the Negro, for such a mixture would produce "the worst results"—but rather between "marginal varieties of the primary races" who approached each other in characteristics. Le Conte did not spell out how such gradual melting down of the primary races by fusion around the edges could be applied to the American racial situation. Presumably the only thing that could save the American blacks from ultimate doom would be the importation of an intermediate racial group from, say, North Africa, to intermarry with both the blacks and the darker-skinned European immigrants.[32]

32. Le Conte, "The Race Problem in the South," in *Man and the State*, pp. 359, 365-374.

Another writer who examined Negro prospects in the light of science in the early 1890s was Dr. Eugene Rollin Corson, an erudite Savannah physician who contributed a paper on "The Vital Equation of the Colored Race and Its Future in the United States" to a *Festschrift* honoring his former professor at Cornell University. Unlike Le Conte, Corson provided specific data on the physical condition of American Negroes to support his general conclusions. On the basis of the 1890 census, he found that blacks were rapidly migrating southward, not just to seek a more congenial climate but principally to escape the unequal competition provided by a concentrated white population. He presented figures on the high black mortality rate and added that "many of these negroes, now rapidly passing away, are survivors of the old regime, where they were well cared for, and had reached at emancipation a safe age which kept them out of the struggle for life." The younger generations, deprived from birth of the paternalistic protection of slavery, were liable to succumb at an even greater rate to a variety of diseases which supposedly hit Negroes harder than whites. Corson maintained in answer to those who would attribute the high mortality rate, and especially infant mortality, to environmental conditions that similarly situated whites survived in much greater numbers. The excessive black death rate simply bore out "the teachings of ethnology and biology" about the anatomical and physiological inferiority of the Negro. Negroes also lacked the intelligence to care for themselves properly; once freed from the control of slaveholders they quickly reverted to savagery. Corson's final verdict was that the Negro race was destined to disappear, a victim of "the struggle for existence against a superior race." From a somewhat unorthodox position, he saw miscegenation as facilitating this process, although presumably not in the form of legalized intermarriage. "In the process of fusion and assimilation, there will be great loss of life, but there will be a Caucasianized element, becoming larger and larger up to a certain point . . . where it will be hard to trace the alien blood." All this would occur over a long period of time, during which the whites would be firmly in control; for there was "no ground for fear of any great clash between the races, so much dwelt upon by certain writers. This is a problem which will solve itself."[33]

A more thoroughgoing and detailed exposition of exactly how and why blacks were losing out in the struggle for existence came in the 1890s from Frederick L. Hoffman, a German-born insurance statistician who made an important analysis of Negro mortality. Hoffman's findings had great impact, not only because they were presented under the prestigious imprint of the American Economic Association but also because Hoffman's foreign origin allegedly made him unbiased. Actually, Hoffman was not an objective outside observer. Prior to his emergence as an authority on the Negro, he had spent several years in the United States, and as an immigrant trying to get ahead in the insurance business had undoubtedly learned to conform to the racial beliefs of his clients and associates. His racist predispositions, coupled with his mastery of the currently fashionable statistical approach to social problems, made his book, *Race Traits and Tendencies of the American Negro,* published in 1896, the most influential discussion of the race question to appear in the late nineteenth century.[34] As the black sociologist Kelly Miller noted somewhat ruefully in his review, Hoffman's study "may be regarded as the most important utterance on the subject since the publication of 'Uncle Tom's Cabin,' for the interest which the famous novel aroused in the realm of sentiment and generous feelings, the present work seems destined to awake in the field of science and exact inquiry."[35] *Race Traits and Tendencies of the American Negro* became a prized source of information and conclusions for anti-Negro writers for many years to come and also had the practical effect of helping to convince most white insurance companies that they should deny coverage to all Negroes on

33. Eugene Rollin Corson, "The Vital Equation of the Colored Race and Its Future in the United States," in *The Wilder Quarter-Century Book. A Collection of Original Papers Dedicated to Prof. Bert Green Wilder* (Ithaca, N.Y., 1893) , pp. 123, 124–127, 139, 164–165, 173–174.

34. For biographical information on Hoffman see *The National Cyclopedia of American Biography* (New York, 1948) , XXXIV, 66–67.

35. Kelly Miller, *A Review of Hoffman's Race Traits and Tendencies of the American Negro* (Washington, D.C., 1897) , p. 3.

the grounds that membership in the race by itself constituted an unacceptable actuarial risk.[36]

Hoffman presented the case for black degeneracy and impending extinction with teutonic thoroughness and with all the callous insensitivity characteristic of the quantification of social pathology during the heyday of social Darwinism. He first made his findings known in *Arena* magazine in 1892, stating that "the time will come, if it has not already come, when the negro, like the Indian, will be a vanishing race."[37]

In the book-length version, Hoffman emerged as an articulate philosopher of racial Darwinism who did not hesitate to point up the policy implications of his statistics. He suggested that previous efforts to improve "the condition of lower races" had failed because "racial traits and tendencies were almost entirely ignored." His own forthright conclusion was that racial characteristics "lie at the root of all social difficulties and problems." In his effort to present "a scientific and factual approach" to the race problem, Hoffman quickly disposed of Gilliam and the fear of black numerical supremacy by pointing to the census of 1890. The white population was outstripping the black through a radical increase in the Negro mortality rate since emancipation, he contended, explaining this phenomenon in terms of ineradicable "race traits and tendencies." Most of the diseases that wreaked havoc among blacks were not simply the product of environmental conditions. Some were the result of "inferior organisms and constitutional weaknesses, which . . . is [*sic*] one

36. In a letter to Edward Eggleston, dated August 5, 1910, Hoffman stated that, partly as a result of his findings, "our company [the Prudential] has not for a number of years insured Negroes except in cases where we were compelled to do so in compliance with the Law." (Edward Eggleston, *The Ultimate Solution of the American Negro Problem* [Boston, 1913], p. 272.) Rayford W. Logan refers to Hoffman's influence on the practices of white insurance companies in *The Betrayal of the Negro: From Rutherford B. Hayes to Woodrow Wilson,* New York, 1965) ; see p. 324. Eggleston (a Virginian, not the Indiana novelist) was only one of a number of racial propagandists who were strongly influenced by Hoffman. Among the others were Paul M. Barringer, whose ideas are discussed in this chapter, and William B. Smith (*The Color Line* [New York, 1905]), who is treated in Chapter Nine, below.

37. Frederick L. Hoffman, "Vital Statistics of the Negro," *Arena,* V (April, 1892) , 542.

of the most pronounced race characteristics of the American negro." Others resulted from "the fact of an immense amount of immorality which is a race trait, and of which scrofula, syphilis, and even consumption are the inevitable consequences." The Negro had been in good physical condition at the time of emancipation but had steadily degenerated ever since: "The tendency of the race has been downward. This tendency if unchecked must in the end, lead to a still greater mortality, a lesser degree of economic and social efficiency, a lower standard of nurture and a diminishing excess of births over deaths. A combination of these traits and tendencies must in the end cause the extinction of the race."[38]

Hoffman flatly asserted that religion and education had made little or no contribution to "the moral progress of the race," because such external influences did not affect basic hereditary characteristics. More significant than the decline in black illiteracy was the rise in the Negro crime rate. As for Negro poverty, it was not the result of white discrimination or lack of opportunity but stemmed directly from an innate tendency toward "crime and immorality." Hoffman drew inspiration from the hardest school of social Darwinism and condemned philanthropists who would interfere with the struggle for existence by seeking what amounted to the artificial preservation of the unfit. Education and philanthropy had made the blacks even more dependent than under slavery. Their only hope—and it was a very slight one—was to struggle without white help of any kind against the most adverse conditions. In the unlikely event that they acquired sexual purity and economic efficiency through their own efforts, they could be expected to survive and develop; otherwise they were condemned to a lingering racial death.[39]

Hoffman's conclusions won quick and general acceptance from leading students of American demography. In 1900 Walter F. Willcox, the New England-born Chief Statistician of the United States Census Bureau, assured the delegates to the Montgomery,

38. Frederick L. Hoffman, "Race Traits and Tendencies of the American Negro." *Publications of the American Economic Association*, 1st Ser., XI (August, 1896), v–vi, 1–3, 66, 95, 176, and *passim*.

39. *Ibid.*, pp. 236, 241–242, 328–329, and *passim*.

Alabama, conference on Race Problems of the South that all the evidence seemed to demonstrate that "the Negroes will continue to become, as they are now becoming, a steadily smaller proportion of the population." Looking farther ahead, Willcox predicted that "the race will follow the fate of the Indians, that the great majority will disappear before the whites, and that the remnant found capable of elevation to the level of the white man's civilization will ultimately be merged and lost in the lower classes of the whites, leaving almost no trace to mark their former existence." The blacks would succumb, he suggested, to the effects of the "disease, vice, and profound discouragement" that generally accompanied the feeble efforts of a "lower people" to compete with their racial superiors. Like Hoffman, he stressed the increase of "sexual vice" and crime as factors leading to black extinction, in addition to constitutional weakness.[40]

A similar prediction was made at the same conference by Dr. Paul B. Barringer, a professor of medicine and chairman of the faculty of the University of Virginia. Barringer's defamation of the Negro was more strident and uncompromising than Willcox's, and like Hoffman he went out of his way to demonstrate the futility of philanthropic efforts to uplift the blacks. In his opinion the only "intelligent, upright, honest" Negroes were ex-slaves; the rest were so much human rubbish to be sacrificed on the altar of evolution. "Survival of the fittest" also implied "the death of the unfit." The Negro had been artificially introduced into the United States as a slave, and it was only the protection of servitude that had allowed him to survive until emancipation. Barringer concluded that "all things point to the fact that the Negro as a race is reverting to barbarism with the inordinate criminality and degradation of that state. It seems, moreover, that he is doomed at no distant day to ultimate extinction." An open apologist for the most repressive kind of racial policies he had in effect succeeded in translating the proslavery racial argument into turn-of-the-century evolutionary terminology.[41]

40. Southern Society for the Promotion of the Study of Race Conditions and Problems in the South, *Race Problems of the South: Proceedings of the First Annual Conference* (Richmond, Va., 1900), pp. 155–156.

41. *Ibid.*, pp. 185, 193.

In another address of the same year—this one to an assemblage of Southern physicians—Barringer developed more fully the scientific side of his argument. Once again following Hoffman's example, he emphasized the newly recognized role of heredity in human affairs, demonstrating how the Darwinian intellectual revolution had led to the conviction that heredity was the basic determinant of social problems—a belief that was soon to culminate in the eugenics movement. Barringer argued in *The American Negro: His Past and Future* that "sociological problems are in most cases biological problems," because "the ontogeny is the repetition of the phylogeny" and "the life history is the repetition of the race history." The inborn characteristics of the Negro had been formed by natural selection during "ages of degradation" in Africa and his savage traits could not have been altered in any significant way by a mere two centuries of proximity to Caucasian civilization in America. Thus his present "reversion to type" was understandable. Lacking the discipline of slavery, "the young negro of the South . . . is reverting through hereditary forces to savagery."[42]

The historian Joseph A. Tillinghast applied the same Darwinian concepts of racial heredity to Negro history in his study *The Negro in Africa and America,* published by the American Economic Association in 1902. Describing the black man's African background in a way that was to influence a generation of scholars, he argued that the only way racial heredity could be changed was by "slow infinitesimal degrees" through the process of "selection, which tends to accumulate advantageous variation in offspring and to eliminate unfavorable ones." It was vain to think that heredity could be "manipulated by purposive human devices." The Negro character had been formed in Africa, a region which supposedly showed an uninterrupted history of stagnation, inefficiency, ignorance, cannibalism, sexual licence, and superstition. The climate, according to Tillinghast, had been a major factor determining the Negro's unfortunate bio-

42. Paul B. Barringer, *The American Negro: His Past and Future* (Raleigh, N.C., 1900), pp. 3, 5, 14–15. The general impact of hereditarianism on American thought is described in Mark H. Haller, *Eugenics: Hereditarian Attitudes in American Thought* (New Brunswick, N.J., 1963).

logical inheritance: "It is obvious that in West Africa natural selection could not have tended to evolve great industrial capacity and aptitude, simply because these were not necessary to survival. Where a cold climate and poor natural productiveness threaten constant destruction to those who cannot or will not put forth persistent effort, selection operates to eliminate them, and preserve the efficient. In torrid and bountiful West Africa, however, the conditions of existence have for ages been too easy to select the industrially efficient and reject the inefficient." Similarly, the alleged sexual promiscuity of the blacks could also be explained as a product of natural selection. A high mortality rate had always existed in Africa because of wars, slavery, famine, and the neglect of children, Tillinghast argued, and therefore a high birth rate was also necessary—hence polygamy, promiscuity, and a general lack of sexual purity. With such a background, it was no wonder that "an overwhelming majority of the race in its new struggle for existence under the exacting conditions of American industry is seriously handicapped by inherited characteristics."[43]

By 1900 Darwinism provided the basis for a necessary reformulation of the set of racist concepts originally developed in the middle of the nineteenth century as a rationale for slavery. The "ethnological" defenders of servitude had of course anticipated "reversion to savagery" and ultimate black extinction as the fruit of emancipation but had lacked a world view that would make such developments part of nature's plan for continuing biological progress. It is doubtful, moreover, that apologists for slavery would have grasped at Darwinism even if it had been available. Since they were defending a set of fixed relationships that they hoped would remain unchanged forever, they were prone to be uncomfortable with any application of evolutionary theory to human society. What was more, the view that elimination of the blacks through direct competition with whites was a necessary and salutary working out of nature's plan was actually an argument against slavery, as its use in rudimentary form by proto-Darwinist free-soil theorists had clearly demonstrated. Ra-

43. Joseph A. Tillinghast, "The Negro in Africa and America," *Publications of the American Economic Association*, 3d Ser., III (May, 1902), i–ii, 2, 29–30, 64–65, 193.

cial Darwinism, therefore, was a philosophy appropriate to anti-Negro thinkers during what Pierre L. van den Berghe has called the postemancipation "competitive" stage of race relations.[44] Its function was to justify a policy of repression and neglect. Coming in the wake of the supposed "failure" of blacks during Reconstruction, it not only served to underline the alleged futility of the kind of policies that the radicals had espoused but even raised doubts whether the blacks should receive any help at all from paternalistic white philanthropists and reformers. Furthermore, it constituted a convenient rationale for new and more overtly oppressive racial policies. If the blacks were a degenerating race with no future, the problem ceased to be one of how to prepare them for citizenship or even how to make them more productive and useful members of the community. The new prognosis pointed rather to the need to segregate or quarantine a race liable to be a source of contamination and social danger to the white community, as it sank ever deeper into the slough of disease, vice, and criminality.

There was, of course, a terrible truth in the figures demonstrating black "degeneracy"; to the extent that they were valid they constituted a powerful indictment of white injustice. But few whites read them that way. By appealing to a simplistic Darwinian or hereditarian formula, white Americans could make their crimes against humanity appear as contributions to the inevitable unfolding of biological destiny.

44. Pierre L. van den Berghe, *Race and Racism: A Comparative Perspective* (New York, 1967), pp. 25–34.

Chapter Nine

•

The Negro as Beast:
Southern Negrophobia
at the Turn of the Century

THE CONCLUSIONS OF "experts" like Hoffman, Willcox, and Tillinghast were widely accepted as the fruit of disinterested scholarly inquiry—which in itself reveals how ready white Americans were by the end of the century to believe the worst about Negro character and prospects. Other spokesmen, more generally recognized as apologists for repressive racial policies, seized upon the findings and interpretations of the racial Darwinists to buttress their position and lend it an aura of intellectual respectability. In general, the Darwinist concepts of racial degeneracy and extinction provided the "scientific" basis for most of the virulent anti-Negro propaganda that spewed forth in unprecedented volume around the turn of the century. In 1905, for example, Professor William B. Smith of Tulane University published *The Color Line,* a polemical book describing and celebrating the Negro's alleged failure in the struggle for existence. Smith had to make an effort—or so he claimed in his introduction—to guard "against the emotion of sympathy, of pity for the unfortunate race . . . which the unfeeling process of Nature demands in sacrifice on the altar of the evolution of Humanity," but there are no signs in the text of a struggle with humane sensibilities. He cited Willcox as his authority on the impending extinction of the blacks, and concluded that there was no reason

to "weep and wail and gnash our teeth" over "a racial di-
minuendo" or "thanatopsis." "The vision . . . of a race vanishing before its superior is not at all dispiriting, but inspiring
rather. . . . The doom that awaits the Negro has been prepared
in like measure for all inferior races." Even if humanitarians had
it in their power to reverse the accelerating rate of disease and
death they should not do so; for there were "diseases whose evolutionary function is to weed out the weak, and so preserve the
future for the strong." Hence "all forms of humanitarianism that
tend to give the organically inferior an equal chance with the
superior in the propagation of the species are radically mistaken;
to the individual and society they would sacrifice the race."[1]

Such beliefs were not limited to racist professors. In another
book, published in 1906, a Southern woman concluded her
reminiscences about the "horrors" of Reconstruction by predict-
ing that the "negro race in America is to be wiped out by the
dual process of elimination and absorption." "The elimination
of the negro," she wrote, "will be in ratio to the reduction of his
potentiality as an industrial factor. Evolutionary processes reject
whatever has served its use."[2] The following year, Senator Benjamin R. Tillman of South Carolina, the chief Congressional
spokesman for extreme Southern racism, argued in similar fashion
that the blacks were losing ground in the industrial competition
of the races: "The old struggle of survival of the fittest is beginning in dead earnest, and it is not saying too much to predict that
the negro must do better or 'move on.' " He referred to the data
gathered by physicians and scientists suggesting that tuberculosis
and syphilis would bring about a natural solution to the race
problem.[3] That same year, Senator John Sharp Williams of
Mississippi, a more genteel exponent of Southern Negrophobia,
noted that Negroes were migrating in great numbers to the cities,
where their birth rate was falling below their death rate. There,
he contended, "God's law of evolution, the survival of the fittest,

1. William Benjamin Smith, *The Color Line: A Brief in Behalf of the
Unborn* (New York, 1905), pp. x, 186–187, 190–191.
2. Myrta Lockett Avary, *Dixie After the War* (Boston, 1906), p. 393.
3. Senator Ben R. Tillman, "The Race Question," *Van Norden's Magazine,*
II (April 1907), 25, 27.

and the extinction of the unfit, is operating"; as a result of "the existing process of natural selection" there would be a gradual whitening of the South.[4]

Most Southern prophets of black extinction were unwilling to wait passively while nature took its course. It was acknowledged that evolutionary processes took a long time, and meanwhile it was necessary to deal in some fashion with a degenerating race that was still a large element in the population. For Southern Negrophobes the prospect of black extinction was at most a comforting thought; it did not remove the pressing problem of how to prevent the contamination of the white community while the doomed race reverted to savagery and declined morally, physically, and economically. Central to the new anti-Negro propaganda was the current "degenerate" state of the Negro, rather than the racial "thanatopsis" at the end of the evolutionary process.

II

Although the concept of black degeneracy was amenable to Darwinian explanation and defense, it would be wrong to see the rise of evolutionary thought as the sole, or even the most important, intellectual basis of the South's conversion after the late 1880s to the view that the black community was retrogressing instead of advancing. The degeneracy myth was actually promulgated well before apologists for the South's caste system had fully assimilated Darwinian phrases and concepts. More fundamental was a social and historical perspective deriving less from scientific dogma than from what passed for a direct, empirical, and "common-sense" perception of past and present racial realities.

4. Senator John Sharp Williams, "The Negro and the South," *Metropolitan Magazine*, XXVII (November, 1907), 147–148. The most comprehensive and detailed presentation of the case for Negro extinction to appear in the period between 1900 and the First World War was Edward Eggleston, *The Ultimate Solution of the Negro Problem* (Boston, 1913). Such predictions continued to appear despite the fact that the censuses of 1900 and 1910 showed the Negro increasing at a rate much closer to that of the whites than the census of 1890 had led people to anticipate.

Indeed, the whole notion sprang readily from deeply rooted traditions of Southern thought. The proslavery theorists had argued that the "brute" propensities of the blacks were kept in check only as a result of the absolute white control made possible by slavery and that emancipation in the South would bring the same "reversion to savagery" that had allegedly taken place after the blacks had been freed in Haiti and the British West Indies. Many Southerners of the Reconstruction era professed to find confirmation for this theory in the behavior of the freedmen under Radical leadership. But after "Redemption," there was, as indicated above, some propensity to reject the full implication of proslavery argument in favor of an expectation of Negro "progress" and racial development under a form of white supremacy supposedly compatible with the protection of black liberties.[5] Even during the 1880s, an undercurrent ran counter to the assertion that the overthrow of the Radicals had set the stage for controlled Negro advancement and a restoration of racial harmony. Many Southern clergymen of that decade saw nothing in the development of an independent Negro religious life but emotional excess, moral decline, and a general falling away from the Christianity originally inculcated by whites on the slave plantations.[6] By 1889 Philip Alexander Bruce was launching a comprehensive attack on the optimistic racial philosophy presented as part of the "New South" creed. In his influential book *The Plantation Negro as a Freeman,* he argued on the basis of his own observations, and without recourse to explicitly Darwinian theorizing, that the Negro race had degenerated since emancipation and would continue to do so. As evidence he pointed especially to an alleged rise in crime and sexual immorality, reflected most ominously in an increasing number of sexual assaults on white women. Bruce saw the old "spirit of loyal affection" which had bound master and slave together and which the new "paternalists" hoped to restore as surviving only in attenuated form among the older blacks who had grown up under slavery; it was totally lacking in the new generations who

5. See Chapters Two, Six, and Seven, above.
6. See the quotations from a number of clergymen in Francis G. Ruffin, *The Negro as a Political and Social Factor* (Richmond, 1888), pp. 14–20.

were taking their place. "The influences that are shaping the character of the younger generations," he wrote, "appear to be such as must bring blacks in time to a state of nature. . . . All search for some means of completely arresting the moral decline of the negro seems to be in vain."[7]

Such ideas soon became commonplace. They were popularized, for example, in the essays and novels of Bruce's brother-in-law, Thomas Nelson Page, who drew a sharp distinction between the "old-time darkies" who were passing away and the "new issue," whom he described as "lazy, thriftless, intemperate, insolent, dishonest, and without the most rudimentary elements of morality." Unlike Joel Chandler Harris, who also glorified the faithful slave, Page made it clear that the amiable qualities of the "good darkies" who appeared in his popular stories of antebellum life could not be passed on to subsequent generations of blacks, for they were not part of the essential Negro character but a special product of a set of relationships permanently destroyed by the Civil War and Reconstruction. Page believed that some "improvement" of the blacks was possible once they were disfranchised and placed under firmer white control, but on the whole he presented an ominous picture of Negro potentialities and probable future race relations.[8]

In 1899 Bruce reasserted the case for moral retrogression among the blacks and argued that the past decade had borne out his worst fears.[9] By then, even the surviving paternalists of the 1880s were having second thoughts about how the Negro responded to efforts to improve his character and situation. J. L. M. Curry, for example, gave the readers of *Popular Science Monthly* what could easily have been interpreted as a confession that his program for Negro uplift had failed: "When the interest and authority of owners was removed and former religious instruction was crippled or withdrawn, the negroes fell rapidly

7. Philip A. Bruce, *The Plantation Negro as a Freeman* (New York and London, 1889) , pp. 246, 249, and *passim.*

8. Thomas Nelson Page, *The Negro: The Southerner's Problem* (New York, 1904) , pp. 80, 163, and *passim;* see also *The Old South* (New York, 1892) , another collection of Page's essays.

9. Philip Alexander Bruce, "The Negro Population of the South," *Conservative Review,* II (November, 1899) , 262–280.

from what had been attained in slavery to a state of original fetishism. . . . many, especially of the younger generation of both sexes, gave proof of what degeneracy can accomplish in a quarter of a century. . . . The danger of doing harm, or injustice, restrains my pen from disclosing material which would only shock senses and stagger credulity." He *was* willing to reveal, however, that "testimony to satisfy the most skeptical, could be adduced, *ad nauseam* from men and women doing educational and missionary work among the colored people, to show the deplorable depths to which multitudes have sunk." Curry was not ready to concede that benevolent work should be given up as hopeless, but his readers might have been tempted to draw that conclusion.[10]

Bruce, Page, the Curry of 1899, and others who claimed that Negroes had retrogressed invariably put some of the blame for the growing gulf between the races on the alleged aftereffects of Radical Reconstruction. The Radicals were berated for having permanently destroyed the Negro's trust in his "only true friends"—the Southern whites—and for having filled his head with false hopes of equality. In a curious way, degeneracy was often identified with the persistence since Reconstruction of a desire for equal rights which prevented the blacks from assuming their "natural place" as a docile, subordinate population.[11] There was, of course, some inconsistency between the notion that the Negroes had been ruined by Reconstruction and the classic argument that freed blacks always reverted to savagery; for if moral decline was the inevitable result of emancipation, Reconstruction had simply made a bad situation worse rather than making any fundamental difference. This inconsistency could

10. J. L. M. Curry, "The Negro Question," *Popular Science Monthly,* LV (June, 1899) , 181.

11. See Bruce, *Plantation Negro,* Chapter V; Page, *The Negro,* pp. 247–248; Curry, "The Negro Question," p. 181; George T. Winston, "The Relation of the Whites to the Negroes," *Annals of the American Academy of Political and Social Science,* XVII (July, 1901) , 113–115; Speech of the Hon. Clifton R. Breckinridge, in Southern Society for the Promotion of the Study of Race Conditions and Problems in the South, *Race Problems of the South: Proceedings of the First Annual Conference* (Richmond, 1900) , pp. 173–174; and John Ambrose Price, *The Negro: Past, Present, and Future* (New York and Washington, 1907) , pp. 100–102.

have been removed if Southern racists had been willing to admit that what they really desired was the re-establishment of slavery; they were prevented from doing so by their knowledge that literal re-enslavement was impossible.

III

The concept of black degeneracy, however explained, was clearly central to the ideology of extreme racism that historians have described as engulfing the South after 1890, virtually submerging the moderate position. The new polemical literature on the "black peril," when placed in its political, social, and economic context, provides some clues as to why this "capitulation to racism" took place when it did.

As early as the late 1880s there was a preliminary outpouring of anti-Negro writing, suggesting, among other things, that the "Bourbon" leadership of the South was losing its faith in a paternalistic "alliance" with the Negro. One of the factors behind this dissatisfaction with the racial *status quo* was the continued threat of an independent Negro vote. Many blacks persisted in voting Republican when they got the chance; and in 1889 President Benjamin Harrison, in his first annual message, called for new legislation to protect the black franchise, sending a wave of apprehension through the South and temporarily undermining expectations of sectional "reunion" on the basis of white supremacy. Such fears seemed confirmed when Representative Henry Cabot Lodge, acting with Presidential encouragement, placed his "Force Bill" in the Congressional hopper in 1890. In addition, there was the possibility that the Negro vote would assume new importance as the object of competitive bidding by white factions because agrarian grievances against the dominant elements created the prospect of political division within the white community.

The growing dissatisfaction with the blacks also had a regional economic side, in that the declining situation of Southern agriculture cast doubt on the promise of a general prosperity made by proponents of the "New South" and invited racist explanations for the South's economic shortcomings. Finally, there was a growing uneasiness about what was happening in the segregated black community; whites found that the price of increasing social separation was a lack of knowledge about how blacks were living and what they were thinking that bred suspicion and fed fears that chaos, violence, and disease would overflow from the black sector and "contaminate" or debase the white community.[12]

The fruit of these anxieties was a major revival of deportationist thinking in the South between 1887 and 1891, stemming largely from respectable "Bourbon" or conservative sources—from the kind of men who had previously advocated an optimistic paternalism. H. S. Fulkerson of Mississippi, a state where "fusion" arrangements between white conservatives and black Republicans were being threatened by insurgent whites from the hill country, presented a detailed exposition of the case for black expatriation in 1887.[13] In 1889, Carlyle McKinley, an editor of the Charleston News and Courier, published a reply to Tourgée's An Appeal to Caesar, entitled An Appeal to Pharaoh, pointing to colonization as the only way of resolving the racial antagonisms Tourgée had perceived. Soon the News and Courtier—an influential voice of the New South movement—was editorializing for colonization or deportation of all Southern Negroes.[14] At the same time, Philip Alexander Bruce was arguing for the desirability of "withdrawing" the black population, and conservative Senators Morgan of Alabama and M. C. Butler of South Carolina

12. On the crisis of the late 1880s and early 1890s, see C. Vann Woodward, The Strange Career of Jim Crow, 2d rev. ed. (New York, 1966), Chapter III; Rayford W. Logan, The Betrayal of the Negro: From Rutherford B. Hayes to Woodrow Wilson (New York, 1965), Chapter Four; Vincent P. De Santis, Republicans Face the Southern Question—The New Departure Years, 1877–1897 (Baltimore, 1959), pp. 196–214; C. Vann Woodward, The Origins of the New South (Baton Rouge, 1951), Chapters VII, VIII, and passim.

13. H. S. Fulkerson, The Negro: As He Was; As He Is; As He Will Be (Vicksburg, Miss., 1887). The unsettled political situation in Mississippi at this time is well described in the opening chapters of Albert D. Kirwan's Revolt of the Rednecks: Mississippi Politics, 1876–1925 (Lexington, Ky., 1951).

14. [Carlyle McKinley,] An Appeal to Pharaoh: The Negro Problem and Its Radical Solution (New York, 1889); Charleston News and Courier, December 16, 1889.

were introducing bills "to provide for the migration of persons of color from the Southern states."[15]

In 1890 Wade Hampton, previously the major spokesman for political paternalism, published an article condemning the granting of Negro suffrage as "a crime against civilization, humanity, constitutional rights, and Christianity," and like the others ended up calling for a total separation of the races. The advocacy of deportation by South Carolina conservatives like Hampton and Butler seems to have resulted, at least in part, from their fear of the agrarian insurgency within the state's Democratic Party. Recognizing that Ben Tillman and other spokesmen for the "dirt farmer" were in a position to use a racial appeal to win and hold power in the state, conservatives sought to associate themselves with the cause of black expulsion, in an unsuccessful effort to preempt the race issue and absolve themselves from anticipated charges of Negrophilia.[16]

Deportation proposals, besides reflecting the political insecurity of the class that had assumed leadership during the 1870s, revealed an ominous tendency to use the blacks as scapegoats for the real or apparent failures of the New South program of sectional reunion, capitalist prosperity, and benevolent white supremacy. Fulkerson and McKinley, for example, emphasized the continuing role of the Negro as a "bone of contention" between North and South, a "source of profound estrangement" which prevented the achievement of American nationality.[17] Fulkerson and Bruce stressed the Negro's economic inefficiency as a cause of the South's failure to achieve the general prosperity promised by New South spokesmen.[18] All the advocates of expatriation argued the extreme and ineradicable inferiority of the blacks, the inevitability of bitter racial antagonism, and, in conclusion, the insolubility of the Southern race problem on any basis other than complete separation.[19]

15. Logan, *Betrayal of the Negro*, pp. 142–143.
16. Senator Wade Hampton, "The Race Problem," *Arena*, II (July, 1890), 135, 138; and William J. Cooper, *The Conservative Regime: South Carolina, 1877–1890* (Baltimore, 1968), pp. 110–111.
17. Fulkerson, *The Negro*, pp. 6–7; McKinley, *Appeal*, p. 9.
18. Fulkerson, *The Negro*, pp. 103–105; Bruce, *Plantation Negro*, p. 261.
19. For another expression of this viewpoint, see Henry A. Scomp, "Can the Race Problem Be Solved?" *Forum*, VIII (December, 1889), 365–376.

Southern deportationists, fully aware that their scheme required the active support of the rest of the country, anticipated that the North might be sympathetic to their program because a contemporaneous rise in Northern nativism was giving rise to a demand for some form of immigration restriction. In his appeal for the preservation of the Aryan homogeneity upon which he claimed the country had been founded, Fulkerson implicitly related the cause of Negro expulsion to the call for curbs on immigration. Denying the thesis that "a man from any clime is fitted for our institutions," he argued that "it may become, if it is not already so, necessary to *close our doors* even at the expense of our reputation for hospitality. Our 'asylum for the oppressed of other lands' is fast becoming a lazar house, or infirmary, a breeding place of corruption and of political and social heresies. . . . Our institutions have cost too much and are too valuable to be vandalized thus."[20] Hampton lumped together the Republican Party's defense of Negro suffrage and its willingness to offer American citizenship to "the Anarchist, the Communist, the Nihilist, and all the other scum of European nations."[21] It was McKinley, however, who made the most direct connection between the deportation of the blacks and the erection of barriers to immigration. Noting that President Harrison had said in his speech accepting the Republican nomination that the nation had a duty to exclude alien races that could not be assimilated, McKinley concluded that "our duty to expel alien races is as clear as the duty to exclude them."[22]

The suggestions of the deportationists, of course, came to nothing. Not only was black expatriation an impossible task, but the South was in fact unwilling to dispense with the exploitation of black labor. As James Bryce pointed out in 1891, colonization proposals would come to nothing because "the Southern whites, as uneasy as they are in states like South Carolina and Mississippi, would not wish to lose this vast body of workers, who cultivate the soil of regions where white labor cannot contend

20. Fulkerson, *The Negro,* pp. 40, 68.
21. Hampton, "The Race Problem," p. 21.
22. McKinley, *Appeal,* p. 202. On the development of Northern nativism in the 1880s see John Higham, *Strangers in the Land* (New Brunswick, N.J., 1955), Chapter Three.

with heat and malaria."[23] But the proposals are significant because they indicate that a mood of racial reaction gripped some "New South" conservatives even before the full flowering of racist demagoguery during the struggle against Populism in the 1890s.

They reveal the persistence in the white imagination of the impossible dream of absolute racial homogeneity, a dream which tended to become vocal in the nineteenth century whenever the racial situation reached a certain level of tension and ambiguity. The psychology of Southern colonizationism or expulsionism would appear to be similar to a characteristic attitude of European colonialists toward the native populations they exploit. At times, Albert Memmi points out, the colonialist is "fed up with his subject, who tortures his conscience and his life. He tries to dismiss him from his mind, to imagine the colony without the colonized. A witticism which is more serious than it sounds states that 'Everything would be perfect . . . if it weren't for the natives.' "[24]

During the 1890s, the unrealizable urge for true homogeneity was sublimated and put in the service of a campaign to achieve a closer approximation to the pseudo homogeneity of the slave era. The white political divisions of that decade, occasioned by the agrarian-Populist revolt against a conservative, business-oriented leadership, led briefly to a competition for the black vote which tended to be disastrous to the side that most openly courted Negro support because opponents could then resort to race baiting. In the end, the Negro became the scapegoat for the political and economic tensions of the period. The result was legal disfranchisement, the passage of rigorous Jim Crow laws, new and more horrible forms of lynching, and a series of one-sided race riots which took a heavy toll of defenseless blacks.[25] Disfranchisement and the extension of legalized segregation corresponded, as C. Vann Woodward has observed, to the rising influ-

23. James Bryce, "Thoughts on the Negro Problem," *North American Review,* CLIII (December, 1891) , 652.
24. Albert Memmi, *The Colonizer and the Colonized* (Boston, 1965) , p. 66.
25. See Woodward, *Jim Crow,* Chapter III.

ence of "the tide of political democracy" among whites.[26] But this did not mean that lower-class whites successfully displaced the planter-capitalist elite. As in the Old South, the dominant elements retained much of their power in the face of a popular democratic consciousness by making concessions to the Southern folk ideology of *Herrenvolk* democracy; they discarded their paternalistic rhetoric and adopted the slogans of white equality and black proscription.

Although the immediate concern of Southern apologists in the 1890s and thereafter was explaining, justifying, and strengthening the racial caste system that was being written into law, proposals for carrying segregation to its logical extreme by deporting or colonizing the blacks continued to be made by men—like Charles H. Otken and John Temple Graves—who were by no means isolated eccentrics.[27] Defenders of segregation were never quite satisfied with the edifice they were helping to construct and could not conceal misgivings about the consequences of attempting to "segregate" two races living and working in close proximity.

Henry A. Scomp had put his finger on the problem in 1889. In an essay advocating colonization, he wrote that segregation, as it was actually taking place in the South, was leading to "an alienation of sympathies," and a decline in white influence over blacks, which could only result in a growth of racial friction—unless of course segregation was carried to its logical extreme of geographical separation.[28] Similar anxieties were expressed by Southern racists who acknowledged that black expulsion was impossible or even undesirable. For them, the real problem was how to achieve a proper balance between the segregation supposedly necessary to save the whites from "mongrelization" and the measure of control over blacks seemingly required to protect the interests and safety of the community. They foresaw real dangers in a system

26. Woodward, *Origins,* pp. 211–212.
27. Otken, a leading interpreter of the South's agrarian problems, advocated deportation in *The Ills of the South* (New York, 1894) ; and John Temple Graves, an influential Atlanta editor, called for geographical separation at the 1900 Montgomery race conference (Southern Society . . . , *Race Problems,* pp. 48–57) .
28. Scomp, "Can the Race Problem Be Solved?," p. 369.

of segregation which meant simply that blacks were allowed to withdraw completely, if only for "social" purposes, into separate communities beyond the reach of effective white surveillance.

In a pamphlet of 1891, William Cabell Bruce, a Baltimore lawyer and brother of Philip A. Bruce, contended that most Southern Negroes still remained under "the spell of the conscious mastery" of the whites; but he warned that "the process of segregation" was creating a situation where the Negro, increasingly isolated from "the direct influence of the whites," would become "more and more aggressive." To the extent that segregation meant simply separation, Bruce regarded it as a dangerous tendency that needed to be modified.[29] In an 1899 article, "The Negro Population of the South," Philip Alexander Bruce betrayed some of the same concerns. Disfranchisement, he pointed out, meant that Negroes were "no longer a menace to organized government, but they continue not the less to be a menace to the moral well-being of the communities in which they live." Whites, he indicated, no longer exercised a beneficial influence over the blacks now that they were concentrated in separate enclaves. He went on to describe these enclaves as centers of filth and debauchery, sources of "endless annoyance and trouble to white people."[30] Bruce of course regarded these conditions as the inevitable result of Negro retrogression; and such an image of the fruits of racial separation could easily lead to efforts to strengthen the barriers of segregation, in an effort to approximate total separation without actual deportation. In 1903 William Lee Howard, a Baltimore physician writing in *Medicine* of the diseases rampant in a degenerating black community, contended: "There is every prospect of checking and reducing these diseases in the white race, if the race is socially—in every aspect of the term—quarantined from the African."[31]

Some spokesmen who shared the belief of Howard and Philip A. Bruce in the Negro's biological doom nevertheless wanted some modification of racial separation to guarantee a greater degree of

29. W. Cabell Bruce, *The Negro Problem* (Baltimore, 1891), pp. 24–26.
30. P. A. Bruce, "Negro Population of the South," 262, 277.
31. William Lee Howard, "The Negro as a Distinct Ethnic Factor in Civilization," *Medicine*, LX (May, 1903), 424.

white control—purely, it was claimed, as a device to protect the whites from unhealthy influences emanating from the black side of the color line. Paul B. Barringer, for example, proposed that the black teachers in segregated Negro schools be replaced by whites who would impose a kind of quasi-military discipline. Regimentation of blacks under white officers in the regular Army had proven effective, he said, recommending such institutional arrangements as a model for the South.[32]

Barringer's proposal suggests that education was an area of special anxiety for those concerned with achieving a proper balance between racial separation and white control. No white supremacist questioned the dogma that the races must go to separate schools, and there was not even much support for Barringer's proposal. The real question that racists debated among themselves was whether a system of Negro education could be devised to keep dangerous ideas and aspirations out of the heads of its beneficiaries. A division of opinion developed in the South in the 1890s and the early twentieth century between those believers in the black-degeneracy hypothesis who thought that a properly conceived program of black education could contribute to the security of white rule and those extremists who argued, in effect, that black education of any kind was a danger to the white community.

Although men of the former persuasion denied that blacks were capable of significant intellectual or economic advancement, they contended that the full implementation of their own version of Booker T. Washington's program for industrial education might bring a measure of discipline to the black character. Philip A. Bruce, for example, favored a combination of rudimentary intellectual and industrial training for blacks, although he saw little economic opportunity for black mechanics and artisans and believed no educational program could permanently arrest the long-range trend toward degeneracy and extinction. Such training, he suggested, would make a bad situation a little better by "cultivating a spirit of steadiness . . . and raising the

32. P. B. Barringer, *The American Negro: His Past and Future* (Raleigh, N.C., 1900), pp. 20–21.

dignity of manual labor in [the Negroes'] eyes."[33] Joseph A.
Tillinghast described the kind of education blacks received at
Tuskegee and Hampton as involving essentially the inculcation
of morality rather than the teaching of skills; and George T.
Winston, president of the North Carolina College of Agriculture
and Mechanic Arts, who had a gloomy view of Negro prospects in
general, professed to find in the tutelage of industrial schools a
possibility of "character building by honest work and honest
dealing" which would lead to "good habits and good manners"
and "respect for elders and superiors."[34]

Other militant racists, however, questioned the whole concept
of Negro education, even in its Washingtonian form. For them
segregation did not mean that the blacks should reproduce basic
white institutions—with appropriate differences in function—on
their own side of the color line, but rather that they should be
discouraged from having *any* institutions predicated on the
allegedly false and dangerous assumption that Negroes could
make even the most limited and temporary advances in intelligence, morality, and economic well-being. Industrial education,
according to one of the earliest and most persistent arguments
against it, prepared blacks for vocations also coveted by lower-
class whites, thus inspiring ambitions that could not be realized
and setting the stage for an increase in racial competition and
antagonism.[35]

By 1900 the case against the very concept of black education
tended to become synonymous with a peculiarly thoroughgoing
and consistent application of the black-degeneracy hypothesis. In
that year John Roach Straton, a Baptist clergyman and professor
at Mercer University in Georgia, argued in the *North American
Review* that education would not help solve the racial problem

33. Bruce, *Plantation Negro*, pp. 164–165.
34. Joseph A. Tillinghast, "The Negro in Africa and America," *Publications
of the American Economic Association*, 3d Ser., III (May, 1902), Chapter IV;
George T. Winston, "The Relation of the Whites to the Negroes," 115, 118.
35. Scomp, "Can the Race Problem Be Solved?," 370–371; John Temple
Graves, in Southern Society . . . *Race Problems*, p. 55; Thomas Dixon, *The
Leopard's Spots: A Romance of the White Man's Burden* (New York, 1902),
p. 335.

because the present tendencies of the Negro race pointed to "permanent decay and degeneracy in every particular." According to Straton, the development of black education since the Civil War had been accompanied by an increase in "crime and immorality . . . in even greater ratio," and he suggested a correlation between the decline of illiteracy and the rise in criminality. The Negro had been least criminal in those areas where he had made the fewest educational advances: ". . . the more the negroes live to themselves and the nearer they remain to the simple life which formerly characterized them, the better they are, while the more they scatter as a race and the closer they come in contact with our civilization and the more they endeavor to take it on, the worse they become. . . ." Straton's solution was an increase in the segregation and localization of the blacks and a de-emphasis on ill-advised efforts to uplift and improve them.[36] In 1903 Dr. William Lee Howard made a similar assertion of the utter futility of educating a degenerating race.[37] Such pronouncements on the more sophisticated level of racist discourse were accompanied after 1900 by the campaigns of race-baiting politicians like James K. Vardaman of Mississippi to withdraw white tax support from Negro schools. Although these efforts failed to effect formal constitutional changes in the procedure for allotting school funds, they did contribute to a climate of opinion that excluded blacks from the benefits of the early twentieth-century campaign for Southern educational reform. The result was an increasing gap between expenditures for white education and what was grudgingly vouchsafed to black schools.[38]

If the question of Negro education presented problems for the theoreticians of segregation, even greater difficulties were encountered by those who attempted to evaluate the practice of lynching. The vicious custom of taking accused Negro offenders out of the hands of the authorities and hanging, shooting, or

36. John Roach Straton, "Will Education Solve the Race Problem?" *North American Review*, CLXX (June, 1900) , 786–787, 789–790, 793–794.
37. Howard, "The Negro as a Distinct Ethnic Factor," 423–426.
38. See Louis R. Harlan, *Separate and Unequal: Public School Campaigns and Racism in the Southern Seaboard States* (Chapel Hill, N.C., 1958), *passim*.

burning them alive reached a high point in the 1890s and persisted on a somewhat diminished scale into the twentieth century.[39]

Lynching represented an ultimate sociological method of racial control and repression, a way of using fear and terror to check "dangerous" tendencies in a black community considered to be ineffectively regimented or supervised. As such it constituted a confession that the regular institutions of a segregated society provided an inadequate measure of day-to-day control. Ideally speaking, racists admitted, lynching should not have been necessary; and the more educated and sophisticated Southern Negrophobes of the period generally condemned the practice in the abstract, on the conservative grounds that lynching destroyed respect for law and order and precipitated Southern society toward anarchy. But since they themselves had no real substitute to offer as a way of achieving objectives they shared with the impassioned mobs, these spokesmen often ended up apologizing for the practice as virtually unavoidable under existing circumstances. They were compelled, in fact, to devote a great deal of time and energy to the "explanation" of these extralegal executions, because lynching tended to be shocking to the kind of "civilized" sensibilities that were willing to condone milder manifestations of racism. After 1890, lynching constituted the single Southern racial practice calculated to horrify a substantial segment of Northern opinion. Northern opposition to lynching was actually a limited and ineffectual phenomenon during this period, but it was vocal enough to arouse Southern fears of renewed Federal intervention or "interference" with the South's efforts to deal with its black population. In the early 1890s serious proposals were introduced for Federal legislation against the lynching of aliens (occasioned initially by the protest of the Italian government against the murder of eleven Italian immigrants in Louisiana), and a few prominent Northern Republi-

39. Woodward, *Origins*, pp. 351–352; Thomas F. Gossett, *Race: The History of an Idea in America* (Dallas, 1965), pp. 269–273. The best general study of lynching is still Arthur F. Raper, *The Tragedy of Lynching* (Chapel Hill, 1933).

cans urged that the Federal government be empowered to protect Southern blacks from mob action.[40]

In 1893 there was an especially urgent need to head off outside criticism. The number of lynchings had reached its all-time peak during the previous year, and newspaper reports revealed that Southern mobs were beginning to torture and burn their black victims, instead of simply stringing them up in time-honored vigilante fashion.[41] In the October issue of the *Forum*, two Southern spokesmen, one considered a hard-liner and the other a moderate, discussed the reasons for the current increase in the number and brutality of lynchings. Charles Henry Smith, an undisguised Negrophobe who had won some fame as a humorist under the pseudonym Bill Arp, addressed himself to the question "Have American Negroes Too Much Liberty?" He concluded that they did, and that this was why lynchings took place. The central problem was not lynching itself but "the rapid increase of crime among the negroes of the South and the alarming frequency of the most brutal outrages upon white women and children." Those who protested against lynchings, Smith charged, "make no effort to stop the outrages that provoke them." The brutality of the white retaliation against black rapists and murderers was more than justified by the increasing "horror and brutality" of the crimes allegedly committed by blacks. The only answer to the problem, according to Smith, was the complete disfranchisement of the blacks and the enactment of a separate penal code to cover Negro offenses.[42]

The other article was written by Atticus G. Haygood, long the leading Southern spokesman for a moderate and "paternalistic"

40. See Logan, *Betrayal of the Negro*, pp. 85–87, 226–227, and Stanley P. Hirshon, *Farewell to the Bloody Shirt: Northern Republicans and the Southern Negro, 1877–1893* (Bloomington, Ind., 1962), pp. 237–238, for evidence of sincere but ineffectual national concern about Southern lynching in the 1890s.

41. In 1892, 162 Negroes and 69 whites were lynched in the United States. (See *The Negro Handbook* [New York, 1949], p. 99.) See Logan, *Betrayal of the Negro*, p. 224, for examples of sensational newspaper reports on the new-style lynchings of 1892 and 1893.

42. Charles H. Smith, "Have American Negroes Too Much Liberty?," *Forum*, XVI (October, 1893), 176, 181.

approach to the black population. Haygood began by denouncing lynching as a barbarous "crime against society." But he went on to ask critics of the South to "consider the provocation": "Sane men who are righteous will remember not only the brutish man who dies by the slow fire of torture; they will also think of the ruined woman, worst tortured than he." Such lynchings as had recently taken place were the result of "the elemental forces that control human nature throughout all time and the world over" and must be understood as the reaction to a recent wave of sexual assaults committed by blacks against women. Lynching would not stop, he suggested, until black leaders and Northern liberals moderated their one-sided denunciation of the practice and prevailed upon Negroes to stop raping white women. Haygood, who had previously argued that blacks were making substantial moral progress, was now in effect lending his support to a defensive Southern reaction based on the characterization of the "new issue" Negro as a brute and a savage.[43]

Smith and Haygood established the narrow limits within which subsequent Southern apologists operated. The general strategy was to concede that lynching had many evil consequences but could not be prevented so long as Negroes committed bestial sexual crimes and necessarily drove the whites mad with fury, arousing, as a Virginia writer put it, "the deepest passions . . . , the fiercest instincts of the race."[44] It must be recognized, a speaker told the Montgomery race conference in 1900, that "the white race regards the rape of white women by Negroes not as ordinary criminality," but as "an attack on the integrity of the race."[45] Thomas Nelson Page, in discussing lynching in his book *The Negro: The Southerner's Problem*, went further than most in condemning the practice, but even he was ready to maintain that "the stern underlying principle of the people who commit these barbarities is one that has deep root in the basic passions of humanity: the determination to put an end

43. Atticus G. Haygood, "The Black Shadow in the South," *Forum*, XVI (October, 1893), 167–169, 173.

44. Marion L. Dawson, "The South and the Negro," *North American Review*, CLXXII (February, 1901), 282.

45. Address of the Hon. Alex C. King, Southern Society . . . , *Race Problems*, p. 163.

to the ravishing of their women by an inferior race. . . ." He explained lynching as an inevitable response to the black rapist, although his own statistics showed conclusively that the victim was not even accused of rape in the overwhelming majority of cases.[46]

All this discussion can be reduced to a claim that lynching was a "necessary evil" in a segregated society, pending more effective methods to control the black population and curb its "criminal" tendencies. Proposals for reform generally pointed in the direction of a separate judicial system and penal code for blacks, changes which would in effect legalize the existing practice of summary "justice" and unusual punishments.[47] Lynching was thus symptomatic of a conviction that the legal mechanisms of repression that accompanied segregation and disfranchisement did not go far enough and that a satisfactory balance between separation and control had not yet been established.

IV

These efforts to "explain" or justify lynching help account for the popularity around the turn of the century of the stereotype of the "Negro as beast." Public segregation could be defended in terms of "racial instincts"—if it needed to be justified at all during a period when the North raised little objection to the "social" separation of the races. (The United States Supreme Court put its stamp of approval on legalized segregation in the *Plessy* v. *Ferguson* decision of 1896.) Disfranchisement was more controversial, but it was not necessary to portray the blacks as lustful brutes to make a case for their unfitness for self-government; it could as easily be done, as it often was, by pointing to the supposed intellectual shortcomings of the race and its simple-minded willingness to follow the leadership of demagogues. But

46. Page, *The Negro*, pp. 91, 100.
47. For various "reform proposals" see C. H. Smith, "Have American Negroes Too Much Liberty?," p. 182; Dawson, "The South and the Negro," 283; C. R. Breckinridge, Southern Society . . . *Race Problems*, p. 176; Bourke Cockran, *ibid.*, p. 203.

the only way to meet criticisms of the unspeakably revolting practice of lynching was to contend that many Negroes were literally wild beasts, with uncontrollable sexual passions and criminal natures stamped by heredity. The incredible cruelty and barbarity of lynching thus led to the most extreme defamation of the Negro character that had yet been offered and helped provide the tone and substance for the race-hate literature of the period.

Of course the image of the Negro as (in Ben Tillman's words) "a fiend, a wild beast, seeking whom he may devour" did not spring full-blown in the 1890s.[48] Like so many other elements in the racist rhetoric and imagery of 1900, it had its origins in the proslavery imagination, which had conceived of the black man as having a dual nature—he was docile and amiable when enslaved, ferocious and murderous when free. The notion that blacks could be seized by uncontrollable fits of sexual passion was derived in part from the traditional picture of Africa as a land of licentiousness. As early as the 1840s, Josiah Priest, one of the antebellum proponents of the Biblical argument for slavery, attempted to prove from Scripture that the descendants of Ham had overdeveloped sexual organs and were the original Sodomites of the Old Testament, guilty in ancient times of all conceivable forms of lewdness. "The baleful fire of unchaste amour rages through the negro's blood, more fiercely than in the blood of any other people," wrote Priest, "inflaming their imaginations with corresponding images and ideas . . ."[49] Later the racist propaganda directed against emancipation and Reconstruction laid heavy stress on the contention that freed blacks had an uncontrollable desire to violate white women.[50] There is little reason to doubt the conventional notion that a fear of oversexed "brute" Negroes has been a constant and deeply rooted feature of the white racist imagination. But it remains true that this

48. Quoted in Francis Butler Simkins, "Ben Tillman's View of the Negro," *Journal of Southern History*, III (May, 1937), 166.

49. [The Reverend Josiah Priest], *Slavery, As It Relates to the Negro or African Race . . .* (Albany, N.Y., 1843), pp. 150–153. (Reissued as *Bible Defence of Slavery* [Glasgow, Ky., 1852].)

50. Forrest G. Wood, *Black Scare: The Racist Response to Emancipation and Reconstruction* (Berkeley and Los Angeles, 1968), pp. 65, 145–148.

image came to the surface in a new and spectacular way around the turn of the century.

In 1900 a religious publishing house brought out *"The Negro a Beast,"* by Charles Carroll, a bizarre work that revived the pre-Adamite arguments of Dr. Samuel Cartwright and "Ariel" by describing the Negro as literally an ape rather than a human being. According to Carroll, the apelike Negro was the actual "tempter of Eve," and miscegenation was the greatest of all sins—the true reason for God's destruction of slavery. As for the mulatto, the offspring of an unnatural relationship, he did not have "the right to live"; for it was the mulattoes, Carroll contended, who were the rapists and criminals of the present time.[51]

Most racists did not accept Carroll's Biblical arguments, but there was some support for his theory that a mixture of blood was responsible for the rise of crimes against white womanhood. In 1899 a Southern woman, Mrs. L. H. Harris, wrote to the editor of the *Independent* that the "negro brute" who attacked some Southern women and struck fear and terror in the hearts of all others was "nearly always a mulatto," with "enough white blood in him to replace native humility and cowardice with Caucasian audacity." This monster had "the savage nature and murderous instincts of the wild beast and the cunning and lust of a fiend." As a result of his presence, the South had become "a smoldering volcano, the dark of its quivering nights lighted here and there with the incendiary's torch or pierced through by the cry of some outraged woman."[52]

51. Charles Carroll, *"The Negro a Beast," or, "In the Image of God"* . . . (St. Louis, 1900), pp. 161, 197 ff. 290–292. Pre-Adamitism had acquired some apparently respectable scientific backing in 1880 when Alexander Winchell, a professor of geology and paleontology at the University of Michigan, published his *Preadamites, Or a Demonstration of the Existence of Men before Adam* (Chicago, 1880). Winchell was a quasi Darwinist who conceded that Adam had not been created directly by the hand of God but had emerged from a prior evolutionary process as the first white man. According to him, Adam may also have been the progenitor of the red and yellow races. The blacks, however, were genuine pre-Adamites, survivals of an earlier stage of human development who could never attain the cultural level of other races. Winchell's book was an important source for Carroll, who cited carefully selected portions as authoritative evidence for his theories.

52. Mrs. L. H. Harris, "A Southern Woman's View," *Independent,* LI (May 18, 1899), 1354–1355.

Attributing the worst outrages to the mulatto was clearly one way of reconciling the traditional stereotype of black docility with the image of bold and violent offenders against the color line which was central to the new propaganda. Such a viewpoint even led some Southern commentators to toy with the idea of recognizing a separate mulatto caste, such as existed in Latin America, as a way of isolating the otherwise peaceable blacks from the inflammatory leadership and example of the mixed-bloods.[53] But for many the distinction between violent mulattoes and docile purebloods was less important than a concept of the basic Negro or African character which supposedly accounted for extremes of submissiveness and violent audacity. Charles H. Smith, for example, said there was a "contrast between the negro's good nature and his bad nature [which] is perhaps more marked than the same contrast in any other race. When a desire to indulge his bad passions comes over him, he seems to be utterly devoid of prudence or of conscience. . . . A bad negro is the most horrible creature upon the earth, the most brutal and merciless."[54] Clifton R. Breckinridge of Arkansas, formerly United States Minister to Russia, told the Montgomery race conference in 1900: "We have a race, the most negative and tractable of which we have any considerable knowledge; but when it does produce a desperado, he is the worst desperado in the world. When it produces a brute, he is the worst and most insatiate brute that exists in human form."[55]

One of the most vivid descriptions of such a "desperado" in action was provided in 1901 by George T. Winston in describing the events preceding a lynching: ". . . when a knock is heard at the door, [the Southern woman] shudders with nameless horror. The black brute is lurking in the dark, a monstrous beast, crazed with lust. His ferocity is almost demoniacal. A mad bull or a tiger could scarcely be more brutal. A whole community is frenzied with horror, with the blind and furious rage for vengeance."

53. See especially Alfred Holt Stone, *Studies in the American Race Problem* (New York, 1908) , pp. 398–435.
54. C. H. Smith, "Have American Negroes Too Much Liberty?," 181.
55. Breckinridge, address, in Southern Society . . . , *Race Problems,* p. 174.

Winston, who clearly rejected the mixed-blood theory by arguing that the mulatto was morally superior to the pure black, attributed such unspeakable acts to "the generation of Negroes who have grown up in the South since slavery." This generation, he contended, had committed "more horrible crimes" than the "six preceding generations of slavery."[56] For him and for many others, therefore, it was not the mixture of blood that was the key to the problem but the degeneration and reversion to savagery that had allegedly occurred in the younger members of the race since the abolition of slavery. Such an explanation was calculated to obscure fine distinctions between "good" and "bad" Negroes and to turn accusations against a few "desperadoes" into an indictment of the entire race, excepting only the diminishing number of elderly ex-slaves who had not lost the habit of submission.

A lurid and detailed account of the supposed susceptibility of all Negroes to "sexual madness" was published in a respected journal, *Medicine*, in 1903. "In the increase of rape on white women," wrote Dr. William Lee Howard, "we see the explosion of a long train of antecedent preparation. The attacks on defenseless white women are evidence of racial instincts that are about as amenable to ethical culture as, is the inherent odor of the race." The physiological basis of the problem, Howard contended, was "the large size of the negro's penis" and the fact that he lacked "the sensitiveness of the terminal fibers which exists in the Caucasian." It followed, therefore, that "the African's birthright" was "sexual madness and excess."[57]

The promulgation of the beast image was also reflected in the literary portrayal of the Negro, although the Victorian taboo against the explicit discussion of sexual matters made it difficult for novelists to be as forthright as Dr. Howard. Thomas Nelson Page, whose stories of the Old South had helped popularize a view of the genial and lovable "old-time darky," was also one of the first to experiment with a different kind of Negro character. His Reconstruction novel, *Red Rock*, published in 1898, intro-

56. Winston, "The Relation of the Whites to the Negroes," 108–109.
57. Howard, "The Negro as a Distinct Ethnic Factor," 424.

duced the repellent figure of Moses, a black politician with sinister ambitions, who is compared to a "beast" or a "reptile." At one point Moses tries to assault a white woman: "He gave a snarl of rage and sprang at her like a wild beast." Thwarted by chance in this particular attempt, he is lynched several years later for a "terrible crime."[58]

The novelist who most fully exploited the literary possibilities arising from the fear of "the black brute" was Thomas Dixon, whose novels of race hate were best sellers in the early twentieth century. Dixon, a prominent Baptist minister before he became a sensational novelist, thought of his work as an evangelical effort to transform the stereotype of the Negro. As he wrote of his first novel, *The Leopard's Spots:* "It may shock the prejudices of those who have idealised or worshiped the negro as canonized in 'Uncle Tom.' Is it not time they heard the whole truth? They have heard only one side for forty years."[59] The side presented by Dixon was the extreme racist side, the full literary development of the concepts of black degeneracy, animality, and "sexual madness." *The Leopard's Spots,* published in 1902, described how the war and Reconstruction had turned the Negro from "a chattel to be bought and sold into a possible beast to be feared and guarded." Since the Negro was a "menace . . . , throwing the blight of its shadow over future generations, a veritable Black Death for the land and its people," Southern whites were justified in using any means necessary to maintain dominance.[60]

In his most popular novel, *The Clansman,* published in 1905 (a decade later the basis of the highly successful film "The Birth of a Nation"), Dixon intensified his efforts to demonstrate the bestial propensities of the blacks. The character who speaks most directly for the author describes the Negro as "half child, half animal, the sport of impulse, whim, and conceit, . . . a being

58. Thomas Nelson Page, *Red Rock: A Chronicle of Reconstruction* (New York, 1898), pp. 356–358, 582.

59. Quoted in Maxwell Bloomfield, "Dixon's *The Leopard's Spots:* A Study in Popular Racism," in Charles E. Wynes, ed., *The Negro in the South since 1865* (University of Alabama, 1965), p. 91. A strangely uncritical biography of Dixon which has recently appeared is Raymond A. Cook, *Fire in the Flint: The Amazing Careers of Thomas Dixon* (Winston-Salem, N.C., 1968).

60. Dixon, *The Leopard's Spots,* pp. 5, 33, and *passim.*

who, left to his will, roams at night and sleeps in the day, whose speech knows no word of love, whose passions, once aroused, are as the fury of the tiger." The climax of the book is the rape of a young white virgin. As Dixon described this event, before discreetly lowering the curtain: "A single tiger spring, and the black claws of the beast sank into the soft white throat." The act results in the suicide of the victim and her mother, followed by a solemn, portentous lynching by the Ku Klux Klan. Dixon's fictional glorification of such vigilante action during Reconstruction served to justify similar retaliation by white mobs in his own time.[61]

Although rape was the central and most horrifying example of the Negro's allegedly inherent criminality, some writers took a broader approach and emphasized the increase of Negro crimes of all sorts. In an address to the American Social Science Association in 1899, Walter F. Willcox demonstrated statistically "that the liability of an American Negro to commit crime is several times as great as the liability of the whites."[62] Such figures were cited again and again by propagandists of race hate who sought to prove that the Negro by nature was a criminal type.[63] Some even attempted to use the new "science" of criminal anthropology to demonstrate that most blacks had the inborn physical features of the hereditary criminal.[64] In 1908 the Negro sociologist Kelly Miller described the climate of opinions resulting from this literature. "The criminal propensity of the Negro," he wrote, "is the charge that is being most widely exploited in current discussion. By fragments of fact and jugglery of argument he is made to appear a beast in human form whose vicious tendency constitutes a new social plague."[65]

The most obvious and immediate function of this kind of

61. Thomas Dixon, *The Clansman: An Historical Romance of the Ku Klux Klan* (New York, 1905) , pp. 293, 304, and *passim*.

62. Walter F. Willcox, "Negro Criminality," in Alfred Holt Stone, *Studies in the American Race Problem*, pp. 443–444. (Originally delivered before the American Social Science Association, Sept. 16, 1899.)

63. See, for example, W. B. Smith, *Color Line*, pp. 249–261.

64. See Charles H. McCord, *The American Negro as a Dependent, Defective, and Delinquent* (Nashville, 1914) , especially pp. 28–31, 42–44.

65. Kelly Miller, *Race Adjustment: Essays on the Negro in America* (New York and Washington, 1908) , p. 95.

propaganda was to counter doubts about the necessity of lynching and other extreme measures to control the black population.
Many Southern apologists contended that criminal and "brute"
tendencies of the new generation of blacks constituted the crown-
ing and conclusive argument for strengthening the whole system
of racial repression. The granting of political rights, it was
argued, had led to dreams of "social equality" and had encouraged blacks to expropriate white women by force. Thus the
Negro's overpowering desire for white women was often described as the central fact legitimizing the whole program of
legalized segregation and disfranchisement.[66]

It would probably be misleading, however, to describe the
purveyors of a brute image of the Negro as simply a group of
cynical propagandists, consciously exaggerating black crime and
sexuality as a way of increasing the pressures for a more thoroughgoing system of black subjugation and exploitation. Many
were probably expressing their own genuine fears and hatreds,
feelings so intense that they suggested dissatisfaction with any
conceivable relationship with the Negro. What white extremists
may have confronted in the image of the black brute was not so
much a Negro as a projection of unacknowledged guilt feelings
derived from their own brutality toward blacks. In order to deserve the kind of treatment he was receiving in the United States
in 1900, the black man presumably had to be as vicious as the
racists claimed; otherwise many whites would have had to accept
an intolerable burden of guilt for perpetrating or tolerating the
most horrendous cruelties and injustices. But in seeing blacks as
bad enough to deserve what they got, racists undoubtedly conjured up a monster that was capable of frightening its creators
and driving them to new frenzies of hatred. By thus feeding on
itself, such a process could easily pass beyond the realm of rational calculation and defensive propaganda. In the end, even
the most oppressed and rigidly subordinated black sharecropper
could serve as a symbol of terror for the white-supremacist
imagination.

66. See for example C. H. Smith, "Have Negroes Too Much Liberty?"
181–182; and Henderson N. Somerville, "Some Co-operating Causes of Negro
Lynching," *North American Review*, CLXXVII (October, 1903) , 509–510.

Chapter Ten

•

Accommodationist Racism
and the Progressive Mentality

THE BLACK-DEGENERACY hypothesis and the concomitant "beast" image failed to win universal acceptance in the South, even at the height of campaigns for Jim Crow and disfranchisement. Dissenting from extreme manifestations of Negrophobia, a group of white moderates took it upon themselves to work for interracial harmony and accommodation. Since they did not usually object to the notion that blacks were inferior or even to the dictum that they remain a separate caste, moderate "liberalism" was seriously flawed and doomed to ineffectuality; it may even strike modern readers as an exercise in hairsplitting to distinguish the moderates from the militant racists with whom they professed to disagree. But in the early twentieth century there did seem to be a substantive difference between their approach and that of the extremists. Even comparatively militant black spokesmen, like W. E. B. Du Bois and Kelly Miller, were ready and willing to differentiate between "friendly" Southern whites and such apostles of discord as Tillman, Vardaman, and Thomas Dixon—and they openly and sincerely prayed for the triumph of the former, not because the moderates promised full equality but because they appeared to offer certain immediate and tangible benefits which might make the difference between a better future and further oppression.[1] In an effort, therefore, to capture the full range and flavor of white discussion of Negro character and prospects between the 1890s and the outbreak of the Great War in Europe, it is useful to distinguish between two forms of racism—the competitive racism of the "survival of the fittest" school and the accommodationist racism that was in part a reaction against the brutality of the extremists.

The foremost Southern exponent of the new accommodationism was Edgar Gardner Murphy, an Episcopal clergyman in Alabama turned social reformer.[2] In his writings and addresses between 1900 and 1909, Murphy developed all the implications of a "liberal" alternative to extreme racism. After Murphy withdrew from the fray because of ill-health, his role as the principal philosopher of racial moderation was taken over by Willis D. Weatherford, a leader in the Southern YMCA movement, who for the next half century would be a major spokesman for inter-

1. See Miller's praise of "the advocates of humane and tolerant treatment" in *Race Adjustment: Essays on the Negro in America* (New York and Washington, 1908) , pp. 64–65; and Du Bois's admission in *The Souls of Black Folk* (Chicago, 1903) that Southern blacks would probably benefit from the guidance and assistance that they would receive "if the representatives of the best white Southern opinion were the ruling and guiding powers in the South today" (pp. 176–177) .

2. Murphy (1869–1913) was born in Arkansas, raised in Texas, and educated at the University of the South in Sewanee, Tennessee, and at the General (Episcopal) Seminary in New York City. Subsequently he was an Episcopal minister at Laredo, Texas, Chillicothe, Ohio, and Kingston, New York, before answering a call from St. John's in Montgomery, Alabama, in 1898. In Montgomery, Murphy's reform interests came to the fore. He organized the Montgomery Conference on Race Problems of the South in 1900; argued, when faced with Negro disfranchisement, for an approach that would ensure that literacy and property qualifications were equally applicable to both races; led the campaign against child labor in Alabama; and acted as executive secretary of the Southern Education Board, a Rockefeller-supported organization working for the improvement of Southern schools. His increasing involvement in reform and philanthropic activities forced him to give up his post at St. John's in 1901 and then to leave the ministry entirely in 1903. He was a prolific writer of books, pamphlets, and articles which attempted to awaken the South to the need for moderate social and humanitarian reform. For biographical information and assessments of Murphy's career see Hugh C. Bailey, *Edgar Gardner Murphy: Gentle Progressive* (Coral Gables, Fla., 1968) ; Maud King Murphy, *Edgar Gardner Murphy* (New York, 1943) ; and the chapter on Murphy in Daniel Levine, *Varieties of Reform Thought* (Madison, Wis., 1964) .

racial cooperation.[3] These writers and others who expressed the same viewpoint spoke for a modicum of decency and humanitarianism in an age of racist demagoguery. Their influence for good may have been severely limited by their own underlying racial preconceptions, but those preconceptions were shared by almost all white Americans, North and South, during this period.

To some extent, the new accommodationists were the heirs of the "paternalists" of the 1880s. Like Atticus Haygood, Joel Chandler Harris, and Henry W. Grady, they heralded the coming of a "New South" in which the hum of industrial progress would be accompanied by interracial harmony. Unlike their predecessors, however, they confronted an ascendant Negrophobia, which made their position by necessity both defensive and, in a limited sense, reformist. As reformers they reflected not only the ideals of Southern paternalism but also, and perhaps more significantly, the new hopes for social cooperation and human betterment characteristic of the Progressive era. Socially conscious intellectuals like Murphy—who also led Southern campaigns for improved white education and the abolition of child labor—constituted the humanitarian wing of the Southern Progressive movement and must be distinguished from the political Progressives, who sometimes combined with militant racists to promote disfranchisement and segregation in addition to such characteristic Progressive causes as the regulation of corporations and the extension of public services.[4]

In describing the black character, the accommodationists strongly emphasized the child half of the perennial racist dichotomy between the Negro as child and the Negro as beast. Part of

3. Weatherford's long and distinguished career as a Southern interracial and antipoverty reformer, which extended into the 1960s (he was still active at ninety), is described in Wilma Dykeman's *Prophet of Plenty: The First Ninety Years of W. D. Weatherford* (Knoxville, 1966). Weatherford's views, like those of some other Southern liberals who began as accommodationist racists, became increasingly egalitarian as time went on.

4. On political Progressivism in the South, see C. Vann Woodward, *Origins of the New South, 1877–1913* (Baton Rouge, 1951), Chapter XIV. Woodward treats the Southern humanitarian and educational reformers of the period in Chapter XV of the same work. Dewey Grantham's "The Progressive Movement and the Negro," *South Atlantic Quarterly*, LIV (October, 1955), 461–477, provides a good brief analysis of Progressive racial attitudes and policies.

their strategy was to call for kindness toward the blacks on the grounds that they retained under freedom many of the amiable characteristics of the faithful slaves of Southern tradition. Such a racial image had been implicit in the paternalistic rhetoric of the 1880s, but it took the active promulgation of the counterimage of the Negro as beast to make it a matter of urgency for paternalists and accommodationists to rekindle the dying embers of romantic racialism. As early as 1889, Julius D. Dreher, president of Roanoke College in Virginia and a contributor to George W. Cable's short-lived Open Letter Club for Southern liberals and moderates, attacked the growing tendency to view the Negroes as a physical threat to the whites by arguing that such a conception was incompatible with the black personality. The Negro, Dreher wrote, "is naturally docile and peacable; and if we treat him with anything like the fairness, justice, and consideration we claim for ourselves as men, we shall hear less of race antagonism in the future. Knowing the peaceable disposition of the Negroes as we do, is it not strange how often the spectre of a 'Negro uprising' or a 'Negro riot' is conjured up by heated imaginations and published throughout the Union as an imminent danger to the white race?"[5]

In 1895 a Charleston aristocrat named Isaac DuBose Seabrook wrote (but did not publish) a long essay on the Negro question intended as an attack on Ben Tillman's campaign for disfranchisement. Despite their biological inferiority, Seabrook argued, blacks should be protected in their political rights; because Negro voters were no real threat to white supremacy: "Their docility and good will are very marked, nor have they as a people been hostile to the interest of the whites, except when made so by the action of the whites or excited by shameless leaders. . . . their faith in any white man who shows kindly intentions toward them is indeed marvellous."[6]

5. William Baskervill, et al., "Shall the Negro Be Educated or Suppressed? Dr. Haygood's reply to Senator Eustis," *Independent*, XLI (Feb. 21, 1889), 227.
6. Isaac DuBose Seabrook, *Before and After; or, The Relations of the Races at the South*, ed. John Hammond Moore (Baton Rouge, 1967), p. 117, and *passim*.

Such arguments did not seriously hinder the campaign for disfranchisement, but after 1900 they began to raise doubts in the minds of some Southerners on how far the campaign to "put the Negro in his place" really needed to be carried. In his influential *Problems of the Present South*, published in 1904, Edgar Gardner Murphy maintained that the Negro did not have to be held down by force or terrorized into submission, because he belonged to a race which possessed a powerful instinct for "self-conservation"—"a preference for amnesty" when confronted with the superior power of the whites. The Negro, according to Murphy, "will accept in the white man's country the place assigned him by the white man, will do his work, not by stress of rivalry, but by genial coöperation with the white man's interests, will take the job allotted him in that division of the world's work which is made by the white man's powers, and will do that work so well that the white man can make more from it by leaving it with the negro than by doing it himself." In his view, therefore, it was cruel and unnecessary to terrorize such a people by lynching and other devices or to deny that they had a future in America.[7]

The paternalistic racial philosophy accompanying such a conception of the Negro character was summed up by Charles T. Hopkins, the leader of a group of prominent whites who met in Atlanta after the race riot of 1906 to condemn the behavior of the white mob. "The Negro race," Hopkins admonished the purveyors of fear and defenders of violence, "is a child race. We are a strong race, their guardians. We have boasted of our superiority and we have now sunk to this level—we have shed the blood of our helpless wards. Christianity and humanity demand that we treat the Negro fairly. He is here, and here to stay. He only knows those things we teach him to do; it is our Christian duty to protect him."[8]

To uphold their view of the Negro as a harmless child or "helpless ward," the neopaternalists of the Progressive era had to meet the charge that the Negro's fundamental bestiality was re-

7. Edgar Gardner Murphy, *Problems of the Present South* (New York, 1904), pp. 81–84, and *passim*.
8. Quoted in Ray Stannard Baker, *Following the Color Line* (New York, 1908), p. 19.

flected in a growing incidence of sexual attacks on white women. In general, they did so by pointing out that such crimes remained so rare and exceptional that they revealed nothing about the essential Negro character. Nathaniel Southgate Shaler, a Kentucky-born geology professor at Harvard, who helped to popularize paternalistic doctrines of racial accommodation among educated Northerners, argued in 1900 against "the common assertion that male negroes are sexually dangerous animals" by contending that Negro rape was overpublicized. In Shaler's opinion, "violence to women is not proved to be a crime peculiarly common among blacks." He was inclined to believe that "there is less danger to be apprehended from them than from an equal body of whites of like social grade."[9] According to Murphy, who took a similar view, the fact that Negro rapists were "so few in number, should make the attitude of the public mind in dealing with them a task of simplicity and ease." It was "because of the deep forces of interracial suspicion" that Negro rape had become "the most complex and difficult of 'questions.' "[10]

The image of the Negro as a harmless child, whose criminal tendencies were marginal or due to special circumstances, received its fullest expression later in the Progressive era in the writings of Benjamin F. Riley and Weatherford. Both were fervent exponents of "social Christianity," and their praise of Negro docility and kindheartedness carried them close to the romantic racialism of the Northern Christian reformers of the Civil War era. Riley, a Baptist minister with an Alabama background, was superintendent of the Anti-Saloon League of Texas when he wrote *The White Man's Burden,* a monument of sentimental paternalism and apparent Negrophilia, published in 1910. "The dominant characteristic of the Negro is that of sub-

9. N. S. Shaler, "The Negro Since the Civil War," *Popular Science Monthly,* LVII (May, 1900), 38–39. Shaler wrote several articles on the race question for *Popular Science* and the *Atlantic Monthly,* all of which expressed the philosophy of accommodationist racism. In 1904 he published *The Neighbor: A Natural History of Human Contacts* (Boston and New York), in which he developed a theory about the origins of group consciousness and prejudice similar to the sociological concept of "consciousness of kind," discussed later in this chapter.

10. Murphy, *Present South,* pp. 173–174.

mission and tractableness," Riley wrote. And such traits had served him well; for without this "quiet submissiveness to wrong," he would long ago have been "pulverized" by the aggressive whites: "He has met the repeated shocks of racial revolution with a resiliency that has saved his race from utter dissolution. This passive virtue has been his greatest means of conservation." Although Southern whites had historically mistreated them in a variety of ways, the blacks had always managed to act like true Christians by turning the other cheek. Such virtues were at last beginning to reap their reward, Riley asserted, because of the appeal that they made to "the really chivalric white man" of the South: "Left to himself, the Negro raises no tumults, incites no strikes; and when smitten smites not again. . . . Where others would resist, he tamely submits, and where others would cherish malice and hatred, he returns a quiet good humor. Eliciting, as this does, the impulse of the old-time chivalry of the South, the Negro will find that as he establishes his genuine worth in his effort to improve, public opinion in his behalf will increase on the higher levels of the stronger race."[11]

In his *Present Forces in Negro Progress*, published in 1912, Weatherford went even further in celebrating the Negro "virtues" that had been obscured by the propaganda of the extremists: "Those who talk about the angelic qualities of 'the old time darky' (I do not like the term), and damn with every breath the new Negro, simply prove their shallow thinking. They ought to know that a race characteristic cannot be developed in two or three generations unless its essential elements are there at the beginning." Arguing in effect that the accommodationists were more consistent in their racialism than the Negrophobes, Weatherford said fidelity, gratitude, generosity, lack of malice, kindliness, sense of humor, and a peculiar aptitude for music and religion—qualities allegedly characteristic of the beloved retainer of the slave era—constituted ineradicable racial traits. "What a catalogue of splendid qualities is this," he proclaimed. It was a small matter to him that the race was "not the most

11. B. F. Riley, *The White Man's Burden* (Birmingham, Ala., 1910), pp. 119, 127, and *passim*. For biographical information on Riley, who was a significant Baptist leader, see *The Dictionary of American Biography*.

brilliantly intellectual," was "lacking in self-mastery," and was deficient in "industry and thrift." The virtues it did possess were sufficient "to make any race happy, virtuous, useful, and even great." If the cardinal Negro virtue of fidelity was less in evidence than formerly, it was the fault of the whites who had not found "the means of bringing it to the surface."[12]

Two years later, in speaking to the Southern Sociological Congress, Weatherford repeated his optimistic analysis and claimed that whites were coming to acknowledge that blacks still possessed "those fine qualities of character displayed by the faithful slave." The belief that the good darky was gone forever was no longer tenable; the white South was "beginning to see that the nobler qualities of the past are rebudding after the rude transplanting of the sixties, and that additional qualities of nobility begin to show themselves which could never have appeared under older conditions."[13] Weatherford made it clear that his concept of black character and temperament allowed for change and modification within a flexible framework of racial traits. If the Negro had the endearing qualities of a child, some of which he would presumably never lose, he also had the child's capacity for growth. Emphasis on "the nobler qualities of the past" was both a safe and patriotic way of appealing to Southern whites to give the Negro a better chance and an assertion that blacks had latent capacities worthy of cultivation. Indeed, it was essential to the neopaternalist case against the theory of Negro degeneracy and "reversion to type" to maintain that the race was capable of progress and that this capability had already been demonstrated.

The Southern liberals readily conceded the existence of some evidence of a deterioration in Negro morality since emancipation. "The masses of the race," Murphy acknowledged, ". . . have shown many of the tendencies of moral and physical reversion." But he attributed this trend solely to the fact that blacks had been "isolated, through the pressure of political exigencies, from the sympathetic guidance of the better South . . ." The

12. W. D. Weatherford, *Present Forces in Negro Progress* (New York and London, 1912), pp. 26–31.
13. James E. McCulloch, ed., *Battling for Social Betterment: The Southern Sociological Congress, 1914* (Nashville, 1914), p. 184.

extreme detractors of the Negro did not recognize, he wrote, what real progress a growing minority had made, as revealed by the "persistently increasing number of true families and real homes . . . homes in which with intelligence, probity, industry, and an admirable simplicity, the man and the woman are creating our fundamental institution."[14] Riley outdid Murphy in celebrating the extent to which some blacks were acquiring white middle-class standards. Indeed, black achievements since emancipation were "astounding." "The Negro," he wrote in 1910, "has made himself an exception among the peoples of the earth in the rapidity of his advancement."[15]

Another writer who called attention to the new kind of "good Negro"—"well-educated, courteous, God-fearing"—was Andrew Sledd. A 1902 article, which cost him his position as a professor of Latin at a Georgia college, included the heretical statement that such black paragons were "in everything save color, superior to many white men"; it was grossly unjust that they were treated contemptuously in public places.[16] Also accused of Negrophilia at about the same time was the historian John Spencer Bassett of Trinity College, now Duke University. Unlike Sledd, however, Bassett weathered the storm resulting from an outspoken attack on the purveyors of racial hatred. In a controversial article published in the *South Atlantic Quarterly* in 1903, Bassett wrote, among other things: "No sensible man in the North or in the South who is not blinded by passion will deny that the better Negroes of the country have made a remarkable record since the days of emancipation."[17]

In an effort to explain why such progress had not prevented the whites from developing a hostile view of the Negro, spokesmen like Murphy and Riley pointed to the effect of segregation on the pattern of interracial contacts. Under slavery, it was suggested, there had been real intimacy between the better class

14. Murphy, *Present South*, pp. 164–166.
15. Riley, *White Man's Burden*, pp. 92, 116.
16. Andrew Sledd, "The Negro: Another View," *Atlantic Monthly*, XC (July, 1902), 68.
17. John Spencer Bassett, "Stirring Up the Fires of Race Antipathy," *South Atlantic Quarterly*, II (October, 1903), 299.

of whites and the best specimens of the Negro race; as a result of this relationship, "the conception of the old-time darky" had become "a national heritage." Under the new conditions of segregation, however, exemplars of Negro progress had little or no contact with whites, who encountered only the servants, loafers, and criminals of the race. The new black middle class, the hope of the future and gauge of racial potentialities, was hidden within the separate black community, and the races confronted each other largely on the lower rungs of the social ladder where conflict and distrust were inevitable.[18] As a remedy for this situation, the liberals might have proposed the substantial modification or elimination of segregation, but they did not in fact do this, because they adhered as strongly as other Southerners to the dogma that social separation was necessary to "race integrity." Men of this persuasion did eventually suggest the development of "co-operative" contacts between the new black bourgeoisie and the upper strata of the white community to discuss ways to eliminate racial friction and ensure mutual progress. In one way or another, they hoped to establish—or, as they saw it, re-establish—friendly relations between "aristocratic" whites and the better elements in the Negro community, as a way of countering the rising influence of the whites of nonslave-holding or lower-class background, a group they characteristically blamed for the excesses of Southern racism.[19]

The model for the advancing contingent of moral and upright Negro leaders who could be expected to co-operate with "the better class" of Southern whites was Booker T. Washington, who was everything that the Southern liberals professed to desire in a black spokesman. John Spencer Bassett called Washington "a great and good man, . . . all in all the greatest man save General Lee, born in the South in a hundred years." Bassett made it clear that Washington was a very exceptional Negro, but this statement, more than anything else in his provocative article,

18. See Murphy, *Present South*, pp. 167–181; and Riley, *White Man's Burden*, pp. 61–62.

19. See Riley, *White Man's Burden*, p. 174; Sledd, "The Negro," p. 68; and Edgar Gardner Murphy, "The Task of the Leader," *Sewanee Review*, XV (January, 1907), 15–16.

aroused the controversy in North Carolina that almost caused him to be fired from his professorship in 1904.[20] Other opponents of demagogic racism did not go so far, but their respect for the principal of Tuskegee Institute was obvious. Murphy had a close working relationship with Washington, and Riley, who praised Washington and his program in *The White Man's Burden*, was to become an early and sympathetic biographer of the great proponent of Negro self-help and industrial training.[21] What Southern moderates saw in Washington is obvious: he was willing to work with the "better class" of Southern whites; he counseled blacks to accept at least a temporary racial subordination and segregation; and, above all, he represented a gradual program for black progress designed to bring racial peace by converting the whites to a more favorable view of Negro character and capacity. Although they did not agree with everything he said or did, the Southern white accommodationists were so close to Washington in their basic racial philosophy and drew so much inspiration from him that it would not be far from the mark to call them white Washingtonians.

These men took stands on specific issues involving the Negro which followed naturally from their understanding of Negro character and Southern racial realities. They departed from the standard quasi-apologetic approach to lynching by forthrightly denouncing the practice as totally inexcusable. But because of their fear of "centralization" and their belief that Reconstruction had demonstrated the evil effects of outside interference with the South's effort to solve its own racial problem, they did not even consider the desirability of Federal antilynching legislation.[22] In the area of voting rights, they accepted disfranchisement based on literacy tests but said the new restrictions should be applied equally and fairly to both races. Such an administra-

20. Bassett, "Race Antipathy," 199. An account of the Bassett controversy can be found in Edwin Mims, *The Advancing South: Stories of Progress and Reaction* (Garden City, New York, 1926), pp. 147–158.
21. Bailey, *Murphy*, pp. 36, 109, 119, 133–134; Riley, *White Man's Burden*, 134–135; B. F. Riley, *The Life and Times of Booker T. Washington* (New York, 1916).
22. Murphy, *Present South*, pp. 176–182; Sledd, "The Negro," pp. 68–71; Riley, *White Man's Burden*, pp. 153–164.

tion of the suffrage restrictions would, in their opinion, "reward" the better element among the blacks and keep from the polls the white riffraff who were the primary target of race-baiting demagogues.[23]

If the danger from suffrage limitation was unequal enforcement, the danger from social segregation was unequal public facilities. The Southern liberals believed wholeheartedly in segregation but argued that it could not achieve its real purpose—the maintenance of "racial integrity"—so long as the blacks received inferior treatment. Miscegenation, Murphy and others pointed out, resulted from black degradation and lack of opportunity; for most race mixing occurred between white men and lower-class Negro women who had not had a chance to develop middle-class standards of sexual purity. As blacks became educated, acquired property, and learned to expect "separate but equal" treatment in public facilities and impartial justice in the courts, they would naturally develop a pride of race which would discourage sexual liaison with whites, because educated and self-respecting blacks allegedly understood the need for racial purity and social separation. Anything that demoralized the blacks, put obstacles in the way of their progress, or hindered their self-realization as a distinct people in the United States encouraged the very "mongrelization" the advocates of black repression professed to fear. Here again the liberal accommodationists sought to put themselves forward as the only consistent and intelligent exponents of basic Southern racial doctrines—in contrast to the confused and self-contradictory advocates of blatant repression. If the blacks were given the opportunity for a self-sufficient social and cultural life on their own side of the color line, Murphy argued, they would develop their latent racial genius, evolve a worthy and distinct culture of their own, and, as a result, lose all desire to amalgamate with the whites.[24]

The primary mechanism for Negro advancement along lines

23. Murphy, Present South, pp. 191–198; see also Hon. William H. Fleming, Slavery and the Race Problem in the South (Boston, 1907), pp. 44–45, 55–57, 62. Fleming was an ex-Congressman from Alabama.

24. Murphy, Present South, pp. 270–274; Murphy, The Basis of Ascendancy (New York, 1909), Chapter VI; Riley, White Man's Burden, p. 133.

separate but parallel to those of the whites was education, and especially the kind of education carried on at Tuskegee or Hampton. In a reply to white extremists who would undermine all black education, Murphy pointed out that "the industrial education of the negro is intended to supply under the conditions of freedom, those elements of skill, those conditions of industrial peace, which our fathers supplied under the conditions of slavery. It is not without significance that no graduate of Hampton or Tuskegee has ever been charged with assault upon a woman." Such a description of Negro education suggested that the Southern white liberals did not go all the way with Washington, who implied that industrial training and self-help were the first steps in a transformation of the Negro's character and condition that would eventuate in full equality. In their view, the Negro could be made substantially better, but it was doubtful if he could ever be raised to the level of the whites. "It is certainly no tribute to the Caucasian," wrote Murphy, "to assume that his own proud and historic race, with its centuries of start and the funded culture of all civilization at its command, cannot keep ahead of the negro, no matter what the negro can know or do."[25] The accommodationists merely postulated that more could be made of the Negro, permanently inferior though he was, than the popularizers of the concept of black degeneracy were willing to admit. As Alabama Congressman Hilary A. Herbert, one of the moderate spokesmen at the Montgomery race conference of 1900, put it: ". . . we can lift up the Negro—not to make him equal to the foremost races of the world, but improve him till he becomes a better laborer, a better citizen, and more useful to himself and to the country. . . ."[26]

One of the best summations of this confidently white-supremacist program for Negro uplift appeared in Walter Hines Page's novel *The Southerner*, published in 1909. Page, a North Carolinian who had gone to New York to become a leading editor and publisher, remained an important promoter of any and all

25. Murphy, *Present South*, pp. 80–81.
26. Southern Society for the Promotion of the Study of Race Conditions and Problems in the South, *Race Problems of the South: Proceedings of the First Annual Conference* (Richmond, Va., 1900) , p. 38.

"progressive" tendencies that appeared in his native region; and in the novel his *alter ego,* Nicholas Worth, gives a speech in defense of Negro education as the high point in his election campaign against a race-baiting demagogue. "The Negro was brought here," Worth tells his audience. "He will stay here. We will make the most of him. He is a burden and a menace unless he is trained. So too, is the white man. But the Negro is a child in civilization. Let us train him. That is our economic duty, our economic necessity. Let us teach him to do productive work, teach him to be a help, to support himself, to do useful things, to be a man, to build up his family life. Let his women alone. Help him. He is docile, grateful, teachable. He is a man. Our civilization menaced by the Negro? That's a lie, and you know it. The only way in which the Negro can be a menace to our civilization is by his ignorance. The state must train him."[27]

Statements of this kind suggest that the Southern Progressive or "liberal" alternative to extreme racism was at bottom a rather conservative doctrine. It constituted no real break with the fundamentals of racist ideology but attempted rather to bring that ideology into harmony with such conservative goals as law and order, social harmony, and rule by a benevolent elite.

The trouble with the extremists and purveyors of the image of the Negro as beast, according to Southern liberals, was that they whipped the masses into frenzies of race hate which endangered the very foundations of the social fabric. In his second book, *The Basis of Ascendancy,* published in 1909, Murphy stressed the point that the accommodationists were the South's true conservatives. During Reconstruction and after, he wrote, the campaign for white supremacy had been necessary to preserve civilization itself. This campaign had been genuinely "conservative," but its success had led to a "new mood" which not only made "few professions of conservatism" but was actually radical and "destructive" rather than "protective" of the best interests of society. The once-noble white-supremacy movement was now drawing on "some of the basest of our factions and impulses." The only force restraining the extremists from attacking "every privilege" the

27. [Walter Hines Page], *The Southerner, A Novel* (New York, 1909), p. 251.

Negro possessed was a genteel minority "made up of the remnant of the older aristocracy and . . . many of the representatives of our professional and commercial classes." Unless the current aggression against the Negro was resisted, Murphy warned, it would destroy "not the negro, nor the white man only, but society itself,—society as a sufficient instrument of equitable and profitable relations." He then went on to show convincingly that injustice against the blacks harmed the whites by lowering the standards of Southern social, economic, and political life. His fondest hope, he indicated here and elsewhere, was for the return of the descendants of the old aristocracy and their middle-class allies to positions of leadership, thereby restoring a decent tone to Southern race relations.[28]

II

The "liberal" paternalists did not convert the South as a whole to their point of view. Their influence on the sources of power in Southern communities was limited, because they were, for the most part, intellectuals—clergymen and professors—attempting in vain to shape public policy in a profoundly antiintellectual society.[29] Their position was further weakened because of their identification with a class-oriented paternalistic tradition which had never succeeded in weaning most Southerners away from "Herrenvolk egalitarianism" with its refusal to differentiate among Negroes or accept the possibility of black advancement. When Dr. Thomas Pearce Bailey, dean of the Department of Education at the University of Mississippi, summed up "Race Orthodoxy in the South" in 1914, he included such doctrines as the following: "in matters of civil rights and legal adjustments give the white man, as opposed to the colored man, the benefit of

28. Murphy, *Basis of Ascendancy*, pp. 25, 138, 28–29, 126–127. Murphy's fullest discussion of the role of the aristocracy appears in his *Sewanee Review* article, "The Task of the Leader," cited above.

29. Many of Gunnar Myrdal's perceptive observations about the situation and influence of the Southern interracial liberals of 1940 (see *An American Dilemma* [New York, 1944], I, 466–473) apply equally well to the Southern liberals of 1910.

the doubt and under no circumstances interfere with the prestige of the white race"; "in educational policy let the negro have the crumbs that fall from the white man's table"; "the status of peasantry is all the negro may hope for, if the races are to live together in peace"; and "let the lowest white man count more than the highest negro"—none of which the accommodationists could have accepted without major qualification.[30]

Although they failed to change popular opinion in the South, the moderates did exercise some restraining influence on the extremists: they contributed to the successful effort to prevent the permanent throttling of an already impoverished Negro school system through a formalized racial division of the educational tax fund, and began a campaign against lynching, helping to bring about a gradual decrease in racial murders of this type; eventually their call for cooperation between the leaders of the white and black communities to improve race relations led to the Southern interracial movement of the 1920s and 1930s which had some success in upgrading separate facilities for Negroes, although it fell far short of its announced goal of equalization.[31]

During the Progressive era itself, however, Murphy and his Southern sympathizers had their greatest impact on a national rather than a regional level. Outside the South, Murphy's views were widely hailed by the leaders of Progressive opinion as constituting a sane and reasonable approach to the race problem. Dovetailing programmatically with the thinking of Booker T. Washington, Murphy's combination of racialism and benevolence was congenial to educated Northerners who acknowledged that Negroes were inferior but were reluctant to exclude them entirely from the benefits of a continuing movement for social

30. Thomas P. Bailey, *Race Orthodoxy in the South, and Other Aspects of the Negro Question* (New York, 1914), p. 93.

31. W. E. B. Du Bois wrote in 1903, "It has been only by the most strenuous efforts on the part of the thinking men of the South that the Negro's share of the school fund has not been cut down to a pittance in some half dozen states" (*Souls of Black Folk,* p. 180). On the later history of the Southern interracial movement see Dykeman, *Prophet of Plenty,* and Dykeman and James Stokely, *Seeds of Southern Change: The Life of Will Alexander* (Chicago, 1962). Alexander was the guiding spirit of the Commission for Interracial Co-operation in the 1920s and 1930s.

betterment. The views of the Southern accommodationists are significant, therefore, because they helped establish a new national consensus of "enlightened" and "liberal" opinion on the race question.

In 1905 Edwin Mims, professor of English at Trinity College, North Carolina, described this emerging consensus in an article defending President Theodore Roosevelt against bitter Southern attacks stemming from Roosevelt's entertainment of Booker T. Washington at a White House dinner in 1901 and his efforts to appoint Negro Republicans to patronage jobs in the South. Mims saw Roosevelt as one of a group of "liberal Northerners" who were opposed to extremes of racial injustice in the South but were in perfect agreement with those "liberal Southerners" like Murphy, who opposed lynching, peonage, and unequal enforcement of the suffrage restrictions, favored industrial education for Negroes, but acknowledged that *"segregation in school, church and society is in the interest of racial integrity and racial progress."*[32] This was a fairly accurate statement of Roosevelt's position in 1905. Earlier in his Presidency he had talked and acted as if he had some concern with maintaining the rights of Negroes to citizenship and political participation, but by 1905 he had obviously decided that the best approach was one which relied on the paternalistic mercies of the "better class" of Southern whites.[33]

Like the Southern liberals, Roosevelt appealed to the gospel of Washington to justify a paternalistic program for racial uplift. "It always seemed to me," he wrote in 1900, "that the salvation of the Negro lay in the development of the Booker Washington theory—that is, fitting him to do ever better industrial work." His strongest statement on the importance of Washington's example is contained in a 1906 letter to the novelist Owen Wister. Although he agreed with Wister that the blacks "as a race and as a mass . . . are altogether inferior to the whites," he dissented

32. Edwin Mims, "President Theodore Roosevelt," *South Atlantic Quarterly*, IV (January, 1905) , 59–60.

33. On the development of Roosevelt's racial attitudes and policies, see Seth M. Scheiner, "Theodore Roosevelt and the Negro, 1901–1908," *Journal of Negro History*, XLVII (July, 1962) , 169–182.

from the latter's extremely low opinion of the race: ". . . admitting all that can truthfully be said against the Negro, it remains true that a great deal that is untrue is said against him . . ." He went on to describe the belief of Southern extremists that the Negro had degenerated since emancipation as "the veriest nonsense." "He has on the whole become better. Among the Negroes of the South when slavery was abolished there was not one who stood as in any shape or way comparable with Booker Washington. Incidentally, I may add that I do not know a white man of the South who is as good a man as Booker Washington today."[34]

In his 1905 Lincoln Day speech, Roosevelt contended that right-thinking Northerners sympathized with the problems faced by white Southerners and "had the heartiest respect for those brave and earnest men of the South who in the face of fearful difficulties are doing all that men can do for the betterment alike of white and black." The problem, as he saw it, was how to train "the backward race so that it may enter the possession of true freedom, while the forward race is allowed to preserve unharmed the high civilization wrought by its forefathers." Such a task, involving, as it did, the "moral and industrial uplifting" of the blacks, was bound to be difficult and would take a long time to accomplish. Black advancement of any sort, Roosevelt believed, must be made compatible with the Southern ban on "social intermingling of the race"; for, as was obvious to "all reflecting men," "racial purity must be maintained."[35]

Edgar Gardner Murphy, it turns out, had some direct influence on the development of Roosevelt's policy position on the South and the Negro. In 1904 Murphy was summoned to the White House to advise the President on how he should respond to the furor resulting from his nomination of a Negro Republican to be Collector of Customs for the port of Charleston. The Southerner counseled Roosevelt to prevail upon the nominee to withdraw voluntarily, arguing that blacks should not seek public office until the race had made progress in other areas. "Wisdom and patience and faithful service must be for the time the Ne-

34. Theodore Roosevelt, *Letters*, ed. Elting E. Morison (Cambridge, Mass., 1951–1954) , II, 1169; V, 226–227.
35. Theodore Roosevelt, *Works* (New York, 1925) , XVIII, 463–465.

groes' way of advancement," Murphy said. Roosevelt attempted, unsuccessfully in this instance, to follow Murphy's advice, and he subsequently reduced the number of Negro officeholders and worked openly for the development of a "lily-white" Republican party in the South.[36] In 1907 Roosevelt openly acknowledged his debt to Murphy's racial philosophy, writing to the Alabamian that "I have grown accustomed to looking to you as one of the men to follow in reference to the Negro question."[37]

Five years later, the influence of Southern liberal paternalism on Roosevelt's thinking was demonstrated again when, as the Presidential candidate of the Progressive Party, Roosevelt published an article on "The Progressives and the Colored Man." In it, he openly repudiated the traditional Republican emphasis on Federal protection of Negro rights in the South, a policy he described as having encouraged racial antagonism, and he called upon blacks to appeal for help to the "competent, high-minded white men of the South." He quoted Julian Harris, son of Joel Chandler Harris, a Southern supporter of the Progressive Party and a racial moderate in the Murphy tradition. According to Harris, the Negro could best make progress "under the supervision and with the cooperation of his white neighbor," and Roosevelt endorsed this point of view as the basis of a "Progressive" solution to the race problem.[38]

Roosevelt was the most important of the many spokesmen for Northern Progressivism who endorsed Murphy's racial philosophy. The *Outlook,* a Progressive weekly, described *Problems of the Present South* as the most illuminating contribution to the study of Southern problems to appear since the Civil War. Many Northern newspapers were equally fulsome in their praise, and Murphy received warm letters of congratulation from the leaders of Northern philanthropy and even from surviving veterans of Radical Republicanism like Carl Schurz and the economist Edward A. Atkinson. It is difficult to read the reviews and notices of Murphy's book without concluding that he had said just what

36. Bailey, *Murphy,* pp. 115–118; Scheiner, "Theodore Roosevelt," 179–181.
37. Bailey, *Murphy,* p. 171.
38. Theodore Roosevelt, "The Progressives and the Colored Man," *Outlook,* CI (August 24, 1912) , 909–912.

liberal opinion in the North wanted to hear about the race question in 1904.[39]

Nowhere were Murphy's views more welcomed than among Northern Progressive clergymen—the leaders of the "social Gospel" movement. The Reverend Lyman Abbott, who during Reconstruction and for some time afterward had favored unlimited Negro suffrage and integrated schools in the South, changed his mind by 1903; in that year he came out for suffrage restrictions based on education and other moderate applications of Southern racial doctrines. In his autobiography Abbott acknowledged Murphy's influence, describing him as "at once a prophet, a reformer, and a historian."[40] In a 1907 article by Washington Gladden, perhaps the most famous exponent of the social Gospel, Murphy was quoted as an example of an enlightened element in the South innocent of "sectional fanaticism" which needed Northern support and encouragement against the "reactionaries" who were presently in control.[41]

For the most part, Gladden and other Northern proponents of "social Christianity" ignored the Negro, concentrating on developing a "Christian" approach to the social problems resulting from industrialism and urbanization; but on the rare occasions when they did address themselves directly to the race problem, they came to conclusions strikingly similar to Murphy's.[42] In *Socialism and Christianity* (1910), the Reverend Percy Stickney Grant called for a new philosophy of race relations, based on a recognition of the inadequacy of the idealism of the Reconstruction era. According to the theory of evolution, Grant argued, the Negro was not entitled to equal rights, because he had not yet developed sufficiently to share fully in the privileges of the more

39. Bailey, *Murphy*, pp. 128–129; see also the selection of favorable comments on *The Present South* in the back of Murphy's subsequent book, *The Basis of Ascendancy*.

40. Lyman Abbott, *Reminiscences* (Boston and New York, 1915), pp. 270, 423–424, 276.

41. Washington Gladden, "The Negro Crisis," *American Magazine*, LXIII (January, 1907), 296–297.

42. On the over-all failure of the social Gospel movement to confront racial injustice, see David M. Reimers, *White Protestantism and the Negro* (New York, 1965), pp. 53–54.

advanced race. This did not mean, however, that blacks should be neglected or oppressed. If inequality between the races authorized differences in privilege, it also imposed duties on the higher races and invited "the missionary and pedagogical spirit." Giving a curious twist to the social Gospel campaign against the ideology of *laissez-faire* individualism, Grant wrote that "a democracy of *inequality* and of *education* is more humane than a democracy of equality and *laissez-faire*."[43]

The Reverend John R. Rogers reached similar conclusions in a pamphlet entitled *The Importance of Time in the Solution of the Negro Problem*, published during this period by the American Missionary Society. Speaking for an organization that had been begun as an outlet for Christian abolitionism and had then led the campaign for freedmen's aid during the Civil War and Reconstruction, Rogers addressed himself to "a sense of disappointment that after the expenditure of millions and millions of dollars and hundreds of devoted lives, the typical negro is still lazy and shiftless and fails to distinguish between meum and teum, especially in the case of chickens and watermelons." Such a feeling of frustration resulted from the fact that too much had been expected of the blacks, who, after all, belonged to a child race: "In the light of common sense, can we expect the Negro to traverse the steps from savagery to civilization in a generation when it took the Anglo-Saxon a thousand years to climb?" Rogers argued that the blacks had reached a difficult stage of childhood, resembling a growing boy who is a trial to his parents. It behooved the whites to be patient and to continue with the slow and expensive process of education and uplift.[44]

Walter Rauschenbusch, the foremost theologian of the social Gospel movement, turned his attention to the Negro problem for the first time in 1914. In an article in the *American Missionary*, Rauschenbusch admitted that the problem seemed "tragic" and "insoluble." But he warned the South that it could not succeed

43. Percy Stickney Grant, *Socialism and Christianity* (New York, 1910), pp. 127–139, 142–143, 146.
44. John R. Rogers, *The Importance of Time as a Factor in the Solution of the Negro Problem* (New York, n.d.), pp. 6, 8–10.

in implementing a policy "which does not satisfy the Christian consciousness of the whole nation." No solution would satisfy the nation, he argued, unless it provided for "the progressive awakening of race pride and race ambition in all Negro communities." It was the duty of the white man to take "our belated black brother by the hand" and "urge him along the road of steady and intelligent labor, of property rights, of family fidelity, of hope and self-confidence, and of pride and joy in his race achievements."[45]

Rauschenbusch was right in his sense of the imperatives of a certain kind of national opinion. The gospel of extreme Southern racism with its concept of inevitable black degeneracy and probable extinction, its implicit or open justification of lynching and extreme forms of oppression, was, in the last analysis, unacceptable to the keepers of the national conscience during the Progressive era. Benevolent and progressive Northerners, who thought they had learned a "tragic" lesson from Reconstruction, were not prepared to intervene in the South in order to ensure that the blacks had an environment conducive to "the progressive awakening of race pride and race ambition," nor were they ready to deny the popular belief in the Negro's inferiority; but they did try to reconcile this posture with social optimism and humanitarian concern. They derived such a mode of discourse from the Southern moderates with their quasi-missionary concept of training and uplifting a child race, as well as from the self-help ideology and black accommodationism of Booker T. Washington. A small minority, representing the extreme left wing of the Northern Progressive movement, went beyond paternalism and white Washingtonianism and came out for the immediate implementation of full equality, but this group, which helped found the National Association for the Advancement of Colored People in 1910, would not become influential until later. In a sense, then, Southern paternalism lost the South to the extremists but won the North, or an articulate segment of it, to its way of thinking.

45. Professor Walter Rauschenbusch, "The Problem of the Black Man," *American Missionary*, LVIII (March, 1914), 732–733.

III

The doctrines of accommodationist racism were well received in educated and philanthropic circles after the 1890s because they were more in tune with the broader intellectual currents of the Progressive era than was the competitive racism of the extremists. This compatibility came out in a striking and paradoxical way in the discussion after the Spanish-American War of America's new imperial role in the world. Some historians have associated the triumph of the imperialist impulse at the end of the nineteenth century with the influence of extreme racist ideas in American thought.[46] But an examination of what was actually being said on the subject of race by imperialists and by anti-imperialists suggests that competitive racism did not, in fact, harmonize readily with the new expansionist ideology.

An understanding of the turn-of-the-century debate on America's proper relationship with "inferior" races abroad requires a recognition of the extent to which racism had been a barrier to imperialism before 1898. The decision not to annex all Mexico in 1848 had been based partially on a distaste for the racial stock south of the Rio Grande; similarly, one of the principal arguments against President Grant's unsuccessful effort to get Congressional approval for the annexation of the Dominican Republic in the early 1870s had stemmed from revulsion against the idea of bringing under the American flag "millions of tropical people, people of the Latin race mixed with Indian and African blood; people who . . . have neither language nor traditions nor habits nor political institutions nor morals in common with us . . ."[47] When it was proposed in 1899 to annex the Philippines, antiimperialists came forth once again with the

46. See, for example, Rayford W. Logan, *The Betrayal of the Negro: From Rutherford B. Hayes to Woodrow Wilson* (New York, 1965), pp. 268–272; and Julius W. Pratt, *The Expansionists of 1898* (Baltimore, 1936), pp. 3–11.

47. Frederick Merk, *Manifest Destiny and Mission in American History* (New York, 1963), pp. 191–192. Carl Schurz, speech in U.S. Senate, Jan. 11, 1871, in *Speeches, Correspondence, and Political Papers*, ed. Frederic Bancroft (New York and London, 1913), II, 99.

traditional arguments that possession of foreign dependencies was a violation of American traditions and that the racial composition of the islands made it unthinkable that Filipinos could be given self-government under American institutions.[48]

Not only were most of the antiimperialists believers in racial inequality, but the extreme racists in Congress and elsewhere, including Senator Benjamin R. Tillman and most of his Southern colleagues, also tended to oppose Philippine annexation, because, as Tillman put it, "we understand what it is to have two races side by side that can not mix or mingle, without deterioration and injury to both and the ultimate destruction of the civilization of the higher." Senator John W. Daniel of Virginia added that the United States had previously experienced "but one impediment to our national harmony and to our national growth": the Negro population. "The interjection of a race nonassimilable with the American people has been the fly in the ointment of American institutions, of American peace, of American history." Why, he asked, should the nation invite more of this kind of trouble?[49]

Viewed from the perspective of a simple dichotomy between racism and egalitarianism, the presence of such attitudes among the antiimperialists demonstrates nothing more than the strength of the underlying racial consensus in the United States at the turn of the century. The departure of the imperialists from the traditional American view of proper contacts with "tropical peoples" came less from a re-evaluation of the potentialities of

48. See Christopher Lasch, "The Anti-Imperialists, The Philippines, and the Rights of Man," *Journal of Southern History*, XXIV (August, 1958), 319–331; and Robert L. Beisner, *Twelve Against Empire: The Anti-Imperialists, 1898–1900* (New York, 1968), p. 219.

49. From a speech in the Senate, Feb. 7, 1899, reprinted in *Republic or Empire: The Philippine Question* (Chicago, 1899), pp. 122, 375–377. Similar views were expressed by some Northern Senators. Henry M. Teller of Colorado claimed that tropical peoples were permanently incapable of adjusting to the American system of government (*ibid.*, p. 240); and Senator William V. Allen of Nebraska contended that the United States already had "a great race problem" and was not in a position "to take within our population 12,000,000 people alien in race, alien in language, and in purpose to a popular government like ours" (*ibid.*, p. 301). On the importance of Southerners and Southern attitudes in the opposition to acquisition of tropical dependencies, see Lasch, "Anti-Imperialists," 324–325.

non-white races than from a desire to reap the economic, political, and psychological benefits that allegedly went with the possession of overseas colonies. But the presence of racism, often of an extreme variety, in antiimperialist thinking suggests that the relationship between overt and virulent Negrophobia at home and colonialism abroad was not really as close as historians have sometimes assumed. Thomas Dixon appears to have been the only significant proponent of the doctrine of inevitable racial antagonism and competition to the death who was also an outspoken imperialist.[50] It was logical that few of the believers in American Negro degeneracy and impending extinction in "the struggle for existence" were excited by the prospect of foreign dependencies. It was one thing to look forward to the extinction of a black population already present in the United States, it was something else again to seek out peoples living in distant and uncongenial climes and enter into competition with them on their own soil. The whites might emerge victorious, but it would be a costly and frustrating struggle; the combination of a climate unsuited to white settlement and a native population productive only under conditions of forced labor meant, antiimperialists said, that tropical colonies were likely to be far more trouble than they were worth.[51]

Imperialists did not deliberately and self-consciously reject a racist tradition when they first argued that the United States could establish a new and fruitful relationship with Asians, Polynesians, or Latin Americans. It appears unlikely, in fact, that racial thinking of any kind was an important factor in the original imperialist impulse: economic motives, concepts of national prestige and influence borrowed from Europe, and the "psychic crisis" arising from the domestic situation of the 1890s were all apparently more significant in stimulating the taste for foreign adventures and involvements than concepts of white supremacy or extrapolations from the Negro's domestic situa-

50. See Thomas Dixon, *The Leopard's Spots: A Romance of the White Man's Burden, 1865–1900* (New York, 1902), pp. 435–436.
51. See Lasch, "Anti-Imperialists," 328; and David Starr Jordan, *Imperial Democracy* (New York, 1899), pp. 31–32, 44–45.

tion.[52] But after America's bid for world power was already well launched, and more or less a *fait accompli,* a racialist rationale emerged to serve the new imperialism that fitted in perfectly with the accommodationist ideology and contributed to its popularity and plausibility.

Imperialists promulgated the concept of "the white man's burden" to justify the new expansionism. Borrowed from Kipling's poem, this phrase did not, in its original context, mean the white man could actually do much to uplift those "lesser breeds" over whom he established dominion.[53] But in the hands of apologists for American expansionism, "the white man's burden" often became indistinguishable from what Percy Stickney Grant called "the missionary and pedagogical spirit." In this vein Theodore Roosevelt—who loved to expatiate on the international "duties" of "the mighty civilized races"—defended the annexation of the Philippines. In an address of 1901 he said: "It is our duty toward the people living in barbarism to see they are freed from their chains, and we can free them only by destroying barbarism itself. The missionary, the merchant, and the soldier may each have a part to play in this destruction, and in the consequent uplifting of the people."[54] On another occasion he argued that "if we do our duty aright in the Philippines, we . . . will greatly benefit the people of the Philippine Islands, and above all we will play our part well in the great work of uplifting mankind."[55]

52. Frederick Merk has cast considerable doubt on the proposition that a burgeoning racism contributed in direct and significant ways to the ideological preparation for imperialism in the years before 1898 (*Manifest Destiny*, pp. 237–247). He concludes with this question: "Is it not likely that racism, prior to the war with Spain, was a deterrent to imperialism rather than a stimulant of it?" (p. 247). For a provocative discussion of some of the more important factors in American expansionism at the turn of the century, see Richard Hofstadter, "Cuba, The Philippines, and Manifest Destiny," in *The Paranoid Style in American Politics, and Other Essays* (New York, 1967), pp. 145–187.

53. On the use and misuse of the phrase from Kipling's poem, see Albert K. Weinberg, *Manifest Destiny: A Study of National Expansion in American History* (Baltimore, 1935), pp. 301–305.

54. Theodore Roosevelt, *The Strenuous Life: Essays and Addresses* (New York, 1900), pp. 38, 293–294.

55. *Ibid.,* p. 19 (from the address entitled "The Strenuous Life," delivered in April, 1899).

Such statements need not be taken seriously as explanations of basic imperialist motivation, but they do suggest that expansionism was unacceptable to many Americans unless it could be sugar-coated with professions of benevolent intent toward the "weaker races." Expansionism had to be justified by reference to lofty humanitarian motives in order to counter fears that the nation was embarking on a career of international plunder leading to larger wars or to the decadence and corruption popularly associated with empires. The concept of "the white man's burden" did not usually carry with it the expectation that "our little brown brothers" could in time be raised to the level of the Anglo-Saxons, and it even remained doubtful when, if ever, they would be ready for full independence. But the very idea that they could be substantially "elevated"—and especially while they remained in their supposedly debilitating tropical environment—was in conflict with the assumptions of the straitest sect of American racists.

It would appear then that the basic assumptions implicit in the concept of a "white man's burden" were identical with the paternalist or accommodationist approach to the American Negro. It was not accidental or contradictory that Roosevelt and like-minded leaders, who advocated an allegedly benevolent imperialism abroad, also endorsed the domestic racial programs of Booker T. Washington and Edgar Gardner Murphy. Both the blacks in the United States and the new dependents in the Philippines were offered the "lasting benefit" of a tutelage in civilization. Although neither were promised ultimate equality and assimilation, the expectation of even a relatively limited improvement in the character and prospects of nonwhite dependents constituted a break with the hard racist doctrine that "lower races" should be strictly quarantined—geographically or socially—and left to degenerate or die out because they were hopelessly immoral and incapable of progress.[56]

56. The concept of "the white man's burden" and the ideological needs it served in the United States are ably discussed in Weinberg, *Manifest Destiny*, Chapter X. In *Theodore Roosevelt and the Rise of America to World Power* (Baltimore, 1956), Howard K. Beale makes the point that Roosevelt's racism was not of the extreme variety then being promulgated by Southern Negrophobes and strict hereditarians (see pp. 27–34). Roosevelt, Beale argues, was

Perhaps the best proof of a mutually reinforcing interrelation-
ship between the rhetoric of expansionism and the quasi-
paternalist concept of racial accommodation can be found in the
writings of the Southern liberals, who constantly likened their
program to the imperialist effort to "uplift the backward races"
in distant dependencies. In his address to the Montgomery Race
Conference of 1900, the Reverend W. A. Guerry, chaplain of the
University of the South (Sewanee), contended that the elevation
of the Negro was "the white man's burden here, as it is elsewhere
throughout the world today," and, as we have seen, Benjamin F.
Riley called his appeal for a moderate racial policy in the South
The White Man's Burden.[57]

The fullest development of the analogy between a "liberal"
policy of racial adjustment at home and an enlightened imperialism abroad appeared in Murphy's *The Basis of Ascendancy.* The
South must see its efforts at racial accommodation in the light of
world-wide developments, Murphy wrote. Everywhere, he noted,
"the isolation of weaker groups is being broken up, and the
'inferior' peoples are being . . . included and reorganized
within the life of the stronger aggregates." This imperial movement was occurring simultaneously with a growth of democracy
and a recognition of the need for "a broader distribution of
power." The result was that the necessities of imperialism were
"modifying certain of our older conceptions of democracy, cor-
recting some of our doctrinate conceptions as to the natural
equality of men," while at the same time the democratic impulse
was making demands on the imperialists. "It is no easy problem,"
he conceded, "this problem of the strong living with the weak
. . . so living as to assure peace without afflicting desolation, as
to preserve order without defeating justice, as to uphold a state
which will express the life of its higher group without en-
feebling or destroying that waiting manhood of weaker peoples

---

essentially a Lamarckian who attributed racial differences to acquired characteristics, which meant that he viewed the "backward races" as capable of
progressive development. Of course Roosevelt's resistance to the theories of
racial extremists was no consolation to the "backward races" who became
subjects of colonial domination.

57. Southern Society . . . , *Race Problems,* p. 128.

which itself craves and deserves expression." Here indeed was not only the problem of the South but also the problem of the United States in Cuba, Puerto Rico, Hawaii, Panama, and the Philippines. The biracial South, Murphy concluded, was an excellent "training ground" for dealing with this "characteristic problem of the modern world."[58]

The correlation that Murphy and others made between biracialism in the United States and American imperialism in Asia and Latin America sheds a curiously revealing light on the doctrines of accommodationist racism. Where the competitive racists, many of whom had to be dragged kicking and screaming into the age of imperial expansion, saw the American Negro as a degenerating and vanishing race, the accommodationists envisioned the black future in terms of a permanent and allegedly benevolent domestic colonialism. Their program of moral uplift, industrial training, and racial integrity really meant, therefore, that they regarded the American black population, not as an incorrigible menace to white civilization, but as a useful and quiescent internal colony.

IV

If the proponents of racial "adjustment" were in tune with the new imperialist thought, they were also in harmony with the basic social thinking of the Progressive era. Perhaps the most fundamental concern of the Progressives was what one historian has called "the search for order." It appears that a sense of social disintegration and incipient chaos afflicted the American mentality in the late nineteenth century, primarily as a result of the pressures of industrialism and urbanization. Such concerns persisted after 1900; but the fluctuation between Utopianism and catastrophism which characterized the social thinking of the 1880s and 1890s was replaced by a philosophy of moderate reform cautiously optimistic about disciplining the unruly forces in American life through a reasonable program of regulation and

58. Murphy, *Basis of Ascendancy*, pp. 218–222.

social adjustment.[59] Clearly, lynching and race riots were among the most glaring examples of the failure of orderly processes. Like violent encounters between capital and labor, corruption and vice in the cities, and the machinations of giant trusts, racial antagonism was part of the larger tangle of conflict and fragmentation that the Progressives hoped to straighten out and bring under control. The racial accommodationists appealed to the Progressive mind because they promised order and harmony between the races, much as other reformers proposed to tame the forces of conflict and disruption in industrial relations and between social classes.

The Progressive desire for social cohesion and cooperation was manifested, not only in the thinking of reformers about concrete problems, but also on the level of abstract social thought where academic theorists hammered out a rationale for efforts to improve social relationships. The pioneers of the new discipline of sociology—men like Franklin H. Giddings, Charles H. Cooley, and Edward Alsworth Ross characteristically described society as evolving toward higher forms of cooperative endeavor. In emphasizing the value of a rise in social consciousness or "fellow feeling" and the need for noncoercive forms of "social control," they were reacting against the rugged individualism of the social Darwinists with their view of society as a place where man was set against man in a "struggle for survival." In place of the social Darwinist concept of inevitable conflict and competition between individuals and groups, the new sociologists posited a social order based on co-operation, compromise, and cohesion.[60]

Applied to ethnic groups, such an emphasis suggested that differing races could live together harmoniously in the same social and political system. Professor Giddings of Columbia, one of the most influential sociologists at the turn of the century, implied that advanced societies were thus able to accommodate racial diversity when he made his famous distinction between

59. See Robert H. Wiebe, *The Search for Order, 1877–1920* (New York, 1967) , *passim.*

60. See Franklin Henry Giddings, *The Principles of Sociology* (New York, 1902) [first published in 1896]; Charles H. Cooley, *Social Organization: A Study of the Larger Mind* (New York, 1909) ; and Edward Alsworth Ross, *Social Control* (New York, 1901) .

"primary" and "secondary congregations." The "primary congregation," a basic and primitive form of social organization, was limited to members of the same original nationality, or at least of the same race, while the "secondary congregation" was composed of differing races and nationalities. All the great nations of the modern world were "the product of secondary congregation," and the emergence of these new and more complex social systems was a sign of the enlargement of the notion of what constituted a viable human community. "Ethnical subordination," or the coercive domination of one race by another, was the rule in history, but only as a lower stage of social development: " . . . in advanced stages of the development of highly organized communities . . . the differentiation of the social constitution from the social composition is so nearly complete that all ethnical elements may make their way into any part of the purposive association."[61]

This conception suggested the evolution of society in the direction of assimilation and equality for all its ethnic components. But this long-range expectation did not, in fact, bring the new sociological school into direct collision with basic American racial practices. As evolutionists, these early academic sociologists viewed historical change as a slow process occurring in stages; and when Giddings appended to his prediction of ultimate social integration the comment that the status of the Negro and the Indian in the United States showed "how far from perfect is this differentiation [of social constitution from social composition] in our own nation even now," he seemed to accept such a situation as unavoidable in the current stage of social development.[62] The view that "ethnical" integration was at most a long-range evolutionary prospect was reinforced by particular doubts about black capabilities and by "scientific" concepts of the origin and nature of racial prejudice which could be used to rationalize contemporary patterns of segregation.

On the question of racial capacities most of the social scientists of the Progressive era believed that Negroes were inferior to

61. Giddings, *Principles,* pp. 93, 316.
62. *Ibid.,* pp. 316–317.

whites but capable of improvement. Once again the views of Giddings can be taken as representative. Accepting the concept of higher and lower races as determined by differences in historical achievement, Giddings rated the blacks above the Tasmanians and Red Indians, who had shown no adaptability or capability of improvement. "The Negro," he affirmed, "is plastic. He yields easily to environing influences. Deprived of the support of stronger races, he still relapses into savagery, but kept in contact with the whites, he readily takes the external impress of civilization, and there is reason to hope that he will yet acquire a measure of its spirit." He was far from certain, however, that the Negro would ever become "a truly progressive type"; for the most capable races "must have not only plasticity, but also strength of character to make independent advances, and without outside help to hold an advantage when it has been gained." Giving support to the popular belief in Nordic supremacy, Giddings contended that only the North and West European peoples had shown such capacities in modern times.[63]

In making such statements about the differing potential of races, the social scientists of the Progressive era did not thereby surrender to the rigid hereditarianism of extreme racists like Hoffman and Barringer; they were committed to the importance of environmental influences and managed to resolve the heredity-environment dilemma by maintaining (even while the empirical basis of their position was being undermined by advances in the science of genetics) that acquired characteristics could be inherited. Their Lamarckian view of human evolution, permitting social influences to affect the genetic make-up of individuals and races, was the scientific basis of Giddings's assertion that the Negro could acquire some of the spirit of Nordic civilization and a central assumption of the proponents of Negro "uplift" at home and "the white man's burden" abroad. It not only fitted in with the Washingtonian concept of gradual Negro advancement but also sanctioned differential treatment of blacks so long as they remained in a lower stage of evolutionary development. The Lamarckian concept of racial improvement did not, of course, go

63. *Ibid.*, pp. 328–329.

uncriticized. It was attacked by the strict hereditarians who denied the plasticity of races, and challenged by a new school of cultural environmentalists, principally Franz Boas and his followers, who were developing the discipline of cultural anthropology. Boas's views did not win a wide following until the 1920s, when the new discoveries in genetics had at last forced the Lamarckians from the field and sharpened the conflict between the cultural environmentalists and the hereditarians.[64]

If the evolutionism of the sociologists carried them beyond rigid racial determinism and opened the possibility of improving the character and capabilities of American blacks, their thinking at the same time strengthened the case for segregation, not only because they asserted that blacks were, for the time being at least, decidedly inferior to the whites, but also because of the way they analyzed racial prejudice. Their concepts of socialization and the progressive development of "fellow feeling" had, as it turned out, built-in racial limitations which helped legitimize white opposition to "social equality." In an influential article of 1904, William I. Thomas of the University of Chicago maintained that racial prejudice was an instinct, which "cannot be reasoned with, because, like the other instincts, it originated before deliberative brain centers were developed, and is not to any great extent under their control." The root of this feeling, according to Thomas, was the collective suspicion manifested by human groups toward outsiders, or those who are obviously unlike themselves. He conceded that a prejudice against skin color per se "is easily dissipated or converted into its opposite by association, or a slight modification of stimulus." But when "complicated with 'caste feeling' it becomes "more ineradicable." Race prejudice "is an affair that can neither be reasoned with nor legislated about very effectively."[65]

Giddings elevated this notion of instinctive intergroup antipathy into a grand sociological principle with his theory of

64. See George Stocking's essay "Lamarckianism in American Social Science," in *Race, Culture, and Evolution: Essays in the History of Anthropology* (New York, 1968), pp. 234–269.

65. William I. Thomas, "The Psychology of Race-Prejudice," *American Journal of Sociology*, IX (March, 1904), 607–610.

"consciousness of kind," which he defined as "a state of consciousness in which any being . . . recognizes another conscious being as of like kind with itself." Such a consciousness was "coextensive with potential society" and the basis of racial feelings and other forms of group identity.[66] In an analysis of how "consciousness of kind" functioned in contemporary society, Giddings noted how a sense of kinship became progressively weaker as one moved beyond the family to larger social groups: ". . . there is normally a greater degree of sympathy among the members of a family than among the members of a nation, and a greater degree of sympathy among men of a common nationality than among all men of the same race or color." Included in a syllabus Giddings prepared for students of sociology was a mathematical graph showing the degrees of kinship feeling in American society as native-born whites confronted other elements; it demonstrated that "consciousness of kind" dropped sharply when white immigrants were encountered and disappeared almost entirely with differences in color. Here Giddings clearly portrayed the Negro as outside the community of fellow feeling—an authentic outcast in American society.[67]

Such a view of the racial limitations of "consciousness of kind" may have had some validity as an empirical description of American social attitudes, but, presented as the manifestation of an inescapable law of human association, it became the perfect basis for a sophisticated defense of racial segregation. Edgar Gardner Murphy, for example, used the concept as the cornerstone of his argument for the necessity of separate racial development.[68] Sociologists might postulate a distant future when "consciousness of kind" would extend to people of a different color, but for the moment white prejudice and the segregation of the blacks seemed to be unchangable realities.

The importance social scientists gave to race as a barrier to social solidarity suggests that there was a real tension between their hope for the enlargement of an integrated social conscious-

66. Giddings, *Principles*, pp. 17–18.

67. Franklin Henry Giddings, *The Theory of Socialization* (New York, 1897) , pp. 15–17.

68. Murphy, *Basis of Ascendancy*, pp. xviii–xix.

ness and their concessions to racism. It was a real question whether their prophecy of a co-operative society could be fulfilled in the face of racial differences. Giddings suggested as much when he enunciated the following law about how human associations become more co-operative and perfect their patterns of "socialization" and "assimilation": "Conflict . . . continues until, through the elimination of extremely different and unequal members of the group, such approximation to equality and such diminution of difference is brought about as to produce the equilibrium of toleration."[69] Had he applied this doctrine literally to the American racial situation—which he never did—Giddings might have become another advocate of expatriation or "natural" extermination instead of a proponent of the progressive uplift of the blacks.

In 1907 John R. Commons, professor of economics at the University of Wisconsin and a leading spokesman for the application of social science to Progressive reform, revealed an even more glaring contradiction between empirical analysis and idealistic hopes in his important book *Races and Immigrants in America*. There was an irresistible tendency in the South toward a permanent caste system based on unbridgeable racial differences, he said at one point; but elsewhere he endorsed the hope that "Americanization" or "assimilation" of "all races within our borders" could eventually take place. "A great nation need not be of one blood, but it must be of one mind," and such a unifying consciousness was possible because of the possession of a common language: "Race and heredity may be beyond our organized control, but the instrument of a common language is at hand for conscious improvement through education and social environment."[70]

Charles Horton Cooley, perhaps the greatest American sociologist of the period, attempted a more direct confrontation with the problematical relation between caste feeling and democratic solidarity in his book *Social Organization,* published in 1909. Conceding that "an impulse toward caste is found in human

69. Giddings, *Theory of Socialization,* p. 21.
70. John R. Commons, *Races and Immigrants in America* (New York, 1920) , pp. 8, 16, 20–21. (Originally published in 1907.)

nature itself," Cooley nevertheless described caste as "an inferior principle" which tended "to be supplanted by something freer and more rational." Difference in race, he pointed out, was one of the most fundamental sources of caste: "Two races of different temperament and capacity, distinct to the eye and living side by side in the same community, tend strongly to become castes, no matter how equal the social system may be. . . . The race caste existing in the Southern United States illustrates the impotence of democratic traditions to overcome the caste spirit when fostered by obvious physical and psychical differences. This spirit is immeasurably strong on the part of the whites, and there is no apparent prospect of its diminution." Cooley's tortuous commentary on this situation suggested how difficult it was for the Progressive mentality to harmonize its abstract social ideals with its resigned acceptance of American racial conditions. The arguments for a caste division were, he pointed out, based "on the recognition of the two races as being, for some purposes, distinct organisms. In this regard it is perhaps better sociology than the view that everyone should be considered solely on his merits as an individual." At the same time, he could not conceal his distaste for "that caste arrogance which does not recognize in the Negro a spiritual brotherhood underlying all race difference and possible 'inferiority.'" Whatever their differences in ability all races should share in "a common spirit and service from which no human being can rightly or Christianly be excluded"; for "science, religion, and the democratic spirit" all entitled the Negro to a recognition that "he is fundamentally a man like the rest of us." "Anything in our present attitude which does deny it," he concluded, "we must hope to be transitory, since it is calculated, in a modern atmosphere, to generate continuing disquiet and hatred. It belonged with slavery and is incongruous with the newer world."[71]

Having established that caste feeling was incompatible with the modern democratic spirit, Cooley reverted to "realistic" sociology and the pious hopes of accommodationist racism. "The practical question here is not that of abolishing castes but of

71. Cooley, *Social Organization*, pp. 215–220.

securing just and kindly relations between them, of reconciling the fact of caste with the ideals of freedom or right."[72] It was on this shaky ground that Progressive social scientists and accommodationist liberals took their stand. Somehow caste feelings, by their very nature undemocratic, could be made compatible with democracy; and exclusive "consciousness of kind," although it put the Negro outside the community of social equals, could lead to a larger collective consciousness knitting society together in mutual trust and harmony. It would eventually become obvious that such a program was not only self-contradictory but essentially fraudulent and dishonest. There was, in fact, no halfway house between the injustice of "caste arrogance" and the achievement of full equality.

72. *Ibid.*, p. 220.

Chapter Eleven

•

Conclusion and Epilogue

THIS STUDY has been primarily concerned with the shifting and divergent white conceptions of Afro-American character and destiny between 1817 and 1914. White racialism, considered as an intellectual and ideological phenomenon, was not a monolithic and unchanging creed during this period, but a fluid pattern of belief, affected in significant and diverse ways by the same social, intellectual, and political currents influencing other basic aspects of American thought and experience. But something further may need to be said about the underlying consensus within which much of the debate took place. Obviously the range of views and policy recommendations was severely limited, during most of the period at least, by certain widely accepted and fundamental assumptions about black-white relations. A relative stress on Southern opinion in the discussion of the post-Reconstruction era was inevitable in view of the South's intense preoccupation with a "Negro question" that the North was then trying to ignore and does not mean that many basic Southern attitudes were not shared, at least passively, by whites in other sections. Indeed, the recorded pattern of Northern response to Southern initiatives was clearly indicative of a consensus in favor of white supremacy, although at times the proper mechanism to ensure white domination might be in dispute.

To make certain that the debates and shifts of opinion are seen in proper perspective, we need only enumerate the basic white-supremacist propositions in a form likely to have been acceptable to almost all shades of white opinion—Northern and Southern, Negrophobe and "paternalist"—after the 1830s. Widespread, almost universal, agreement existed on the following points:

1. Blacks are physically, intellectually, and temperamentally *different* from whites.

2. Blacks are also *inferior* to whites in at least some of the fundamental qualities wherein the races differ, especially in intelligence and in the temperamental basis of enterprise or initiative.

3. Such differences and differentials are either permanent or subject to change only by a very slow process of development or evolution.

4. Because of these permanent or deep-seated differences, miscegenation, especially in the form of intermarriage, is to be discouraged (to put it as mildly as possible), because the crossing of such diverse types leads either to a short-lived and unprolific breed or to a type that even if permanent is inferior to the whites in those innate qualities giving Caucasian civilization its progressive and creative characteristics.

5. Racial prejudice or antipathy is a natural and inevitable white response to blacks when the latter are free from legalized subordination and aspiring to equal status. Its power is such that it will not in the foreseeable future permit blacks to attain full equality, unless one believes, like some abolitionists, in the impending triumph of a millenarian Christianity capable of obliterating all sense of divisive human differences.

6. It follows from the above propositions that a biracial equalitarian (or "integrated") society is either completely impossible, now and forever, or can be achieved only in some remote and almost inconceivable future. For all practical purposes the destiny of the blacks in America is either continued subordination—slavery or some form of caste discrimination—or their elimination as an element of the population.

Given the acceptance of this creed by all but a tiny (and often uncertain) minority of white spokesmen, it is hardly surprising that the principal debate after the 1830s occurred between advocates of a permanent hierarchical biracialism and prophets or proponents of racial homogeneity through the eventual elimination of the black population.

The doctrine of hierarchical biracialism, often expressing itself as the ideology of *"Herrenvolk* democracy," began as a defense of slavery widely accepted in the antebellum South. It was embraced by Northerners who valued an economic or political connection with the slave South or feared that emancipation would result in an inundation of the North by Southern blacks competing with white labor and threatening the status of lower-class whites. After the abolition of slavery, hierarchical biracialism was reaffirmed as "white supremacy" and the gospel of segregation.

The ideal of homogeneity originated with men of a moderately reformist persuasion, for it derived initially from the conservative antislavery sentiment of the early Republic. Implicit in the initial colonizationist enterprise, it did not receive full articulation until it became an element in the nationalist thinking of many Republicans and free-soilers in the 1850s. The hope for an all-white America found a final outlet in the Darwinian speculation of the late nineteenth century about the disappearance of the American Negro in a "struggle for existence" with the superior whites. The other possible path to homogeneity—homogenization through intermarriage—was, of course, strenuously rejected by almost everyone except a few romantic racialists who criticized the unadulterated Anglo-Saxon character during the Civil War era and actually hoped to see it improved through a mixture of blood.

The attitudes toward blacks revealed by such conceptualizations had their origins in the institutionalization of slavery based on race during the seventeenth century. But racism did not come to full ideological consciousness until called forth by nineteenth-century developments and given shape and consistency by contemporary trends in scientific and social thought. Racialist thinking crystallized in nineteenth-century America mainly because the presence of blacks was a central fact in the great sectional conflict that almost destroyed the Union.

The first shot in the ideological war over slavery was fired by the abolitionists of the 1830s who sought to apply to blacks, in an immediate and literal fashion, the dictum that "all men are created equal." As a basic Southern response would put it, blacks were actually submen suited only for slavery, to whom the Declaration of Independence obviously did not apply. The ensuing conflict, with its prominent racial dimension, can be summarized briefly. Much of the South desired to keep blacks as slaves and emphasized race as a justification of slavery; and by the 1850s many Southerners had come to regard territorial expansion as necessary for the survival of the institution. The Northern majority, on the other hand, came to oppose slavery as an institution because of its incompatibility with an ascendant "free labor" ideology, and this opposition became vocal in the 1850s because Southern expansionism seemed at that time to pose a serious threat to the manifest destiny of the Northern way of life to spread over, and dominate, all or most of the territory of the United States. But most Northerners were not prepared to accept blacks as equals, especially in substantial numbers; in fact a common Northern dream depicted an all-white America where the full promise of equality could be realized because there was no black population to be relegated to a special and anomalous status.

In the pre-Civil War crisis, then, the South can be described as having manifested a desire for both slavery and Negroes, while a Northern majority provided indications that it wanted neither, at least not on a permanent basis. Abraham Lincoln, it should be recalled, affirmed in this period not only that slavery must be put on the path of "ultimate extinction" but also that blacks could never have equal rights as long as they remained in the United States and should therefore be colonized abroad. But contingencies arising from the war and the subsequent need to reconstruct the Union combined to give an influential segment of Northern opinion the idea that Southern blacks must be given equal rights, principally because their cooperation was essential to the establishment of Northern political, social, and ideological hegemony over the South. Accompanying this sense that blacks could be useful was the growth in popularity of the romantic stereotype of the blacks as a people whose peculiar virtues were submissive gratitude and undying loyalty to benefactors. Consequently, the Reconstruction era saw a temporary subordination of racial nationalism to the overriding political nationalism arising out of the Unionist fervor of the Civil War years.

After the failure of Radical Reconstruction, the North acquiesced in the restoration of white supremacy in the South on the understanding that blacks would not be deprived of their formal rights and would be given some chance to make whatever social and economic progress their capabilities would allow. This compromise was acceptable to an emerging group of Southern spokesmen because it fitted in with their disposition to promote a bourgeois form of "paternalism" that prescribed, somewhat ambiguously, a kind of social and industrial "guidance," not only for blacks but also for a newly dependent class of poor whites. This inherently unstable and ambiguous settlement did not last, however. The economic and social crisis of the late 1880s and early 1890s brought an agrarian insurgence in the South which gave blacks the potential in some areas to decide the political struggle between competing white factions. Panicked by this possibility and disturbed by other uncertainties in white-black relations, politicians and propagandists resorted to virulent race baiting to prevent their opponents from consummating the crucial alliance and to make sure that blacks were kept "in their place."

By the 1890s, therefore, the Negro was again seen as a critical problem, and dreams of homogeneity reasserted themselves in both the North and the South, in the form of deportation schemes and in the wishful thinking of racial Darwinists who predicted that blacks would become extinct in "the struggle for existence." The latter view was especially popular among Northern racial and demographic theorists who could afford to take an Olympian view of immediate Southern difficulties by pointing to a long-term "solution." But in a period of uncertainty some Southerners also longed for total relief from what they considered the disagreeable necessity for eternal racial vigilance. Since the dream of homogeneity was unrealizable, they settled in the end for the continued exploitation of blacks and for an approach to the "pseudo homogeneity" of the slave era, achieved this time through the institutionalization of extreme racism in the form of legalized segregation and disfranchisement.

By the early years of the twentieth century, therefore, there was a renewed disposition to accept blacks as a permanent (but inferior) portion of the population. In the context of Progressivism and imperialism, an ideal approximating a benevolent internal colonialism came to dominate national thinking about the race question. This was a point of view permitting liberals and moderates to manifest some concern about Southern blacks, but it also sanctioned their acquiescence in the basic Southern policies of segregation and disfranchisement.

II

The full story of subsequent white racial thought, theoretical and applied, is beyond the scope of this book. To some extent later thinking took place in a significantly altered context because of the mass migration of Southern blacks to the North beginning in the period of the First World War. The race question had always been a national one because the North in general subscribed to many of the same basic views as the South and because Northerners had directed a surprising amount of antipathy at their own tiny black minority. But for many Northerners the problem of black-white relations had often seemed less critical than other social issues simply because most blacks were in the South. As this situation changed and it became clear that the North had a very serious race problem of its own stemming from the forced ghettoization of masses of blacks in its cities, a new urban-oriented and sociological approach to the black presence came into prominence which was often conservatively geared to the need of an increasingly complex, industrialized, and bureaucratized society for "social engineering" as a means of neutralizing the potentially disruptive tensions of group life. Complicating such efforts at "racial adjustment" were virulent outbreaks of white prejudice, ranging from the race riots of 1919 to the "backlash" of the late 1960s, and violent manifestations of black disgust with the myriad deprivations of ghetto life, expressed most dramatically in the Harlem riots of 1935 and 1943 and in the wave of racial disorders that swept the nation in the 1960s.

It would take another book as long as this one to do justice to the white intellectual response to this changing situation, to say nothing of the discussion that developed in the 1940s and after over the struggle to end legalized segregation in the South. It may be appropriate, however, to describe briefly the fate after 1914 of two of the principal conceptions with which we have been concerned—the ideal of white homogeneity and the variant of white racial thinking I have called romantic racialism.

The dream of an all-white America continued to find expression from time to time in the utterances of the most extreme racists. Its most famous exponents were advocates of black deportation like Senator Theodore Bilbo of Mississippi and Ernest Sevier Cox, a Virginia racial theorist who fed the fires of extreme anti-Negroism in the 1920s and 1930s. But their views were not taken seriously by many whites.[1] The consignment of the recurrent nineteenth-century aspiration for racial homogeneity to the fringes of the white consciousness can be explained in a number of ways. First there was the cumulative effect of the failure of all previous colonization schemes, a record which must have served as a caution to those who would have liked, in the best of all possible worlds, to have dispatched American blacks to some distant shore. The other predicted path to homogeneity, the biological disappearance of the Negro in an evolutionary struggle, had decreasing plausibility partly because of purely demographic developments. The mass movement of Southern blacks to the North and their acclimatization there put to rest once and for all the pseudoscientific myth that blacks naturally migrate southward because they cannot survive in a cold or even a temperate climate. Furthermore, the continued increase of the black population in rough proportion to the whites refuted expectations of gradual extinction. In addition to such practical considerations,

1. See Idus A. Newby, *Jim Crow's Defense: Anti-Negro Thought in America* (Baton Rouge, 1965), pp. 61, 182–184.

there was the effect of a sustained intellectual assault on the theoretical basis of the belief that a biological struggle between the races was inevitable. This assault was part of the general attack on social Darwinism as a false application of evolutionary theory to human societies.

Although there is no longer any obvious and logical basis for racist hopes that the black population will completely vanish, one hesitates to affirm that the desire for white homogeneity is dead. It seems likely that it persists in some form in the minds of many whites, awaiting an opportunity or occasion for renewed expression.

Romantic racialism, on the other hand, did not fade so readily from the articulate levels of white consciousness. In the 1920s a revised form of romantic racialism became something of a national fad, resulting in part, curiously enough, from patronizing white encouragement of the "New Negro" movement and the "Harlem Renaissance." "The New Negro," as perceived by many whites, was simply the old romantic conception of the Negro covered with a patina of the cultural primitivism and exoticism fashionable in the 1920s. In 1918 Robert Park, the distinguished sociologist who would come to be recognized as the foremost white student of race relations in the period between the World Wars, set the tone for subsequent appreciation of black cultural achievements when he wrote that the Negro unquestionably had a temperament which differed from that of whites. The Anglo-Saxon was basically "a pioneer and a frontiersman," while the Negro "is primarily an artist, loving life for its own sake. His *métier* is expression rather than action. He is, so to speak, the lady among the races."[2] But the would-be Negrophiles of the 1920s were not content to allow the Negro to express his artistic temperament and love of life through jazz and the literature of the Harlem school; they took to writing novels and plays of their own emphasizing that the blacks were basically exotic primitives, out of place in white society because of their natural spontaneity, emotionalism, and sensuality.

What was new about the image of blacks conveyed in the

2. Robert E. Park, *Race and Culture: Essays in the Sociology of Contemporary Man* (Glencoe, Ill., 1950), p. 280.

novels of white writers like DuBose Heyward, Julia Peterkin, and Carl Van Vechten was not the stereotype itself but the lack of moralism in the treatment of what would previously have been defined as black immorality or even animality; for these novelists incorporated sexuality into the romantic stereotype without appearing to condemn it. The cultural revolt against "Puritanism" and "repression" in the 1920s could lead some whites to believe that they were being complimentary to blacks when they described them as naturally naïve and primitive creatures who characteristically gave free rein to all their passions. Thus in 1925 the New York critic Heywood Broun could describe Heyward's *Porgy,* a novel of primitive low life and sexual passion among the blacks of Charleston, as demonstrating that Negro life was "more colorful and spirited and vital than that of the white community." "If the two cultures do not readily mix, as many maintain," he continued, "it may well be that it is the Nordic who lags."[3] The new spokesmen for black "superiority," however, tended to overlook some of the real injustices suffered by blacks, and they sometimes implicitly or explicitly justified white-imposed segregation on the grounds that the vast temperamental differences between the races meant in fact that they should not "mix."

In the 1930s romantic racialism, both in its traditional and recently jazzed-up versions, lost much of its credibility among the white liberal intelligentsia. This change can be seen rather dramatically in two editions of the same book by Edwin R. Embree, an architect of philanthropic efforts to aid Negro education and a popular interpreter of black culture. In the 1931 edition, Embree described the Negro as having "gifts of his own quite beyond the American standard." He "is expressive" and "has an amazing capacity for meeting buffets with laughter—not with a smile but with hearty guffaws of olympian laughter." Furthermore, "he sings at his work and plays and dances as soon as his work is done." This innately joyous and aesthetic view of life was now finding expression in elaborate and formalized artistic achievements. After discussing recent Negro literature with its

3. New York *World,* October 14, 1925.

emphasis on folk materials, Embree concluded that "only an adaptable race and one full of emotion craving expression could have taken on the new forms and new ideas and contributed to them the rhythmic sermons and melodious songs that have come from the Negro."[4] In the revised edition of 1943, passages of this sort were deleted and there was no reference whatever to racial temperament or innate gifts.[5]

The decline of romantic racialism in the 1930s was the result of several factors. One was the popularization of the discovery of psychologists that there was no empirical basis for the belief in an inherited racial temperament. Professor Thomas R. Garth concluded in 1931, after an exhaustive review of "such scientific investigations as have been made," that "there are no sure evidences of real racial differences in mental traits."[6] Garth's conclusion was re-echoed by many psychologists and sociologists in the 1930s and 1940s.

A second factor which tended to discredit the romantic stereotype in the thinking of white liberals was the growing tendency of black intellectuals to reject the image *in toto* as part of a more militant protest orientation. In the 1920s the white intelligentsia had responded to a segment of black cultural expression and had seen it as confirming at least part of the traditional stereotype. Such a misconception was no longer possible in the 1930s and early 1940s, as black writers like Richard Wright and William Attaway presented lower-class blacks as products of an oppressive environment, discontented victims of racial and economic injustice who expressed their frustration by lashing out violently against the world around them. In the depression years, when there was a growing recognition of the effects of social and economic deprivation and when Marxism had some influence on American thought, a new image of the Negro as a peculiarly oppressed proletarian gained considerable currency in white

4. Edwin R. Embree, *Brown America: The Story of a New Race* (New York, 1931), pp. 23, 240.
5. Edwin R. Embree, *Brown Americans: The Story of a Tenth of the Nation* (New York, 1943). See pp. 16 and 190 for the sections where the above-quoted passages were deleted.
6. Thomas Russell Garth, *Race Psychology: A Study of Racial Mental Differences* (New York, 1931), p. 211.

liberal and radical circles. Even the most benevolent and well-intentioned romantic racialist concepts came under attack because it was seen that they provided a covert rationale for continued segregation, exploitation, and poverty. If blacks were seen as naturally joyous and capable of deriving aesthetic pleasure from the simplest things of life, it was pointed out, then whites had a perfect excuse for doing nothing about the fact that blacks were an exploited minority.

The decline of romantic racialism was indicative of the most fundamental change that occurred in white racial thinking after the First World War—the rise of liberal environmentalism as a racial creed. Carrying on a struggle that was begun by the anthropologist Franz Boas and by a handful of white radicals and Socialists during the Progressive era, the liberal environmentalists battled during the 1920s and 1930s with a rear guard of hereditarian racists who were often entrenched in the scientific departments of major universities. By the Second World War the egalitarians had come to dominate completely such fields as sociology and anthropology and their views were coming to influence a broadened liberal public. The real triumph of their ideas undoubtedly came during the war in the context of a revulsion against the racism of the Nazis. A full codification of the new egalitarianism was presented to a receptive public in 1944 with the publication of Gunnar Myrdal's *An American Dilemma*.

The liberal environmentalists affirmed that there were no differences between the races which were likely to affect their social, cultural, and intellectual performance; all apparent differences were the result of environment. The policy implications of their views were clear—they argued openly for the possibility and desirability of the full assimilation or integration of blacks into American life. These doctrines, of course, had great influence in that they provided a theoretical basis for the civil-rights and integration movements of the 1950s and 1960s. By arguing that prejudice could be eliminated through education and legislation the new egalitarians raised hopes that America could become, in the relatively near future, a color-blind society.

The influences contributing to the triumph of liberal environmentalism in the respectable thought of the mid-twentieth century were numerous. The growth of an active black protest movement aimed at full equality and desegregation touched the conscience of some whites and appealed to the enlightened self-interest of others. In addition, there was the rise to prominence in intellectual and academic circles of members of white ethnic groups which themselves had been victimized by a form of racial prejudice and discrimination; men of this background were likely to have a strong predilection to reject racist beliefs of all kinds.

One suspects, however, that the measure of popular and official acceptance accorded to this view during and after the Second World War was not due primarily to the decency and rationality of its ideological advocates, or to their ability to galvanize a latent "American creed" which prescribed equality for all. Such factors as the need of a bureaucratized industrial society for social peace, the increasing importance of a black electorate in Northern urban areas, and the exigencies of international conflict, first against the Axis, and later against "world Communism," were probably more significant. As the United States attempted to guarantee its social equilibrium and embarked on efforts to influence the non-Western world in behalf of its interests and ideology, overt and virulent intellectual racism came to be recognized as a dangerous liability.

This is not the place to embark on an extended critique of liberal environmentalism and the integrationist ideology. But events of the late 1960s served to raise doubts about the full adequacy of some of its formulations. Although inherent racial differences of a socially significant kind cannot be demonstrated and probably do not exist, the consciousness of race as a basis of personal identity seems much more difficult to eliminate than the more optimistic liberal environmentalists have led us to believe. The sheer fact of a difference in color seems enough by itself to arouse serious antipathy, at least in our kind of society, when a distinguishable minority is regarded by the majority as potentially competitive—witness the recent rise of racial prejudice among whites in Great Britain. When this consciousness of color is combined, as it is in the United States, with a tradition of slavery and caste so deeply rooted in the white psyche that it often seems impervious to rational argument, it becomes doubtful whether egalitarian indoctrination or meliorative legislation can solve the problem. Furthermore, the blacks' intense search for a racial culture and identity, manifested most dramatically in black nationalist movements, raises the possibility that many blacks would not feel completely at home as minority citizens even in a more genuinely egalitarian society than currently exists in the United States.

Perhaps Tocqueville was right after all when he described the American race problem as insoluble and certain to result in disaster. Or perhaps, and this is only a slightly more hopeful view, the problem can be solved only by a radical change in basic institutions and values, of a kind hardly likely in the foreseeable future. If this latter view is correct, however, and if it is possible to conceive of a social order within which serious race problems can be eliminated, perhaps because the social anxieties fueling prejudiced thought and action have been removed, then it is clearly the responsibility of reflective Americans who believe in the ideal of racial equality to indulge in some serious Utopian thinking; for there is always the slender but precious hope that today's Utopia can be tomorrow's society.

Index

ABOUT THE AUTHOR

George M. Fredrickson, Edgar E. Robinson Professor of United States History at Stanford University since 1984, is the author of *The Inner Civil War: Northern Intellectuals and the Crisis of the Union, The Black Image in the White Mind: The Debate on Afro-American Character and Destiny, 1817–1914* and *White Supremacy: A Comparative Study of American and South African History*. A graduate of Harvard University (A.B. 1956, Ph.D. 1964), he was a Fulbright scholar at the University of Oslo in 1956–57 and a Fulbright professor of American history at Moscow University in 1983. Fredrickson has twice been appointed Senior Fellow of the National Endowment for the Humanities; he is a member of the Executive Board of the Organization of American Historians.